TOLKIEN
and the
INVENTION OF MYTH

TOLKIEN

and the

INVENTION OF MYTH

A READER

EDITED BY

JANE CHANCE

THE UNIVERSITY PRESS OF KENTUCKY

Scholarly publisher for the Commonwealth,
serving Bellarmine University, Berea College, Center
College of Kentucky, Eastern Kentucky University,
The Filson Historical Society, Georgetown College,
Kentucky Historical Society, Kentucky State University,
Morehead State University, Murray State University,
Northern Kentucky University, Transylvania University,
University of Kentucky, University of Louisville,
and Western Kentucky University.
All rights reserved.

Editorial and Sales Offices: The University Press of Kentucky
663 South Limestone Street, Lexington, Kentucky 40508–4008
www.kentuckypress.com

08 07 06 05 04   5 4 3 2 1

Library of Congress Cataloging-in-Publication Data

Tolkien and the invention of myth : a reader / edited by Jane Chance.
    p. cm.
Includes bibliographical references and index.
  ISBN 0-8131-2301-1 (hardcover : alk. paper)
  1. Tolkien, J. R. R. (John Ronald Reuel), 1892-1973—Criticism and
interpretation. 2. Tolkien, J. R. R. (John Ronald Reuel),
1892-1973—Knowledge—Mythology. 3. Fantasy literature,
English—History and criticism. 4. Middle Earth (Imaginary place)
5. Mythology in literature. 6. Myth in literature. I. Chance, Jane, 1945-

  PR6039.O32Z839 2004
  823'.91209—dc22   2003025135

This book is printed on acid-free recycled paper meeting
the requirements of the American National Standard
for Permanence of Paper for Printed Library Materials.

Manufactured in the United States of America.

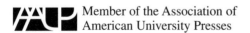 Member of the Association of
American University Presses

For Christopher Tolkien

His father's best reader, editor, and glossator

I have long ceased to invent. . . : I wait till I seem to know what really happened. Or till it writes itself.

—J.R.R. Tolkien, Letter 180, to "Mr. Thompson"

CONTENTS

PREFACE AND ACKNOWLEDGMENTS

How Tolkien turned his knowledge of medieval languages and literatures into the literature and mythology that have become so well known in contemporary culture has become a question of increasing interest to scholars and readers alike. Why he did so has been known for some time: his biographer Humphrey Carpenter has isolated Tolkien's desire to construct a "mythology for England" (Carpenter's phrase) by analogy with those mythologies unique to Greece and Rome in the South and the Scandinavian countries in the North. Tolkien's famous letter to Milton Waldman, of the publishing house Collins, circa 1951, has in this regard come to be seen as a Rosetta stone of aesthetic theory for the study of Tolkien (letter 131).

The title of this volume reflects its nature as an introduction to the complex subject of Tolkien's mythmaking, which rests upon a foundation of Christianity, medieval literature, and philology as well as of those western European mythologies of which Tolkien was so fond. This collection of essays by medievalists and Tolkien scholars and students seeks to advance our understanding of the touchstones (Matthew Arnold's phrase) or anchor holds (Douglas A. Anderson's phrase) used by Tolkien in constructing his mythology. That is, at these points some crucial episode, character, style, language, or concept common to medieval Latin, Old Norse, Old English, or Finnish language and literature—as well as to the mythology that tends to dominate the epic works in these languages—catalyzes Tolkien's imagination in the alchemy of his art. Within such an alembic the transformation of such a catalyst means the final product will both resemble and yet not resemble its paradigm or source. These essays will probe when, where, and how such transformations take place in crucial thematic and symbolic arenas in Tolkien relating to society, culture, history, heritage, tradition, nature, heroism, and love. What becomes apparent by the readings of these essays is Tolkien's especial interest in cross-culturalization among peoples as a resource for social harmony, heroic values as a site for community development and maintenance, and love as a restorative force both individually and politically. All these concerns are, of course, mirrored in the early mythological histories of European nations such as England, Italy, Greece, Finland, Sweden, Norway, and others.

Some of these essays (by Gergely Nagy, Sandra Ballif Straubhaar, Jen Stevens, Marjorie J. Burns, Andy Dimond, Andrew Lazo, Alexandra Bolintineanu, Verlyn Flieger, Richard C. West, and David Elton Gay) grew out of papers presented in the four sessions of the symposium titled "Tolkien and the Emergence of Myth" at the International Congress on Medieval Studies in Kalamazoo, Michigan, under the auspices of the Medieval Institute, Western Michigan University, in 2002, which I organized with the help of Douglas A. Anderson, Flieger, and Nagy. One other (by John R. Holmes) grew out of papers presented in the five sessions on "Tolkien and the Discourses of Medieval Culture" at the same conference in 2003, which I organized with the help of Brad Eden, Nagy, Straubhaar, Rebekah Long, and Anderson. We appreciate the continuing support of director Paul Szarmach for hosting "Tolkien at Kalamazoo" and therefore for the fostering of Tolkien studies under the umbrella of the study of the Middle Ages. Two additional essays (by Tom Shippey and Michael D.C. Drout) were first presented in altered form as lectures delivered, respectively, at Rice University in 1996 and at Bucknell University at a 2003 symposium.

Thanks go to Flieger, Gay, Lazo, Burns, West, Ted Sherman, and Anderson for their valuable comments concerning the title and contents of the volume. Professor Sherman was responsible for suggesting the final title, "J.R.R. Tolkien and the Invention of Myth."

I am grateful to St. Louis University and the Center for Medieval and Renaissance Studies and the Vatican Film Library of the Pope Pius Memorial Library—and respective directors Professor David Murphy and Dr. Gregory Pass—for allowing me to use the computer and library facilities to work on this project while I served as National Endowment for the Humanities and Mellon Fellow in spring of 2003 in researching another project, completion of the third volume of *Medieval Mythography*.

Thanks to Ted Nasmith, Tolkien illustrator par excellence, for once more supplying an image (*Gates of Morning*) for a book cover that fits so well with the mythological/medieval theme of this collection.

The assistance of Andy Dimond, Rice University Century Scholar 2000–2002, in the preparation of this volume—chiefly, rechecking of references and documentation and compiling a bibliography—has been invaluable. The Century Program at Rice University allows the top 5 percent of entering freshmen an opportunity to pursue research with faculty members at the earliest of stages in their undergraduate career. I would also like to thank Rice English graduate student Jeffrey Jackson for his aid in rechecking Tolkien quotations.

Terry Munisteri, editorial assistant for the English Department at Rice, has read and rechecked many of these essays for errors in style and has made many fine suggestions about phrasing and language in all the essays, for which we thank her. Cyndy Brown, editorial assistant for the language departments, ably took over for Terry when necessary for a time at the end of the project. Gina Weaver, a graduate student in English, helped to input changes in the essays; during her absence, she was in turn succeeded by Cynthia Duffy, a second-year graduate student in the department, to whom I am especially grateful for being there when I needed her. Jamie Cook, English department secretary, has kindly printed out essays and mailed manuscripts during the course of this venture. Finally, Terry Munisteri completed the index for this book. To all we are grateful for their help.

And last but not least: We wish to dedicate this volume to Christopher Tolkien for his lifelong efforts to elucidate his father's mythology by means of his careful and conscientious editing of the unpublished materials that make up the twelve volumes of *The History of Middle-earth* and *Unfinished Tales* (and the many other works Christopher has brought to light and allowed to be published). While it is unusual to find a son becoming the premier glossator of his father's literary works, it is not unheard of: I think of Pietro and Jacopo Alighieri writing the earliest commentaries on Dante to explain their father's monumental *Divina commedia* to the world. In that same medieval tradition, Christopher returns to us what Tolkien offered first to his children—always his first and best audience—and then to the world by means of his remarkable mythology.

Several essays have been reprinted (and revised) from their previous incarnations; we are grateful to the respective authors and the journals in which they appeared for permission to reprint them in this collection.

Catherine Madsen's "'Light from an Invisible Lamp': Natural Religion in *The Lord of the Rings*," originally appeared in *Mythlore* 53 (spring 1988): 43–47; Mary E. Zimmer's "Creating and Recreating Worlds with Words: The Religion and Magic of Language in *The Lord of the Rings*," originally appeared in *Seven: An Anglo-American Literary Review*, in issue 12 (1995): 65–78, as did David Lyle Jeffrey's "Tolkien as Philologist," in issue 1 (1980): 47–61. Kathleen E. Dubs's "Providence, Fate, and Chance: Boethian Philosophy in *The Lord of the Rings*," was first published in *Twentieth-Century Literature* 27 (1981): 34–42.

The edition of *The Lord of the Rings* used throughout is the single-volume standard revised edition of its previously published three volumes, *The Fellowship of the Ring, The Two Towers*, and *The Return of the King*. This single-volume edition, based on the revised edition published in London by Allen and Unwin in 1966 and in Boston by Houghton Mifflin in 1967, was reissued by HarperCollins in London in 1993, reset in 1994, and published in Boston by Houghton Mifflin in 1994. References to *The Lord of the Rings* (henceforth *LR* in my text) appear within parentheses and indicate book, chapter, and page number(s)—*The Fellowship of the Ring* (*FR*) being volume 1; *The Two Towers* (*TT*), 2; and *The Return of the King* (*RK*), 3, each volume having two books. Permission to quote from *The Fellowship of the Ring*, *The Two Towers*, and *The Return of the King* has been granted by HarperCollins.

Note: Tolkien generally prefers certain spellings that are used where appropriate in this study—for example, Dwarves (not Dwarfs), Middle-earth (not Middle Earth), Faërie, King of Faery (in "Smith of Wootton Major"), fairy-stories, sub-creation (not subcreation), and so forth. I capitalize the names of his species for consistency.

Jane Chance
Houston, Texas

ABBREVIATIONS

"Beowulf"   J.R.R. Tolkien. "Beowulf: The Monsters and
               the Critics." *Proceedings of the British
               Academy* 22 (1936): 245-95. Reprinted in *An
               Anthology of Beowulf Criticism,* ed. Lewis E.
               Nicholson, 51-104. Notre Dame, Ind.:
               University of Notre Dame Press, 1963; and
               *"The Monsters and the Critics" and Other
               Essays*, ed. Christopher Tolkien, 5-34.
               London: George Allen and Unwin, 1980.

Biography   Humphrey Carpenter. *Tolkien: A Biography*.
               London: George Allen and Unwin; Boston:
               Houghton Mifflin, 1977.

BLT1   J.R.R. Tolkien. *The Book of Lost Tales, Part 1*.
               Vol. 1 of *The History of Middle-earth*. Ed.
               Christopher Tolkien. London: George Allen
               and Unwin, 1983; Boston: Houghton Mifflin,
               1984; New York: Ballantine, 1992.

BLT2   J.R.R. Tolkien. *The Book of Lost Tales, Part 2*.
               Vol. 2 of *The History of Middle-earth*. Ed.
               Christopher Tolkien. London: George Allen
               and Unwin, 1984; Boston: Houghton Mifflin,
               1984; New York: Ballantine, 1992.

EPCW   C. S. Lewis, ed. *Essays Presented to Charles
               Williams*. London: Oxford University Press,
               1947. Rpt., Grand Rapids, Mich.: William B.
               Eerdmans, 1966.

FGH   J.R.R. Tolkien. *Farmer Giles of Ham*.
               London: Allen and Unwin, 1949; Boston:
               Houghton Mifflin, 1950. Rpt. in *Smith of
               Wootton Major and Farmer Giles of Ham*.

	New York: Ballantine, 1969; and in *The Tolkien Reader.* New York: Ballantine, 1966.
FR	J.R.R. Tolkien. *Fellowship of the Ring.* Vol. 1 of *LR.*
H	J.R.R. Tolkien. *The Hobbit; or There and Back Again.* London: George Allen and Unwin, 1937, 1951; Boston: Houghton Mifflin, 1938, 1958. New York: Ballantine, 1966; London: George Allen and Unwin, 1978.
"Homecoming"	J.R.R. Tolkien. "The Homecoming of Beorhtnoth Beorhthelm's Son." *Essays and Studies by Members of the English Association,* n.s., 6 (1953):1-18. Rpt. in *The Tolkien Reader.* New York: Ballantine, 1966.
"Leaf"	J.R.R. Tolkien. "Leaf by Niggle." *Dublin Review* 216 (1945): 46-61. Rpt. in *Tree and Leaf.* London: Allen and Unwin, 1964; Boston: Houghton Mifflin, 1965; and in *The Tolkien Reader.* New York: Ballantine, 1966. Rpt. in *Tree and Leaf Including the Poem Mythopoeia.* London: Unwin Hyman, 1988; Boston: Houghton Mifflin, 1989.
Letters	J.R.R. Tolkien. *The Letters of J.R.R. Tolkien.* Ed. Humphrey Carpenter with assistance from Christopher Tolkien. London: George Allen and Unwin, 1981; Boston: Houghton Mifflin, 1981; London: HarperCollins, 1995.
LR	J.R.R. Tolkien. *The Lord of the Rings.* 3 vols.: *The Fellowship of the Ring, The Two Towers,* and *The Return of the King.* 2nd. ed. London: George Allen and Unwin, 1966; Boston: Houghton Mifflin, 1967. First published in a single vol. 1968; London: HarperCollins, 1993. Reset ed., HarperCollins, 1994; Boston: Houghton Mifflin, 1994.

Road	J.R.R. Tolkien. *The Lost Road and Other Writings*. Vol. 5 of *The History of Middle-earth*. Ed. Christopher Tolkien. London: Unwin Hyman, 1987; Boston: Houghton Mifflin, 1987; New York: Ballantine, 1987, rpt., 1996.
Monsters	J.R.R. Tolkien. *"The Monsters and the Critics" and Other Essays*. Ed. Christopher Tolkien. London: George Allen and Unwin, 1983; Boston: Houghton Mifflin, 1984.
"OFS"	J.R.R. Tolkien. "On Fairy-Stories." In *Essays Presented to Charles Williams*, ed. C.S. Lewis. London: Oxford University Press, 1947. Rpt., Grand Rapids, Mich.: William B. Eerdmans, 1966. 38-89. Rev. and reprinted in *Tree and Leaf.* London: Allen and Unwin, 1964; Boston: Houghton Mifflin, 1965. Rpt. in *The Tolkien Reader.* New York: Ballantine, 1966; *Tree and Leaf Including the Poem Mythopoeia.* London: Unwin Hyman, 1988; Boston: Houghton Mifflin, 1989.
RK	J.R.R. Tolkien. *The Return of the King.* Vol. 3 of *LR*
Shadow	J.R.R. Tolkien. *The Return of the Shadow: Part 1 of "The History of The Lord of the Rings."* Vol. 6 of *The History of Middle-earth*. Ed. Christopher Tolkien. London: Unwin Hyman, 1988; Boston: Houghton Mifflin, 1988.
Sauron	J.R.R. Tolkien. *Sauron Defeated. The End of the Third Age, The Notion Club Papers and The Drowning of Anadûné: Part 4 of "The History of The Lord of the Rings."* Vol. 9 of *The History of Middle-earth*. Ed. Christopher Tolkien. London: HarperCollins, 1992; Boston: Houghton Mifflin, 1992.

Shaping	J.R.R. Tolkien. *The Shaping of Middle-earth: The Quenta, the Ambarkanta and the Annals.* Vol. 4 of *The History of Middle-earth.* Ed. Christopher Tolkien. London: George Allen and Unwin; Boston: Houghton Mifflin, 1986; New York: Ballantine, 1995.
Silm	J.R.R. Tolkien. *The Silmarillion.* Ed. Christopher Tolkien. London: George Allen and Unwin, 1977. Boston: Houghton Mifflin, 1977.
"Smith"	J.R.R. Tolkien. "Smith of Wootton Major." In *The Tolkien Reader.* London: Allen and Unwin; Boston: Houghton Mifflin, 1967; *Redbook* 130 (1967): 58-61, 101, 103-7. Rpt. in *Smith of Wootton Major and Farmer Giles of Ham.* New York: Ballantine, 1969. Rpt. in *The Tolkien Reader.* New York: Ballantine, 1966.
TR	J.R.R. Tolkien. *The Tolkien Reader.* New York: Ballantine, 1966.
TL	J.R.R. Tolkien. *Tree and Leaf.* London: Allen and Unwin, 1964; Boston: Houghton Mifflin, 1965; rev. ed. *Tree and Leaf Including the Poem Mythopoeia.* London: Unwin Hyman, 1988; Boston: Houghton Mifflin, 1989.
Treason	J.R.R. Tolkien. *The Treason of Isengard: The History of The Lord of the Rings, Part Two.* Vol. 7 of *The History of Middle-earth.* Ed. Christopher Tolkien. London: George Allen and Unwin; Boston: Houghton Mifflin, 1989.
TT	J.R.R. Tolkien. *Two Towers.* Vol. 2 of *LR*
UT	J.R.R. Tolkien. *Unfinished Tales.* Ed. Christopher Tolkien. London: George Allen and Unwin, 1980; New York: Ballantine, 1980.

Introduction

A "Mythology for England"?

Jane Chance

Much has been written about Tolkien's mythology in *The Silmarillion* and *The Lord of the Rings*, its nature, form, and origin, often with varying degrees of success (a firm definition of "mythology" would help make his purpose clearer).[1] It has become well known among scholars that Tolkien yearned to create a "mythology for England" that would accomplish for his country what mythologies had done for other countries such as Greece, Italy, Iceland, and Norway: create a religious pantheon of the gods attached to a creational act of genesis that functioned as an expression of national origin and identity.[2] What is still uncertain is what Tolkien may have meant in creating a "mythology for England," and where he turned for models. Generally he appeared to be looking for some uniquely British (probably Celtic) paradigm that might be celebrated as a national myth.

But however one might strive to identify some system of Celtic supernatural for the British, particularly one associated with Wales and the myth of King Arthur, it was nearly impossible to differentiate Arthurian legend from the French contamination of chivalry, an institution that Tolkien loathed (as we can see in the afterword to his verse drama sequel to "The Battle of Maldon," "The Homecoming of Beorhtnoth Beorhthelm's Son"). As much as Tolkien wished to incorporate a system of faërie and perilous realm in his own fiction, and as much as he realized the counterpart to it existed in Celtic mythology, it was impossible for him to accept Arthurian legend as indubitably English. In "On Fairy-Stories," he even sets up the hero's journey in an Arthurian realm as a venture into a perilous realm that marks the mythological

1

form of this adventure as a fantasy, a journey from a primary (real) world into a secondary world of sub-creation that permits escape, consolation, and recovery. Given this frustration with extant models, it should come as no surprise that Tolkien created his own mythology of Middle-earth, related to its cosmogony and history and its system of languages, particularly the Elvish (Quenya and Sindarin). Nor should it come as a surprise that Tolkien appropriated from other systems for the gods, heroes, and cosmogonies interwoven so successfully in his own mythology.

But given the extraordinary nature of his creation of an entire mythology, we might well ask: At what moment in Tolkien's reading of other literatures and mythologies did he conceive of the mythology of Middle-earth? At what flash points did medieval epic and legend spark Tolkienian myth (at least in our attempts to reconstruct the process)— the very instant at which myth emerged (hence the title of this volume)? Scholars usually point to the poem "The Voyage of Eärendil" (September 1914) as the earliest emergence of the mythology, but the drafts of Tolkien's early poetry make clear (according to Douglas A. Anderson) that the mythology did not truly coalesce until around July 1915—with the poem "The Shores of Faery."[3] What catalyzed this emergence is Tolkien's reading of other medieval mythologies or epic works of national identity, most especially Roman and Greek, Old Norse, Old English, and Finnish.

Discovering how Tolkien appropriates medieval idea is not just a matter of establishing source and influence, in the way we look at Chaucer's text and note how he adapts to his own ends some source romance or chronicle entry. This is so because within Tolkien's mythology, story evolves vertically, through a historical trajectory, in his delineation of time on Middle-earth. Simultaneously, a whole cultural macrocosm is represented within the many recensions of his own stories, as if he had incorporated within his mythology the equivalence of a Middle Ages of western Europe, complete with different scribes, authors, and commentators adding new glosses and phrasings to an extant story, and therefore different perspectives. In this sense, Tolkien's mythology is an "asterisk-cosmogony," to borrow the terminologies of John William Houghton and Tom Shippey.[4] Houghton defines "asterisk-cosmogony" in terms of the Elves' "cosmogonical myth" of the *Ainulindalë*, that is, as "an imagined account of the creation of an asterisk-reality."[5] By "asterisk-reality,"

T.A. Shippey means a hypothesized ur-language and its concomitant world-view, or, in Houghton's words, "the tendency of philologists to reconstruct not only the forms of lost words (typically marked by a prefixed asterisk) and lost languages, but also the world-views that those words and languages described."[6] Houghton's final point is that the *Ainulindalë* has a cosmogony not so different from others in western Europe in the early Middle Ages, just as the name "Hobbits" bears an Old English derivation.

The Silmarillion and *The Lord of the Rings* also, *Beowulf*-like, assimilate legend and digression as a means of layering cultural reality, as Gergely Nagy has argued; they are works having what Shippey calls "depth."[7] About the relation between Tolkien's works and his mythology, Nagy notes that:

> Tolkien's texts and the background mythological system they succeed in creating are essentially similar to real-world mythological corpora and the way they invoke their mythological system because of the basically similar relation of text to myth. Mythology traverses the definitions of textuality in the overlay of textual on oral and makes it clear that *no text is myth by genre*. The texts are mythological and together they form a *mythology*, the "*telling* of myths" contained in the background mythological system. [Nagy's emphasis][8]

Nagy concludes that Tolkien's mythology, modeling itself on real-world paradigms, consists of pseudo-text and retextualization:

> What I propose is the handling of *myth as a pseudo-text*, with an indefinite number of retexts, which is a way to account for both the differing story versions and the complex textual tangle. As mythology is the articulation of (in that form doubtless fictitious) events in linguistic form, oral or textual, which is then used for various cultural aims and is retextualized in various forms and genres, it is not in any way different from the retextualizations of an ultimate "pseudo-event" that we see in Tolkien's texts, where even the cultural, historical, and political context of the texts is supplied and simulated. [Nagy's emphasis][9]

Tolkien's mythology encompasses both of these, "asterisk-cosmogony" and "retextualization," and more. In understanding Tolkien's unique assimilation, scholars must invent new terminology and types of discourse to comprehend fully his intentions in creating Middle-earth. Douglas A. Anderson has for this reason identified Tolkien's explicit mentions of Anglo-Saxon nations and legends the "anchors" by which he was attaching his material to the extant body of Germanic legends, not because they were in any sense mutually exclusive, but precisely the reverse. Those connecting points became obscured, however, as his own legends took on lives of their own.

This collection, *Tolkien and the Invention of Myth: A Reader*, consisting of an introduction and eighteen essays, will isolate the backgrounds of Tolkien's mythmaking in theories of folklore, Christianity, and language and literature. *Inventio*—"invention" but as "discovery" or "finding"— in medieval rhetoric referred to the technique for justifying and ordering an idea. Although *inventio* came to be associated with the arts of the poet and the preacher, from antiquity through the early Middle Ages the technique represented an art of composition within the discipline of rhetoric used for oratory and often was listed among the *colores rhetorici*, rhetorical figures.[10] Cicero's *De inventione* defines *inventio* as the "discovery of valid or seemingly valid arguments that render one's thoughts plausible"; these appear with other appropriate techniques, among them, arrangement (*dispositio*), expression (*elocutio*), memory (*memoria*), and delivery (*pronuntiatio*).[11] By the thirteenth century, however, when the mendicant movement blossomed, *inventio* came to refer to written composition and became part of the *ars versificandi*, or the poet's skill in composing texts (which often involved using allegory), and the *ars praedicandi*, or the preacher's skill in composing sermons.[12] For Tolkien, neither poet nor preacher, but familiar with the skills of both in the Middle Ages, invention involved borrowing from and assimilating into his own structures the mythological constructs and paradigms most akin to his own vision of Middle-earth. This collection will demonstrate how some of these "inventions" happened—how particular mythological features crept into his fiction and how they were reworked and adapted to suit Tolkien's differing purpose.

Specifically, after an introductory section on methodologies, the four main sections will explore the ancient Greek and classical and medieval Latin, Old Norse, Old English, and Finnish touch points through which Tolkien's scholarly interests as a medievalist catalyzed concepts, images, characterizations, contexts, and theories that metamorphosed into the myths found in his own fictional narratives in *The Lord of the Rings* and *The Silmarillion*. Although individual scholars may have explored aspects of these medieval influences on Tolkien's fiction, no one volume has attempted to deconstruct these touch points to understand the vertical and horizontal genealogies of influence in his mythology.

In the first essay, in the methodologies section, "J.R.R. Tolkien: A Rediscovery of Myth," Michaela Baltasar provides an overview of Tolkien's exploration of myth in folklore and allegory. Baltasar argues that *The Lord of the Rings* embodies Tolkien's creative principles and beliefs about mythology, in particular, that myth is neither allegory nor representation/symbolism, that its basis is language, and that it cannot be excavated but only experienced. If Tolkien was critical, then he criticized by example; when he disliked how something was done, he provided an alternative. His famous *Beowulf* essay, "Beowulf: The Monsters and the Critics," for example, offered a fresh and original approach to the *Beowulf* poem. *The Lord of the Rings* also offered a new approach to folklore in response to two major contemporary folklorists, Friedrich Max Müller and Andrew Lang, who perceived myth as valuable for historic and not literary reasons. This essay contrasts their definitions of myth with Tolkien's "folklore alternative" in *The Lord of the Rings*, in relation to its origins, its influences, and its audience.

In the second essay, "'Light from an Invisible Lamp': Natural Religion in *The Lord of the Rings*," Catherine Madsen outlines the ways in which Tolkien's Christianity has been assimilated in what she calls "natural religion" in *The Lord of the Rings*. The assumption that the Christian underpinnings of *The Lord of the Rings* work themselves out in directly evangelical ways is often advanced simplistically and without a sympathetic feel for either Tolkien's piety or his purposes. Tolkien's aversion to the use of historical elements in fairy stories and his assertion that Middle-earth is "a monotheistic world of 'natural theology,'" however, suggest another approach. The characters' handling of moral choices and their discovery of awe in the world that surrounds them are consistent with an essentially secular cosmology. The elegiac feeling and tone of the book and its compelling presentation of a world whose beauty and moral gravity seem to derive from nature rather than from God may have the unexpected effect of creating a religious feeling quite unlike that of Christianity in the reader.

In the third essay, "Creating and Re-creating Worlds with Words: The Religion and Magic of Language in *The Lord of the Rings*," Mary E. Zimmer links Tolkien's love of philology—with languages and with the idea of language—with his Christianity. The essay provides a systematic explanation of verbal magic in *The Lord of the Rings*. Concentrating on two types of verbal magic, this essay demonstrates that in the *Rings* "[a]ll word magic and name magic is based on the assumption that the world of things and the world of names form a single undifferentiated chain of causality and hence a single reality."[13] This essay further demonstrates that this "chain of causality" between language and things is forged by the Christian-Neoplatonic principles presented in Tolkien's *Silmarillion* as underlying Middle-earth's creation. In sum, this essay argues that the verbal recreation of material reality in the *Rings* operates according to the same Christian-Neoplatonic principles that first created that reality.

In the fourth essay—last in this section—David Lyle Jeffrey introduces us to "Tolkien as Philologist" and thereby weaves together these different strands of folklore, allegory, religion, magic, and philology in a tapestry of the mythology Tolkien created. This article suggests that through names and invented language Tolkien endeavored to induce in his readers recovery of a mythic sense of history. Tolkien's own work as a philologist and on the *Oxford English Dictionary* as well as his prodigious command of northern European languages suited him well for the imaginative exploration of linguistic consciousness he attempts in his fiction—including its "scholarly apparatus." Speculative etymology of the name "Aragorn" instances Tolkien's construction of names for historical and quasi-allegorical reasons, as well as to evoke what he believes to be an innate disposition to myth.

After this introductory section on the backgrounds, the volume is organized into four main sections, on the ancient Greek and classical and medieval Latin, Old Norse, Old English, and Finnish components that make up the mythology we define as uniquely Tolkien's. Like Chaucer and Shakespeare before him, Tolkien transforms aspects of his sources into a new and wonderful thing.

In the section on ancient Greek and classical and medieval Latin, Gergely Nagy, in the fifth essay, "Saving the Myths: The Re-creation of Mythology in Plato and Tolkien," investigates the similarities between Plato's and Tolkien's relationship to mythology and the creation and use of myths in writing. The similarity between their myth-creating activities becomes discernible when one compares the way these two authors related to tradition (both the "mythical tradition" and its meta-level, the "tradition of the use of myth"). Their own aims and methods in actually using myth consolidate the connection; finally, their attitudes to myth as their own written text make it evident. Both authors are concerned with an activity of *rewriting*, in a variety of senses and with surprisingly similar aims, producing the effect of "saving the myth." After the general and theoretical similarities of the conceptions, some central and crucial details are examined which make it clear that even in its topics and imagery, there is a close connection between Tolkien's mythopoeic work and Plato's writings. These examined details include the role and importance of vision and light as central cosmological/theological concepts; the concept of what Tolkien calls "Recovery" as related to Platonic *anamnesis*; the Platonic analogues of Tolkien's "sub-creation" concept; and the problems with the transmission and the interpretation of myth, to be found with both authors.

The sixth essay, "Myth, Late Roman History, and Multiculturalism in Tolkien's Middle-earth," by Sandra Ballif Straubhaar, explores the subtlety of changing intercultural relations in Tolkien's "calqued postcolonial world," using attitudes through time toward mixed marriages in the Gondorian dynasties as a central case study. A persistent error has been to equate Tolkien's own thinking with that of his characters. In point of fact, however, much of Tolkien's irony resides in the fact that no character, however sympathetic, actually articulates what might be extrapolated as the author's point of view on multicultural issues; created beings display fallibility. Tolkien's fictional constructions of "race" and "nationality" among created beings emerge not only out of his background as a medievalist, a linguist, and a believing Catholic, but also out of his own experiences as a twentieth-century European academic, born in an imperial colony at the moment of imperial decline, and more ruminative than most on these subjects. The assumptions of "civilized" imperial writers from Europe's real historical past, such as Tacitus and Procopius, concerning outlying barbarians such as the Goths, are nicely anticipatory (as, Straubhaar believes, Tolkien intended) of the sentiments of characters such as Faramir of Gondor on entirely parallel themes. Straubhaar maintains that Tolkien would have his readers notice that all such assumptions about the Other are absurd, as much as the Hobbitic one ("They're queer folk in Buckland") is.

The seventh essay, by Jen Stevens, "From Catastrophe to Eucatastrophe: J.R.R. Tolkien's Transformation of Ovid's Mythic Pyramus and Thisbe into Beren and Lúthien," traces the origins of one important—perhaps the most important—tale in *The Silmarillion*, the love story of Beren and Lúthien. Tolkien drew on many literary and mythological traditions in his works, including classical Greek and Roman myths and literature. In particular, there are substantial similarities between Tolkien's *Silmarillion* and Ovid's *Metamorphoses*, a collection of mythological stories from sources such as Homer and Latin folk tales. Among the most famous of these is Ovid's story of the lovers Pyramus and Thisbe, barred from being together by their parents, who plan to run away together but die tragically. Tolkien transforms the tale of Pyramus and Thisbe, used by a number of writers, including Chaucer and Shakespeare, into his story "Of Beren and Lúthien." Although Beren and Lúthien do ultimately die, they succeed in being united despite the initial disapproval of Lúthien's father and are granted another life together in Middle-earth. Tolkien effects his transformation partly by adding a quest to the Pyramus and Thisbe story in which he gives Beren and Lúthien a chance at succeeding, which infuses their story with greater meaning and depth within the framework of Middle-earth. Tolkien also grants Lúthien far more agency than Ovid gave to Thisbe, so that Lúthien both aids Beren in his quest and successfully petitions Mandos to unite her with Beren. Tolkien uses these and other elements to derail the story from its original tragic path, making it an example of a Tolkienian "eucatastrophe," or "joyous turn."

The last essay in this section on ancient Greek and classical and medieval Latin, essay eight, by Kathleen E. Dubs, "Providence, Fate, and Chance: Boethian Philosophy in *The Lord of the Rings*," explores the concepts of fate, providence, and chance, and their complex relationships to each other, as well as to the concepts of free will and choice, in *The Lord of the Rings*. To sort out these concepts and relationships, this article begins with definitions from *The Consolation of Philosophy* by Boethius and then proceeds to apply them to Tolkien's work. Boethius's classic text presents itself not only because it was surely known to Tolkien the medievalist, but more importantly, because it provides definitions in a general—that is, non-Christian—context that matches the world of Tolkien's fantasy. By focusing on specific instances in the first part of the trilogy, where the foundations of Tolkien's universe are laid, the article shows how, by applying Boethius's definitions and distinctions, the reader can reconcile the seemingly contradictory, and arrive at an understanding of Tolkien's cosmos.

In the third section, four essays explore Old Norse antecedents. The ninth essay in the collection, Tom Shippey's "Tolkien and the Appeal of the Pagan: *Edda* and *Kalevala*," centers on Tolkien's attraction to northern European mythologies, both Norse and Finnish. What is not so clear is why a devout Christian should wish to imitate and in a way to revive them. This essay accordingly tries to determine the nature of the appeal of such works as the *Poetic Edda*, Snorri Sturluson's prose epitome of the *Edda*, and Elias Lönnrot's *Kalevala* and the way in which this appeal was communicated over the centuries before Tolkien. Shippey argues that the myths of northern paganism had a powerful effect on the learned world, precisely because they were completely unknown to begin with, and utterly unlike the familiar myths of the Bible and the classics. For Tolkien they offered a new philosophical perspective, and a new literary taste, or flavor. Aspects of these include: fatalism; laconism; a close connection between realism and fantasy; the "theory of courage," as Tolkien called it; and perhaps above all a surprising and deeply unclassical indecorum. Shippey argues that Tolkien tried to imitate all these features, as well as some more accidental ones, such as the survival of mythological material only as epitome. This analysis may help to explain not only where Tolkien's *legendarium* began, but also where it might have headed, if it had ever reached completion.

The tenth essay, by Marjorie J. Burns, "Norse and Christian Gods: The Integrative Theology of J.R.R. Tolkien," leads into the issue of Tolkien's use of Old Norse mythology. Tolkien was strongly attracted to those pagan beliefs that had once belonged to England's past. He was, as well, a devoted Christian committed to the idea of a single God. Burns's essay looks at how Tolkien's mythology borrows from early Norse belief but still maintains the idea of a godhead compatible with Christian tastes. He does this through his figure of Eru, a supreme being who creates the Ainur. The Ainur are in essence a pantheon, but a pantheon designed to serve their creator, Eru, "The One," in essence a Christian God. In character, the Ainur are closely based on the gods of Norse mythology, and they give Tolkien dramatic possibilities that could not exist with Eru on his own. Aspects of the Norse pantheon, however, trouble Tolkien. In early drafts, he refers to the Ainur as "gods," but over time he lessens this idea and begins to insist that they are only called that—erroneously—by Men. At the same time, Tolkien also lessens the Ainurs' physicality. In late versions his Ainur no longer have spouses or children in a physical sense but only in a spiritual one. Changes of this sort detract from his pantheon's vitality, but they also allow Tolkien to stay true to his Christian beliefs while creating a cast of powerful, interactive beings.

Andy Dimond, in the eleventh essay, also writes about Tolkien's use of Norse mythology, in "The Twilight of the Elves: Ragnarök and the End of the Third Age." Tolkien's lifelong love of Norse mythology has been a subject of much discussion among critics, and this essay seeks to track the influence of one particular area of Norse legend on Tolkien's work, the concept of Ragnarök. The Ragnarök myth foretells the end of the world, and more specifically the death of Odin's pantheon of Norse gods, taking place in a climactic battle with the forces of evil headed by Loki. The influence of this myth on Tolkien has been hitherto mentioned only parenthetically in Tolkien studies, and this essay is the first to focus on the topic. Its broad subject is the similarity between Ragnarök and the situation Tolkien describes in *The Return of the King*, not only in their superficial resemblance as apocalyptic "last battles" and specific literary echoes, but as each tale represents for its author a mythological link between the beloved fairy tales of the past and the accepted (Christian/modern secular) cosmology. The written source of the Ragnarök legend, known as the *Voluspa*, dates from soon after the conversion of Iceland to Christianity. This essay demonstrates that the significance of the myth is in explaining this transition, and thereby reconciling for the Icelandic people their two very different views of the universe. Tolkien, a devout Catholic who revered old myths and fairy tales, had much the same dilemma. The thesis proposes that he used the *Voluspa* as a model for the end of his own created universe (which derives much of its power from its credibility), in its passing into the "Fourth Age"—our modern, human-dominated world.

The final essay in the Old Norse section—the twelfth in the volume—is by Andrew Lazo, "Gathered Round Northern Fires: The Imaginative Impact of the Kolbítar," and explains some of the reasons for Tolkien's interest in Norse mythology and literature. One of the methods Tolkien employed to explore the world of Norse myth was his foundation of and participation in the Kolbítar, a literary group he formed in the 1920s in Oxford. Devoted to reading the sagas in Old Norse, the Society became the basis for the deep and far-reaching friendship between Tolkien and C.S. Lewis, another devotee of "Northerness." This paper examines the Kolbítar and their readings, focusing on the importance of these myths to many aspects of Tolkien's life and work. It also explores three ways in which the Kolbítar served as a foregrounding for three important events in Tolkien's literary life. First, Lazo examines the way in which meetings of the Kolbítar served in many ways as the model for the Inklings, a literary society that centered around Lewis, of which Tolkien was a essential and founding member. Second, Lazo addresses how these two literary clubs initiated and fostered the friendship between Tolkien and Lewis, a relationship deeply formative to both men. Finally, Lazo looks into the ways this friendship sponsored the fiction of both writers, particularly toward how Tolkien's work affected Lewis, and how both men hearkened back to Norse myth in their own imaginative works, most of which they wrote in the crucible of each other's company, fueled in many ways by Northern fires.

In the fourth section, Tolkien and Old English, three essays explore the ways in which Anglo-Saxon heroic and religious literature influenced Tolkien's own mythological fiction. The thirteenth essay in the volume, Michael D.C. Drout's "A Mythology for Anglo-Saxon England," argues that, in attempting to create a "mythology for England," Tolkien was by necessity creating a mythology for Anglo-Saxon England and that this mythology ended up pervading not only *The Lord of the Rings*, but Tolkien's entire *legendarium*, including *The Silmarillion* and the materials published as *The History of Middle-earth*. Previous critics have acknowledged and examined Tolkien's use of Old English in Rohan, and of course Tolkien's use of *Beowulf* as a source is well documented, but the ways in which Tolkien created an Anglo-Saxon prehistory of mythology are only apparent in *The History of Middle-earth* materials and so have received less scrutiny.

Drout notes that Tolkien used names and stories from Anglo-Saxon history and literature to link his invented mythology to real English history. For example, Tolkien knew very well that the Geatas of *Beowulf* were almost certainly a tribe of southern Sweden. Yet in the appendices to *The Lord of the Rings*, *Unfinished Tales*, and *The Book of Lost Tales*, *Part 2*, a mythological history emerges in which the Geatas were in fact Goths and the Goths were the ancestors of the Anglo-Saxons, thus explaining why *Beowulf* would be an epic of England rather than of Denmark or southern Sweden (that is, telling of the glories of the Goths, ancestors of the Anglo-Saxons). When this information combines with the frame narrative of the journey of Ælfwine of England, Tolkien's creation of mythology represents not only the development of stories that he hoped would provide a mythic background for England but an attempt to integrate factual history, mythical desired-history (or "invented tradition"), and presumed proto-Germanic mythic patterns. But before Tolkien published *The Lord of the Rings*, he removed the overt connections to English history, particularly by means of the complex frame narrative created by Appendix F. Nevertheless, the links remain beneath the surface of *The Lord of the Rings* and the mythical and historical connections pervade Tolkien's Middle-earth, forging his invented creation to the real background of England and English.

While much linguistic study of Tolkien's fiction involves his invented language, or Old Norse and Old English, semantic studies of the way his characters use language can be revealing. In the fourteenth essay, "Oaths and Oath Breaking: Analogues of Old English *Comitatus* in Tolkien's Myth," John R. Holmes isolates the concept of oath breaking—*āðbrice*—found in Wulfstan's "Sermon to the English" as central to *The Lord of the Rings*. The centrality of the *comitatus* oath in Old English heroic poetry and the seriousness with which Old English sermons chastise oath breaking suggest that a semantic analysis of oaths and oath breaking in Tolkien's fiction might yield parallels to ancient literature as instructive as the philological ones. The model of the fealty oath in northern culture is the Germanic social contract which Tacitus called *comitatus*. Both Merry and Pippin model this type of oath in *The Lord of the Rings*, but the most important variation is the very Fellowship of the Ring itself. For Holmes, morally superior characters such as Gandalf, Elrond, and Treebeard show surprisingly lax attitudes toward the oath, but this can be explained by analyzing their relationship to the oath takers.

In the fifteenth (and last) essay in this section on Old English, "'On the Borders of Old Stories': Enacting the Past in *Beowulf* and *The Lord of the Rings*," Alexandra Bolintineanu compares the Old English epic with Tolkien's modern equivalent. In *Beowulf*, numerous episodes from the legendary past resurface in the present, either through narrative allusion or in a character's voice, often echoing or glossing the situation in the poem's present. In *The Lord of the Rings*, Tolkien makes similar use of the legendary background of his invented world. The carefully culti-vated parallelism between past and present suggests that, in both texts, the legendary past is real, operative, and manifoldly enacted in the present. This interplay between past and present is of great importance in two works purporting, to different degrees, to be based on historical/legend-ary material, be it an oral account of the Spear-Danes' deeds, or a trans-lation of Shire records. *Beowulf* and *The Lord of the Rings* function, in relation to the reader's present, as what the legends are to the central narratives of the two texts. Accordingly, the treatment of the legendary past is often self-reflexive, suggesting ways to interpret the two texts themselves.

In the fifth and last section of this collection, three essays examine the Finnish connection in Tolkien, particularly in relation to the *Kalevala*. The sixteenth essay is by Verlyn Flieger, "A Mythology for Finland: Tolkien and Lönnrot as Mythmakers." Tolkien's stated desire to create a mythology to dedicate "to England" was not the product of ambitious imagination only, but had a real-world exemplar in the Finnish *Kalevala*, Elias Lönnrot's compilation of Finnish folk songs, or *runos*. The impact of Lönnrot's discovery of their national mythology on the disenfran-chised Finns endowed Finland with a mythic past and a cultural identity that it had hitherto not known it possessed. Tolkien's own words show how keenly he felt that England (not Britain or the British Isles) needed something of the same. In addition, his statements to W.H. Auden and others about the effect of the *Kalevala* on his writing show how deeply he was influenced not just by Lönnrot's general example but by the struc-ture and tenor of some of the songs themselves. His original effort to put one of the *Kalevala* stories, that of Kullervo the Hapless, into his own prose, was the heroic germ of his own *legendarium*.

The seventeenth essay is by Richard C. West, "Setting the Rocket Off in Story: The *Kalevala* as the Germ of Tolkien's *Legendarium*." At an early age, Tolkien was deeply impressed by the Finnish language and, as Verlyn Flieger notes in her essay, by Elias Lönnrot's compilation of the folklore and myths of his country in the *Kalevala*. Tolkien set out to retell the story of Kullervo from the Finnish epic, but this grew enor-mously in the telling, and became radically transformed into the tale of Túrin Turambar. He said later that it was this experience that "set the rocket off in story." This paper examines the influence of the Finnish *Kalevala* on the stories (such as those of Túrin and of Beren) that became the centerpieces of Tolkien's *legendarium* and shaped the development of his own "mythology for England."

The eighteenth and final essay is by David Elton Gay, "J.R.R. Tolkien and the *Kalevala*: Some Thoughts on the Finnish Origins of Tom Bombadil and Treebeard." Although much has been written on Tolkien's use of Finnish as the basis for Elvish and his use of the Kullervo story from the *Kalevala* in *The Silmarillion*, far less attention has been given to his restricted but significant use of the *Kalevala* in *The Lord of the Rings*. Several descriptive passages appear to have been inspired by the *Kalevala* (the description of the destruction of Mordor after the Ring is destroyed, for example), but the most important use is as the source for two characters in particular: Tom Bombadil and Treebeard are based in large part on Väinämöinen, the great singer and the key character of the *Kalevala*, especially in the second and third poems. Neither character simply imitates Väinämöinen; rather, each reflects different aspects, much as the avatars of Hindu gods in Indian mythology and epic reflect various aspects of the gods. Through an examination of parallel passages from the *Kalevala* and *The Lord of the Rings*, Gay shows how Tolkien made use of his source to create two of the more enigmatic, yet popular, characters of *The Lord of the Rings*.

What is clear from all these essays is the masterful way that Tolkien adapted from and changed his medieval sources in myth to suit his own cosmogony and literary purposes. Where he obtained his materials over the course of his lifetime is so obvious as not to need repeating—he was, after all, a medievalist. And yet when his readers wonder anew how any one man could have created in one lifetime fourteen languages and a world called Middle-earth (not to say multiple recensions of different works, like the manuscript of any medieval author), it is hoped this collection may provide a bridge to understanding.

Notes

1. See, for example, essays on specific influence, such as Lynn Bryce, "The Influence of Scandinavian Mythology on the Works of J.R.R. Tolkien," *Edda: Nordisk Tidsskrift for Literaturforskning* 2 (1983): 113–19; or the typing of Tolkien's mythology by means of a specific work, for example, Andrzej Wicher, "The Artificial Mythology of *The Silmarillion* by J.R.R. Tolkien," *Kwartalnik Neofilologiczny* 28 (1981): 399–405. Other, more broadly based, approaches to Tolkien's mythology examine the relationship between his medieval sources and his mythology, such as Jane Chance (Nitzsche), *Tolkien's Art: A Mythology*

for England (London: Macmillan Press.; New York: St. Martin's Press, 1979; rpt. pb. London: Papermac, 1980; rev. ed., Lexington, Ky.: University Press of Kentucky, 2001); or compare his mythology with features common to myths found in Sir James Frazer's *The Golden Bough* and Irish myth, as in Ruth S. Noel, *The Mythology of Middle-earth* (Boston: Houghton Mifflin, 1977); or with the anthropological types of myth advanced by Joseph Campbell, Vladimir Propp, and Claude Lévi-Strauss, as in Anne C. Petty, *One Ring to Bind Them All: Tolkien's Mythology* (University: University of Alabama Press, 1979); or with the theory of power and knowledge advanced by Michel Foucault, as in Jane Chance, *The Lord of the Rings: The Mythology of Power* (New York: Twayne/ Macmillan, 1992; rev. ed., Lexington, Ky.: University Press of Kentucky, 2001).

2. The phrase was Carpenter's, mentioned first in his *Biography* and derived from Tolkien's letter 131 to Milton Waldman of Collins in 1951; the "mythology for England" concept was explored in relation to his own scholarship on Old and Middle English in Chance, *Tolkien's Art* and debated at the Centennial Conference held at Oxford, with presentations by Carl F. Hofstetter and Arden R. Smith, "A Mythology for England?" and Anders Stenström, "A Mythology? For England?" published in Patricia Reynolds and Glen H. GoodKnight, eds., *Proceedings of the J.R.R. Tolkien Centenary Conference, Keble College, Oxford, 1992*, combined issue of *Mythlore* 80; *Mallorn* 30 (Milton Keynes, Eng.: Tolkien Society; Altadena, Calif.: Mythopoeic Press, 1995). See the discussion in Michael D.C. Drout and Hilary Wynne, "Tom Shippey's *J.R.R. Tolkien: Author of the Century* and a Look Back at Tolkien Criticism since 1982," *Envoi* 9, no. 2 (2000): 101–34, here, 111–13.

3. Douglas A. Anderson, e-mail to Jane Chance, Summer 2002.

4. See John William Houghton, "Augustine in the Cottage of Lost Play: The *Ainulindalë* as Asterisk Cosmogony," in Jane Chance, ed., *Tolkien the Medievalist* (London and New York: Routledge, 2003), 171–82; and T.A. Shippey, *The Road to Middle-earth* (London: Allen and Unwin, 1982; Boston: Houghton Mifflin, 1983; rev. ed., London: Harper Collins, 1992), 15–17.

5. Houghton, 171.

6. Ibid.

7. See Gergely Nagy, "The Great Chain of Reading: (Inter-)textual Relations and the Technique of Mythopoesis in the Túrin Story," in Chance, ed., *Tolkien the Medievalist*, 239–58.

8. Nagy, 252.

9. Ibid.

10. According to the *Oxford Latin Dictionary*, *inventio* involves, first, "the discovery (of facts)" and, second, "[t]he action of devising or planning," rhetorically, "the devising (of arguments)," or "the devising of the subject matter of a speech." See the *Oxford Classical Dictionary*, fascicle 4, ed. P.G.W. Clare (Oxford: Clarendon Press, 1973), 858, for the citation of examples from rhetorical texts: Cicero, *Div.* 2.85; *Tusc.* 3.1; Pliny, *Nat.* 5.67; *Vitr.* 2.1.5; Cicero, *De inventione* 1.50; Quintilian, *Inst.* 12.1.30; *Rhet. Her.* 1.3; Cicero, *Orat.* 176; and Quintilian, *Inst.* 2.5.7, among others. For a survey of *inventio* from antiquity

and the Middle Ages to the Renaissance and Baroque era, see M. Kienpointner, in *Historisches Wörterbuch der Rhetorik*, ed. Gert Ueding et al., vol. 4 (Hu-Ki) (Tübingen: Max Niemeyer, 1998), cols. 561–74.

11. The major points from *De inventione* 1.5 are summarized by James J. Murphy, in *Rhetoric in the Middle Ages: A History of Rhetorical Theory from St. Augustine to the Renaissance* (Berkeley, Los Angeles, and London: University of California Press, 1974), 10.

12. For the former skill, Geoffrey of Vinsauf's *Poetria nova* in the thirteenth century includes it within the discussion of allegory. For the latter skill, *inventio* was used in the construction of the sermon—an oral, intentionally public, form requiring the techniques of ancient rhetoric. For the *ars praedicandi*, beginning with Thomas of Salisbury's *Summa de arte praedicandi* in the early thirteenth century, see Murphy, *Rhetoric in the Middle Ages*, 323. For an overview, see Harry Caplan, "Rhetorical Invention in Some Medieval Tractates on Preaching" (1927), rpt. in *Of Eloquence: Studies in Ancient and Medieval Rhetoric*, ed. A. King and H. North (Ithaca: Cornell University Press, 1970), 79–92.

13. Ernst Cassirer originally made this observation in describing traditional verbal magic, in *The Philosophy of Symbolic Forms*, vol. 1: *Language*, trans. Ralph Manheim (New Haven: Yale University Press, 1953).

Part I

BACKGROUNDS

*Folklore, Religion, Magic,
and Language*

Chapter 1

J.R.R. TOLKIEN

A Rediscovery of Myth

MICHAELA BALTASAR

The Lord of the Rings successfully illustrates J.R.R. Tolkien's principles and beliefs about mythology. The novel arose in part due to Tolkien's response to the folklore studies of the late nineteenth and early twentieth centuries. Though Tolkien did not call himself a critic (*Biography*, 126), he strongly disagreed with the established treatment of mythology, arguing that myth is neither allegory nor historical document, but a true secondary world born out of language, to be experienced, not excavated ("Beowulf," 5). Because he considered himself a maker or storyteller rather than a critic or reader (*Letters*, 126–27), Tolkien voiced his dissatisfaction through his own writing, thus creating an alternative by example. *The Lord of the Rings* functions as such a piece, dispelling the methods of the folklorists of Tolkien's time by showing the way he felt mythology operated.

Tolkien's reaction was directed at two folklorists in particular: Friedrich Max Müller and Andrew Lang. Though both men hailed from opposing schools of thought, they were primarily concerned with the origin of myth rather than with its literary effects, a practice Tolkien viewed as "placing the unimportant things at the centre and the important things on the outer edges" ("Beowulf," 5). He addressed Müller and Lang in his essay "On Fairy-Stories," indirectly referring to them as "people using the stories not as they were meant to be used, but as a quarry from which to dig evidence, or information, about matters in which they are interested" ("OFS," 18).

Müller's interests lay in philology, and though Tolkien, who was also a philologist, experienced a similar attraction to language, he did not concur with Müller's interpretation of its role in mythmaking. Müller, a comparative philologist, believed myth was used to explain the phrases and proverbs resulting from the splintering of a parent language.[1] In other words, myth came from "a disease of language,"[2] and stories existed merely as explanatory, or allegorical, devices used to alleviate anomalies. Thus Müller favored the "nature-myth," with special focus on solar mythology, by which he believed humans attempted to understand the existence of natural phenomena, such as the sun, the dawn, and the sky: "Clearly, mythopoeic man constructed his pantheon around the sun, the dawn, and the sky. How could it be otherwise?"[3]

But it was indeed otherwise, according to Tolkien, who saw the variances in language as indicative of its ability to create anew, not merely to retell or represent another story: "It is precisely the colouring, the atmosphere, the unclassifiable individual details of a story, and above all the general purport that informs with life the undissected bones of the plot, that really count" ("OFS," 18–19). Through *The Silmarillion*, the mythological history of which *The Lord of the Rings* is a part, Tolkien began to counter Müller's claims, constructing a world from language on both exterior and interior levels. He created Middle-earth as a home for his invented languages (*Biography*, 93), for "language . . . only springs into being as it is uttered by men, or heard by men, or thought by men,"[4] and could therefore only find life through usage. Tolkien also made Middle-earth so it was born out of song—sound and vocalization—and not of light: "A marked difference here between these legends and most others is that the Sun is not a divine symbol, but a second-best thing, and the 'light of the Sun' (the world under the sun) become terms for a fallen world, and a dislocated imperfect vision" (*Letters*, 148).

Though Tolkien's use of light as malleable element rather than signification of God in *The Silmarillion* tended to mirror his understanding of language[5]—how it can be fractured, remolded, engulfed, and diffused to craft something entirely new ("OFS," 21–22)—he did not intend for his mythology to be translated as allegory. Light and language may appear related, but the connection is one of applicability rather than symbolism.[6] Tolkien understood that allegory had its uses; he utilized it himself to advance an argument, inserting the metaphor of a man and a tower in his "Beowulf: The Monsters and the Critics" essay to pointedly criticize *Beowulf* scholarship of that time.[7] Allegory was also present in his short story "Leaf by Niggle,"[8] a brief personal account of the way in which he viewed his writing process; he felt writing the tale was necessary for the completion of *The Lord of the Rings* (*Biography*, 196). However, Tolkien found allegory to be "less interesting" in terms of art because of its close proximity to its archetype ("OFS," 23). In his mind, allegory was defined as a series of equivalents, in which symbols consistently and correctly corresponded to their primary-world counterparts, leaving little room for creation.[9] His desire to present Middle-earth as a secondary world, one similar to yet not dependent on reality, dismissed allegory as a method.

Yet there is no doubt that *The Silmarillion* and, subsequently, *The Lord of the Rings* appear to contain allegorical elements. Readers have sent Tolkien letters questioning what they perceived to be religious and historical symbols: Galadriel as the likeness of the Virgin Mary (*Letters*, 172), *lembas* as a depiction of the Eucharist (*Letters*, 288), the scouring of the Shire as a commentary on the Industrial Revolution and Tolkien's dislike for machines (*Letters*, 288), Orcs as the image of communists (*Letters*, 262). But there are no exact links to prove any of these connections true and definite; unlike the *Beowulf* essay and Müller's interpretation of mythology, Tolkien's writing here seeks neither to make an argument nor to attempt to explain natural phenomena or rewrite history. The novels are perhaps more a case of the "coming to life" of a story (*Letters*, 212), rather than direct representation. Characters contain universals, such as traits of good or evil, only so they might relay themselves to the reader as "real" and believable, but Tolkien never tried to portray them as absolute truths (*Letters*, 121).

An example of Tolkien's preference for applicability over allegory is the Ring. The publication of *The Lord of the Rings* following World War II seemed to suggest that the Ring symbolized nuclear weapons[10] and was a commentary on the rise of atomic power (*Letters*, 246). Yet the series of equivalents that Tolkien used to define allegory is not present. If the Ring were indeed a representation of nuclear weapons, it would have been utilized against Sauron,[11] and its power would have been revealed. Instead, the Ring's power occurs only in story; the horror it can inflict if utilized lives solely in memory and in tales passed down from one generation to another: "That is a very long story. The beginnings lie back in the Black Years, which only the lore-masters now remember. If

I were to tell you all that tale, we should still be sitting here when Spring had passed into Winter" (*LR* 1.2, 50). In a sense, the Ring itself is a type of myth at work, and rather than show the reader what to make of the Ring, Tolkien chose to rely on its applicability, the way in which the reader related to and experienced it.

It is this interaction with story that Tolkien found so important in his portrayal of myth at work. The scene on the steps of Cirith Ungol, in which Sam realizes that Frodo possesses the light of the Silmarils in the phial of Galadriel, illustrates myth as very much alive, not merely representative of the past or as a mode of explanation. Here, myth is an active component of the present and of the future, and those who are confronted by it find themselves engaged in it:

> "Beren now, he never thought he was going to get that Silmaril from the Iron Crown in Thangorodrim, and yet he did. . . . But that's a long tale . . . and goes on past the happiness and into grief and beyond it—and the Silmaril went on and came to Eärendil. And why, sir, I never thought of that before! We've got—you've got some of the light of it in that starglass the Lady gave you! Why, to think of it, we're in the same tale still! It's going on. Don't the great tales never end?"
>
> "No, they never end as tales," said Frodo. "But the people in them come, and go when their part's ended." (*LR* 4.8, 696–97)

Though the text seems aware of itself and its shape, the passage does not dictate how *The Lord of the Rings* should be read. Instead, it portrays myth in full function, as a means of experience, a continuous story changed by its progression, shifting according to those who become involved in it. To use the words of Owen Barfield's *Poetic Diction,* while Müller believed language and therefore myth to be "solid chunks with definite boundaries and limits, to which other chunks may be added as occasion arises,"[12] Tolkien, in contrast, was more apt to see words as the "ever-flickering vestiges of the slowly evolving consciousness beneath them."[13]

Thus words provided a type of "architectural pleasure" for Tolkien;[14] though he opposed Müller's understanding of myth, he did agree with the concretization of language. Not only did the intricacies of language please Tolkien, as they reminded him of his own past and ancestral history—giving him the sense that he, too, was part of a great story: (*Biog-*

raphy, 34–35) "It was not an arid interest in the scientific principles of language [that motivated him]; it was the deep *love* for the look and the sound of words, springing from the days when his mother had given him his first Latin lessons" (*Biography*, 35)—but language also provided him with the tools he needed to create his secondary world. Those tools were essential, for he was not constructing Middle-earth from nothing, but "bringing further into consciousness . . . something which [he felt] already exist[ed] as unconscious life."[15] Tolkien called this process "sub-creation," the crafting of a secondary world to exist on its own plane, "rather than representation or symbolic interpretation" of the primary world ("OFS," 23). "[I]n such 'fantasy,' as it is called, new form is made; Faërie begins; Man becomes a sub-creator" ("OFS," 22).

Through the method of sub-creation, Tolkien invented the Elvish languages of Quenya and Sindarin and borrowed and diffused forms of, respectively, Finnish and Welsh (*Biography*, 94). Tolkien was careful to stress that though his fantasy languages were rooted in "real" phonology, what was important was not so much their origins, but the "colouring" and "individual details" ("OFS," 18) that differentiated them from anything in the primary world: "how powerful, how stimulating to the very faculty that produced it, was the invention of the adjective" ("OFS," 22). In fact, Tolkien allowed himself to become so engrossed in the "colouring" of his languages, the way in which their minutiae brought them to life, that he often felt they were "real" languages that merely needed to be elucidated (*Biography*, 94).

Tolkien's process of naming in *The Silmarillion* illustrates how this diffusion in language is an important and essential characteristic of the act of sub-creation: "And Oromë loved the Quendi, and named them in their own tongue Eldar, the people of the stars; but that name was after borne only by those who followed him upon the westward road" (*Silm*, 49). The naming of the Elves in their own tongue suggests their identity stems from their language, and therefore the two are inherently intertwined. Yet the fact that not all Elves become known as Eldar—only those who make the journey to Valinor continue to bear the name—shows language as malleable. Though every Elf first exists by the name Eldar, distinctions that are the direct result of the Elves' actions re-create their identities and differentiate one group from the next. Thus the focus of the story becomes not so much the singular origin of the Elves, but the multiple tales that result from variation.

This is where Tolkien's principles of mythology begin to oppose those of Andrew Lang, the other popular folklorist of Tolkien's time. Lang's notions of myth "led from Darwin's *On the Origin of Species* (1859) and the theory of biological evolution to the science of anthropology and the theory of cultural evolution."[16] Lang's studies of folklore emphasized myth's relationship to anthropology. He interpreted, for example, the myth of Cronus swallowing his children as a story about an era of cannibalism.[17] For Lang, the study of myth assisted in "reconstructing the earliest stages of human life and culture, much as the fossil bones of a prehistoric creature could conjure up an extinct species."[18]

If Lang had investigated Tolkien's work, he would have doubtless discovered moments in which the author appeared to be borrowing from other, older sources. For example, the story of Beren and Lúthien seems to follow the traditional folk motif of the suitor confronted with the impossible task: "Bring to me in your hand a Silmaril from Morgoth's crown; and then, if she will, Lúthien may set her hand in yours. Then you shall have my jewel" (*Silm*, 202). Túrin Turambar is "derived from elements in Sigurd the Volsung, Oedipus, and the Finnish Kullervo" (*Letters*, 150). Tom Bombadil can be likened to the legend of the Green Man, "or the spirit of the (vanishing) Oxford and Berkshire countryside" (*Letters*, 26) and his wife, Goldberry, the "actual seasonal changes in such lands" (*Letters*, 272).

Lang might also have argued that Tolkien's work attempts to reconstruct early medieval theology—particularly that of Saint Augustine of Hippo—because of its seeming commentary on Genesis.[19] In *The Silmarillion*, Tolkien's portrayal of the Ainur is similar to Augustine's angels, or "gardeners" of creation,[20] in *De Genesi*, and Ilúvatar is much like the medieval Christian God.[21] Yet while these similarities do exist, Tolkien differs from Augustine through his discussion of sub-creation; he suggests that the created world is flawed, or fallen, and beings other than the one God have the ability to make it better.[22] If Tolkien were indeed trying to act as historian explaining theology in the Middle Ages, such emphasis on sub-creation would not have been possible because "the late-antique world in which Augustine wrote . . . militated against a Christian author giving too much attention to angelic sub-creation."[23]

And neither is Tolkien's writing purely autobiographical, though it does contain such elements, both in echoes of previous literary endeavors as well as in scenes that seem flavored by experiences in the author's life. Eärendil and Tom Bombadil originally existed as characters in Tolkien's early, unrelated poems before they became part of his mythology. Tolkien wrote "The Voyage of Earendel the Evening Star" in the summer of 1914, prior to beginning *The Silmarillion*; the poem marked his first exploration of the world that would later become Middle-earth (*Biography*, 71). Tom Bombadil came from "The Adventures of Tom Bombadil," and Tolkien admitted he "put him in [*The Lord of the Rings*] because I had already 'invented' him independently . . . and wanted an 'adventure' along the way" (*Letters*, 192). Drawing from events in his own life, Tolkien fashioned Lúthien after his wife, Edith Bratt. The story of Beren and Lúthien arose from what he called "the dreadful suffering of our childhoods, from which we rescued one another, but could not wholly heal wounds that later often proved disabling. . . . For ever (especially when alone) we still met in the woodland glade and went hand in hand many times to escape the shadow of imminent death before our last parting" (qtd. in *Biography*, 97–98). Further, Hobbits seem to be shaped after Tolkien's own personality:

> "I am in fact a hobbit," he once wrote, "in all but size. I like gardens, trees, and unmechanized farmlands; I smoke a pipe, and like good plain food (unrefrigerated), but detest French cooking; I like, and even dare to wear in these dull days, ornamental waistcoats. I am fond of mushrooms (out of a field); have a very simple sense of humor (which even my appreciative critics find tiresome); I go to bed late and get up late (when possible). I do not travel much." (qtd. in *Biography*, 176)

Biographical associations are also suggested in Tolkien's portrait of the Shire, which seems to be based on the West Midland county of Worcestershire from which Tolkien's mother's family had come (*Biography*, 176), and in his descriptions of war, which were perhaps influenced by Tolkien's own experience in the trenches during World War I: "We must walk open-eyed into that trap, with courage, but small hope for ourselves. For, my lords, it may well prove that we ourselves shall perish utterly in a black battle far from the living lands. . . . But this, I deem, is our duty" (*LR* 5.9, 914).

Though Tolkien admitted these connections were indeed present in his writing—he even denoted many of them himself, as can be seen above—he disagreed with the use of biographical information as an element of criticism, arguing that facts such as these "distract attention from an author's works" (*Letters*, 288). Tolkien felt Lang's practice of reading mythology was incorrect and misleading because it turned the focus away from the story and centered instead on its potential role as a historical document: "[T]o rate a poem . . . as mainly of historical interest should *in a literary survey* be equivalent to saying that it has no literary merits, and little more need in such a survey then be said about it" ("Beowulf," 7). Tolkien believed great stories could and do exist outside the purpose of history and illustrated this point especially in two specific instances in *The Lord of the Rings*.

The first example occurs when Gandalf returns after falling from Durin's Bridge and into the abyss. The wizard describes his fight with the Balrog and his journey back to the living world in the following manner: "There was none to see, or perhaps in after ages songs would still be sung of the Battle of the Peak. . . . I threw down my enemy, and he fell from the high place and broke the mountain-side. . . . Then darkness took me, and I strayed out of thought and time, and I wandered far on roads that I will not tell" (*LR* 3.5, 491). Because no one is present to witness Gandalf's encounter with the Balrog, the fight cannot be chronicled in the annals of history; it will not be turned into song by a minstrel or documented by a lore-master. However, this does not mean the incident did not occur, or that the story itself does not exist, for Gandalf's own words give it life. But what to make of the phrase "out of thought and time"? It appears to pose a counterargument, for it suggests "out of memory and history," and Gandalf's refusal to elaborate on this segment of his experience seems to imply that his story ceases here because it is neither vocalized nor recorded. Again, this is a case of what Tolkien termed "applicability," not absolute equivalence. "Out of thought and time" denotes a departure from the perceived world, and though the phrase can indicate "out of memory and history," it can also be interpreted as a reference to death (*Letters*, 201). Tolkien viewed death as perhaps the greatest untold story, and this elegiac mood pervaded all of his fictions.[24] He alluded to it in "Athrabeth Finrod Ah Andreth":

As may a master in the telling of tales keep hidden the greatest moment until it comes in due course. It may be guessed at indeed, in some measure, by those of us who have listened with full heart and mind; but so the teller would wish. In no wise is the surprise and wonder of his art thus diminished, for thus we share, as it were, in his authorship. But not so, if all were told us in a preface before we entered in![25]

Therefore Gandalf's spoken decision to not tell the details of his death is an indication of a tale that is being kept hidden, and though such a story occurs outside "thought and time" and hence history, the story is still very much alive. The key lies in the telling; language is shown once more to possess the power to create, and this making of art so it comes to be in the present is what Tolkien deemed most important.

Death is also a factor in the second example of Tolkien's argument against Lang's reading of story as historical document. In this next passage, Théoden speaks of his decision to ride to battle against the army of Isengard, despite the fact that the Orcs outnumber him: "But I will not end here, taken like an old badger in a trap. . . . When dawn comes, I will bid men sound Helm's horn, and I will ride forth. Will you ride with me then, son of Arathorn? Maybe we shall cleave a road, or make such an end as will be worth a song—if any be left to sing of us hereafter" (*LR* 3.7, 527). Théoden's bravery does not stem from a desire to be remembered in history, but from a sense of duty. Neither is his speech a form of rhetoric, for he does not seek to convince Aragorn to go into the fray alongside him; he says, "*I* will ride forth" (emphasis added), and thus his decision has been made regardless of Aragorn's response. Théoden is compelled to fight, even in the face of hopelessness, and he is willing to die in battle and thus pass from the annals of time. Again, Tolkien illustrates that documentation has little to do with heroism; even if great deeds go unsung and forgotten, they still exist as deeds. Similarly, mythology, though it may possess historical elements, does not arise solely from historic events. Rather, myth comes from a type of responsibility, a need to tell, to give words, and thus life, to an emotion. *Beowulf* was not written to prove that dragons and other monsters roamed the earth at one point in history, but to relay the story of "man at war with the hostile world, and his inevitable overthrow in Time" ("Beowulf," 18).

This sense of inevitability is important, as Tolkien believed man to be "fallen" and thus engaged in a continuous struggle to regain the vision he possessed before his fall (*Biography*, 147). Yet this "fall" occurred outside history, apart from reality as mankind has come to know it. For this reason, Tolkien felt fantasy—the construction of a secondary world—was the mode by which man could gain a glimpse of the "state of perfection" (*Biography*, 147) that was lost after the fall: "You call a star a star, and say it is just a ball of matter moving on a mathematical course. But that is merely how *you* see it. By so naming things and describing them you are only inventing your own terms about them. And just as speech is invention about objects and ideas, so myth is invention about truth" (*Biography*, 147). Mythmaking, then, is a type of speculation, an imagining, and though Tolkien understood that myths would undoubtedly contain errors, he believed they were also capable of possessing fragments of truth: "Our myths may be misguided, but they steer however shakily towards the true harbour" (*Biography*, 147). Every story is based on a fall, or conflict, and mythmaking illustrates man's longing for a resolution, for a smoothing-over and a return to a blissful, unmarred way of life (*Letters*, 147). "In Tolkien's view, the impulse toward artistic creativity and the motives for the Fall are inextricably wedded."[26] Thus mythology, for Tolkien, seemed spiritual in nature as it illustrated the innate desire to use art to overcome flaws.

On this subject, Tolkien found himself again at odds with Lang, who believed "mythology and religion (in the strict sense of the word) are distinct things that have inextricably become entangled, though mythology is in itself almost devoid of religious significance" ("OFS," 25–26). Lang listed animism, totemism, and fetishism—practices in which he felt people mistakenly attributed mystical powers to natural objects—as important examples of the misguided assumption that mythology and religion are linked.[27] Tolkien disagreed, saying "fantasy is a natural human activity" ("OFS," 54), and therefore it is not incorrect or implausible for man to create myths about the objects that surround him. Such an action simply illustrates his desire for truth: "Yet these things [myth and religion] have in fact become entangled—or maybe they were sundered long ago and have since groped slowly, through a labyrinth of error, through confusion, back towards re-fusion" ("OFS," 26). Because of this bleeding of myth onto religion, as well as the synthesis of myth with personal fact, Tolkien felt it humanly impossible to "unravel" or excavate mythology (*Letters*, 288), in the way that Lang attempted to do.

Tolkien also deemed such dissection pointless, as the reader would gain little by approaching literature in this manner. Instead Tolkien believed the real value of myth lay in the experience it offered its audience, and his understanding of the secondary world supports this. Tolkien defined fantasy as the combination of imagination with the "freedom from the domination of observed 'fact'" ("OFS," 47). Successful fantasy produces secondary belief, through which a reader comes to think he or she is actually living in the secondary world, a place in which a green sun is possible ("OFS," 48–49), or where humans can intermarry with Elves. "The experience may be very similar to Dreaming and has (it would seem) sometimes (by men) been confounded with it" ("OFS," 51–52). Hence Merry describes the Hobbits' adventure in *The Lord of the Rings* in the following terms: "'Well here we are, just the four of us that started out together,' said Merry. 'We have left all the rest behind, one after another. It seems almost like a dream that has slowly faded'" (*LR* 6.7, 974). Merry's quote carries the sense that there is an interior and exterior to the secondary world; inside fantasy exist quests, escapades, and battles, while outside lie reality and the normalcy of the Shire. Yet such a duality of worlds is necessary to and even inherent in sub-creation. As Barfield says in *Poetic Diction*: "In order to *appreciate* it, he himself must also exist, consciously, outside it; for otherwise, the 'felt change of consciousness' cannot come about."[28]

The short story "Leaf by Niggle" illustrates this theory. Though the piece is unrelated to Tolkien's mythology, "it probably did arise out of the author's 'preoccupation' with *The Lord of the Rings*"[29] and "it helped to exorcise some of Tolkien's fear and get him to work again on [his project]" (*Biography*, 196). An allegorical autobiography, "Leaf by Niggle" seems to offer a "personal apologia" for Tolkien's absorption in his writing—in "niggling," or working in a trifling and ineffective way[30]— as well as to relay a sense of self-criticism, for Tolkien portrayed Niggle as "too large and ambitious for his skill."[31] But "Leaf by Niggle" also offers a textual example of Tolkien's sentiments regarding his work as a writer and sub-creator; the short story was meaningfully published alongside the essay "On Fairy-Stories," in the volume *Tree and Leaf*. In Niggle's life, there are two worlds: the inner, creative world, where he begins to paint his leaf and create the country that surrounds it ("Leaf," 88); and the outer, "real" world, full of what Niggle calls "interruptions"—the neighbor who calls to ask a favor, the errands that must be run in town, the garden that requires tending ("Leaf," 89–90). Tolkien reveals that though the two worlds seem to oppose each other at times, both play a necessary role in what he saw as man's search for truth, or the state of perfection before the fall. In other words, a juxtaposition of reality and fantasy is necessary in mythmaking: "For creative Fantasy is founded upon the hard recognition that things are so in the world as it appears under the sun; on a recognition of fact, but not a slavery to it" ("OFS," 55). Niggle's painting is not only completed at the end of his journey, but it is actualized, and the goal he aspired to through the process of art and sub-creation indeed becomes tangible, a living, breathing, growing thing: "'Leaf by Niggle' ends as a comedy, even a 'divine comedy,' on more levels than one. But while it looks forward to 'divine comedy' it incorporates and springs from a sense of earthly tragedy: failure, anxiety, and frustration."[32]

Perhaps an even better example of the relationship between fantasy and the primary world is the Shire. Here is a place Tolkien described as remarkably suburban and bourgeois (*LR* Prologue, 1–2), where being "respectable" means never having any "adventures" or doing "anything unexpected" (*H*, 15). War and violence do not figure prominently into Shire history, and therefore government offices exist more as titles than forms of duty—the mayor's primary obligation is to "preside at banquets" (*LR* Prologue, 10). In fact, life in the Shire is so uneventful that Hobbits chronicle the years not through songs or lore-making, but by the construction of extensive genealogies and family trees (*LR* Prologue, 7). But this does not mean the Shire is a type of Utopia (*Letters*, 197); rather, the Hobbits' lack of imagination and their ignorance of a world apart from their perception of reality become their undoing, as they are unprepared to deal with the entrance of ruffians such as Bill Ferny and Sharkey.

For the Shire, in all of its normalcy, cannot exist without the "adventures" and fantastic deeds that occur beyond its borders. The Rangers, "mysterious wanderers" whose unanticipated and enigmatic habits incite suspicion in Hobbits (*LR* 1.9, 146, 149), are actually protectors of the Shire. It is not until the Rangers ride south to join Aragorn in Rohan that the Hobbits and Bree-landers realize the effect of their absence. Butterbur says: "You see, we're not used to such troubles; and the Rangers have all gone away, folk tell me. I don't think we've rightly understood till now what they did for us" (*LR* 6.7, 971). Similarly, and perhaps with more urgency, the quest to destroy the Ring illustrates the need for a departure from reality and predictability in order to ensure the preservation of the primary world. Frodo says:

> I should like to save the Shire, if I could—though there have been times
> when I thought the inhabitants too stupid and dull for words, and have

felt that an earthquake or an invasion of dragons might be good for them. But I don't feel like that now. I feel that as long as the Shire lies behind, safe and comfortable, I shall find wandering more bearable: I shall know that somewhere there is a firm foothold, even if my feet cannot stand there again. (*LR* 1.2, 61)

Thus Tolkien believed fantasy neither "destroyed" nor "blunted the appetite for . . . the perception of scientific verity. On the contrary: "The keener and the clearer is the reason, the better fantasy it will make" ("OFS," 54).

Fantasy done well, however, can also cause a reversal of what is perceived as reality. For instance, while Merry likens the adventure to a dream, Frodo considers the experience the most real thing he has ever done, and thus the return home becomes somewhat of a disappointment in comparison: "'Not to me,' said Frodo. 'To me it feels more like falling asleep again'" (*LR* 6.7, 974). Frodo appears to be suffering from what Tolkien referred to as delusion, when the potion of the secondary world is, in fact, too strong ("OFS," 52). Frodo's reason has been damaged, perhaps as a result of the effects of the Ring and the vision it gave him when he bore it. For though the Ring is misguided in its purpose, its power allows its bearers to imagine themselves as strong, infallible, and capable of achieving the state of perfection to which Tolkien felt all people aspired: "Already the Ring tempted him. . . . Wild fantasies arose in his mind; and he saw Samwise the Strong, Hero of the Age, striding with a flaming sword across the darkened land, and armies flocking to his call as he marched to the overthrow of Barad-dûr" (*LR* 6.1, 880). Even the immortal Elves wish to avoid the inevitable march of time and the conflict and change the passage of years would doubtless bring with it: "Hence the making of the Rings; for the Three Rings were precisely endowed with the power of preservation, not of birth. Though unsullied, because they were not made by Sauron nor touched by him, they were nonetheless partly products of his instruction" (*Letters*, 177). The loss of this "precious" illusion of perfection is therefore painfully jarring to Frodo, and his return to the primary world of the Shire is empty and numbing. Despite the danger that exists in the act of secondary belief, Tolkien still held fantasy as both an inherent human right and a natural tendency ("OFS," 55), and he chided Lang for reducing it to nothing more than savagery.[33]

But Tolkien did not disagree with all of Lang's teachings. For instance, Tolkien supported Lang's notion that fantasy requires an audience, for Tolkien felt in order to construct a secondary world, a sub-creator must first understand what others define as "reality." But while Lang dedicated his *Fairy Books* to "children to whom and for whom they are told," claiming children "represent . . . the young age of man true to early loves, and have his unblunted edge of belief, fresh appetite for marvels" ("OFS," 36), Tolkien claimed his mythology was for adults, describing it as "a monster: an immensely long, complex, rather bitter, and very terrifying romance, quite unfit for children" (*Letters*, 136). Though he did not deny Lang's claim that "humility and innocence" are traits present in children ("OFS," 43), Tolkien felt this did not mean children were the only audience receptive to fantasy. Just as adults are capable of possessing what Lang called "the heart of a child," children can also maintain the critical view ascribed to older readers ("OFS," 43). Fantasy has to be intelligent and meaningful, regardless of the age of its audience, or it will fail to result in the type of interaction Tolkien felt so necessary to myth.

Perhaps Tolkien's decision to direct his mythology toward an adult audience was more of an example of a preference of style rather than a preference of audience. He was, in fact, very conscious of the expectations of his readers as he began to write *The Lord of the Rings*. He knew both his publisher and his fans were clamoring for another book about Hobbits, but he was unsure as to how he should approach the making of such a sequel:

> I think it is plain that . . . a sequel or successor to The Hobbit is called for. I promise to give this thought and attention. But I am sure you will sympathize when I say that the construction of elaborate and consistent mythology (and two languages) rather occupies the mind. . . . So goodness knows what will happen. Mr. Baggins began as a comic tale among conventional and inconsistent Grimm's fairy-tale dwarves, and got drawn into the edge of it—so that even Sauron the terrible peeped over the edge. (*Letters*, 26)

Tolkien was not purposely shying away from children when he began *The Lord of the Rings*; rather, he was answering his natural compulsion to draw from the rich mythological world he had created in *The*

Silmarillion. He tried to compose *The Lord of the Rings* in the same voice as he did *The Hobbit*, but the result was forced and awkward, the writing too laughable and quaint, for Hobbits are "suburban unless . . . set against things more elemental" (*Letters*, 26). The style of *The Hobbit* barely took him past the first chapter of *The Lord of the Rings*, and he rewrote "A Long-Expected Party" six times before he was satisfied that it possessed the type of depth and consequence he sought to create (Foreword, *Shadow*, 3).

Though Tolkien admitted that "some of the details of tone and treatment [in *The Hobbit*] are . . . mistaken" when seen in comparison to *The Lord of the Rings*, he did "not wish to change much" (*Letters*, 159). For *The Hobbit*, despite its "fairy-story" style, was responsible for creating the link that allowed Tolkien's greater, more complex mythology to find an audience. Tolkien needed the "reality" of the seemingly simple, ordinary tale of *The Hobbit* to decide what his goal was as a writer and where his heart truly lay: in the Silmarils and their ongoing, ever-evolving story (*Letters*, 26).

Thus in *The Lord of the Rings*, Tolkien not only rediscovered his own mythology, but conveyed to his readers the manner in which he felt mythology truly functions: as a living thing, born of language, born of humanity, born of the desire for the divine. Tolkien succeeded in his intent to "make a body of more or less connected legend, ranging from the large and cosmogonic, to the level of romantic fairy-story . . . which I could dedicate simply to: to England; to my country" (*Letters*, 144), for his writing did what the folklore studies of his time could not. Tolkien's work revealed an alternate universe in which his readers could immerse themselves, taking the echoes of Middle-earth into their own primary worlds, for the fantasy was theirs to live and the truth theirs to discover.

Notes

1. Richard M. Dorson, *The British Folklorists: A History* (Chicago: University of Chicago Press, 1968), 162.

2. Ibid.

3. Dorson, 163. Dorson is paraphrasing Müller here.

4. Owen Barfield, *Poetic Diction* (London: Faber and Faber Limited, 1964), 41.

5. Verlyn Flieger, Lecture on "Splintered Light: Logos and Language in Tolkien's World," in a course on "J.R.R. Tolkien: A Mythology for England," University of Maryland, College Park, 1 October 2002.

6. T.A. Shippey, *J.R.R. Tolkien: Author of the Century* (Boston: Houghton Mifflin Company, 2001), 164.

7. Ibid.

8. Ibid.

9. Dorson, 163.

10. Ibid.

11. Ibid.

12. Barfield, 75.

13. Ibid.

14. Barfield, 96.

15. Barfield, 112.

16. Dorson, 160.

17. Dorson, 208.

18. Ibid.

19. John William Houghton, "Augustine in the Cottage of Lost Play," in *Tolkien the Medievalist*, ed. Jane Chance (London: Routledge, 2003), 173.

20. Houghton, 179.

21. Houghton, 178.

22. Houghton, 180.

23. Ibid.

24. Jonathan Evans, "The Anthropology of Arda," in *Tolkien the Medievalist*, ed. Jane Chance (London: Routledge, 2003), 218–19.

25. J.R.R. Tolkien, "Athrabeth Finrod Ah Andreth," in *Morgoth's Ring*, ed. Christopher Tolkien (Boston: Houghton Mifflin Company, 1993), 319.

26. Evans, 216–17.

27. Dorson, 208.

28. Barfield, 103.

29. Shippey, *J.R.R. Tolkien: Author of the Century*, 266.

30. Shippey, *J.R.R. Tolkien: Author of the Century*, 267.

31. Quoted in Shippey, *J.R.R. Tolkien: Author of the Century*, 269.

32. Shippey, *J.R.R. Tolkien: Author of the Century*, 277.

33. Dorson, 208.

Chapter 2

"Light from an Invisible Lamp"

Natural Religion in The Lord of the Rings

Catherine Madsen

It was in 1971 that a reader wrote to Tolkien, calling himself "an unbe-liever, or at best a man of belatedly and dimly dawning religious feel-ing" and saying how profoundly he had been moved by *The Lord of the Rings*. "You create a world," he said, "in which some sort of faith seems to be everywhere without a visible source, like light from an invisible lamp" (*Letters*, 413).

Some eight years earlier, though I was too young to put it so clearly, I had had a similar response upon first reading the "book," as Tolkien tended to call it. There seemed both a brightness and a severity in it, an intensity of focus, that was plainly religious in character, the plainer for not being specifically Christian. In those days I was very impatient with evangelism, and fairly good at detecting it; but what Tolkien seemed to be doing was something quite different. He seemed to present religious feeling, and even religious behavior, without ritual, revelation, doctrine—indeed without God, except for two fairly cryptic and untheological ref-erences in the appendices. The book seemed to have far less to do with the New Testament than with the mountains I could see out my win-dows, but it moved me to religion. Indeed, having once goaded my par-ents in an argument into asking me, "Well, what *do* you believe?" I ran to my room, brought out the three volumes, and presented them, saying, "I believe *this*." It was youthful extravagance; but I have never since been sure that it was false.

Subsequently for several years, on the advice of the critics, I tried faithfully to discover in Christianity what I had found in *The Lord of the Rings*, and on the whole did not find it there. It was not for lack of expectation; I thought, as certain critics seem to have thought before the publication of Tolkien's biography and letters, that all the Inklings thought the same about Christianity, and that when Lewis spoke Tolkien could not be far behind. But neither Lewis nor Williams, nor indeed Dante or Augustine or Paul or the evangelists, struck the same note. I had a bad dream during that time in which the Elves came sailing back to Middle-earth from the West, and disembarking prostrated themselves before a cross upon an altar, repenting of their love for Elvenhome and confessing Christ. I believe this is the situation in which much of the Christian critical opinion has placed *The Lord of the Rings*: it has tried to take the enchantment out of it. It has tried to make an independent imagination a means to a religious end. Finding myself strongly drawn to faith by the book, and yet not particularly to the Christian faith, I think this effort to see it as Christian is essentially mistaken.

The critics who have undertaken to "prove" the book's Christianity have used some interesting methods; they have mined it for Christian content with the same ingenuity their spiritual forbears used to find foreshadowings of Jesus among the law and the prophets. The late Clyde S. Kilby, in his *Tolkien and "The Silmarillion,"* [1] lays much stress upon motifs that appear both in Tolkien's work and in the Hebrew scriptures (such as the long lives of the patriarchs and the unions between earthly and angelic beings), as though such borrowings were necessarily done for devotional reasons—as though any writer might not borrow powerful images from what is, after all, the urtext of Western civilization. Jared Lobdell, in his otherwise insightful *England and Always*,[2] employs the curious expedient of searching through *The Lord of the Rings* for examples of the gifts of the spirit from Paul's list in First Corinthians, an exegetical effort that has nothing to do with how a storyteller thinks. Lobdell also identifies several characters as "unfallen," an impression that the subsequent publication of Tolkien's letters has shown to be inaccurate (see especially *Letters*, 203–4 and 286–87). These methods strike me as a kind of pious occultism, which takes to uncovering resemblances and correspondences and hidden meanings simply because the overt meanings the critics look for are not there. One might as well try to prove that Tolkien was interested in ceremonial magic because Gandalf, Aragorn, and Bombadil chant spells. But Tolkien insisted, over and over again, that he was writing a story, not a homily. He was not trying to encode Christian ideas in his work any more than he was trying to deny them. "Nobody believes me," he complained, "when I say that my long book is an attempt to create a world in which a form of language agreeable to my personal aesthetic might seem real. But it is true" (*Letters*, 264).

It is clear enough from his own statements elsewhere that Tolkien was a Roman Catholic and took his religion with profound seriousness all his life. But he was not a simple person, and how his Christianity worked on his storytelling is not a simple matter. He disliked preaching, not only in stories but in most sermons (*Letters*, 75), and his religious feeling was founded not on a sense of the logic of Christianity but on a love for the sacramental Body of Christ (*Letters*, 53–54 and 338–40). Also, his sense of the purpose of fairy-stories prevented him from making any literal reference to the world's history in his own stories. "[I]f a waking writer tells you that his tale is only a thing imagined in his sleep," he said in his essay "On Fairy-Stories," "he cheats deliberately the primal desire at the heart of Faërie: the realization, independent of the conceiving mind, of imagined wonder" ("OFS," 45). The effect of any open reference to Christianity in his stories would have been equally fatal. He felt that the Arthurian legend failed as a fairy-story partly because "it is involved in, and explicitly contains the Christian religion. . . . Myth and fairy-story, as all art, reflect and contain in solution elements of moral and religious truth (or error), but not explicit, not in the known form of the primary 'real' world" (*Letters*, 144).

Why a man who was clearly committed to his religion should have had an even deeper allegiance to the laws of the fairy-story, I hope to suggest. But it is clear that he did not intend his work to argue or illustrate or promulgate Christianity. Any Christian-seeming images in it are precisely not witnesses to the Gospels; they are echoes. If Elbereth owes something to the Virgin Mary—if one can never again hear the phrase *stella maris* without thinking *o menel aglar elenath*—it is her starriness that crosses over into Faërie, not her miraculous motherhood or her perpetual virginity. If *lembas*, the Elves' waybread, clearly recalls the sacramental wafer as Frodo and Sam subsist on it in Mordor, it is the idea of spiritual food that comes through, shorn of all suggestion or argument of Christ's presence in it. Tolkien borrows Christian magic, not Christian doctrine; and Christianity without doctrine is a shadow of itself.

No one, I think, should imagine that by avoiding mention of Christianity Tolkien was in the least attempting to supplant it or subvert it. Nonetheless, his story is not that story. The sub-creator makes something different from the creation. By recombining the elements of which the world is made—by translating the Old English *Eala earendel engla beorhtost* into the Elvish *Aiya Eärendil elenion ancalima*—he makes something unknown and new. What he imagines he makes imaginable. If, for whatever purpose of his own, he imagines a world without Christianity, he makes that world imaginable to his readers; he may even make it worth longing for.

Tolkien's own statement on the religion of Middle-earth is that "it is a monotheistic world of 'natural theology'. . . the Third Age was not a Christian world" (*Letters*, 220). Elbereth and the other Valar are not worshiped, though they are praised and invoked (and in *The Silmarillion* they are called "the gods"). To explain the relationships of God, the Valar, the Elves, and Men, Tolkien wrote: "Elves and Men were called the Children of God; and hence the gods either loved (or hated) them specially: as having a relation to the Creator equal to their own, if of different stature" (*Letters*, 203–4). The Elves have "no religion (or religious practices, rather) for those had been in the hands of the gods" before their exile from the Blessed Realm (204). The Men of Númenor "escaped from 'religion' in a pagan sense, into a pure monotheistic world, in which all things and beings and powers that might seem worshipful were not to be worshipped, not even the gods . . . being only creatures of the One. And He was immensely remote" (204).

Indeed, the word "worship" is only used in *The Lord of the Rings* to denote *illegitimate* worship. The Men of the Mountains would not fulfill their oath to Isildur because "they had worshipped Sauron in the Dark Years" (*LR* 5.2, 765); when Gollum encountered Shelob he had "bowed and worshipped her" and promised to bring her food (*LR* 4.9, 707); Galadriel, enacting what she would become if she took the Ring, appears "terrible and worshipful" (*LR* 2.7, 356). There is no example of permissible worship to set against these; only the Elves' praise of Elbereth and the moment of silence Faramir's men observe before supper (*LR* 4.5, 661). No one ever names the One, except Arwen at Aragorn's deathbed, and then not to worship but to protest the bitterness of the gift of death.

The Hobbits, who seem to know nothing of the Valar and little enough of the Elves, have no customs even approaching religion. For those who come into contact with the wider world, love of the Elves becomes the way to religious feeling; but even then there is no deliberate ritual acknowledgment of it, only moments of wonder. Bilbo in Rivendell makes verses on the stories of the Elder Days, but one feels this is because he has become *cultured*, not devout. At one point he says to Frodo, "I'll take a walk, I think, and look at the stars of Elbereth in the garden" (*LR* 2.1, 232), but he says it with the gentle urbanity a polite unbeliever might use of the religious observances of his adopted country. It is left to Frodo, whose task leads him into horrors Bilbo cannot imagine, to invoke Elbereth and Eärendil as the Elves do—because they are the highest powers he knows; and to Sam, who in Shelob's lair cries out four lines of Sindarin as though pentecostally inspired (*LR* 4.9, 712–13) and later chooses the name *Elbereth* as a password because it is "[w]hat the Elves say" (*LR* 6.1, 891). In the end all three Hobbits are taken up entirely into the Elvish cosmology—they cross the sea to Elvenhome—but there is never the faintest hint that this has anything to do with God. It has to do with morality, and with extraordinary beauty, and with loss; but none of these things are founded on worship. Worship is not an act the Free Peoples engage in.

It is rather like the epigram of the contemporary secularist Sherwin T. Wine: "The true refusal of idols is the unwillingness to worship anything."[3] Middle-earth is a monotheistic world—remotely; it has no theology, no covenant, and no religious instruction; it is full of beauty and wonder and even holiness, but not divinity. Even the reader need not worship anything to comprehend it. It is more important for the reader to love trees.

"Natural theology," in the *Oxford English Dictionary*'s definition, is "theology based upon reasoning from natural facts apart from revelation." Unless one is willing to call God a natural fact it is difficult to see how this can be theology at all. The related term "natural religion" suffers from a similar confusion, but less so: it is defined as "The Things knowable concerning God, and our Duty by the Light of Nature"; that "which men might know . . . by the meer principles of Reason . . . without the help of Revelation." Of the two terms, "natural religion" seems to me better suited to *The Lord of the Rings*, in which the essential fact about God is his distance. It is other "natural facts" such as the Elves, the Ents, the longing for the sea, and the very geography of Middle-earth, on which the religious feeling of the book depends. And it is a kind of religious feeling that is curiously compatible with a secular cosmology.

For example, divine authority is never invoked in the making of moral decisions; and yet moral decisions get made, and often made conscientiously. "We may not shoot an old man so, at unawares and unchallenged," says Aragorn to Gimli (*LR* 3.5, 482); he quotes no chapter and verse, nor does it seem odd that he does not, since by any civilized standard it is difficult to make sniping seem morally defensible. "We must send the Ring to the Fire," says Elrond (*LR* 2.2, 260), again not through any compliance with a divine command but through a kind of high and desperate pragmatism: nothing else will effectively put an end to Sauron's power. Frodo takes on the quest of Mount Doom because no one else is willing to and it must be done. He has no law to guide him, beyond his feelings for Bilbo and Gandalf and the Elves and the Shire—that and a little knowledge of history—yet these are enough to move him to the most painstaking thought and the severest sense of duty of which he is capable. Though Gandalf and Elrond both believe him fated to go on the quest, the fate that chooses him is unnamed and inaccessible; what matters is not to identify the prime mover but to undertake the task.

In this and other respects I think the "natural religion" of Middle-earth is similar to what believers and unbelievers alike experience in daily life. Whether or not we invoke divine authority, all of us essentially have only our emotional ties and a little knowledge of history. We can build on these, but we cannot outdistance them; in all our heaviest decisions we try to keep faith with the best judgments of those we love and to act on what we know about the past. "Good and ill have not changed since yesteryear," says Aragorn to Éomer (*LR* 3.2, 428), "nor are they one thing among Elves and Dwarves and another among Men. It is a man's part to discern them"—the crucial word being *discern*, for even if good and ill are unchanging, we are bound by the limits of our discernment.

The relationships of Frodo, Sam, and Gollum are one illustration of this pattern. Frodo has no pity for Gollum at the beginning of the story, but he loves and respects Gandalf who tells him he ought to. By the time he actually meets Gollum, he has also met Aragorn and Elrond and Galadriel—that is to say, he understands much more about the Ring and its place in the history of Middle-earth—and he has also suffered terror and hardship, the wound from the Morgul-knife, the loss of Gandalf in Moria, Boromir's assault, and the growing burden of the Ring. He is keeping faith with Gandalf, but also genuinely feels pity, when he tells Sam not to kill Gollum. Gollum, on the other hand, keeps faith with no one but his Precious: he guides Frodo to Mordor simply because he has sworn by the Ring, and he agonizes over a way to circumvent the intent of his promise while keeping the letter of it. His sole emotional bond is to the Ring. It is the possibility of another emotional bond that almost saves him—on the stairs of Cirith Ungol, when he finds Frodo and Sam asleep and loves them. And here it is Sam's untaught emotions, his lack of discernment, that wreck any further hope for Gollum.

Frodo's capacity for pity is what makes the destruction of the Ring possible even when he himself is overthrown: because he let Gollum live, Gollum can challenge his ownership of the Ring. At the same time, the scene at the Crack of Doom is one of immense moral ambiguity: good does not triumph over evil, but depends on evil to deliver it. Good and evil change places for a moment when Frodo claims the Ring and Gollum attacks him. As a child I felt that one of the crowning delights of the book—it would not be speaking too strongly to call it a eucatastrophe—was that Gollum got his Precious back: that his wickedness, his horrid speech, his murderous craving, and his pitiful existence were taken up into the center and solution of the story, and not by being redeemed but by being allowed to play themselves out. His very nastiness and spite become the necessary tools, shadow and foil to Frodo's decency and courage; the fate that chose Frodo chose Gollum too. Even sin is not wasted but woven into the pattern. In natural religion as in the Gospels, pity is a mystery at the heart of the world; but here it *encompasses* evil without either punishing or converting it. Gollum is the sacrificial goat that takes away the sins of the world. His life was its own punishment; his death is also his reward.

This ambiguity is surely a necessary quality of religion without revelation, for without the possibility of direct supernatural intervention it is the natural beings, incapable of being entirely good, who must bring everything about. Therefore all triumphs are mixed; every victory over evil is also a depletion of the good. They diminish together. Indeed, all of Middle-earth is in a state of devolution, a long decline from Elder Days to after-days. The Elves are fading; the Men of Númenor are becoming like "lesser" men. Even the landscape is broken: Beleriand is gone, and Arnor is uninhabited, and Hollin is deserted. The drowning of Númenor has changed the shape of the world.

It is clear that both the light and the darkness in Middle-earth are less than they once were. Morgoth was a greater enemy than Sauron, and the Elves were stronger in resisting him; Morgoth took away the light by stealing the Silmarils, whereas Sauron only blocks the light with a vast cloud of smoke; Elbereth scattered the stars and sent Eärendil among them in his ship, but Galadriel only seals a little of that light in a glass. Aragorn is a hero and a descendant of heroes, but he is brought up in hiding and given the name of Hope; Arwen possesses the beauty of Lúthien, but she is born in the twilight of her people and her title is Evenstar; these two restore the original glories only for a little while, before the world is altered and "fades into the light of common day" (William Wordsworth, "Ode on Intimations of Immortality," line 76). Indeed *The Lord of the Rings* may be read as the story of how the Elves vanished from Middle-earth, fully as much as the story of the unmaking of the Ring. The tragedy of the Ring's destruction is that it cannot do anything positive, only prevent the great evil of Sauron's domination; in fact it guarantees the lesser evil, the departure of the Elves and the beginning of the Dominion of Men. The story has a eucatastrophe, but it has no happy ending.

Whether or not the sense of "fading" is compatible with Christianity may be debated. Certainly Tolkien did not feel it to be contrary. Verlyn Flieger sees it as evidence of the "precariousness" of his faith: "however he may qualify the pagan point of view, his heart is with the tragedy."[4] But Tolkien himself, in a letter to a reader, takes it entirely into the Christian framework: "I am a Christian and indeed a Roman Catholic, *so that* I do not expect 'history' to be anything but a 'long defeat'" (emphasis added; *Letters*, 255). On the other hand one may legitimately wonder how good he felt the news of the Gospels to be, given the opposing strength of the tragic feeling. For he himself did not live out of history; he suffered loss without reparation as everyone suffers it, Christian or not. The sense of "fading" is rooted in the central fact of the human condition, prior to all creeds and covenants. We are mortal: we do not see our own works come to fruition, but look back to those who went before us and are gone. Those we most admire we will never meet; we can only try to be worthy of them in our own work. Those we love die, and we lose not only their presence but even a sufficient memory of what they were. Our life is not even a there-and-back-again journey that leaves us in good health and good condition; inasmuch as we take on the responsibilities it lays on us ("I will take the Ring, though I do not know the way" [*LR* 2.2, 264]), it brings us to the limit of our endurance—our real limit, not our imagined one—and then, if we are still alive, it sends us home to discover that we are not even whole enough to live there. Frodo's woundedness after his journey is not only the inexorable outcome of his ordeal with the Ring, but the thing that happens to all of us. The Christian hope of resurrection is one way of enduring this devastation, but it is one faint possibility in a world of crushing actualities. In the whole long story of the War of the Ring, the one challenge to the mortality of Men is Aragorn's last assertion, "Behold! we are not bound for ever to the circles of the world, and beyond them is more than memory" (*LR* Appendix A.1.v, 1038). But what he says just before that carries far more conviction, and its language is direct and not speculative: "there is no comfort for such pain within the circles of the world" (*LR* Appendix A.1.v, 1037). His final hope does not cancel this: in fact it seems only to try to soften what cannot be softened. Certainly it does not seem to comfort Arwen.

To answer mortals' suffering on earth with the hope of a compensation from beyond the earth is in fact unconvincing. Any answer to the pain inflicted by nature must come from within nature. A supernatural answer deliberately cheats the primal desire of all rational beings, to have their lives make sense in the terms on which they are lived. But there is another kind of hope in the book, one that has nothing to do with overcoming death, and has little even to do with the future. It is attached to the present, sometimes to the past, and its effect is not to override despair but to give people small measures of strength to keep acting in spite of it. It is what the Hobbits feel when they see Elves, or the stars; it is what the reader feels about the languages and the half-told histories and the sense of beholding a separate world. It is what Tolkien, in the essay "On Fairy-Stories," calls Recovery: awakened senses, immediate attention, "'seeing things as we are (or were) meant to see them'—as things apart from ourselves" ("OFS," 74). It is the sense Frodo has in Lórien the moment his blindfold is removed and he first sees the land:

> A light was upon it for which his language had no name. . . . He saw no
> colour but those he knew, gold and white and blue and green, but they

were fresh and poignant, as if he had at that moment first perceived them and made for them names new and wonderful. (*LR* 2.6, 341)

This is a gratitude to other beings for their otherness: a gratitude the Hobbits feel most of all toward the Elves and their landscapes, and in a smaller degree toward the Ents, and which extends for the reader over the whole book, into Moria, and the fields of Rohan, and Dunharrow, and even into the Dead Marshes and the barren plains of Mordor, because they are all seen with awakened senses. To my mind, it is the most compelling thing about the book—and also the least Christian: for this kind of attention is unmediated, available to anyone of any persuasion, and not contingent upon belief. (And it is not taught as a part of Christian learning, except to aspiring mystics as an "advanced" technique of prayer.) Nothing in the awakening of the senses points one inevitably toward Christ; if anything, it points one to the world, since it is so often the landscape or the heavens or the beauty of other people that startles the mind into attention. It is true that, in the cosmology of *The Lord of the Rings*, the Valar shaped the landscape and Elbereth sowed the stars, but Tolkien never forces cosmology into these moments of attention. Most often, the means by which hope comes is indistinct, but the fact of it is clear, as when Sam looks up from the darkness of Mordor by night:

> There, peeping among the cloud-wrack above a dark tor high up in the mountains, Sam saw a white star twinkle for a while. The beauty of it smote his heart, as he looked up out of the forsaken land, and hope returned to him. For like a shaft, clear and cold, the thought pierced him that in the end the Shadow was only a small and passing thing: there was light and high beauty for ever beyond its reach. (*LR* 6.2, 901)

There is nothing in this to suggest hope in the sense of personal immortality; even the star may not be immortal, though it will outlast Sam and all his people. For that moment, the unexpected presence of beauty in the midst of desolation is enough to assure that beauty will endure forever—because of the otherness of the other, because of its very distance, perhaps (could one see it as beauty) because of the very distance of God.

There is another writer whose work is concerned with this kind of direct attention, and who says in philosophical form what Tolkien's story says implicitly; there is no evidence that either had read the other, but the similarities in image and temperament are striking:

> [I]t is from the wastes of waters that [pity] reaches our heart. It is from the solemn march of the high stars that it melts the soul. Can pity come from the rocks and forgiveness from the wet sea-sands? Why not? Everything comes from the encounter of the Self with the Not-Self.[5]

This is John Cowper Powys, like Tolkien a rather unplaceable figure on the margins of twentieth-century English literature. His great project as a writer was to delineate a religious outlook that in his book *A Philosophy of Solitude* he called "Elementalism." In his view, power and solace derive directly from nature, and the capacity for kindness grows out of a knowledge of one's own loneliness, one's direct connection to the elements. It is very much like the phenomenon Tolkien calls "recovery"—and he uses another word to which Tolkien attaches importance:

> The clue-word, and it is tragically significant that it has become what it has, to all our modern pleasures, is the word "escape." Escape from what, and into what? Alas! escape from ourselves and into the whirlpool of the crowd! There is only one true escape . . . and this is a sinking down into the mystery of the inanimate.[6]

The formal theological views of the two men are almost opposite: Powys was an unabashed pagan, and intentionally used the word "worship" toward the elements, meaning that very attitude of mind which Tolkien describes as "seeing things . . . as things apart from ourselves." Powys also refused to contemplate worshiping God: he was implacably at odds with a Creator whose designs could permit cruelty to exist. Yet between the orthodox teller of fairy-stories and the unorthodox maker of philosophies there is a curious common ground. Both of them cared profoundly about pity; both attached great importance to the otherness of the other; and both showed the spirit's sustenance coming from solitary moments of attention to the natural world. I will give one more example:

> Under our feet the earth, above our heads the sky; while the murmur of the generations . . . mingles with that deeper sound, audible only to ears

purged by solitude, whereby the mystery of the Inanimate whispers to itself below the noises of the world.[7]

Thus John Cowper Powys. And Tolkien:

I was alone, forgotten, without escape upon the hard horn of the world. There I lay staring upward, while the stars wheeled over, and each day was as long as a life-age of the earth. Faint to my ears came the gathered rumour of all lands: the springing and the dying, the song and the weeping, and the slow everlasting groan of overburdened stone. (*LR* 3.5, 491)

Whoever sent Gandalf back from the dead in this scene is never (except sketchily, in the *Letters*, 201–3) identified, and in the end it does not matter to the story. What the rocks said mattered too much to be left out. Their "slow everlasting groan" is the theological statement at the heart of the book. The world itself and its wearing—time, and the body, and the elements—is the only revelation we have. Not through our beliefs, but through loneliness, pity, and unmediated attention to these present and imperfect things, do we attain what strength and solace we can have. Tragedy and hope are simultaneous and not sequential. It is a religion more truly catholic than the one Tolkien professed.

This may be the reason for his allegiance to the laws and form of the fairy-story above those of his own religion. He wished, it seems, to show a world on its own terms, in which both catastrophe and eucatastrophe developed from natural facts, because these carry a weight which the supernatural cannot; they are internally consistent and satisfy a deep desire. In the essay "On Fairy-Stories," Tolkien suggests that while the stories of mortals are often occupied with the escape from death, those of the Elves must be concerned with the escape from deathlessness ("OFS," 81). But might not a Christian imagine the escape from Christianity? I do not mean the abandonment of it, which at present is relatively easy for those who incline that way. I mean the escape from its history, its accretions of theology which have put such a strain on both reason and kindness; its exclusiveness of doctrine which has caused such suffering to pagans and heretics, and to Jews; the ugliness and want of intellect in most of its daily celebrations; and the burden of evangelism, which sets the individual Christian in a position of superiority that is always impossible to defend. The escape from all this into some state where the heart's reasons for believing can be remembered, some landscape illumined with a light for which our language has no name—perhaps not even the name of Jesus, so weighted down and so abused.

Yet having imagined such a place, how different must be the possible responses among those who read the story. For the writer remains a Christian; he has simply made a new approach to the heart of his faith, more bearable to his mind and character. But not all his readers will be led to Christianity by his work. Or if led there, some may conclude that the fire they sought has in fact struck a different altar: that for them Tolkien has simultaneously made holiness imaginable and made it imaginable apart from Christianity. For Christianity is above all concerned with *showing forth*, making God visible: either in the Incarnation, in which he is said to have become a man, or in the Eucharist, in which he is said to enter bread and wine. In *The Lord of the Rings* God is not shown forth, nor does he even speak, but acts in history with the greatest subtlety. He does not violate the laws of flesh or of food, but remains the last Other behind all otherness that may be loved. Those who are struck by this reticence will not turn to the Nicene Creed's formula *et incarnatus est* but to a more obscure and paradoxical Hebrew saying: *lo sh'mo bo sh'mo*, "Where the Name is not uttered, there the Name is present."[8] For some thousand pages Tolkien refrained from taking the Lord's name in vain; invisible, it illuminates the whole.

Notes

1. Clyde S. Kilby, *Tolkien and "The Silmarillion"* (Wheaton, Ill.: Harold Shaw Publishers, 1976).

2. Jared Lobdell, *England and Always: Tolkien's World of the Rings* (Grand Rapids, Mich.: Eerdmans, 1981).

3. Sherwin T. Wine, *Judaism beyond God* (Farmington Hills, Mich.: Society for Humanistic Judaism, 1985), 107.

4. Verlyn Flieger, *Splintered Light: Logos and Language in Tolkien's World* (Grand Rapids, Mich.: Eerdmans, 1983), 22.

5. John Cowper Powys, *A Philosophy of Solitude* (New York: Simon and Schuster, 1933), 161.

6. Powys, 112.

7. Powys, 130.

8. Eric Gutkind, *The Body of God: First Steps toward an Anti-Theology* (New York: Horizon, 1969), 26.

Chapter 3

CREATING AND RE-CREATING WORLDS WITH WORDS

The Religion and Magic of Language in The Lord of the Rings

MARY E. ZIMMER

THEN GOD SAID, "LET THE WATERS UNDER THE HEAVENS BE GATHERED TOGETHER INTO ONE PLACE, AND LET THE DRY LAND APPEAR," AND IT WAS SO.
—Genesis 1:9

[W]E MAKE IN OUR MEASURE AND IN OUR DERIVATIVE MODE, BECAUSE WE ARE MADE: AND NOT ONLY MADE, BUT MADE IN THE IMAGE AND LIKENESS OF A MAKER.
—J.R.R. Tolkien, "On Fairy-Stories"

In his essay "On Fairy-Stories," Tolkien likens verbal magic to everyday language, declaring, "[I]ncantations might indeed be said to be only another view of adjectives." Both incantations and adjectives modify reality through the human "powers of generalization and abstraction," which allow us to disconnect adjectives from nouns and abstract properties from substances. Tolkien gives an example of such activity when he observes that we see "not only green-grass, discriminating it from other things, but we see that it is *green* as well as being *grass*" ("OFS," 22). In other words, we are not doomed to the mere identification of things given in the world, but instead, recognizing that the adjective "green" can be disconnected from the noun "grass," we are able to conceive that things could be different. Having realized the nonnecessity of this world, we are free to conceive of any number of adjective-noun and property-substance combinations: "The mind that thought of *light, heavy, grey, yellow, still, swift,* also conceived of the magic that would make heavy things light and able to fly, turn grey lead into yellow gold, and the still rock into a swift water. If it could do the one it could do the other. It inevitably did both" ("OFS," 22). The magician, in other words, merely strives to realize the possible worlds implied in the structure of language; all magic is linguistic in inspiration.

The magic of Tolkien's *The Lord of the Rings* is linguistic in another sense as well. For in this trilogy, magic is not only inspired by the structure of language but is also effected through actual language use. Unfortunately, criticism that addresses verbal magic in *The Lord of the Rings* does so inadequately. For example, one critic observes that there is "a kind of magic" in the power words have over things, but she does not specify what "kind" of magic that is;[1] another critic asserts that because "there is a thing for each word and a word for each thing . . . [the] signifier then *naturally* has power over signified" (emphasis added), but he does not identify the law of nature to which he alludes.[2]

This essay provides a systematic explanation of verbal magic in *The Lord of the Rings*. The similarities between verbal magic in Tolkien's text and the accounts of verbal magic given in such anthropological classics as *The Golden Bough* are numerous and striking. I concentrate here on two types of verbal magic found in both and, following Ernst Cassirer, term these "word magic" and "name magic." Specifically, we examine the "word magic" of incantations and two forms of "name magic": the tabooing of proper names and the changing of a person's name to signify a substantial change in the person. This examination demonstrates with regard to Middle-earth a conclusion advanced by Cassirer with regard to this earth—namely, that "[a]ll word magic and name magic is based on the assumption that the world of things and the world of names form a single undifferentiated chain of causality and hence a single reality."[3] This essay further demonstrates that this "chain of causality" between language and things in *The Lord of the Rings* is forged by the Christian-Neoplatonic principles presented in Tolkien's *Silmarillion* as underlying Middle-earth's creation. In sum, this essay argues that the verbal re-creation of material reality in *The Lord of the Rings* operates

according to the same Christian-Neoplatonic principles that first created
that reality.

Carveth Read divides the development of this earth's magic into
four stages, only the first two of which concern us here. The first stage is
that of "direct magic," comprised of "merely wishes, or commands, or
warnings."[4] There are a few examples of this relatively primitive type of
magic in *The Lord of the Rings*, such as when Aragorn heals Éowyn
from her deathly rest, calling to her: *"Éowyn Éomund's daughter, awake!*
For your enemy has passed away!" (emphasis added; *LR* 5.8, 849). But
for the most part, verbal magic in *The Lord of the Rings* is "indirect"
magic, which operates "not upon persons or things themselves, but . . .
upon imitations of them."[5] Read notes that such magic depends on the
assumption "that to operate upon a likeness or representation, or by analogy, affects the person, or object, or process imitated or represented as if
it were directly assailed."[6] The barrow-wight's incantation operates by
such analogy, portraying a situation in words analogous to the situation
the wight wishes to realize in the material realm: "Cold be hand and
heart and bone, / and cold be sleep under stone: / never more to wake on
stony bed, / never, till the Sun fails and the Moon is dead" (*LR* 1.8, 138).
The barrow-wight's incantation is only partially effective on Frodo, who
"felt as if he had indeed been turned into stone" when in fact he had only
been "chilled to the marrow" (*LR* 1.8, 137). But the magic works so well
on Merry, Pippin, and Sam that Frodo needs to call on Tom Bombadil to
cure them. Tom does so through a counterincantation that works by the
same logic; using language to create a situation contrary to the one created
by the barrow-wight, Tom reverses the effect of the barrow-wight's spell:
"Wake now my merry lads! Wake and hear me calling! / *Warm now be*
heart and limb! The cold stone is fallen" (emphasis added; *LR* 1.8, 140).

The wizard Gandalf also works verbal magic. Most of his incantations cannot be analyzed because they are not fully translatable from the
Elvish, or else they remain implied, with the actual words not recorded.
The one incantation of Gandalf's that is fully analyzable, however, fits
the above pattern. As Gandalf banishes Saruman from the Council, he
creates in language the effect he wishes to realize in the material realm:
"He raised his hand, and spoke slowly in a clear cold voice. 'Saruman,
your staff is broken.' There was a crack, and the staff split asunder in
Saruman's hand, and the head of it fell down at Gandalf's feet" (*LR*
3.10, 569).

As is evident in the preceding examples, "indirect" verbal magic follows the principle that effects resemble their causes, that "as like produces like, so a result can be obtained by imitating it."[7] In other words, if one wishes to produce an effect in the material realm, one models in language a cause resembling that effect. An extensive example of such modeling is provided by Tom Bombadil's dealings with Old Man Willow. Responding to Frodo and Sam's distressed pleas for help, Tom agrees to free Merry and Pippin from the willow by singing the tree's "tune," which is in fact a verbal incantation: "I know the tune for him. Old grey Willow-man! I'll freeze his marrow cold, if he don't behave himself. I'll sing his roots off. I'll sing a wind up and blow leaf and branch away" (*LR* 1.6, 117). What is Old Man Willow's "tune"? Although we do not hear the entire incantation, the parts we do hear are as follows: "You let them out again, Old Man Willow! . . . What be you a-thinking of? You should not be waking. Eat earth! Dig deep! Drink water! Go to sleep!" (*LR* 1.6, 118). Tom does not merely command the willow to let go of the imprisoned Hobbits. In fact, the bulk of Tom's song is not concerned with the Hobbits at all, but only with the tree, as Tom creates in language a normative model of the tree's being.

Behind the principle that verbal magic works through resemblance lies the more fundamental assumption that verbal magic works at all—in other words, the assumption that language can directly affect the world of things. Although seemingly contrary to fact, the assumption that language can re-create material reality is understandable in the context of the Christian-Neoplatonic belief that language first created that reality.

Verlyn Flieger speaks for a number of critics in her observation that the *Silmarillion*'s story of Middle-earth's creation is deeply influenced by Neoplatonic thought. Flieger focuses on the transcendent nature common to both the Neoplatonic god and the *Silmarillion*'s god, Eru. She also notes the similarity between these gods' primary acts of creation (*Silm*, 131); in both the Neoplatonic and *Silmarillion* accounts, the primary act of creation is god's eternal act of self-consciousness, an act by which all creation is known: "[T]he divine essence as known by the divine intellect is known as imitable in a plurality of creatures, as the exemplar of many objects."[8] In the *Silmarillion*, Eru's act of self-consciousness, in which he listens to his thoughts—i.e., the Ainur—"sing," creates an ideal model of the world that will be realized in time.

Here, as in Neoplatonism, creation "pre-exists intelligibly in the intellect of [g]od before [i.e., logically prior to] its actualization in time."[9]

In the Christian tradition of Neoplatonism, the account of creation given above is formulated in explicitly linguistic terms. While in non-Christian-Neoplatonic thought the eternal act that constitutes the divine mind is termed the "nous," in the Christian tradition the *nous* is reformulated as the Word. Like the *nous,* the Word contains within itself all of creation as it exists eternally in the form of archetypal ideas. However, the Word is not only the eternal and ideal structure of creation; it is also this structure's realization in time and matter: "[T]he ideas in God exercise causality in every way over the things of which they are the forms . . . according to the mode of the exemplary formal cause . . . from the idea ratio in God, the first essence of the creature flows forth into its being of essence, and secondly, through the mediation of the divine will, this same essence flows forth in its being of existence."[10] This double quality of the Word as both the intelligible structure and the willed act of creation is expressed in the *Silmarillion* by the single word "Ea," which means both "It is" and "Let it be" (*Silm*, 404), and which refers both to the vision of the Ainur—i.e., the structure of creation—and to that vision's realization in time and matter—i.e., the act of creation. Like God's Word and Eru's Ea, the magic word has the power to do what it says, to "realiz[e] what it signifies."[11] In the example above, by singing the willow's "tune" Tom Bombadil not only models in language the tree's normative being but also realizes this model in material reality, as the tree returns to its proper, inert state (and, in doing so, releases the imprisoned Hobbits).

Up to this point we have been examining the word magic of incantations. Now we turn to the magic of names, a type of verbal magic found throughout *The Lord of the Rings* and elucidated by the Christian-Neoplatonic cosmology sketched (albeit only in the broadest strokes) above.

Name magic and Christian-Neoplatonic thought meet in the concept of the "true name"; for the true name is to human language what the divine idea is to the Word: both the true name and the divine idea express the intelligible form of the thing whose name or idea it is.[12] The art of the true name is a subdivision in the broader field of etymology. Tolkien's interest in etymology shows clearly not only in background sources such as his letters, but also in the *The Lord of the Rings* itself, where its manifestations range from obvious to subtle. At the obvious end, the topic of etymology is explicitly included in the "Note on the Shire Records" that prefaces *The Fellowship of the Ring*. Here, we read that Merry's interest in etymology has left us with "a short treatise on *Old Words and Names in the Shire*" (*LR* Prologue, 14–15). The more subtle manifestations of Tolkien's interest in etymology include his composition and use of words that resemble, i.e., share a likeness with, their referent and, in this sense, manifest what they signify. One type of such resemblance is onomatopoeia, in which the resemblance between the word and its referent is audible. An example of this is Gollum's name; the name "Gollum" signifies the Hobbit Gollum through the word's audible similarity to the guttural (and unappealing) sound its referent (i.e., Gollum the Hobbit) makes. We find a sophisticated play on onomatopoeia in the drumbeats of Moria: "*Doom, boom, doom* went the drums in the deep" (*LR* 2.5, 315). Here, the onomatopoeic relationship of "doom" and "boom" to the drumbeats they denote is enriched by the homonymic relationship between "doom" signifying drumbeat and "doom" signifying the hopeless situation in which the characters presently find themselves.

Most often, the resemblance between the word and its referent is not perceptual, as above, but intelligible, in which case the word's meaning includes a concept (or concepts) associated with the referent. Examples of such "intelligible resemblance" abound in the *The Lord of the Rings* and its appendices. For example, unexpectedly faced with the task of naming a maid child, Sam consults Frodo on suitable names. Frodo suggests following "the old custom" of naming female children after flowers. Sam agrees with this wisdom, but stipulates that: "if it's to be a flower-name, then I don't trouble about the length: it must be a beautiful flower, because, you see, I think she is very beautiful, and is going to be beautifuller still" (*LR* 6.9, 1003). Here, language has very little to do with communication. In fact, the utility of a short name is cast aside in light of the more important consideration that the name be a "true name"—in this case, that the name's association with a beautiful flower will allow the name to refer to the child not only by convention, but also by signifying her beauty. The name chosen is "Elanor." Engaging in an etymological practice dating back at least to Socrates,[13] we can divide this compound word into its root elements, "el" and "anor," which, according to *An Introduction to Elvish*, mean "star" and "sun" respectively. "Elanor" thus signifies sun-star and refers to that which it resembles—

namely, a flower (grown in Cerin Amroth) that is sunlike in color (i.e., golden) and starlike in shape. Furthermore, because the flower Elanor is beautiful, the meaning of the name "Elanor" comes to include the concept of beauty, thus making it suitable to serve also as the "true name" of Sam's beautiful child. Here we see how the "construction of language reproduces the structure of reality";[14] as the child and the flower are related in reality by their beauty, so too they are related in language through their shared name Elanor.

Many more examples could be given. But the fact that naming by "true names" is common in Middle-earth is clear not only by the number of instances of such naming, but also by the characters' attitudes towards the practice. We earlier saw Sam and Frodo's assent to naming female children after flowers. As Frodo comments: "Half the maidchildren in the Shire are called by such names, and what could be better?" (*LR* 6.9, 1003). Gandalf also seems to regard the practice as universally accepted, and if anyone knows the ways of Middle-earth it should be Gandalf, personal messenger of the Valar who created it. When Théoden questions Gandalf about the Ents, Gandalf admonishes him for not paying attention to the structure of language; for in the structure of language is revealed the structure of reality. Gandalf responds to Théoden's questioning about the Ents by saying that the Ents "are the shepherds of the trees . . . You have seen Ents, O King, Ents out of Fangorn Forest, which in your tongue you call the Entwood. Did you think that the name was given only in idle fancy? Nay, Théoden, it is otherwise" (*LR* 3.8, 536). Here, Gandalf expresses the ancient belief that the relationship between names and what they signify ought to be one of "right reasoning" rather than "idle fancy."[15] The relationship between a word and its referent is based on "right reasoning" if one is able to reason from the word to that which it denotes. We practiced such reasoning when reading the word "Elanor" as signifying both the sun-star flower and Sam's beautiful maid child. Gandalf provides another example above. For taking the name "Entwood," in which "Ent" is a possessive prefix of "wood," one can reason from this name that the denoted woods belong to the Ents who, then, must be its keepers, or its "shepherds," as Gandalf calls them. In these examples, "the etymologies of the names for things constitute epistemic access to things themselves."[16]

If words provide "epistemic access" to their referents, one can know the world through language. The language of the Ents typifies such thinking, taking it to (and arguably beyond) the limits of its usefulness in constructing language. In the Ent language, "real names" are not arbitrary, but instead "tell you the story of the things they belong to" (*LR* 3.4, 454). Because these names intelligibly resemble the things they denote, as those things grow and change, so too do their names. While we do not get many examples of Ent speech, the Ents' name for the Orcs is given—in abridged fashion, of course: "evileyed–blackhanded–bow-legged–flint-hearted–clawfingered–foulbellied–bloodthirsty, *morimaite-sincahonda*." This, however, is not their "full name," which is coextensive with their existence and thus "as long as years of torment" (*LR* 6.6, 957).

The above example of the Entish for Orc demonstrates that the Ent language strives to duplicate in the realm of language the realm of material creation. Such duplication is the Middle-earth analogue of the Christian-Neoplatonic relationship between the divine Word and material creation. However, because the Christian God is a personal God, in Christian Neoplatonism the divine Word must include not only the eternal forms of species but also the life history of each individual creature: "God exercises Providence over each and every individual creature, so the one divine Mind must contain the distinct knowledge of every creature as well as the universal archetypal ideal patterns guiding the creation of the world according to reason."[17] In other words, God knows each of us by our "Entish" name. While the following quote is about Ents and Entish, it could also be applied to God and God's Word: "Entish may have lacked anything that might be called a common noun, for Ents would be able to take the time and use the complexities of their own tongue to describe every object and person in a way that would, in effect, give it a distinct proper name of its own."[18]

The view of true names as analogous to divine ideas explains the practice of tabooing such names. For like a divine idea, a true name is the exemplary cause of the material thing to which it refers; the "name of a thing is not a mere label or symbol but the true reality," with "the material object [being] but a shadow/image projected forward by the true reality behind it."[19] Thus, to protect oneself from the effects of magic, one must protect one's true name, preventing its use and employing false names instead.

The fact that the practice of tabooing names is common in Middle-earth is shown by Treebeard's shock when the Hobbits tell him that they are Hobbits. Treebeard responds to the Hobbits' "hastiness" with their own names with the guarded reply: "I am not going to tell you *my* name, not yet at any rate" (*LR* 3.4, 454). For the meantime, "*Fangorn* is my name according to some, *Treebeard* others make it. *Treebeard* will do" (*LR* 3.4, 453). Here, "Treebeard" will serve the function of a name, and yet it is not this Ent's proper name at all. Treebeard's caution with his true name is shared by the Dwarves. Like the Ents, the Dwarves keep their true names hidden within their own secret language. The names of Dwarves given in *The Lord of the Rings* "are of Northern (Mannish) origin," for "[t]heir own secret and 'inner' names, their true names, the Dwarves have never revealed to any one of alien race. Not even on their tombs do they inscribe them" (*LR* Appendix F.1, 1106). Sauron also does not "use his right name, nor permit it to be spelt or spoken" (*LR* 3.1, 406); rather, he answers to as many as twenty-two pseudonyms.[20]

Another name-magic practice found in *The Lord of the Rings* is the taking on of a new name to signify a change in being. Examples of this practice abound in *The Lord of the Rings*. For example, as the Ring changes Sméagol's nature for the worse, he becomes Gollum: "He took to thieving, and muttering to himself, and gurgling in his throat. So they [all his relations] called him *Gollum*, and cursed him, and told him to go far away" (*LR* 1.2, 52). Likewise, Gandalf dies as Gandalf the Grey and is reborn as Gandalf the White. Legolas and Gimli first mistake Gandalf the White for Saruman but then recognize him as Gandalf, a recognition that Gandalf does not wholly accept: "'Gandalf,' the old man repeated, as if recalling from old memory a long disused word. 'Yes, that was the name. I was Gandalf.'" Gandalf the White makes clear that his change in name denotes also a change in being; by taking on Saruman's name, Gandalf is taking on the exemplary form of being up to which the previous Saruman did not live: "Indeed, I *am* Saruman, one might almost say, Saruman as he should have been" (*LR* 3.5, 484). In taking Saruman's name and color, Gandalf takes Saruman's position in the "Middle-earth equivalent of the medieval Chain of Being."[21] "Behold! I am not Gandalf the Grey, whom you betrayed. I am Gandalf the White, who has returned from death. You have no colour now, and I cast you from the order and from the Council" (*LR* 3.10, 569). Saruman loses all the power that his previous, high position in the hierarchy of being had brought him. From now on he is only known as "Sharky," a common name for a common criminal.

The loss of being concomitant with a loss in name also appears in connection with "the mouth of Sauron." This "mouth," which has no proper name of its own, also has no being of its own. Rather, it is merely an appendage to Sauron's being: "The Lieutenant of the Tower of Barad-dûr he was, and his name is remembered in no tale; for he himself had forgotten it" (*LR* 5.10, 870). When we consider that Entish names are like "the story of the things they belong to" (*LR* 3.4, 454), and that these stories have been likened to our lives as they exist in the divine mind, the fact that this lieutenant's name is remembered in no story takes on particular resonance—for to exist in no story means to be absent from the divine mind. It is not surprising, then, that Sauron is referred to as the "Nameless Enemy" (*LR* 2.2, 239); banished from the divine mind, evil things become nameless: "[T]here were murmured hints of creatures more terrible than all these, but they had no name" (*LR* 1.2, 43).

The re-creation of Middle-earth through verbal magic operates according to the Christian-Neoplatonic principles that first created that earth. Since these principles are immanent to Middle-earth, verbal magic does not require the suspension or reversal of Middle-earth's natural order. Accordingly, performing such magic does not require supernatural power, a point made clear by the Doors of Durin. No physical force can open the doors; only speaking a certain word can open them. Yet to know and speak this word is, like a riddle once solved, "absurdly simple," for the word is written on the doors themselves. In short, anyone who can use language can work magic in Middle-earth.

The view of Middle-earth's creation presented in the *Silmarillion* is the view of this earth's creation presented by "all mythical cosmogonies" of this world, in which "the Word [is] a sort of primary force, in which all being and doing originate . . . in all mythical cosmogonies this supreme position of the Word is found."[22] Given the widespread nature of this belief that creation proceeds through language, it is not surprising that a traditional belief in verbal magic is widespread as well; if the world was first created through language, it seems reasonable to try this same means when re-creating it. Both Tolkien and the magicians of this world join the world's great religions in using "speech . . . as the paradigm for understanding the process of creation"[23] and, we might now add, re-creation. We hear echoes of both religion and magic in Galadriel's song: "I sang of leaves, of leaves of gold, and leaves of gold there grew: / Of wind I sang, a wind there came and in the branches blew" (*LR* 2.8, 363).

Notes

1. Judy Winn Bell, "The Language of J.R.R. Tolkien in *The Lord of the Rings*," in *Mythcon I: Proceedings of the Mythopoeic Society* ed. GoodKnight (Los Angeles: Mythopoeic Soc., 1971), 35.

2. T.A. Shippey, *The Road to Middle-earth* (Boston: Houghton Mifflin, 1983), 81.

3. Ernst Cassirer, *The Philosophy of Symbolic Forms* (New Haven: Yale University Press, 1953), 118.

4. Carveth Read, *Man and His Superstitions* (Cambridge: Cambridge University Press, 1925), 60.

5. Read, 59.

6. Read, 66.

7. Alfred C. Haddon, *Magic and Fetishism* (London: Constable, 1921), 15.

8. Frederick Coplestone, *A History of Philosophy*, vol. 2, *Augustine to Scotus* (New York: Doubleday, 1985), 360.

9. Hampus Lyttkens, *The Analogy between God and the World: An Investigation of Its Background and Interpretation of Its Use by Thomas of Aquino* (Uppsala, Sweden: Almqvist and Wiksells, 1952), 176.

10. W. Norris Clarke, "The Problem of the Reality and Multiplicity of Divine Ideas in Christian Neoplatonism," in *Neoplatonism and Christian Thought,* ed. Dominic J. O'Meara, Studies in Neoplatonism: Ancient and Modern, no. 3 (Albany: State University of New York, 1982), 124.

11. John F. Boler, "Isomorphism: Reflections on Similitude and Form in Medieval Sign Theory," *Livstegn: Journal of the Norwegian Association for Semiotic Studies* 7, no. 2 (1989): 75.

12. As the father of Neoplatonism, Plato is quoted as saying, "A true name . . . refer(s) to the intelligible form" (Lyttkens, *Analogy*, 64).

13. Mark Amsler, *Etymology and Grammatical Discourse in Late Antiquity and the Early Middle Ages,* Studies in the History of the Language Sciences, vol. 44 (Amsterdam: John Benjamins, 1988), 21.

14. Amsler, 80.

15. Ross G. Arthur, *Medieval Sign Theory and "Sir Gawain and the Green Knight"* (Toronto: University of Toronto, 1987), 28.

16. Amsler, 12.

17. Clarke, 113.

18. Jim Allan et al., *An Introduction to Elvish* (Frome, Somerset, Eng.: Bran's Head, 1978), 18. Of course, as seen above, God's Word would *also* include common nouns, such as those for species.

19. Kimball Young, "Language, Thought, and Social Reality," in *Social Attitudes,* ed. Young (New York: Henry Holt, 1931), 113.

20. Robert Foster, *A Guide to Middle-earth* (New York: Ballantine, 1974), 227–28.

21. Jane Chance [Nitzsche], *Tolkien's Art: A "Mythology for England"* (London: Macmillan; New York: St. Martin's Press, 1979), 107.

22. Ernst Cassirer, *Language and Myth,* trans. Susanne K. Langer (New York: Harper, 1946), 46. See also Joyce O. Hertlzer, *A Sociology of Language* (New York: Random House, 1965), 268.

23. Marcia L. Colish, *The Mirror of Language* (Lincoln: University of Nebraska Press, 1968), 97.

Chapter 4

TOLKIEN AS PHILOLOGIST

DAVID LYLE JEFFREY

Allegory and Allusion

Readers of Tolkien have often noted that, while he emphatically denied that *The Lord of the Rings* was in any received sense allegory, the trilogy seems to have, nonetheless, allegorical features.[1] Among these, for example, are evocative incidents such as Gollum's (Sméagol's) Cain-like murder of his brother Déagol in the story's ur-past, the tree symbolism analogues with Genesis, the departure of the Fellowship on December 25, and the fall of Sauron on March 25 (which Tolkien certainly knew to be the date of the Feast of the Annunciation).[2] Typically, these elements have been acknowledged, out of respect for Tolkien's apparently unequivocal testimony that he was not an allegorist, merely as part of his richly allusive narrative style or characterization.

Yet there is another notable component of the texture of his trilogy that Tolkien did not deny and that evokes a sense of reference in his stories that may seem, likewise, almost allegorical. I am referring, of course, to his countless evocations of old Germanic and Gaelic mythology along with deliberate traces of their original languages. It has long been observed that the Ring and Faramir and Éowyn are to be found in thirteenth-century German literature: Isildur's story may be read in the *Poetic Edda* and *Nibelungenlied*,[3] and the speech of the Rohirrim is "very close to Old English."[4] (It is actually, in some respects, closer to Icelandic or Old Norse.) Typically, these elements have also been regarded, in tribute to Tolkien's formal scholarship, as deliberate attributes of the writer's richly allusive philological style.[5]

Yet it should be seen, I think, that both philological allusion and what sometimes appears to be allegory (but which in Tolkien ought to be called, as he calls it, "Recovery") are intrinsic and fundamental expressions of Tolkien's sub-creative method. Philology and allegory both offer ways of looking back. Tolkien was, most of us would agree, heartily interested in looking back, and it was natural for him that by retrospective and synthetic definition he should offer us access to an understanding of his "sub-creation": "To ask what is the origin of stories," he says, "(however qualified) is to ask what is the origin of language and of the mind" ("OFS," 17).

This is the statement of a writer who was first and foremost a philologist in the old European tradition. It reminds us that there can be no adequate appreciation of Tolkien's work that does not root itself in a recognition that, long before he took up fiction, he was regarded as one of the most gifted scholars of language of his day.

Humphrey Carpenter and others among Tolkien's biographers have already noted that his route to an Oxford chair at the age of thirty-three was marked by admirable achievement as a linguist and philologist. For several years he worked as a research associate on the *Oxford English Dictionary*, checking and detailing hundreds of etymologies, particularly for words of Anglo-Saxon origin or old Germanic relation. Tolkien's suitability for this work was exceptional. He had extensive knowledge of the Romance languages generally and of Anglo-Saxon, Welsh, Finnish, Old Norse, Old Icelandic, German (from Old High German to the modern), Gothic, Old Friesian, Afrikaans, and Dutch. Henry Bradley, the successor to Sir James Murray as general editor of the *O.E.D.*, is reported to have said that he never knew Tolkien's equal for the Germanic languages (*Biography*, 101).

Moreover, it is apparent that Tolkien thoroughly enjoyed this part of his work—that it was to him intrinsically interesting. He had the etymologist's conviction that behind words, however much they might appear to be simply tags of convention, lay wider significance—indeed, basic truths about man and his world that deserved to be recovered.[6] In his work for the *O.E.D.* he was respected for being meticulous in his use of established sources, yet his colleagues were confident enough of his general intuition in these matters that they did not shy away from his filling gaps in the evidence with a leap of the trained imagination: some of his best etymologies for the *O.E.D.* involved a portion that is necessarily speculative (*Biography*, 101).

Much of his scholarship, of course, would not seem to most observers to be speculative at all. Tolkien was not only a philologist but also an editor—something fairly common for a scholar of language in the English tradition. His most notable edition, that of *Sir Gawain and the Green Knight* (in collaboration with the Canadian E.V. Gordon), became a standard text.[7] Yet one feels that it was the speculative side of philology that most interested him, and that it was to the more suggestive and imaginative aspects of his discipline that he was regularly drawn. Soon his work broadened in its scope: he also became a translator (something less common in a traditional philologist) and a teller of tales—as had philologists before him, such as Grimm. This literary bias is apparent even in his scholarship by the time of his brilliant British Academy lecture, "Beowulf: The Monsters and the Critics" ("Beowulf," 51–104).

Jane Chance (Nitzsche) turns our attention to the several facets of Tolkien's scholarly and artistic activity in her book *Tolkien's Art*, asking us to see these various activities as roles, and part of a complex psychological warfare in Tolkien's conscious and subconscious mind.[8] When he works with the divergent demands of his various roles consciously, Chance suggests, Tolkien plays one off against the other almost whimsically, with a kind of magical Byzantine orchestration of his own many inner and professional "voices." This perspective has one clear advantage: it causes us to look afresh at Tolkien in the context of his principal métier and his academic, intellectual history. But I wonder if Chance's view does not offer us a more complex and schizophrenic Tolkien than is warranted by the mere (or apparent) diversity of his academic pursuits. Chance tries to "save the appearances" for allegory in Tolkien by showing him to be deliberately posturing as a bad exegete when he plays the part of a critic, and thus as speaking disingenuously in his now famous disavowal:

> Interestingly, Tolkien as critic refers pejoratively to himself as an "old man" in the Foreword to *The Lord of the Rings*: "I cordially dislike allegory in all its manifestations, and always have done so since I grew *old and wary enough* to detect its presence" (emphasis added; *LR* Foreword, xvii). That Tolkien's old critic was meant to embody St Augustine's Old Man becomes more convincing within the context of the same passage, wherein St Augustine also blames the Old Man for adhering to the letter in reading the Bible instead of preferring the spirit, or an understanding of figurative signs and expressions of allegory.[9]

I think, however, we may reasonably doubt that in describing himself as an "old and wary" reader Tolkien meant us to see him (at least in *this* context) deliberately identifying himself with St. Augustine's (or St. Paul's) "old man."[10] To put it another way: the plight of the old man is that he is always taking the dead letter instead of the spirit, and we can be almost certain that Tolkien would never have taken philology for the science of the letter only. Chance is right, I think, to suggest to us that we may easily misconstrue what Tolkien meant by "allegory," as opposed to "allegorical." But much of the "allegorical" in which Tolkien engages is fairly simply to be realized in terms of the natural complementarity and unity of his scholarly interests rather than of a contest between them. I am inclined to doubt that there is such a "split between the academic and the critic," or writer and philologist, as Chance suggests.

Tolkien was above all a philologist—and a very good one. In his varied activities as a philologist, we can find important elements of his sense of creative purpose and even of his basic writer's tools. Among the first of these is a knowledge of, love of, and commitment to *history*. In contextualizing his "cordial dislike" for "allegory in all its manifestations," Tolkien asserts that he "much prefer[s] *history* true or feigned, with its varied applicability to the thought and experience of readers" ("Beowulf," 51–104). He believed, with other philologists, that behind present words (and stories) lies the history of their speakers (and tellers), and that a trained imagination and the tools of linguistic "archaeology" are well employed in searching out this "past" toward the creation of a richer meaning in present experience. Like all philologists, he was incessantly engaged at the business of making a better *history of the language*. The linguistic histories of the trilogy are philologists' play— an opportunity to "participate" in the history of language[11]—they are a kind of philological laboratory in which an otherwise untenable hypothesis can be set to experiment. But the experiment in *The Lord of the Rings* is not entirely abstract. Even so great a philologist as Tolkien could not, ex nihilo, create several interesting languages, positing their historical (and moral) development, and make this bewildering inventiveness innocent of his prior love for real historical language. He used elements of the Western languages of the Middle-earth he knew, playing with them speculatively so as to try to recover a richer sense of the *history* of consciousness—shadowing the evanescent history of speaking in an "after Babel" world.

Leaf as Pattern

In relating the origin of stories to the origin of language and the mind, Tolkien suggests how it is that what he calls "Secondary Belief" must be the consequent arena of artistic "sub-creation." He thereby doubly demonstrates how fundamental his evident acceptance of a traditional Christian doctrine of Creation is to his own art. Yet one must in the end agree with those who feel that his work resists Christian allegory. In acknowledging that, in the traditional sense, a one-to-one allegory is not to be found in *The Lord of the Rings*, R.J. Reilly has offered a description of the allusive, quasi-allegorical "numinous elements" in the trilogy especially as "inherent morality" and recalled for comparison "the sense of a cosmic moral law" as found in C.S. Lewis and George MacDonald.[12] One supposes that it is these same "numinous elements" that lead enthusiasts to speak of the trilogy as a "personal theology," "like a Bible," or as containing "all the necessary materials for a religion."[13] And the same elements, fairly enough, lead Patrick Grant to a sustained Jungian analysis of the archetypal patterns in Tolkien's characterization, and to speak of the trilogy's allusive texture as metaphorical and ethical in the Jungian sense, rather than, in the received sense, allegorical.[14] Although Tolkien himself was neither a theologian nor a psychologist, properly speaking, each of these approaches seems to me to be responding to a discernible pattern. One might add dimension to their perceptions, nonetheless, from something closer to Tolkien's primary métier, a more philological point of view.

What does Tolkien actually mean when he avers that as opposed to allegory he prefers "history"? Here one needs to consider first Tolkien's close familiarity with the perspective of medieval writing, which saw the act of writing as sub-creation. For the medieval writer, writing was always an analogous activity, a repetition in history of patterns first translated in Creation, and in the Garden of Eden. In the medieval view all writing that is true will inevitably, even in the world of fallen fantasy ("OFS," 23), exemplify. The medieval writer believed that except in primary Creation and in the Incarnation nothing happens for the first time. The men and events of the Old Testament are prefigurations of the New, and the lives of the fathers and the saints repeat the pattern laid down from the beginning. History patterns: the medieval view is a view of representative history, of history *sub specie aeternitatis*, or of history as poetry.

In quite traditional vocabulary, then, it is possible to see how Tolkien's philological medievalism makes available insights into sub-creation (and Secondary Belief) which are parallel to those afforded by the vocabulary of Carl Jung. I say "parallel," not "coeval," because Tolkien, like Lewis and Owen Barfield, submits his appreciation of archetypes to a traditional acknowledgment of the biblical doctrine of Creation. As Patrick Grant puts it, "Lewis' criticism, that Jung offers a myth to explain a myth, can be met only by assertion: there is a myth which is true, and fundamental."[15] In everything he writes, but particularly clearly in "On Fairy-Stories," a fundamentally "true" creation is Tolkien's working premise. From out of the world of fallen fantasy—as he calls it— students (or writers) gather leaves. But this, though secondary, is far from invidiously reductive or simply repetitious:

> Who can design a new leaf? The patterns from bud to unfolding, and the colours from spring to autumn were all discovered by men long ago. But that is not true. The seed of the tree can be replanted in any soil. . . .
> Spring is, of course, not really less beautiful because we have seen or heard of other like events: never from world's beginning to world's end the same event. Each leaf, of oak and ash and thorn, is a unique embodiment of the pattern, and for some this very year may be the embodiment, the first ever seen and recognised, though oaks have put forth leaves for countless generations of men. ("OFS," 26)

Leaf is pattern. Yet since even fallen leaves are not authorized by men, in the pattern of story the focus is not on the leaves as words or allegories but on the art of their ingathering. Or to put the same thought in another way: where the medieval writer would say that allegory was not so much a way of writing as a theory of history (in which men and events signify, as do words), for Tolkien the activity he calls "Recovery" (as of leaves) likewise exemplifies such a view (or theory) of history.

The term "Recovery" presupposes that something has been lost. The idea, Tolkien tells us, "includes [the] return and renewal of health" ("OFS," 57), and here his recurrently chthonic vocabulary reminds us how his doctrines of creation and sub-creation consistently interpret the matrix of art as "the fantasy of fallen Man" and interpret the role of poetry and language (i.e., of philology) as recovery of the meaning our fallenness has left behind.

The Allegory of Language

In the dissipation of the strength and power of Lothlórien, a Lothlórien largely recalled in mysterious and powerful utterances of its ancient tongue, we see *The Lord of the Rings* as a work of art that develops an acute sense of fallenness. Lothlórien, we read, though diminished, is even yet a place without shadow (*LR* 2.6, 340), with a different sense of time (*LR* 2.6, 340), a place of *light* and "no stain" (*LR* 2.6, 341), characterized by a garden, and by harmony.

But then came a time, as Gloin puts it, "that a shadow of disquiet fell upon our people" (*LR* 2.2, 234). The power of the Dark Lord is shown in estrangement (*LR* 2.2, 238; *LR* 2.6, 339), a separation of Men from Men, Men from Elves, and Elves from each other. And we are told that the Elves that fell, fell by "their eagerness for knowledge, by which Sauron ensnared them" (*LR* 2.2, 236).[16] We see that the knowledge by which Sauron ensnares, symbolized by Orthanc, is very different from the kind of knowledge desired by the Elves when they first made the Elf-rings (not as weapons of war or conquest). Those who made them "did not desire strength or domination or hoarded wealth, but understanding, making, and healing, to preserve all things unstained" (*LR* 2.2, 262). The Elves of old, in a sense, were proto-recoverers. And "recovery," in every sense in *The Lord of the Rings*, seems within the pale of belief because the universe is, if diminished, not totally corrupted. We are shown that the *language* of the Elves still has the power to recover, to still Shelob, the watchers, the Nazgûl. That is, it is *language* that most powerfully preserves the traces, the pattern in the leaf of the world's first forest. The great opposition in *The Lord of the Rings* is an opposition between a recovery of old Elven wisdom and a present obtrusiveness of the knowledge of Orthanc. It is expressed as a struggle between the mellifluous language of Elves and the grating gobble of Orcs.

Language makes recovery possible. For a medieval philologist there is a rich and multivalent sense in which language itself always intimates allegory. Or at least the modern philologist recognizes this view of language in the medieval writers he studies. To express this idea in the simplest terms, we might say that for a medieval writer language had central value because it mediates between mankind's two appreciations of reality: the causal limitations of history and the freer syntax of memory and dream. (One could describe the two aspects of medieval reality reflected in its poetry in other terms, of course—for example, as a dialogue between time and eternity or nature and grace—each in the end meaning much the same thing. But the important point is that between history and dream comes language.)

For a medieval Christian, St. Augustine, for example, language provided a paradigm for all human understanding because it seems to express timeless truth through an utterance in time.[17] *Verbum caro factum est* [The Word was made flesh] models, in the Word, the relationship of God to the world. But Christian reality contains both appreciations. It is neither the Platonic dream of a disembodied logos, an intellectual reality totally divorced from the world, nor an unintelligible (historical) nightmare irredeemably lost in the world.[18] In medieval Christian reality the Word of God is external, eternal, from the beginning. History is a kind of continuous unfolding of God's Word in time, until at last, as in the words of Isaiah's vision or recollection by St. John on Patmos, "the heavens shall be folded together as a book" (Isa. 34:4; Rev. 6:14).

In the medieval texts Tolkien studied, edited, translated, and taught, the primary book, like the primary creation, remains under the authorship of God. All literature, for the Middle Ages, forms a present gloss on an absent text, or, in Dante's words, "l'ombra del beato regno"[19] [the shadow of the blessed Kingdom]. Yet shadowy or no, fallen or no, in a logocentric perspective language itself, like literature, lives as a mediator, as a conjoiner of the two realities. Tolkien affirms this medieval view of language emphatically, both in historical terms and as personal perspective, already in his monumental *Beowulf* essay.[20] But Tolkien also knew that the very closest and most faithful mediation of language— especially between present and shadowy past—can come in the recovery made possible by the meaning of *names*, and it is unsurprising that he gave so much attention to names in his fiction.

Names *mean*—signifying whole stories, even moral histories. They are, in this sense, also "allegorical." Once one has considered this aspect of nomenclature in *The Lord of the Rings*, then an appreciation of what formerly may have appeared to be merely imaginative sonority or "rich allusion" is likely to be heightened to a new understanding of names as one of the trilogy's most basic (and allegorical) vocabularies.

One is startled to discover that the index to *The Silmarillion* lists over eight hundred names. While there are, happily, fewer to learn in *The Lord of the Rings*, even very young readers quickly sense that the names are a very important part of the story itself—indeed, the author works everywhere to ensure that it cannot be otherwise. In his own guide to the nomenclature of *The Lord of the Rings*, Tolkien insisted that his translators discern *two categories* of names. One category could be translated following the "theory" of Appendix F in volume 3 of the trilogy, according to which "[t]he names in the English form should . . . be translated into the other language *according to their meaning* (as closely as possible)."[21] He goes on to point out that

> Names (of places and persons) occur, especially in the Shire, which are not "meaningless," but are English in form (that is, in theory the author's translation of Common Speech names), containing elements that are in the current language obsolete or dialectical, or are worn down or obscured in form.[22]

Following, Tolkien lists the names that may be translated and offers with them annotations, etymologies, and relationships. Some of these are straightforward Germanic etymologies and offer little difficulty. An example is *Ent*:

> *Ent*. Retain this, alone or in compounds, such as *Entwives*. It is supposed to be a name in the language of the Vale of Anduin, including Rohan, for these creatures. It is actually an Old English word for "giant," which is thus right according to the system attributed to Rohan, but the *Ents* of this tale are not in form or character derived from Germanic mythology.[23] *Entings* "children [of Ents]" [*LR* 3.4, 464] should also be unchanged except in the plural ending. The Greyelven (Sindarin) name was *Onodrim LR* 3.2, 431.[24]

But we see how quickly Tolkien's knowledge and his instinct for good speculative etymology could produce a really intricate "derivation." Here is only part of his entry for Isengard and Isenmouthe:

> *Isen* is an old variant form in English of *iron*; *gard* a Germanic word meaning "enclosure," especially one round a dwelling or group of buildings; and *mouthe* a derivative of *mouth*, representing Old English Mūða (from mūð "mouth") "opening," especially used of the mouths of rivers, but also applied to other openings (not parts of a body). *Isengard* "the Iron-court" was so called because of the great hardness of the stone

in that place and especially in the central tower. The *Isenmouthe* was so called because of the great fence of pointed iron posts that closed the gap leading into Udun, like teeth in jaws. . . . [*LR* 6.2, 809, 906]

In the Dutch and Swedish versions *Isengard* is left unchanged. For Isenmouthe the Dutch uses *Ixenmonde*, translating or assimilating to Dutch only the second element (a more complete translation to *Ijzermonde* would seem to me better). The Swedish renders it *Isensgaþ*, which is incorrect, since *Isen* is not a proper name but adjectival.

The *gard* element appears in Old Norse *garðr*, whence current or dialectal Swedish *gård*, Danish *gaard*, and English *garth* (beside the original English form *yard*); this, though usually of more lowly associations (as English *farmyard*), appears for instance in Old Norse *As-garðr*, now widely known as *Asgard* in mythology. The word was early lost in German, except in Old High German *mittin-* or *mittil-gart* (the inhabited lands of Men), Old Norse *miðgarðr*, and Old English *middan-geard*: see Middle-earth. Would not this old element in German form *-gart* be suitable for a translation or assimilation to German such as *Eisengart*?

Of *-mouthe* the German equivalent appears to be *Mundung* (or in place-names *-munde*); in Scandinavian, Danish *munding*, Swedish *mynning*.[25]

For the words and names that *may* be translated, then, there is an extensive and thoroughly rationalized philological system available. Moreover, it is clear that Tolkien regarded the recovery of these names by translation as essential for readers in other languages.

But of the other category of names he takes an even "higher" view, asking that they remain "*entirely* unchanged in any language used in translation, except that the inflexional *-s*, *-es* should be rendered according to the grammar of the language."[26] What is it about these names that causes Tolkien to stand so fiercely against any chance that they might be misrendered? Can we trace etymologies or derivations for some of them that might indicate to us how they are to be understood or their focus of reference recovered? If we pursue just one character, and some of the names immediately associated with him, outlines for an understanding of Tolkien's method begin to emerge.

Aragorn: Name and Incarnational History

"Aragorn" is a name carefully compounded from elements which are highly evocative for a philologist who has studied European languages of the last millennium. The first syllable, *ar*, is one of the most richly meaningful monosyllabic words in the Old English language and is found with cognate meaning in many other Indo-European languages (e.g., Gr. *arêtê*; OI *ara*; Gothic *áirus*; OSw *êru*; ON *árr, éru, aeru*; OHG *êra*).[27] A cognate use in Tolkien's *Silmarillion* comes in the very first sentence: "There was Eru, the One." It is glossed in early texts in four ways, three of which are correlative: as a person, as a quality of character, and as a personal action. When *ar* is applied to a person, it is glossed as *nuntius, apostolus, angelus, minister*: e.g., "Ða com dryhtnes *ar*, halig of heofonum" [Then came the messenger of the Lord from heaven].[28] When *ar* signifies a quality of character, the glosses are *honor, dignitas, gloria, magnificentia, honestas, reverential*: e.g., "sie him *ar* and onweald in rodera rice" [may he have *glory* and power in the kingdom of heaven]; "ióva us þa *ar*, þe þe Gabriel brohte!" (to Blessed Virgin Mary at the Annunciation) [Reveal to us the *glory* which Gabriel brought to you]; "Bringað nu drihtne bu ætsomne wlite and *ar*" [Offer the Lord glory and *honor*].[29] When *ar* indicates a personal action, glosses read *gratia, misericordia, beneficium, favor*: for example, "cymeð him seo *ar* of heofnum" [*grace* comes to him from heaven]; "þam þe *ar* seceð, frofre þe fader on heofnum" [to him who seeks *favor*, relief from the father in heaven], and so on.

The middle syllable of Strider's higher name might possibly be construed as an infix, but, if we are to speculate, it is more likely that the last two syllables should be taken together as *agorn*, perhaps alluding to OE *agan*, "to possess," or to the OE verb *agangan*, "to pass by unnoticed," but also "to surpass"; "to travel quickly"; "to come forth"; "to come to pass": "Geseah ða swiðmond cyning, ða he his sefan ontreowde, wundor on wite *agangen*" [He saw a miracle come to pass];[30] "aer his tid *aga*"; "þa *agangen* wæs tynhund wintra geteled rimes fram";[31] "Wyrd ne cuþon, / . . . swá hit *ágangen* wearð / eorla manegum" (*Beowulf*, lines 1233– 35).[32]

It is in the context of all of these associations that we begin to acquire a fuller understanding of the name of Arwen, the Elven lady whom Aragorn loves and for whom he works and waits. The second syllable of her name, *wen*, is related to OE *wyn* (joy), yielding therefore "the joy of *ar*" (see *LR* 2.1, 221—Arwen *Undomiel*, [OW] "Evenstar . . . of her people"). But the form *wen* (as opposed to *wyn* in Éowyn), though it is related to "joy"—"hearpan *wyn*, gomen glēobeams"—can have the meanings "prospect," "conviction," "belief," and "expectation": "him sēo *wēn* gelēah" (*Genesis*, lines 49, 1446; *Beowulf*, line 2323), in the sense of "faith," or "hope."[33]

We see then that, for one with an ear for the philological memory, Aragorn and Arwen are names charged with meaning, which, even in their application as character history, are seen to be incarnational of the tale's deepest structure. But we see something more: that in these names the encounter of history and dream is laden with other fruit—its recollection of another Incarnation. The association with biblical language is "accidental," tacit rather than explicit, in that Tolkien has chosen to anchor his referential language beneath the conscious structure of other mythic formulations (biblical or Germanic) in the subconsciously meaningful deep structure of Western language itself. Here, then, is the realm of the hypothesis: the weightiest register of Strider's full name lies in its radicals, its philological access to a language spoken before any of the contending tongues of Middle-earth in which his name still dimly "means," recalling a time when all languages were much closer to one. This conjecture is itself mythopoeic, whether in philology or in poetry, and has evident theological undertones.

The register of deep meaning in Tolkien's names also helps, I think, to see as sub-creation and individual (in the old sense) some events that might otherwise too conveniently be construed as "mere allegory." Even as we recall these events we appreciate how they might well evoke interpretations both allegorical and archetypal: Aragorn comes to the great battle out of the paths of the Dead and from the sea (*LR* 5.6, 829). He is the exiled king who returns. It is suggested of him that he is related to Gandalf (*LR* 5.8, 852); he is the Elf-man, the one by whom that which was long ago separated and estranged is now joined. He speaks of Elrond as the "eldest of all our race" (*LR* 5.8, 845), he takes the Elf-name Elessar ON one who appears in another manner, and he marries at last an Elven lady who is his perfect complement and the recovery of a joy that overcomes his eros-longing (*Ar*-wen, "the joy of *ar*"). Appropriately, as symbol of an old wound healed, he is the king who heals, the "Renewer" (*LR* 5.8, 845). He employs, symbolically, the *athelas* [OE spirit of the King, or God],[34] breathing on it, creating and restoring to health. As Faramir (ON *fara*, "to travel") awakens, he speaks:

"My lord, you called me. I come. What does the king command?"

"Walk no more in the shadows, but awake!" said Aragorn. "You are weary. Rest a while, and take food, and be ready when I return."

"I will, lord," said Faramir. "For who would lie idle when the king has returned?" (*LR* 5.8, 848)

Like the whispering of wind amongst the leaves that one takes sometimes for voices, other associations spread outward from the name: the reign of Aragorn, and that of his heirs, is to have dominion over all Middle-earth, "unto the ending of the world" (*LR* 6.5, 946). He ushers in a New Law, of mercy (*LR* 6.5, 947), and a New Age: it is no longer the Third Age of Middle-earth. Symbolically, there is a new tree. And though Aragorn dies, his death is not a cause for despair; in fact it is despair that his coming is meant to banish. His final speech is that which promises the transformation of history:

But let us not be overthrown at the final test, who of old renounced the Shadow and the Ring. In sorrow we must go, but not in despair. Behold! we are not bound for ever to the circles of the world, and beyond them is more than memory. Farewell! (*LR* Appendix A.1.v, 1038)

Measured against the backdrop of culminating events, we see even more clearly that the meaning of Aragorn's name is, philologically speaking, an incarnation. For Tolkien the philologist, language remembers much, and in the perspective provided by names, the quasi-allegorical characterization in parts of *The Lord of the Rings* can be seen, mythologically, archetypally, and philologically, as a pattern of "recovery." Characterization and action become a kind of "gloss on the name." Or we could say that Tolkien's sub-creation, in respects both psychological and philological, constitutes, in a manner analogous to medieval writing, a manner of present gloss on an absent text. That the gloss is not systematic but rather poetic is of the essence of his philological understanding.

This insight could be extended much further in the whole of Tolkien's fictional work. For example, the sensitive handling of Éowyn's love (OE *eo*, "thou"; *wyn*, "joy") for Aragorn, which he must restrain in favor of Arwen, can be more deeply understood through a comparison of the meaning of their names in relation to his own.

That Tolkien is trying to achieve much more with the idea of recovery than a mere tour de force display of his command of individual Indo-European languages is made evident in his selection of language elements that remain powerfully evocative for the residual collective memories of less learned folk. In key names from Aragorn to Legolas to Mordor the careful morphology and lexicology is so close to "roots" (cognate radicals) that the names are open to understanding in nearly all the tongues of modern Middle-earth.[35] The function of philological recovery, as of the recovery of history, is here much more than the surface illusion of being conversant in strange tongues: it is a participatory inculcation in an ancient depth of language (of word and of name) accessible to us all through the subliminal, often unacknowledged, but persistent half-conversance that we still share.

In Tolkien's fiction the business of names is, admittedly, a game—a more extravagant form of speculation than is found in most of his work for the *O.E.D.* Yet the principles are not substantively different. Each name may be perceived as metonymic—a miniature myth, a poem, a story in itself. Behind the Adamic playfulness, therefore, is a high seriousness—the desire to imply or recover truths of a prior order, to engage an understanding that informs and creates history. In pursuing those things that really matter by the route of philology and "faërie," Tolkien, as Lewis and others knew, chose a courageous, almost audacious route, especially for an academician. One wonders if he drew courage from some whimsical appreciation of the "allegory" in his own Germanic name.[36]

Eucatastrophe and Anagogy

Perhaps too much has been written about Tolkien's eucatastrophe and anagogy.[37] But it is not far from the point at hand to conclude with a suggestion that what Tolkien would have us catch sight of in the "sudden glimpse" of the good fairy-story's eucatastrophe is as much an incarnational reality as his eucharistic (Christian) and historical and philological terminology implies—that its narrative realization, as secondary belief, is the renewed enfleshment of a primally powerful Word, one which, as Word, comprises both aspects of reality, history, and dream. "Recovery," he says, "is a re-gaining—regaining of a clear view" ("OFS," 57). Since now, in the world of fallen fantasy, we see through a glass darkly, we need "to clean our windows" to see "things as we are (or were) meant to see them—as things apart from ourselves" ("OFS," 57).

In the making of his sub-creation and in the response it evokes, Tolkien invites us to see sub-creation in Adam's terms, as *naming*, and to see the meaning of name in *The Lord of the Rings* as pattern in the leaf, and to see the leaf of the world's first forest as the leaf of the world's first book.

Notes

1. See R.J. Reilly, *Romantic Religions: A Study of Barfield, Lewis, Williams, and Tolkien* (Athens: University of Georgia Press, 1971), 194.

2. In his "Guide to the Names in *The Lord of the Rings*," in *A Tolkien Compass*, ed. Jared Lobdell (La Salle, Ill.: Open Court, 1975), 153–201, under the heading for "Yule," Tolkien writes (enigmatically): "The fellowship . . . left on December 25, which then had no significance, since the Yule, or its equivalent, was then the last day of the year and the first of the next year. But December 25 (setting out) and March 25 (accomplishment of the quest) were intentionally chosen by me" (201).

3. J.S. Ryan, "German Mythology Applied—The Extension of the Ritual Folk Memory," *Folklore* 77 (1966): 45–57.

4. John Tinkler, "Old English in Rohan," in *Tolkien and the Critics*, ed. N.D. Isaacs and R.A. Zimbardo (Notre Dame, Ind.: Notre Dame Press, 1968), 164–69.

5. In "Old English in Rohan," Tinkler states that the relationship between Old English and the language of Rohan provides "an added richness in connotation and allusion" (169); and Ryan, in "German Mythology Applied," comments, "The fusion of elements from various sides, Celtic and the Arthurian preliminaries, Germanic primitive, Scandinavian and Middle High German, is necessary as a bridge between this literary world of Middle Earth and our world, the Age of Men, the Fourth Age" (57).

6. Robley Evans, *J.R.R. Tolkien* (New York: Warner, 1972).

7. The text has been revised, subsequently, by Norman Davis. See J.R.R. Tolkien and E.V. Gordon, eds., *Sir Gawain and the Green Knight*, 2nd ed., rev. Norman Davis (Oxford: Clarendon Press, l967).

8. Jane Chance (Nitzsche), *Tolkien's Art* (London: Macmillan, 1979).

9. Chance, *Tolkien's Art*, 26.

10. Ephesians 4:22 (Douay-Rheims trans.).

11. This idea is analogous to Owen Barfield's idea of "participation," in *Saving the Appearances: A Study in Idolatry* (London: Faber and Faber, 1965).

12. Reilly, 202.

13. Patricia Spacks, "Ethical Pattern in *The Lord of the Rings*," *Critique* 3 (1959): 36.

14. See Patrick Grant, "Tolkien: Archetype and Word," *Cross Currents* (1973): 365–79; and his *Six Modern Authors and Problems of Belief* (London: Macmillan, 1979), 93–121.

15. Grant, "Tolkien," 375.

16. Sauron's power to estrange the races of Middle-earth and pervert their desires and aspirations is further seen in the history of Aragorn's ancestors, the Men of Númenor, many of whom were destroyed through the counsel of Sauron (*LR* Appendix A). Similarly, Éowyn becomes dissatisfied with the royal house of Rohan through the teaching of Wormtongue, Sauron's servant. The Dwarves, too, are dispersed by the Dark Lord's power (*LR* Appendix A), and his influence over them, while limited, is described as inculcating a lust for gold and power (*LR* Appendix A.3, 1051).

17. John Freccero, "Dante's Medusa: Allegory and Autobiography," in *By Things Seen: Reference and Recognition in Medieval Thought*, ed. David Lyle Jeffrey (Ottawa: University of Ottawa Press, 1979), 33.

18. Freccero, 33.

19. *Paradiso*, 1.23. *The Divine Comedy of Dante Alighieri*, vol. 3, *Paradiso*, ed. John Sinclair (New York: Oxford University Press, 1948), 19.

20. Cf. Tolkien, "Beowulf," 51–104.

21. Lobdell, ed., *A Tolkien Compass*, 153.

22. Lobdell, ed., *A Tolkien Compass*, 156.

23. See the note for *Ent* in my appendix, below.

24. Lobdell, ed., *A Tolkien Compass*, 164–65.

25. Lobdell, ed., *A Tolkien Compass*, 187–88.

26. Lobdell, ed., *A Tolkien Compass*, 155.

27. Also the OE word for "oar"—cf. Greek *eretmon*, in Homer's *Odyssey* 23.275–76. See *The Odyssey*, ed. and trans. A.T. Murray, rev. by George E. Dimock, Loeb Classical Library Series (Cambridge, Mass.: Harvard University Press, 1995), 404.

28. *Guthlac*, lines 684–85, in *The Exeter Book*, vol. 3, *The Anglo-Saxon Poetic Records*, eds. George Philip Krapp and Elliott van Kirk Dobbie (New York: Columbia University Press, 1936).

29. Psalm 95:7, in *The Paris Psalter and Boethius*, vol. 5, *The Anglo-Saxon Poetic Records*, ed. George Krapp (New York: Columbia University Press, 1932), 68.

30. *Daniel*, lines 268–69, in *The Junius Manuscript*, vol. 1, *The Anglo-Saxon Poetic Records*, ed. George Krapp (New York: Columbia University Press, 1931), 118.

31. "The Coronation of Edgar," in *The Anglo-Saxon Minor Poems*, vol. 6, *The Anglo-Saxon Poetic Records*, ed. Elliott van Kirk Dobbie (New York: Columbia University Press, 1942), 21.

32. See *Beowulf* in *"Beowulf" and "The Fight at Finnsburg,"* ed. Fr. Klaeber, 3rd ed. (Boston: D.C. Heath, 1950), 47.

33. For *Genesis*, see Krapp, ed., *Junius Manuscript*, 4, 45 (the line on the letter reads "Eft him seo wen geleah"); for *Beowulf*, see Klaeber, ed., 87.

34. Tolkien illustrates here how he toys with his readers: the Anglo-Saxon is plain enough. Yet in giving us the alternate name "kingsfoil," he can engage in a kind of philological ruse. The description is straightforward and botanical, except perhaps for the play on "leaf," "foil," and *asëa*. But *athelas* cannot be translated.

35. See my appendix, below.

36. George Swinton, the distinguished Canadian art historian, drew to my attention a relationship between Tolkien and *Tollkühn*, which can hardly have escaped a philologist's fancy. *Toll* suggests a rash fantasy, or daring, almost poetic extravagance; *kühn* is, of course, "daring" and "courageous," in our English sense of it, *keen*.

37. See here Dorothy Barber, "The Meaning of *The Lord of the Rings*," *Mankato State College Studies* 2 (1967): 38–45.

Appendix: Speculative Notes to Some of the Names

Aragorn: (compound)

OE *ar*: a recurrent OE monosyllable, found with cognate meaning in many Indo-European languages; e.g., Greek *arêtê*; OE *ara*; Gothic *áirus*; OSw *êru*; ON *árr*; OHG *êra*; ON *êru*, *æra*. Glossed in early texts as:

(a) a person: *nuntius, apostolus, angelus, minister*; e.g., "þa com dryhtnes *ar* of heofonum" (*Guthlac*, line 656) [Then came the messenger of the Lord from heaven].

(b) a quality of character: *honor, dignitas, gloria, magnificentia, honestas, reverentia*; e.g., "sie him *ar* and onweald in rodera rice" [may he have glory and power in the kingdom of heaven]; "iōva us þa *ar*, þe þe Gabriel brohte!" (to the Blessed Virgin Mary) [reveal to us the glory which Gabriel brought to you]; "bringað nu drihtne wlite and *ar*" [offer the Lord glory and honour] (Ps. 95:7).

(c) a personal action: *gratia, misericordia, beneficium*, favor; e.g., "cymeð him seo ar of heofnum"; "þam þe *ar* seceð, frofre þe fader on heofnum"; etc. [also the OE word for "oar"—cf. Greek *eretmon*, in *Odyssey*, 23.275–76]. *agorn*: related to OE *agan* (to possess, to have) and *a-gangan* (to pass by unnoticed, but also to surpass, to travel quickly, to come forth, to come to pass); e.g., "geseah he wunder on wite agangan" [he saw a miracle come to pass] (*Daniel* 270); "aer his tīd āgā"; "þa agangen was tynhund wintra fram" ("Coronation of Edgar," line 10; and so forth); "[w]yrd ne cūðon, swā hit āgangan wearð eorla manegum" (*Beowulf*, line 1234).

Arwen: *ar* + *wen*; *wen* is related to OE *wyn* (joy, or hope); cf. ON *arwae* (heir); therefore, "joy of Ar." But the form *wen* (as opposed to *wyn* in *Éowyn*), though it is related to "joy"—"hearpan wyn, gomen glēobeames"—has the meanings "prospect," "conviction," "belief," and "expectation"; e.g., "sēo wen gelēah" (*Genesis*, lines 49, 1446; *Beowulf*, line 2323)—in the sense of "faith . . . in the fullness of time."

Athelas: OE spirit of the king.

Balrog: OE *bealu* (evil); *wrēagan* (to arouse).

Bilbo: OE *bil* (a sword); *-bo* (a diminutive): "short sword."

Boromir: ON *boro* (ruler).

Denethor: OE *denu* (valley); *thor* (brave); cf. ON "thunder."

Dunedain: (also Dunharrow, etc.).
ON *duna*, OE *dun* (hill, mountain); cf. OI *dun* (fort, hill).
Edoras: OE *eodor* (limit, boundary; also prince); cf. *geodor* (olden time).
Elendil: OE *ellende*, adj. (foreign, exiled); cf. OE *ellen* (elder), as in "elder tree"; also "courage."
Elessar: ON one who appears in another manner; cf. OF *elestar* (vessel, banner).
Elrond: OE *elra* ([wholly] other); *rond* (shield).
Ent: OE giant; but cf. the *ente* of the *Tydorel* and the ente tree in *Sir Orfeo*, under which Eurydice falls asleep and is rapt into the power of Faërie.
Eorl: OE, ON warrior, leader of fighting men.
Eothain: OE *eo* (thou); *thain* (servant, follower).
Éowyn: OE *eo* (thou); *wyn* (joy).
Fangorn: OE *fang* (booty, plunder); cf. *fōn* (to imprison): "prison-wood" as well as "beard-tree."
Faramir: ON *fara* (travel); OE *fara* (traveling companion).
Frodo: OE wise (neutral), glossed *prudens*, *sciens*; cf. Frodi, King of Denmark.
Galadriel: MW *gala* (light) : "lady of light."
Gandalf: ON magic elf; OE *ginan* (to drive back); OE *delf* (to go into deeply, to seek out); but cf. OI deep-seeker, etc.
Gondor: OE *gond*, *gan*, *geond* (to occupy, conquer, etc.).
Helmingas: OE helmet wearers.
Hobbit: OE *hob* (generic name for clown, rustic); *-bit* (a diminutive suffix).
Isildur: cf. OE *isig*, *dur*; ON *isil* (icy); *dyrr* (door); but cf. OI *isel*, *isil* (low); cf. OI *dur*, *duire*; Lat. *dur* (hardness).
Legolas: OE *lego* from *legu* (elder race, ancestor); *las* from *laes*, a diminutive (less, least); but OI *laigu* (smaller, lesser); *las* (while, time).
Lothlorien: from the *Mabinogion*, the Garden of the Elves; OW, OI *loth* (vale); *lour*, *louri* (bounteous, plenitude).
Orc: Lat. *orcus* (god of the underworld, cf. Pluto; cf. Orpheus); glossed in OE as *hel-deofl*.
Orthanc: OE knowledge of the world; OE gloss for *scientia*, *ingenium*, *astutia*.
Rohan: ON land of the horses.
Rohirrim: ON horsemen.
Saruman: OE *sarū* (pain, sorrow); cf. OE *searu* (contrivance, stratagem).
Sauron: OE *sar* (sickness, wound, affliction).
Shadowfax: c.f. ON *fax* (mane); OE *fēax* (hair).
Shelob: OE *lobbe* (spider); cf. Hebrew *sheol* (place of death)—cf. here also Tolkien's part in translation of New Jerusalem Bible, especially Book of Job.
Smaug: OE *smēocan* (to emit smoke), i.e., "smog."
Sméagol: OE *smēah* (subtle); cf. *smēagan* (to peer into, to think out, to scrutinise).
Thengel: OE prince, lord; gloss on *princeps*, *dominus*.
Théoden: ON, OE chief of tribe (related to OE verb "to translate").
Took: OE verb, "to take"; cf. Lat. *peregrine* (pilgrim, traveller).

Part II

Tolkien and Ancient Greek and Classical and Medieval Latin

Chapter 5

SAVING THE MYTHS

The Re-creation of Mythology in Plato and Tolkien

GERGELY NAGY

As has been proved many times, the antique roots of J.R.R. Tolkien's literary works are a rewarding field of examination, especially when one is looking for similarities of mythopoeic practices. Antiquity as the great age of the epic—as the era when many of the world's great primary mythologies came into being, were used in cultures, and produced works of lasting interest and profound significance—is all the more relevant in relation to Tolkien's work because he himself knew it and its texts very well (having studied them at Birmingham and Oxford). Homer and Virgil (together with some other authors) as sources and analogues to Tolkien have already been studied at some length,[1] and David Greenman's brief article on the Aristotelian organizing principle of *The Silmarillion* ("*The Silmarillion* as Aristotelian Epic-Tragedy")[2] shows a great potential still to be exploited in the comparison of Tolkien's practice and the antique conceptions of poetics.

In the history of reflective thought in antiquity and in the history of mythopoeic practices, the Greek philosopher Plato stands in an undoubt-edly central place. It is all the more surprising, therefore, that his con-nections to Tolkien in this respect have not been fully explored before.[3] Patrick Curry, in a footnote to a paper on Tolkien's critics, mentions "that great enemy of myths, Plato,"[4] and one is left even more surprised why this simplification has not been perceived. Plato was certainly not an "enemy of myth" in any sense that Curry invokes in the passage. His relationship to myth and mythology was much more complex and subtle than that: he actually used myth, not only by way of interpretation and reflection, but even by writing some myths himself, assigning to them an important part in his dialogues. He did not simply hold myths to be lies (as Curry attributes to the tradition he claims to be traceable to Plato)[5] or to be delusive and infantile. Plato is perhaps the most important person in antique mythopoesis, and his work on the creation and use of myth is decidedly focal. At the very least, there is vicious irony in labeling the writer of the *Timaeus* an "enemy of myth." Like Tolkien, he gives thought to myth, transforming and reshaping it to suit his purposes. Both authors stand in a tradition of relating to myth, which they both knew they could not disregard; both sensed that this relation is somewhat problematic (as the very definition and status of myth is problematic), but both responded favorably, integrating myth into their inventory of discourses.

The similarity between Plato's and Tolkien's myth-creating activity is apparent on the theoretical level as an essentially similar way of understanding and applying myth as a discourse; but it is also discernible in many of their common images and conceptions. The ways the two authors related to tradition and the use of myth give the conceptional frame to their own views and uses, situating these frames themselves in a historical context. The aims and methods they employ in actually using myth offer methodological meeting points; finally, Plato's and Tolkien's attitudes to myth as their own written text arrive at a stance that is decidedly in the sphere of cultural theory. Both authors, as will be seen, are concerned with an activity of *rewriting*, in a variety of senses, producing the effect of "saving the myth," defending its integrity and position. In this essay, I deal with the similarities of frameworks, methodologies, and theories between Plato's and Tolkien's creation and use of myth, touching on some central and crucial details of motif and imagery that also demonstrate the affinity between Tolkien's mythopoeic work and Plato's writings. The connection is meaningful, and I believe it casts some light on Tolkien's post-antique, postmodern mythopoeic practice.

Plato and Tolkien both use myth as an obvious sign of their relating to a distinct tradition. This tradition is in both cases primarily historical: with Plato, this is the mythological-poetical tradition of Greek literature, on the one hand, and the philosophical tradition he is reacting to, on the other. Tolkien's relationship is to the narrative and linguistic traditions of the texts and languages he was occupied with studying. While providing a historical context for both their material and their reflections, this also determines the frame in which the philosopher and the writer see themselves and their work. In the following, I will briefly survey the two authors' relationship to this tradition.

Hostility toward poets and myths is most often attributed to Plato on the basis of the *Republic*, but this reading disregards a number of cultural and philosophical considerations. It is true that in books 2 and 10 of the *Republic* Plato seems to oppose poets in rather harsh terms, culminating in his famous turning them out of his state in book 10—but Plato does see the function of poets and their stories, and he does not excise without providing for that function. The critique of poetry and traditional myth (largely along the Platonic lines), already a phenomenon with a history of its own by Plato's time, left poetic conventions and mythological material in use in philosophy.[6] Parmenides used Dike and the myth of the path to wisdom and truth, and even the cynical sophists employed mythological expositions to exhibit their rhetorical prowess (most famous is perhaps Gorgias's "Encomium of Helen," with which he "displays his own particular subtlety in his relationship with tradition.")[7] *Mythos* and *logos* as governing principles were not as clearly separable and opposed as the philosophers themselves would like us to think, and the effect of reevaluating this old binarism can be felt today in current interpretation of Plato as well as of the Pre-Socratic philosophers. It was, in fact, inconceivable to break with poetry altogether: a new discourse, a new mode of language, was needed to break away from poetry.[8] Eric A. Havelock's work has shown how the *Republic* aims its critique, not at poets and poetry as such (this is borne out by the fact that Plato does provide for the function of the exiled poets in requiring well-instructed *mythopoioi* to take their place), but at the orally founded mythological culture, having found it theologically-ethically-methodologically inappropriate for the function it was fulfilling: that of education.[9] It is oral culture to which Plato is an enemy, not myth: oral culture as the epitome of the mythical imagination, mythical thought that is not any longer exact and systematic enough for the philosophers. Plato's "quest [is] for a non-Homeric mind and language."[10] The tradition of relating to myth in Greek philosophy is a tradition of relating to a cultural context, a framework of thought, a conception of language and meaning production.

Myth in orality is an elusive concept. It seems to be an underlying generative force, a traditional and culturally central narrative, which determines the community's relation to the world through its religious application and is preserved (as is all important information) in the performance of the singer. This conception definitely filters through Plato: as Luc Brisson observes, "[F]or Plato, myth in the true sense of the word is a form of discourse which transmits all information that a community conserves in memory of its distant past and passes on orally from one generation to another."[11] This form of discourse is essentially mobile and plural; this is underscored by considerations of the very cultural/ communicational context in which it is transmitted. As each performance—even of the same narrative, even by the same singer—will be different, this concept of myth accommodates the quality of variance as a fundamental definitive factor.[12] This myth is not textual, having no real author, no canon, no orthodoxy. Formulaic diction and other mnemotechnical characteristics determine the linguistic manifestations of the stories as well as the whole framework of thought in which culture exists.[13] Performance, the dynamics of the singer-audience direct relationship, and the social space in which the singer performs shape each retelling from the outside, as it were.[14] Myth, as its tellings, is a very emphatically public and common discourse, a unifying ideology (this is why Havelock calls the Homeric education "indoctrination").[15] Plato judges this framework to be incapable of producing philosophical knowledge and of educating the young; that is, he attacks it for philosophical reasons, and with this he introduces new criteria into the evaluative system, criteria that had for some extent already been pointed out in the tradition of the philosophical relating to myth.

The spread of literacy started the textualization of poetic and mythological tradition, which resulted in different uses of myth. Epic texts now formed the canon of Homer as the *didaskalos Hellados*, the "teacher of Greece"; written accounts of stories could be compared and analyzed by historians. Stories *in texts* became reference points: they could now be criticized and examined, and this led to a completely new way of defining knowledge and the authority of any narrative. Philosophy shaped and defined its conception of knowledge and its criteria of truth with the help of the literate way of thinking.[16] It was engaged in polemics not only with the morals of myth but also with its essential fluidity and variance.[17] In the process, philosophers inevitably used myths as texts and started to develop relations to them as such. Critique, rationalization, and the emergence of allegorical interpretation were parts of the same process.[18] Plato thus stood in both the poetic and mythological tradition (he was doubtless educated on Homer and uses the Homeric register for his own ends, e.g., in the myth of Er in the *Republic*)[19] and the philosophical tradition of relating to mythology. He cannot ignore this latter tradition of the philosophical use of myth, for that is partly what his own philosophical precedents are.

Tolkien's relation to the mythological tradition is also a two-sided one. On the one hand, he relates to the stories that make up Germanic mythology, a system he loved instinctively better than the Greek. His philological inquiries into texts led him naturally to the larger frameworks of these traditions: the reconstructive method produced more or less coherent systems of stories and conceptions from corpora of texts.[20] Tolkien was interested in these stories and their uses in texts, as his articles on the Sigelhearwan and on *Beowulf* suggest; and he was primarily interested because these texts show how language is adapted to conveying new meaning while preserving traces of its old context. The word with the forgotten, old reference coming out of the shadows is a frequent motif of his writing (as the reappearance of the Ents explains the word and the stories for the riders of Rohan and Théoden [*LR* 3.8, 536–37]). It is possible to go back and find the original meanings and to see the original stories again. Germanic myth, like Greek, is also a background system one finds surfacing in texts like the *Eddas*, which themselves partly go back to an essentially oral phase. They are transformed and preserved in medieval orality too, but the other aspect of Tolkien's relating to tradition is also important here. Philology, like Plato's philosophical use of myth, is a critical discipline that is basically textual, and, as the work of T.A. Shippey has shown, Tolkien's work and his relation to myth are also heavily determined by its writing-controlled assumptions and methods.[21] His linking of specific versions of a story with specific authors (as in the "Silmarillion" tradition) shows that he was primarily thinking in terms of text and its textual source.[22] His own mythological stories are presented as texts, written accounts, translations, and redactions of other texts: *The Book of Lost Tales* as Eriol's account from the Golden Book and from what he heard in Eressea (cf. *BLT2*, 283, 287, 290–91, 310),[23] various other texts attributed to Pengolod or Rúmil, and, in the final conception, *The Silmarillion* as Bilbo's "translations from the Elvish" (see *BLT1*, 5–6). One of the points Tolkien was making in his mythopoeic work is about the essential continuity of tradition: the supposition that traditions are an integral part of the present, and that old stories lie behind our new ones.[24] This conception is behind much of the early *Lost Tales* design, especially the Eriol/Aelfwyne frame: at that time, the tradition was to be that of present-day Britain.

Tolkien's work, like Plato's, is a *reaction* to tradition, an apparent breaking point that in fact does more to connect than to separate. Both turn to myth because of the meanings that can be brought into play. The qualities that Plato usually attributes to traditional myth are being "old" and being "authoritative";[25] he will fasten on the traditional meanings and transform them, while preserving the framework (and the authoritative voice). For Tolkien, stories are similarly resonant exactly because they are old, and it is this effect that he will exploit to create stories that create their own age. Plato, moreover, nearly always marks out (his) myths as explicitly in an oral context: they are always referred to as "being told" (*legetai, legontai*).[26] Tolkien also makes much of orality and the "telling" of stories in the way he refers to the sources in *The Silmarillion* ("it is told," "it is said," "said by the wise" usually with details of other, alternative accounts), and oral "tales" (which nevertheless prove to be true) figure in *The Lord of the Rings*, too (as in the case of Théoden and the Ents, Ioreth's knowledge of "old lore" about the king, or the rhyme about *athelas* that "women such as our good Ioreth still repeat without understanding") (*LR* 3.8, 536–37; *LR* 5.8, 842; *LR* 5.8, 847, respectively). The use of myth itself, as we have seen, suggests a similarity of vision between the two authors, but the parallels in the aims and methods of Plato and Tolkien deepen it.

Plato inserts myth into his dialogues of strict dialectical philosophy, which is essentially writing-controlled, constructed in a way that is methodologically enabled only by the use of writing. No such trains of thought, definitions, and analyses would have been possible in orality—the very rhetoric that conducts the dialogues is a fundamentally written product.[27] What Plato ultimately drives at is, however, not a definition or a systematic account of philosophy. He is mirroring the *process of philosophy* in writing. Philosophy is a pursuit, not a state; the state is wisdom.

Writing, as the *Phaedrus* makes clear, is not considered an entirely efficient medium for communicating philosophical insight. It can merely function to remind one of what one already knows.[28] Writing is only a "game," and the writer of the *Seventh Letter* claims never to have written anything on the ultimate things in philosophy.[29] The dialogues, then, seem to be "playful" accounts, records of the process and of the stages of the philosophical quest for truth. Plato is *writing* myth from the writing-controlled standpoint of philosophy and not as a user of a basically oral and mythological central story. Writing is, after all, the structuring technology of philosophy, on a deeper level than its actual articulation; myth is accordingly *rewritten* in this vein.

What Plato does, therefore, is *reshape* and transform the mythological consciousness into a philosophical one.[30] He *overwrites* the mythological background with myth produced in and through writing, with philosophical considerations in mind. He replaces the old and criticized tradition (both in its content and its framework) with one of his own making. *Functionally*, however, it is in the same place as background and performs the same role: it lends involving force to philosophy, determining the structure of discourse one is engaged in and the very way one sees the world. Plato thus overwrites the poets on their own ground.

He does not do this in order to "preserve" philosophical traditions (as the singer of orality sings primarily to preserve and only secondarily to entertain);[31] he does it to point toward philosophical truth. Plato, unlike the sophists and postmodernists (who perhaps would not have differed greatly to his mind), thinks that truth is *not* relative (as Protagoras would measure it by each man) or nonexistent: it exists but is exceptionally difficult to access. "Truth" is in the world of Forms, of which all have a lingering knowledge but which only philosophers can properly open up. He expresses this access in mythological terms: as in the story of Er in the *Republic*, where we see the multiple "frames of reporting" distance Socrates from the source and allow him to attribute his mythical fiction to someone else, as something "told" by Er;[32] or in the numerous expositions of the idea of learning as remembering, anamnesis.[33] According to this, the immortal soul, before being embodied for this worldly life, sees the Forms plainly but in its embodiment forgets them. Learning, knowledge acquired in this world of phenomena, is therefore only remembering what one already knew but forgot. Plato also sets truth itself (the world of Forms) into a mythical framework, which works as an expression of its determining function and justifies the mythological terms in which the access is presented. The world of truth is the "place above the sky" (*hyperouranios topos*) in the *Phaedrus* where the soul-chariots ride in the train of the gods;[34] or, indeed, Er's afterworld where souls choose fates for themselves, to drink of the forgetful waters of Ameles before their embodiment. It is expanded into a whole mythical cosmology in the *Phaedo* and is treated in the context of judgment in the *Gorgias*.[35] The use of traditional discourse and the traditional conceptual framework is in the service of the creation of something fundamentally new; but the function assigned to it will still be the old one.

Tolkien's aims and methods show much the same preoccupation with myth as a device of expression, and it is similarly his most important concerns that are expressed in it. He cannot escape to see myth as *reconstruction*, to start at the philological level. The English and Norse texts he studied were produced much later than the original use of myths; by the time they came to be written down the stories did not function as "myth proper" in their religious determining role, which would have made them all-pervasive in culture. In the twelfth century when they were written (or at least when the first extant manuscript fragments of the *Elder Edda* were written down), the *Eddas* definitely did not carry a "religious" meaning—certainly not for people like Snorri Sturluson, who nevertheless collected and wrote down the *Prose Edda*. Consequently, one has to reconstruct the original state if one wants to look at English and Norse mythology: what it "originally" looked like when it was used as a mythology, a system of religion. As philology works backward to the original, the source, Tolkien also creates myth backwards. The mythical background of *The Hobbit* and *The Lord of the Rings* is projected back by the allusions and hints, but *The Silmarillion* itself, as an account going back to sources, is also only a starting point for reconstruction. Philology, like Plato's philosophy, is also a pursuit; it leads to the recovery of the past. At the end of processes starting from the *empiria* of the world, on the one hand, we thus have Platonic truth, removed from the world in an abstract level but still apparent in it through participation;[36] and Tolkien's past, on the other hand, irrevocably gone but appearing in traces and determining the extant stories through participation in the tradition. Plato's Forms and Tolkien's past are functionally in the same place. Furthermore, if we consider that the truth of the Forms is already known through myth as the "past life of the Soul" in the world of Forms (which, according to the *Phaedrus*, it remembers in anamnesis),[37] we see that truth and the mythical past are for a significant extent similar.

The Platonic remembering soul is like Théoden, who had always known about Ents from the old tales (narrative traditions) of Rohan but never realized he knew something that was a piece of real knowledge, with a real subject and referent.

The creation of myth for Tolkien is determined by the method of philological reconstruction. The stories that make up the mythical history of the Elves all go back to previous recountings: the mythical past itself, the *original story*, is always hiding behind these accounts.[38] Recovery of the past is thus the recovery of mythology to account for the stories in our texts, as Tolkien accounted for the word "Earendel" in Cynewulf's *Crist* in his story of Eärendil. In a sense, Tolkien does not write myth but leaves it to be reconstructed: it is not only the *texts*, not only *in* the texts, but is for a large extent in the *system* of texts. When we speak about "Tolkien's mythology," therefore, we should properly understand the whole corpus—the fixed and finished texts together with the unfinished ones and the variants—*and* the theoretical framework of variance, unfixedness, and plurality that they produce. As mythopoesis has come full circle, this theoretical space is perhaps not entirely unlike the cultural situation of orality, the original condition of mythology, and the cultural context Plato is so much opposed to and attempts to overwrite.

Another significant similarity of the Platonic and Tolkienian paradigms is that Tolkien, too, handles writing as if it were merely a means of *record*. He records the stories of the (Elvish) past in texts—even when in the fiction they are orally told, as in *The Book of Lost Tales* (the frame of tale-telling is, of course, an age-old device for both record and fiction, and Tolkien also inserts a written source, the Golden Book [see *BLT2*, 283, 287, 290–91, 310, and n. 23]).[39] Tolkien records the reconstructive process, working toward the past, in writing: but since he is in fiction all the time, this is at the same time the creation of a context for the implied mythology. The early texts, where Tolkien is seen struggling toward the story of Eärendil, striving to establish a larger framework, illustrate this: when asked by G.B. Smith what the Eärendil lines "were really about," Tolkien reportedly answered, "I don't know. I'll try to find out" (*Biography*, 75). The content of myth is actually the past, and the reconstructive process—as the philosopher's "rising," "going up" to the Forms—leads to knowledge in various senses. Both inside and outside the textual world, this is primarily the knowledge of the "originals" (the languages and stories) that determine what we started with, what we have got now (as do the Forms of the phenomenal world). It is also the knowledge of history and origins *inside* the texts, while it is the knowledge of and the access to *meanings* for the outside interpreter (as the meaning of *empiria* is to be found in the really existent Forms that give grounding to the phenomena: the "meaning" of any "good" act or thing can be given by reference to the Form of the Good).[40] Creating myth is entirely carried out in writing: the result is itself a philological corpus, from which the philological method "backtracks" to the "originals." In writing the texts, Tolkien writes their background: he creates not only texts but also a *tradition* in which those texts stand. It is this that makes the pull of internal interpretation so irresistible. The texts themselves demand to be interpreted in their own implied tradition—hence the temptation to look at events like the War of the Ring not as a narrative element in a literary text in its context of Tolkien's work but in its "historical context," the end of the Third Age.

Tolkien uses a traditional discourse and a traditional conceptual framework to create what is basically a new phenomenon in contemporary literature. Like Plato's, his use also utilizes both the old and the new frameworks and criticizes the contemporary context not only from a literary standpoint but also from a cultural one. At the same time, it asserts continuity and makes use of it; this is a restoration of a functional place to mythology. The function of recovery that Tolkien attributes to the fairy story in "On Fairy-Stories" illustrates this very well: here Tolkien even ventures close to philosophical discourse to define this effect. "Recovery," he writes, "[…] is a re-gaining—regaining of a clear view. I do not say 'seeing things as they are' and involve myself with the philosophers" ("OFS," 77).

But how can it still be said that either Plato or Tolkien writes myth when myth by definition is not, and cannot be, written? Both Plato and Tolkien, as we have seen, use stories recounted in texts to create a system, to make a background, and to insert these texts into that background (a whole culture, in slightly different senses with the two authors). Myth is a culturally privileged story, and you have to have a culture for that culture to privilege anything; but once the context has been created, stories in the text that created it can be reinterpreted and can function in a privileged way. The attitude to their own myths as texts, the ways they handle this, also indicates similarities between the mythopoeic practice of Plato and that of Tolkien.

Plato's myths are integrated into his philosophical discourse, ultimately a written construct. In the *Republic* he analyzes myth and its function in the community at length. First, he associates myth with a "recounted-ness," in the emphasis on myth as "being told" (in the three references to traditional myths in the *Republic*, Plato always refers to these as being "said" or "told," always in the passive).[41] Second, he links myth with poets as their producers and with education as their sphere of use.[42] Third, he sets criteria for them to be effective in and appropriate for that function—and these considerations already show his reworking, since they are undoubtedly philosophical and do not derive from the traditional mythological context. Indeed, Plato attacks the poets (including Homer and the tragedians) for not fulfilling these criteria, and therefore being inappropriate for educational aims. In his fictitious state, Plato proposes to use myths in the same function but has specific *mythopoioi* produce them according to specific instructions.[43] The most basic of these is that the myth should be "well" told (*kalōs*),[44] harmonizing with the true conceptions about the gods and the other subjects of such tales. It is philosophical considerations of theology that determine these conceptions: the gods cannot be conceived to be bad or evil. Socrates sets up "types" (*typoi*) for these poets' use: these are presumably "paradigms" containing subjects and appropriate handlings, guidelines for telling stories "well."[45] The state has various interpretive and regulatory functions in this production (and surely it is partly this fencing myth round with the apparatuses of the state that earned Popper's hostility [see notes 5 and 15]). The point is that a text gets inserted into a nontext position, into the function of nontextual myth. Myth, however, remains to be seen as a nontext inside the dialogue (Socrates and other speakers relate it, not read it out, saying that they are "rulers" and "lawgivers" who make up the rules but need not write myths themselves)[46] while it of course remains a *text* inside the dialogue: both the myth of the *autokhthonia* and the myth of Er are part of the dialogue's text, as told by Socrates. Here Plato is employing the same fictional frame as that of Tolkien when talking about a fictional world where texts our authors (Plato and Tolkien) write can function as myths in contexts these texts create and as texts/ utterances by other fictitious authors (Socrates and Tolkien's author figures, Bilbo, Pengolod, Rúmil, and other named and unnamed authors).

Plato's relation to textuality comes out clearly in the myth of the Egyptian god Theuth at the end of the *Phaedrus*. Here Socrates mounts an explicit critique on writing in general,[47] saying that written texts can never function as proper dialectic: they always say the same thing; they cannot explain what they mean or defend themselves or their positions. Thamus, answering Theuth's claim about the uses of writing, says that writing can only remind: it does not make one wise but only makes one feel wise by giving him the false perception of knowing what he had read. Authority, Thamus argues, does not derive from texts; it derives from knowledge, of which writing can only remind, and which it cannot *construct* in one. But, as G.R.F. Ferrari observed, the whole of the dialogue is also in a way about textuality and authority.[48] Phaidros's problem is exactly that he confuses a text and the control over it with genuine knowledge. The Theuth myth shows text to be a tool for reminding: a cover, a reminder, a sign for what there is behind it. Texts need contexts in which they make sense; but they themselves are suggestive of this context, creating backgrounds for themselves.

The irony of saying this in a written myth is evident; but there is a point in it. When Phaidros gently accuses Socrates of "making up" the Egyptian story, he is told that this is not important: myth is not authentic because it has a definite source the user can point to.[49] It is authentic because it is *true*—true because it has always been told that way, because there is a tradition behind it. Something that had been known to be that way for generations simply *is* that way for subjects in that culture. Authority is not generated by sources (as Thamus says), since myth is in an authorizing system completely disjointed from the textual conceptions of authority and truth value.[50] Myth refers to a system behind it: in Plato, to the philosophical system that got inserted in the place of the old poetic one. And this is exactly Plato's aim: he is not deconstructing his own oeuvre but explaining what he does with myth, how he uses it to provide a wider cultural foundation for his philosophical discourse.

One can immediately see the similarity of Tolkien's strategy. I already remarked that his texts do not simply "add up to" a mythology—the creation of that lies in the system. Without the system, none of Tolkien's stories can be "mythic" in a definition that takes into account the essential cultural and functional context of myth. It is not the corpus, not the individual texts together, but the theoretical effect and context the whole generates: myth is only, and can only be, *implied*. The individual variants, their use as retellings and points of reference, as typological starting points, are the tool (the "text," so to speak, of mythology).

What this serves to remind one about, to speak in terms of the function Plato assigns to writing, is the underlying system of myths. The proliferation of texts is essential, since this implication of tradition (the depth effect) is exactly what leads to the authenticating system of mythology (at least according to Socrates). The trick is, in both Plato and Tolkien, that there is no such system preceding the texts themselves: it is the texts that create it and thus reinterpret their own status.

Tolkien's texts are multiply contextualized and extraordinarily suggestive of background. They not only generate both philological and narrative depth but also project a tradition back for themselves, into the prephilological and pretextual. As with Plato, the ultimate authenticating force is always only implied: one can never actually reach it in a text, since it is embedded deep in the texture of culture. Probably Tolkien would have said it was revelation; his views about the "truth of mythology" come to mind.[51] Plato's Socrates, interestingly enough, sometimes also acknowledges the role of divine inspiration, though he systematically questions the inspiredness of poets.[52]

But there are not only conceptual, methodological, and theoretical similarities between Plato's and Tolkien's myth-creation: the key motifs and images of light and vision in their writings suggest even closer, thematic affinities. The content of Plato's myth, philosophical knowledge (which is expressed in mythic terms, and the access to which is also signaled by mythic tales of the afterworld), and of Tolkien's ultimate theological myth is depicted in strikingly similar terms. Light in both systems fulfills a crucial role, accommodating both a theological and an ontological aspect; this is why Tolkien's creation myth lends itself so readily to comparison with Neoplatonic theories of emanation.[53] Light in Tolkien is an ultimate theological metaphor: cultures and beings in Middle-earth are categorized according to their distance from and relation to it. Light in *The Silmarillion*, as Verlyn Flieger writes, "at its best is meant to reveal, to make visible, so that we may see clearly and judge rightly."[54] But this is true in more than one sense: in a concrete sense, light offers opportunity for physical perception by vision; but in another sense, the light of Ilúvatar also stands for *meaning*, to which cultures of Middle-earth have access in varying degrees, according to their capacities and integration into the hierarchy of authority and knowledge. It is this meaning that is expressed and accounted for in mythical terms; it is this light that splinters and fragments through the history of the ages of the fictitious world (a process which Flieger examines so well in *Splintered Light*), and it is this which, emblematized in the "Flame Imperishable," supplies the whole reality of the World That Is. Plato also finds exactly such a double use for light: in the simile of the Sun, he says that as the sun's light makes physical vision possible, so does the Form of the Good lend *existence* to things: "and even so, you will say that the things known take not only their potential to be known from the Good, but also their existence and their being are provided to them by it; while the Good is not being, but is even beyond being, in rank and power superior."[55] The epistemological consideration is turned into an ontological one, in fact, nearly a theological one, as in Tolkien. The use of the metaphor of light in both authors conveys the same structure in the myth: that light comes from the supreme power, and it connects with (indeed, represents) both being and knowledge.

The concept of the vision as prior to worldly perception, where meanings are contemplated directly, and which is later recalled to make sense of phenomena, is also a common motif. In Plato, the vision of the Forms (as seen by the soul in the "place above the sky")[56] provides the souls with the knowledge they forget with their embodiment and later recall in anamnesis; while in Tolkien's cosmogony, the vision of the Ainur, which Ilúvatar shows them (as a projection of the Music), is also representative of the ultimate meaning, the intention of Ilúvatar. The vision in both systems determines order and defines what there is in the world: its content is the real meaning, of which the world is only a reflection. Even Melkor's ideas, as Ilúvatar says, are already in his plan (*Silm*, 6). It is toward this meaning, toward the recognition of the ultimate guarantee, that Plato's philosopher and the cultures of Tolkien's Middle-earth strive. The role of the Valar, furthermore, opens up another Platonic concept, that of the Demiurge in the *Timaeus*, who, with an eye on the Forms, orders the world.[57] Plato's philosophical truth and Tolkien's mythic past are thus seen to be not only functionally but also thematically, conceptionally similar.

The *Timaeus* and the Demiurge-function in Tolkien's cosmogony further supply another self-reflexive point that bears on the principles of creation and the construction of fictions. As Robert Zaslavsky points out, Plato sees analogies between the creation of a textual work of art and the creation of a world or a creature.[58] The world is like a living being; a well-constructed fiction creates a complex system like this with all its subtleties.[59] The Demiurge, we are told, shapes the world exactly so, as a creature, a living being, with an eye on the models.[60] The author of a text works on the same principle as the shaper of the world (and we already saw how the Demiurge's function fits into the conceptual framework of Tolkien's cosmogony). Tolkien's assertion in his poem "Mythopoeia" that "We make still by the law in which we're made," (line 70, in *TL*, 99), while underscoring and theorizing the very interesting metafictional bent his fiction has, appears to put forward precisely the same claim: that God's world-creation and the human artist's creation of artwork, the "secondary world," are based on the same principle. Furthermore, the effect the sub-created artwork produces also leads us back to Platonic principles: by revealing this theological modeling of the creative faculty of man, sub-creation in fact opens a door on "an already existent truth about the world."[61] It leads us to a forgotten world that we can recover, and reveals the undeniable signs that we belong to that world.

We saw that the practices that Plato and Tolkien adapt toward myth are highly similar in a number of ways. Plato is involved in reshaping and re-creating a mythological world, a whole cultural context; Tolkien's work is aimed at creating it, but this is positioned and thematized as a re-creation, with a strong suggestion of continuity. Of course, the mythological context that Plato re-creates is just as new as Tolkien's and is just as traditional in its inventory of motifs and images, but with the "Platonic difference" of being determined and controlled by philosophy. Both authors use myth as a device of expression. Myth can tell one about the world: how it is structured, how it works, and how we get to know it. In these, it also suggests how we get to know truth—indeed, it points out what truth is. Both Plato and Tolkien find truth expressible in the mythical past, which they both create along the lines and in the discourse of the mythological tradition they are part of and to which they are relating. Both assert criteria that myth, as a device, must fulfill to be able to function appropriately. Relation to tradition is one point; another crucially important one is that of philosophical-theological appropriateness. Myth has to be acceptable by the standards of philosophy and philology, too: the role of the process by which one arrives at myth is also similarly important for them.

Socrates says at the end of the myth of Er in the *Republic* that "the myth was saved . . . and can save us too if we believe in it."[62] In other places he seems to imply that to "save the myth" is to defend its position and its point.[63] What both Plato and Tolkien do, as I hope to have shown, is exactly this. They produce myths, having their good reasons to do so and expressing something centrally important for them. The myth thus communicates a *position*, and both authors go to great lengths to defend that, to show why it is important. They are both working to "save the myths," and let them save us. For both authors believe the myths can.

Notes

For the opportunity to use various articles for this paper, my thanks are due to many people. I would like to register my gratitude here to Verlyn Flieger and Theodore J. Sherman, editor of *Mythlore*; to Tom Shippey; and to the British Council, with whose help (as part of the British Studies Project) I was able to spend a week of research at the British Library, London, in March 2002. The Hungarian Scholarship Board, by whose Eötvös Scholarship I was enabled to work at Wheaton College, Norton, Massachusetts, for three months in the spring of 2003, also gave me important and generous support. Jane Chance gave me valuable advice and help, for which I remain deeply grateful.

1. See Mac Fenwick, "Breastplates of Silk: Homeric Women in *The Lord of the Rings*," *Mythlore* 21, no. 3 (1996), 17–23, 50; David Greenman, "Aeneidic and Odyssean Patterns of Escape and Return in Tolkien's 'The Fall of Gondolin' and *The Return of the King*," *Mythlore* 18, no. 2 (1992), 4–9; John Houghton, "Commedia as Fairy-Story: Eucatastrophe in the Loss of Virgil," *Mythlore* 17, no. 2 (1990), 29–32; James Obertino, "Moria and Hades: Underworld Journeys in Tolkien and Virgil," *Comparative Literature Studies* 30, no. 2 (1993): 153–69; Donald E. Morse, *Evocation of Virgil in Tolkien's Art: Geritol for the Classics* (Oak Park, Ill.: Bolchazy-Carducci, 1986).

2. David Greenman, "*The Silmarillion* as Aristotelian Epic-Tragedy," *Mythlore* 14, no. 3 (1988), 20–25.

3. There have been some articles on Plato and Tolkien, but it is mostly parallels of individual motifs that are discussed (like Gyges' ring in the *Republic* as an analogue to Tolkien's Ring of Power), or on the more general level, similarities of outlook and conceptual system, especially in regard to the cosmologies and creation stories of the two authors. Robert E. Morse's short note "Rings of Power in Plato and Tolkien" *Mythlore* 7, no. 25 (1980), 38; and Frederick A. de Armas's "Gyges' Ring: Invisibility in Plato, Tolkien, and Lope de Vega," *Journal of the Fantastic in the Arts* 3, no. 4 (1994): 120–38, deal with the connections of rings of invisibility in Plato's and Tolkien's work; this motivic parallel is a significant one, leading to considerations of the contexts and other details of the two stories of ring-findings, but it still remains only a detail. Only one article seems to compare general aspects: John Cox's treatment in "Tolkien's

Platonic Fantasy," *Seven* 5 (1984): 53–69, is a good extended study, which relates Tolkien not only to Plato but to the Western tradition of Neoplatonism, connected mainly with Plotinus and St. Augustine of Hippo. Tolkien's Neoplatonic connections are studied further by Verlyn Flieger, in "Naming the Unnameable: The Neoplatonic 'One' in Tolkien's *Silmarillion*," in *Diakonia: Studies in Honor of Robert T. Meyer*, ed. Thomas Halton and Joseph P. Williman (Washington, D.C.: Catholic University of America Press, 1986), 127–32; and by Mary Carman Rose, in "The Christian Platonism of C.S. Lewis, J.R.R. Tolkien, and Charles Williams," in *Neoplatonism and Christian Thought*, ed. Dominic J. O'Meara (Norfolk: International Society for Neoplatonic Studies, 1981), 203–12.

4. Patrick Curry, "Tolkien and His Critics: A Critique," in *Root and Branch: Approaches towards Understanding Tolkien*, ed. Thomas Honegger (Zurich and Bern: Walking Tree Publishers, 1999), 133 n. 71.

5. This view, as Janet E. Smith remarks, goes back to Karl Popper (see Smith's "Plato's Myths as 'Likely Accounts, Worthy of Belief,'" *Apeiron* 19, no. 1 [1985]: 24–42; 40 n. 18). The only sense in which Plato thought myth connected to anything in any sense "infantile" or "childlike" is his taking it (together with writing) as *paidia*, "play" (see the *Phaedrus*, 276D, 277E). All references to Plato's works are to the standard edition of John Burnet, *Platonis opera*, 5 vols., Oxford Classical Texts (Oxford: Oxford University Press, 1899–1906); citations will be indicated by: title of work; book number, if necessary; page number of the Stephanus edition of 1578; and section number(s).

6. See Kathryn A. Morgan, *Myth and Philosophy from the Pre-Socratics to Plato* (Cambridge: Cambridge University Press, 2000), 1–14. On the religious stances of the philosophers, a question intimately connected with their critique of traditional myth and piety, see Simon Price, *Religions of the Ancient Greeks* (Cambridge: Cambridge University Press, 1999), 126–42, especially 128–29, 133–34, and 137–38 for discussions of Plato.

7. Morgan, 127; see also 122–30.

8. Cf. the original etymological meanings of both *mythos* and *logos* as terms of language and discourse: see Kent F. Moors, *Platonic Myth: An Introduction* (Washington, D.C.: University Press of America, 1982), 35; Robert Zaslavsky, *Platonic Myth and Platonic Writing* (Washington, D.C.: University Press of America, 1981), 11–12, and Morgan, 16–18, 23 for a summary.

9. See Eric A. Havelock, *Preface to Plato* (Cambridge: Cambridge University Press, 1963), 29–31, 44–45, 81–82.

10. Havelock, 91.

11. Luc Brisson, *Plato, Myth Maker*, trans. Gerard Naddaf (Chicago and London: University of Chicago Press, 1998), 9.

12. See Morgan, 20–21, especially as she interprets poetic excellence as "the ability to generate superior versions of any story" (21). Very pertinent to my approach is Gregory Nagy's argument for the organic role of *performance* in myth: *Homeric Questions* (Austin, Tex.: University of Texas Press, 1996), 112–46.

13. Walter J. Ong, *Orality and Literacy: The Technologizing of the Word* (London and New York: Methuen, 1982), 33–36.

14. Morgan, 22.

15. Havelock, 27. This is why one could argue that the concept of ideology was in fact discovered by Plato: what he does in analyzing, deconstructing, and then rewriting mythology as a formative discourse, a state-controlled basis of culture, would certainly be called a critique (and practice: hence Popper's hostility) of ideology today and definitely foreshadows Louis Althusser's conception of ideology as the discourse operated by "state apparatuses" in "Ideological State Apparatuses" (in *Lenin and Philosophy, and Other Essays*, trans. from the French by Ben Brewster [London: New Left Books, 1971], 123–73); and Plato is very much conscious of the importance and functioning of this discourse and its political medium.

16. See Ong, 79–81.

17. Morgan, 24–30, 63.

18. Morgan, 24.

19. See Plato, *Republic* 10.617D–E.

20. See T.A. Shippey, *The Road to Middle-earth*, 2nd ed. (London: Grafton, 1992), 17–21.

21. See Shippey, *Road*, 27–50.

22. Cf. his emphasis on "the soup," "the story as it is served by [any story's] author or teller." "OFS," in *The Tolkien Reader* (New York: Ballantine, 1966), 47; and see Iwan Rhys Morus, "'Uprooting the Golden Bough': J.R.R. Tolkien's Response to Nineteenth Century Folklore and Comparative Mythology," *Mallorn* 27 (1990): 5, 8.

23. This reappears as the source for the earliest form of the *Quenta*, with a very unstable authorship all through. See *Shaping*, 77–78, 274, and Shippey, *Road*, 203–4, 278.

24. See Tom Shippey, *J.R.R. Tolkien: Author of the Century* (Boston: Houghton Mifflin, 2001), 21–29, especially 26; Michael D.C. Drout and Hilary Wynne, "Tom Shippey's *J.R.R. Tolkien: Author of the Century* and a Look Back at Tolkien Criticism since 1982," *Envoi* 9, no. 2 (2000): 101–67, here, 111–13.

25. Moors, 58–59, 60–61.

26. Plato, *Republic* 1.330D, 7.521C, 7.565D, 9.588C; *Phaedrus* 229B, C, D; *Phaedo* 107D–108C; *Symposium* 196D, 197B; *Protagoras* 322A, etc., and see further below.

27. Cf. Ong, 109–10.

28. Plato, *Phaedrus* 275A; cf. G.R.F. Ferrari, *Listening to the Cicadas: A Study of Plato's "Phaedrus"* (Cambridge: Cambridge University Press, 1987), 204–20, for a survey of interpretive stances on this Platonic assertion and a valuable interpretation of his own.

29. See Plato, *Seventh Letter* 341C–D, and the following argument as to why writing is inappropriate for the serious uses of serious thinkers, concluding at 344C.

30. Cf. Havelock, 91.

31. Havelock, 89–90, 93–94.

32. The whole text of the myth of Er (Plato, *Republic* 10.614B–621B), with one remarkable "aside" by Socrates (10.618B–619B), is built up of reported structures dependant on Er's verbs of saying and recounting: "he said," "he told" (*ephē, elegon*).

33. Plato, *Phaedrus* 249D–251B, *Phaedo* 72E–77D, *Meno* 81B–82A and the famous demonstration with the slave boy up to 86B.

34. Described in Plato, *Phaedrus* 247C–248E.

35. Plato, *Phaedo* 110A–111E, *Gorgias* 523A–527C, respectively. Concerning the judgment myths, see Julia Annas, "Plato's Myths of Judgment," *Phronesis* 27, no. 2 (1982): 119–43.

36. As the *Symposium* and the *Phaedo* say: Plato, *Symposium* 211B, *Phaedo* 74B–75B. Participation (*methexis*) of worldly things in the Forms always remained a problematic point for Plato. See his own opening up of the question in the late *Parmenides*.

37. Plato, *Phaedrus* 249E–251B; see also *Phaedo* 75C–E.

38. See my examination of the "original" of the Túrin story in "The Great Chain of Reading: (Inter-)textual Relations and the Technique of Mythopoesis in the Túrin Story," in *Tolkien the Medievalist*, ed. Jane Chance (New York and London: Routledge, 2002), 239–58.

39. The Golden Book in fact sometimes functions as a pseudotext (as I used the term in "The Great Chain of Reading"), a fiction of a source which is never actually there but of which the actual text the reader is reading is a transcript.

40. With this, I by no means intend to suggest that, as Plato believed the Forms universal and ultimately knowable, *meanings* in Tolkien's text are likewise universal, knowable, fixed. What *is* universal, however, is the concept of meaning as such, which for Tolkien is to be found or understood from the past.

41. Plato, *Republic* 1.330D, 7.565D, 9.588C.

42. Cf. Havelock, 61–86.

43. The terms by which Plato refers to the producers of myth are, however, various: *mythopoios* appears in *Republic* 2.377B; *poiētēs* in 2.378E–379A, 3.392A–B, 3.398A–B, 10.596B–C; *logopoios* in 3.392A–B (also), and *mythologos* in 3.392D and 3.398A–B (also). For references to the activity as *mythologein*, see 2.378C, and E, 2.379A, 2.380C, 2.392B, 3.415A, and 6.501E. It is significant that Plato in fact refers to the whole fiction of the *Republic* (the imaginary city) as myth: *Republic* 2.376D, 6.501E, and in the *Timaeus* (as the speech delivered the day before: *Timaeus* 26C).

44. Plato, *Republic* 2.377D. The expression could equally well be translated as "beautifully," "appropriately," or "fittingly."

45. Plato, *Republic* 2.378E–379A, 2.380B–C.

46. Plato, *Republic* 2.378E–379A.

47. Plato, *Phaedrus* 274C–275C, supplemented by Socrates's remarks in 275D–E.

48. Ferrari, 216–18.

49. Plato, *Phaedrus* 276B–C.

50. See Morgan, 22–24, and Gregory Nagy, *Homeric Questions*, 122–28, where Nagy analyzes the Homeric usage of *mythos* as connected to the roots *lēth-* and *mnē-* ("forgetting" and "remembering"), referring to a "speech-act of actually *narrating from memory* an authoritative myth from the past" (127). This, coupled with his conception of myth as "performance" (see n. 12), describes the orally based authenticating system of myth that Plato is referring to here.

51. See Morus, 8.

52. For places where Plato discusses divine inspiration and for a critical discussion of the concept, see Penelope Murray, "Inspiration and Mimesis in Plato," in *The Language of the Cave*, ed. Andrew Barker and Martin Warner, *Apeiron* 25, no. 4 (1992), 27–46. See also Morgan, 238–39, on the question of inspiredness and authenticity in the *Phaedrus*.

53. See Flieger, "Naming the Unnameable," and cf. Cox, 58–59, where the Neoplatonic idea of emanation is traced back to the Platonic concept of a "series of imitations" (58), a more conscious model of creation.

54. Verlyn Flieger, *Splintered Light: Logos and Language in Tolkien's World* (Grand Rapids, Mich.: William B. Eerdmans, 1983), 124.

55. Plato, *Republic* 6.509B; my translation.

56. Plato, *Phaedrus* 247C–248E.

57. Plato, *Timaeus* 27C–31A.

58. Zaslavsky, 61, 164. The dialogues from where Zaslavsky derives assertions to this effect are the *Phaedrus*, the *Republic*, and the *Timaeus*.

59. See Plato, *Phaedrus* 264C and Zaslavsky, 61; in this connection it may again be significant that Socrates calls the fictional city, itself a veritable subcreation, a myth: see above in n. 43.

60. Plato, *Timaeus* 30C–D.

61. Clive Tolley, "Tolkien's 'Essay on Man': A Look at *Mythopoeia*," *Inklings-Jahrbuch* 10 (1992): 226 (Tolley here is referring to line 39 of the poem: "digging the foreknown from experience"). See also page 231.

62. Plato, *Republic* 621B–C; my translation.

63. Moors, 46, 51, 53, and 74.

Chapter 6

MYTH, LATE ROMAN HISTORY, AND MULTICULTURALISM IN TOLKIEN'S MIDDLE-EARTH

SANDRA BALLIF STRAUBHAAR

This essay, to paraphrase J.R.R. Tolkien, grew in the writing. Considering its origin in a conference session "Tolkien and the Classical," I shall begin with a classical quotation, and proceed from there:

> Unde habitus quoque corporum, tamquam in tanto hominum numero, idem omnibus: truces et caerulei oculi, rutilae comae, magna corpora et tantum ad impetum valida: laboris atque operum non eadem patientia, minimeque sitim aestumque tolerare, frigora atque inediam caelo solove adsueverunt.

> [The physical type, if one may generalize at all about so vast a population, is everywhere the same—wild, blue eyes, reddish hair and huge frames that excel only in violent effort. They have no corresponding power to endure hard work and exertion, and have little capacity to bear thirst and heat; but their climate and soil *have* taught them to bear cold and hunger.][1]

This is Publius Cornelius Tacitus, writing in the first century A.D. about the Germanic tribes, whom he patronizes for their simplicity and barbarity but admires for other virtues, including valor and loyalty. I will argue below that these rather specific, and certainly culturally biased, assumptions of one dark, sophisticated southerner writing about paler, simpler northerners have directly informed J.R.R. Tolkien's fictional construction of Gondorian attitudes toward the Rohirrim (the Riders of the Mark) and their ancestors from farther north, the chieftains of Rhovanion.

I first conceived of the present study when I came across an excellent article by R.C. Blockley (1982) on marriages between Romans and barbarians in the late empire, containing a good real-world database and some workable conclusions on the shifting meaning of such mixed unions to the greater culture.[2] It struck me that in both narrated Gondor and historical Rome such instances of miscegenation at the royal level could be seen (at least at first) as contraimperial disasters, but the fact that they occurred at all indicates at least some level of tolerance for the concept within the dominant class. The parallels—and there are many—cried out to be explored.

Tolkien stages a long conversation, between Faramir of Gondor and Frodo the Hobbit, in the fastness of Henneth Annûn, in which we learn (among many other things) the Gondorian view of human taxonomy. (Note that there is no indication in this episode that the author does, or does not, validate such taxonomies. On the contrary, I would argue that a good bit of Tolkien's irony on this issue resides in the fact that no character, however sympathetic, actually articulates what might be extrapolates as the author's point of view on multicultural or multiracial issues; created beings display fallibility.) Faramir says:

> For so we reckon Men in our lore, calling them the High, or Men of the West, which were Númenoreans; and the Middle Peoples, Men of the Twilight, such as are the Rohirrim and their kin that dwell still far in the North; and the Wild, the Men of Darkness. (*LR* 4.5, 663)

Earlier in the narrative, Tolkien lets Aragorn express this not dissimilar view of the Rohirrim:

> I have been among them. . . . They are proud and wilful, but they are true-hearted, generous in thought and deed; bold but not cruel; wise but unlearned, writing no books but singing many songs, after the manner of the children of Men before the Dark Years. (*LR* 3.2, 420)

Besides harmonizing with the Tacitus citation above, this last text contains a specific echo of another of Tacitus's observations about the Germanic tribes, namely, that they are illiterate—that their tribal memory consists of oral narratives only:

> Celebrant *carminibus antiquis, quod unum apud illos memoriae et annalium genus est*, Tuistonem deum terra editum.

> [In their *ancient songs, their only form of recorded history*, the Germans celebrate the earth-born god, Tuisto.][3] (emphasis added)

Later on in the Tolkienian narrative, Éowyn, a woman of Faramir's designated "Middle Peoples," confronts Faramir with the following challenge:

> And would you have your proud folk say of you: "There goes a lord who tamed a wild shieldmaiden of the North! Was there no woman of the race of Númenor to choose?" (*LR* 6.5, 944)

Faramir assures Éowyn of his open-mindedness on such matters, and we see this declaration confirmed not only with a kiss in this very scene but elsewhere with another striking physical image, celebrating both human genetic diversity and the union of unlike partners:

> And so they stood on the walls of the City of Gondor, and a great wind rose and blew, and their hair, raven and golden, streamed out mingling in the air. (*LR* 6.5, 941)

Thus we see a mixed partnership, soon to become a mixed marriage, constructed as a desirable match and a happy ending, despite unmistakable culturally driven misgivings from both sides.

There is a clear parallel and counterexample within the Tolkienian narrative, considerably upstream in time (1,600 years or so), although still Third Age, which demonstrates Tolkien's careful attention to these cultural constructs in Middle-earth. This is the marriage between the Gondorian prince Valacar and the Northern barbarian princess Vidumavi, which union produced Vinitharya, later king of Gondor under the name Eldacar, who is, in turn, perhaps best known as the catalyst for the "Kin-strife" in the Gondorian royal line. The Kin-strife, as any Gondorian historians reading this text will recall, centered precisely on the issue of miscegenation and the questionable fitness of half-breeds to rule.

As I have shown via excerpts above, and as further excerpts confirm, the attitudes of imperial culture toward fringe culture can be observed both in Gondor and in Rome (or New Rome further east, as we shall see) as varying between, on the one hand, patronizing and, on the other hand, grudgingly admiring, incorporating a covert agenda toward reform in the imperial culture. For instance, Faramir remarks to Frodo (at an earlier point in the Henneth Annûn conversation cited above) that decadence has marred the Númenorean-descended dynasties and civilizations for some time:

> Kings made tombs more splendid than houses of the living, and counted old names in the rolls of their descent dearer than the names of sons. Childless lords sat in aged halls musing on heraldry; in secret chambers withered men compounded strong elixirs, or in high cold towers asked questions of the stars. And the last king of the line of Anárion had no heir. (*LR* 4.5, 662–63.)

He further states, very much in Tacitus-mode, that the Northern barbarians are in some isolated ways perhaps superior to his own people, presumably because they have *not* achieved the Númenoreans' superannuated decadence:

> [T]hey speak among themselves their own North tongue. And we love them: tall men and fair women, valiant both alike, golden-haired, bright-eyed and strong; they remind us of the youth of Men, as they were in the Elder Days. (*LR* 4.5, 663)

Having observed these close parallels between the approaches to culture taken by Tacitus and Tolkien, then, it was my next thought that additional generative roots for Tolkienian narrative might accordingly be found in the works of the postclassical historians, those who followed in the centuries after Tacitus and chronicled the increasing number of encounters between Romans (and Byzantines) and outlying tribespeople—the "narrators of barbarian history," to borrow Walter Goffart's phrase,[4] who would, coincidentally, have supplied much of the raw data so usefully interpreted by Blockley. We know that Tolkien read these historians. We even know that he had a particular fondness for Paul the Deacon's *Historia Langobardorum*, since he used the Lombardic dynastic names Alboin and Audoin in several unfinished stories, including "The Lost Road" (*Road*, 39–58) and the "Notion Club Papers"—in the latter of which Tolkien even has a character remark, "Odd how the Langobards crop up" (*Sauron*, 301). They certainly *do* crop up out of all ordinary proportion in Tolkien's posthumous material.

However, when we take a closer look at the dynastic names in this essay's central case study, it is clear that we need to turn our attention not to Paul the Deacon this time but specifically to those colleagues of his who chronicled the deeds of the Goths. The non-Gondorian names in our focus episode (namely, the mixed marriage between Valacar and Vidumavi) are quite recognizable as Gothic—the Gothic of our primary world, the Gothic of Wulfila's Bible. We will accordingly visit Cassiodorus, Jordanes, and Procopius in due time below.

First, though, I must refer the reader to the following chart and pay passing notice here to the thorny issue of "translation" in Tolkien's Middle-earth. Suffice it to say that the three languages represented in the dynastic names here are either two-thirds "real" and one-third "unreal" *or* the reverse, seen from a Middle-earth–o–centric worldview or a real-world worldview, respectively. (See the "Simplification" note in the following chart.) I will revisit these paradoxes more closely in due time. The dynastic segment under study, then, includes the following persons in the accompanying table (*LR* Appendix A.1.iv, 1020–22).

We can observe here the following persons: the barbarian father-in-law, Vidugavia; the royal Gondorian father-in-law, Minalcar; the mixed couple, Valacar and Vidumavi; and their son, the half-breed prince Vinitharya/Eldacar, who will have to ascend to the throne twice because of the controversy surrounding his birth. Note also the attitude-revealing description of this hybrid royal heir—"To the lineage of Gondor he added the fearless spirit of the Northmen"—added for us by the Fourth-Age Gondorian scribe Findegil, who, as you may recall, wrote Appendix A for us; and the tree-related names of Eldacar's two sons, probably deliberately referring back to their Northern forest ancestry.

Thus we see two dynastic successions crossing at a single focal point, at the marriage of Valacar and Vidumavi. At that intersection, structuralists would encourage us to note that not only does "lineage" meet "spirit" but also civilization meets noble savagery and long-livedness meets short-livedness.

NORTHERNERS (parent to child)

GONDORIANS (parent to child)
Minalcar (Q., "Prominent helmet?")
Lived 1126-1366 (Third Age)
Regent from 1240
Fought Easterlings 1248
Crowned as **Rómendacil II**
(Q., "East-slayer"), 1304
Built pillars of Argonath

Vidugavia, king of Rhovanion
(G.=Vidugauja, "Woods-dweller")

Valacar (Q., "God-helm")
Lived 1194-432
Sent by father to Rhovanion as
ambassador 1250
Married Vidumavi
Came to throne 1366

Vidumavi (G., "Woods-maiden")
(**Galadwen** [S., "Tree-maiden"])
Married Valacar

Eldacar (Q., "Elf-helm")
[Probably named after his ancestor,
Isildur's grandson, 87-339]
(Known in Rhovanion as
Vinitharya [G., "Bold friend?"]
[thauris, adj., "daring"])
Lived 1255-490
Crowned 1432
Deposed by cousin Castamir and
fled to Rhovanion 1437
Restored to throne 1447
"To the lineage of Gondor he added
the fearless spirit of the Northmen"
(*LR* Appendix A.1.iv, 1022)

Q = Quenya
S = Sindarin
G = Gothic (translated, *standing in
for Proto-Westron/Proto-Adûnaic

(*Simplification: In Middle-earth,
Q and S are the attested languages
and G is a stand-in; in the world as
we know it, G is [or was] real and
Q and S are fictions.)

Ornendil (Q., "Tree-friend"), first son
Killed by Castamir at Osgiliath 1437
Brother of **Aldamir** (Q., "Tree-
jewel"), second son
Lived 1330-540
Crowned 1490
[These names are probably tributes
to their Northern grandmother's tree-
related name.]

And perhaps—as is the case with Faramir and Éowyn much later—black-hairedness meets blondness. Within the Third-Age narrative of *The Lord of the Rings*, all the Númenorean descendants we meet are either dark-haired or too old to tell, and (correspondingly) all the Rohirrim we meet are either blond or too old to tell.[5] But we find in the unfinished stories "Aldarion and Erendis" and "The Lost Road" (*Road*, 66; *UT*, 182), and perhaps elsewhere as well, that in the days when Númenor was still above the waves some of its people were blond—just as many of the House of Hador in the First Age had been, as Faramir remarks to Frodo, "of the youth of Men, as they were in the Elder Days" (*LR* 4.5, 663). In Tolkienian narrative, golden hair (which later darkens with age) seems to have an association with the youth of an entire people, just as it in fact often does with the youth of individuals of western and northern European background in our primary world. The Third-Age Númenorean kingdom of Gondor, in any case—the Gondor we visit in *The Lord of the Rings*—does seem to be chiefly inhabited by dark-haired people. To argue on another front, this trait is perhaps not surprising for a land whose capital city Tolkien situated geographically "at about the latitude of Florence" (*Letters*, 376) and compared to both Byzantium and Egypt (*Letters*, 157, 281). Certainly a case can be made for blondness in Middle-earth to stand as a marker for primevalness; although for Third-Age Gondorians, in all their self-absorbed hauteur, it can hardly be seen to stand for ethnic superiority. It should perhaps be added here that the blondness of a wide array of Tolkienian figures (of varying descent), such as Goldberry, Galadriel, and Éowyn, has caused at least one life-long reader from our world (Anthony Lane, of the *New Yorker*) to form the early impression that:

> all women were milk-pale maidens with waterfalls of yellow hair—a
> delusion that landed me in no end of trouble, and one that, even now,
> pains me like a war wound.[6]

In any case, it would not be far-fetched to argue that these northerners from Rhovanion, whom Findegil chronicles and whose descendants Faramir praises condescendingly, are meant to be seen at least partly as primeval, Garden-of-Eden types, inhabiting as they do the ancient forests and reminding nostalgic Third-Age Gondorians of the youth of Men in the Elder Days.

As is always the case in Tolkien, none of the figures on this dynastic chart is randomly named. In Tolkienian onomastics, sound and sense are always equally significant. The Gothic names in this family—Vidugavia, Vidumavi, Vinitharya—are particularly euphonious[7] and nicely alliterative; semantically, they carry interrelated connotations of woodsiness and valor. Curiously, even the Quenya name of the ambassadorial prince from Gondor, Valacar, alliterates into this Gothic group—reflecting Germanic poetic tradition as well as Germanic familial naming customs. This is odd, since Valacar was certainly his name before he met his future in-laws; perhaps it is at least partially intended to foreshadow his status as their kinsman by marriage. It is instructive to note that all of the Eldarin (i.e., non-Gothic) names in this family are constructed on Tolkienian invented linguistic roots connoting such significant themes as piety, tradition, veneration of nature and ancestors, and military defense. Probably not coincidentally, in Tolkien's generative matrices of aesthetics and meaning, they also echo (in sound) various noble and honored names from the occidental past of the world we know, such as Hamilcar, as well as Clodomir, Casimir, and Vladimir.

The two male Gothic names in our chart, being framed in a language from the world we know, are (not surprisingly) attested in European history and legend. The name Vinitharya (Winitharius) shows up in the writings of two sixth-century historians—Cassiodorus and Jordanes[8]—attached to a Gothic king of the past, specifically praised by Cassiodorus for his *æquitas* (fairness). (Winitharius also turns out to have been the name of an eighth-century scribe at the abbey of St. Gall in Switzerland, but as this Winitharius seems to have been discovered only in the last decade or so, we cannot assume that Tolkien knew about him.) Vidugavia is almost certainly the same name as that borne by Vitiges or Ouittigis (Vittigis), mentioned by Jordanes,[9] Cassiodorus, and Procopius,[10] and the grandson-in-law of king Theodoric of the Ostrogoths. Several centuries later, this name shows up in the Old English poem *Wídsíth* as Wudga—as one of many celebrated warriors, kings, and chiefs of the past. Six hundred to seven hundred years after Jordanes, in *Thidhreks saga af Bern* and in the writings of Walter Map, we find the name Vithga or Widia grafted onto another kind of family tree as the son of the legendary Wayland (Völund) the Smith. The giant Wade (Vathi) has become his grandfather, and his paternal great-grandmother is a mermaid; the connection with Theodoric is still retained. Thus it is a fine, polyvalent cluster of real-world Gothic names, attested in both history and legend, that Tolkien has drawn from to assign names to this kinship group. That there were no matching female names in this database seems to have been no obstacle; Vidumavi (woods + maiden) could be easily extrapolated from Vidugavia (woods + dweller). Similar cut-and-paste creativity can be seen in Tolkien's Old English names for the late–Third-Age Rohirrim: Éowyn (horse + joy), for instance, is not found in any Old English texts, but could be calqued from similarly formed analogues like Jófrídhr (horse + beautiful), which are attested in Old Norse.

Further searches in Procopius, Cassiodorus, and Jordanes for Tolkienian parallels, however—on the narrative level, deeper than onomastics alone—have proved in vain. I could find no narrative parallels or echoes other than the metaparallel I have already spoken of, namely, that tolerance of dynastic interbreeding between imperial and fringe peoples seems to have increased with time in Tolkien (Valacar to Faramir) in the same way Blockley documents that it did in real-world history (four documented instances from the third century A.D., versus thirteen from the fifth).[11] The echoes of Gothic-ness proved to be *not* particularly historically based but linguistically only. Thus Tolkien crafted a text not designed to reflect real history but one that would transact an observably recurring *pattern* of human historical change. This is hardly surprising considering Tolkien's celebrated preference for having his narratives exhibit *applicability* to our primary world rather than simple one-to-one correspondences of a topical and timely nature (*LR* Foreword, 11).[12] I should have anticipated that, as is always the case with Tolkienian narrative, inspiration is to be sought primarily in language itself; that for Tolkien, linguistics and onomastics were not mere surface ornamentation but the *Ding an sich*.

And here we can put our finger on what I think is the greatest paradox within Tolkienian narrative, the one I have already hinted at, the one we face in Appendix F.2 to *The Lord of the Rings* (*LR* Appendix F.2, 1167–72). There we are told that Germanic naming and vocabulary elements, including those we have noted and documented above—Gothic for the chieftains of Rhovanion (as we have seen), Norse for the Dwarves and Dale-men, Old English for the Rohirrim and the Beornings, and rustic English for the Shire—have been *translated* from their linguistically unrelated "originals" into Germanic versions that English speakers are meant to feel more at home with. Presumably this is a late addition to Tolkien's thinking, intended to solve the paradox between the postulated antiquity of his narrated world and the evolution of real languages in our primary world; but what a morass it creates for those of us whose hobgoblin minds expect foolish consistencies!

It is frustrating that a sufficient number of linguistic, narrative, and temporal paradoxes remain even after Tolkien's translation corrective has been applied, perhaps the most notable of them being the handful of puns between Germanic and the Eldarin languages, such as Orc and Orthanc and even Mordor. Thus chronological consistency of cultural artifacts, including language, cannot really be seen as a defining feature of the Tolkienian narrative, however much the author seems to have wanted to make it so—after the fact. As T.A. Shippey has pointed out, the Shire *is* Edwardian England, with postal service, pipes after dinner, teatime and "weskits;"[13] as Tolkien himself hinted, the Bayeux tapestry, an artifact of our primary world's Middle Ages, was not a bad template to have in mind while visualizing the Riders of the Mark (*Letters*, 281). Anachronisms are built into Tolkien's epic just as thickly as they are into the multiculturally narrated tales of the Völsungs or King Arthur or into the plays of Shakespeare. In many ways it works best for Hobbits to *be* Edwardians, for Rohirrim to *be* Anglo-Saxons or Normans, and the chieftains of Rhovanion to *be* Goths, even if we are supposed to visualize the overriding story as predating such people by millennia. It is perhaps most advisable to embrace the simple fact (even though the author himself seems to have had difficulty embracing it) that in Tolkienian narrative, the gyre of history, as we usually construct it, has been flattened into a two-dimensional coil, where all is allowed to exist contemporaneously in a postmodern limbo: Goths and umbrellas, mead halls and vambraces, and (yea, even) express-trains (*LR* 1.1, 36). Again, it is not primary-world history that matters. Narrative matters; language matters; cultural and ethnic diversity matters.

So what exactly *is* the smaller narrative (within the larger one) that grows out of these Gothic/Eldarin naming patterns and their logic of diversity and alterity? As I have said above, Blockley concludes that cultural intermixing became more palatable to Rome with the passage of time; Tolkien similarly narrates that attitudes changed correspondingly in Gondor. The literally health-bringing alliance between Faramir and Éowyn revitalizes Gondorian decadence with a draught of fresh

Northern air. In other words, for a multicultural world to survive, diverse elements must cooperate with and complement each other. T.A. Shippey has already noted a number of distinctly twentieth-century themes in Tolkien's epic;[14] multiculturalism is yet another, which can only come to be more significant in our own century than it was in the last.

With the advent of Peter Jackson's cinematic version of *The Lord of the Rings* trilogy, particularly as seen against the backdrop of the events of the first years of the twenty-first century, the multicultural themes of the story have been explored in public discourse as never before. Widely varying extrapolations on this theme have been explored, up to and including the topical kind that Tolkien decried so passionately. On the one hand, *Newsweek* film reviewer David Ansen, an admitted Tolkien neophyte, suggested in late 2001 a clear (though unspoken) identification between the Fellowship of the Ring and the United States and its (varied) allies:

> [Frodo] must form a coalition among the races of Middle-earth. . . . (Is there an echo here of our current world? If you hear it, it lends this war movie an extra urgency.) With his multispecies band of brothers—the Fellowship—Frodo sets out to the Land of Mordor.[15]

On the other hand, it is probably Viggo Mortensen (the Danish-American actor who portrays Aragorn in the films) who has provided the most public voice against that particular, contemporary reading of the story's topicality. Note that Mortensen stresses Tolkien's multicultural theme just as Ansen does, but suggests an opposite applicability, if any:

> I've seen where people try to relate it [Jackson's film version of the *Lord of the Rings* trilogy] to the current situation—specifically the United States and their role in the world right now. And I—if you're going to compare them, then you should get it right. . . . [I]n *The Two Towers* you have different races, nations, cultures coming together and examining their conscience and unifying against a very real and terrifying enemy. . . . And I don't think that the civilians on the ground in those countries [e.g., Iraq] look at us in the way that maybe Europeans did at the end of World War II, waving flags in the streets. . . . [T]hey're terrified—and have been for a long time—and we are not the good guys, unfortunately, in this case.[16]

[Aragorn is] very aware of the fact that in Middle-earth there are no other men who've traveled as much as he has, who have an understanding of the different cultures and languages, and who realize the benefits of unifying all these people.[17]

It seems to be safe to conclude that a polycultured, polylingual world is absolutely central to Tolkien's narrated Middle-earth and is easily perceptible as such by many readers and filmgoers—while specific topical applicability comes and goes with current events, in addition to clearly running counter to the author's own stated intentions. It remains indubitable, though, that the themes of multiculturalism and hybridity are strongly present in Tolkien's text, as we have seen in microcosm in the case study here of Valacar and Vidumavi.

This is why it is always interesting to see the recurring accusations in the popular media through the years that argue for a specifically racist interpretation of Tolkien's narrative. I will briefly visit two of these, written in conjunction with the releases of Peter Jackson's first and second films respectively.

Aftonbladet, Stockholm's 170-year-old evening paper, ran a series of commentaries in late 2001 and early 2002 in which David Tjeder, cultural studies doctoral candidate at the University of Stockholm, defended himself against all comers (including hordes of enraged Swedish Tolkien fans), insisting that J.R.R. Tolkien promoted pernicious and antiquated models of gender and race in his fiction. Tjeder claimed to find a palpable "skräck för uppblandning" (fear of miscegenation) interwoven throughout Tolkien's text; he did not hesitate to equate this fear to similar attitudes from the eras of Nazism and European imperialism. "White men are best; men and women are different" are the two interrelated ideas Tjeder found in Tolkien and saw as most "livsfarlig" (mortally dangerous).[18] I hope that I have shown that the correct Tolkienian reading on at least the first of these issues is considerably more complex than Tjeder can see. Tjeder's first error, clearly, was that he equated the views of some characters with those of the author.

His second error was that he faulted J.R.R. Tolkien for being a product of his own time. "What is interesting," wrote Tjeder, "is that he could express such antiquated ideas at such a late date." He went on to say that the 1890s (coincidentally Tolkien's own birth decade) would be a better home for these ideas.[19] Tjeder was obviously unacquainted with popular

Anglophone adventure authors, from H. Rider Haggard (publishing from 1885 to 1925) through John Buchan (publishing from 1910 to 1940), Edgar Rice Burroughs (1912 to 1950), and Robert E. Howard (1920s and 1930s), in whose works the construction of race and miscegenation is considerably more embarrassingly retrograde than it is in Tolkien. He had presumably also forgotten Astrid Lindgren's *Pippi Långstrump i Söderhavet* (Pippi Longstocking in the South Seas)—published in 1948, and containing (even in today's editions) some very problematic material on quaint woolly-headed Polynesians. We could certainly argue that Tolkien has largely avoided such gaffes as these. However, Tjeder did find the following description of the warriors of Harad stereotypical and reflective of colonial attitudes. It is, admittedly, possible to read it that way:[20]

> They are fierce. They have black eyes, and long black hair, and gold rings in their ears; yes, lots of beautiful gold. And some have red paint on their cheeks, and red cloaks; and their flags are red, and the tips of their spears; and they have round shields, yellow and black with big spikes. Not nice; very cruel wicked Men they look. Almost as bad as Orcs, and much bigger. (*LR* 4.3, 631–32)

As you have probably gathered, though, this is not an authoritative character speaking. It is Gollum. I would argue that Tolkien would have his readers notice that all such arbitrary and stereotypical assumptions about the Other are absurd—whether they are Gollum's or even Faramir's—just as much as the Hobbitic one, more readily identifiable as laughable, is: "They're queer folks in Buckland" (*LR* 3.1, 68). By contrast, Sam Gamgee's silent encounter with a recently slain warrior of the same people Gollum has described, not too much later, is harder to find fault with:

> His scarlet robes were tattered, his corslet of overlapping brazen plates was rent and hewn, his black plaits of hair braided with gold were drenched with blood. His brown hand still clutched the hilt of a broken sword.
>
> It was Sam's first view of a battle of Men against Men, and he did not like it much. He was glad that he could not see the dead face. He wondered what the man's name was and where he came from; and if he was really evil of heart, or what lies or threats had led him on the long march from his home. (*LR* 4.4, 646)

The Edinburgh-based *Scotsman* ran an op-ed piece on 14 December 2002 presenting the Tolkien interpretations of Yale-trained cultural studies scholar Stephen Shapiro, of the University of Warwick. Shapiro claims:

> Put simply, Tolkien's good guys are white and the bad guys are black, slant-eyed, unattractive, inarticulate and a psychologically undeveloped horde. . . . The fellowship is portrayed as über-Aryan, very white and there is the notion that they are a vanishing group under the advent of other, evil ethnic groups.[21]

Shapiro may have an argument here with regards to "slant-eyed," on which aesthetic point Tolkien seems to have exhibited a kind of racism perhaps not unremarkable in a mid-twentieth-century Western man— and yet certainly milder than that found in the contemporary popular novelists mentioned above (Buchan, Burroughs, Howard). As Tolkien wrote in 1958, with only a mild veneer of apologetics (in the second parenthetical phrase):

> The Orcs are definitely stated to be corruptions of the "human" form seen in Elves and Men. They are (or were) squat, broad, flat-nosed, sallow-skinned, with wide mouths and slant eyes: in fact, degraded and repulsive versions of the (to Europeans) least lovely Mongol-types. (*Letters*, 274)[22]

Like Viggo Mortensen (cited above), and like Karen Durbin of the *New York Times* in a similar op-ed piece,[23] Stephen Shapiro fears that today's audiences will misapply Tolkien's story to contemporary events:

> For today's film fans, this older racial anxiety fuses with a current fear and hatred of Islam that supports a crusading war in the Middle East. The mass appeal of the *Lord of the Rings* [books], and the recent movies, may well rest on racist codes.[24]

However, unlike Mortensen and Durbin, Shapiro has not looked further in Tolkien's writings to find the author's appalled objection to exactly this kind of topical application.

David Tjeder correctly grounded his more sophisticated arguments against Tolkien in *Aftonbladet* in the social constructions of the last four centuries, noting that "Rasismen är inte en underström i den europeiske idéhistorien, utan befinner sig i dess mittfåra" (Racism is not an undercurrent in European intellectual history but runs right through the mainstream).[25] Tjeder and I probably agree here that one of the most problematic ideas in racist thinking (if you will) is the spurious equation of language with ethnicity. Associated with it is the assumption that speakers of languages designated as "superior" are thereby ethnically superior. Tjeder has situated the beginning of this tradition in western Europe in the eighteenth century—presumably with Johann Gottfried Herder and the idea of *Volksgeist*, although he did not name him[26]—followed by an upswing of interest in the late nineteenth century and the worst consequences occurring in the twentieth.

What Tjeder did not see is that Tolkien—and not only in the vignettes I have examined here—made a concerted effort to alter this paradigm as it is usually understood—actually back to something like Herder's original model, which has been pruned and caricatured by subsequent generations, some of them with pernicious agendas.

In our case studies of Vidumavi and Éowyn and, indeed, in many other places—for example, in the stories of the human Elf-friends of the First Age—Tolkien has actually made the argument that those (of any genetic makeup) who choose to affiliate with the speakers of a "superior" language are *de facto* raised by this choice, while also simultaneously improving and revitalizing their patrons, who are situated within the supposedly superior culture. Ethnicity is not really the issue with Tolkien, in the long run; as always, language is: and language is shareable. Éowyn may well bring literacy to the Mark; Vidumavi of Rhovanion learned to pass as "a fair and noble lady" (*LR* Appendix A.1.iv, 1022) at the haughty court of Gondor, certainly learning to speak Sindarin while she was there.

Herder saw the acquisition of language and culture across boundaries as a vital component in human development, although subsequent generations have unfortunately passed over this second half of his thinking. Not only were language and culture able to be passed down in kinship groups, alongside with one's DNA inheritance; they were also *acquirable*, through encounters with the Other:

[M]ithin wird die Erziehung unsres Geschlechts in zweifachem Sinn genetisch und organisch; genetisch durch die Mittheilung, organisch durch die Aufnahme und Anwendung des Mitgetheilten. Wollen wir diese zweite Genesis des Menschen, die sein ganzes Leben durchgeht, von der Bearbeitung des Ackers *Cultur*, oder vom Bilde des Lichts *Aufklärung* nennen: so stehet uns der Name frei; die Kette der Cultur und Aufklärung reicht aber sodann bis an's Ende der Erde.

[The education of our species is in a double sense genetic and organic: genetic, inasmuch as it is communicated; organic, as what it communicates is received and applied. Whether we name this second genesis of man [*sic*] *cultivation* from the culture of the ground, or *enlightening* from the action of light, is of little import; the chain of light and cultivation reaches to the end of the earth.][27]

J.R.R. Tolkien is not likely to have known this passage, but he would not have taken exception to it. It does not celebrate racism; rather it celebrates a delight in the cultural exchange made possible by the kinds of mixed unions and alliances he celebrated in his narratives (*LR* Appendix A.1.i, 1009–13).[28]

Notes

1. Publius Cornelius Tacitus, *Tacitus on Britain and Germany*, trans. H. Mattingly (Harmondsworth, Eng.: Penguin, 1960), 103–4.
2. R.C. Blockley, "Roman-Barbarian Marriages in the Late Empire," *Florilegium* 4 (1982): 63–77.
3. Tacitus, *Tacitus on Britain and Germany*, 102.
4. Walter Goffart, *The Narrators of Barbarian History (A.D. 55-800): Jordanes, Gregory of Tours, Bede, and Paul the Deacon* (Princeton: Princeton University Press, 1988), passim.
5. This neat distinction is, however, patently missing in Peter Jackson's cinematic Middle-earth (*The Fellowship of the Ring*, *The Two Towers*, and *The Return of the King*), for whatever it is worth.
6. Anthony Lane, "The Hobbit Habit: Reading *The Lord of the Rings*," *New Yorker*, 10 December 2001, 98–105.
7. T.A. Shippey engagingly describes the enthusiasm for the Gothic language (which was a relatively new rediscovery) among the philologists of Tolkien's generation, in *The Road to Middle-earth* (Boston: Houghton Mifflin, 1983), 8, 11–14, and passim.
8. Cassiodorus, letter on Amalasuntha, http://freespace.virgin.net/angus.graham/Cass-V10.htm; Jordanes, *Getica*, 14, http://www.thelatinlibrary.com/iordanes.html#XIV.

9. Jordanes, *Getica*, 14 and 60. http://www.thelatinlibrary.com/iordanes.html#XIV and http://www.thelatinlibrary.com/iordanes.html#LX.

10. Goffart, 39–40, 69.

11. Blockley, 66–68.

12. "I much prefer history, true or feigned, with its varied applicability to the thought and experience of readers. I think that many confuse 'applicability' with 'allegory'; but the one resides in the freedom of the reader, and the other in the purposed domination of the author." (*LR* Foreword, 11)

13. Shippey, *Road to Middle-Earth*, 50–54.

14. Specifically: "Power corrupts," which is an idea alien to the ancient or medieval world; and "Chemical addiction is to be avoided at all costs." Shippey, *Road to Middle-Earth*, 104–6.

15. David Ansen, "A 'Ring' to Rule the Screen," *Newsweek*, 10 December 2001.

16. Viggo Mortensen, interview by Charlie Rose, *Charlie Rose Show*, Public Broadcasting System, 3 December 2002.

17. Viggo Mortensen to Ian Spelling, "For Viggo Mortensen, The War of the Rings Gets Serious," *Inside Sci-Fi and Fantasy*, online column for the New York Times Syndicate online, 15 December 2002.

18. David Tjeder, "Tolkiens farliga tankar,"*Aftonbladet*, Kultur section, 20 December 2001 and 11 January 2002. Archived on the Web at http://www.aftonbladet.se.

19. David Tjeder, "En dåres försvarstal," *Aftonbladet*, 11 January 2002.

20. *Aftonbladet*, 20 December 2001.

21. James Reynolds and Fiona Stewart, "Lord of the Rings Labelled Racist," *Scotsman*, 14 December 2002.

22. It should perhaps be noted that Peter Jackson's cinematic Uruk-hai, particularly their captain (played by muscular Maori actor Lawrence Makoare) in the *Fellowship* film, are definitely depicted as slant-eyed; this has not deterred legions of female fans on the Internet from finding him, and them, irresistible. (On the other hand, David Tjeder worries that the flowing Uruk-hai coiffures are meant as a slur against dreadlocked Rastafarians.)

23. Karen Durbin, "Propaganda and 'Lord of the Rings,'" *New York Times*, 15 December 2002.

24. Reynolds and Stewart.

25. Tjeder, "En dåres försvarstal."

26. Johann Gottfried von Herder, *Ideen zur Philosophie der Geschichte der Menschheit* (Leipzig: Johann Friedrich Hartknoch, 1821).

27. Herder, 1:340; quoted in English in Robert J.C. Young, *Colonial Desire: Hybridity in Theory, Culture, and Race* (London and New York: Routledge, 1995), 41.

28. All the above observations apply equally to the "three unions of the Eldar and the Edain," of course. (*LR* Appendix F.2, 1107–12.)

Chapter 7

FROM CATASTROPHE
TO EUCATASTROPHE

J.R.R. Tolkien's Transformation
of Ovid's Mythic Pyramus and Thisbe
into Beren and Lúthien

JEN STEVENS

Tolkien's story of Beren and Lúthien is among his most celebrated. Most readers first encounter it in *The Fellowship of the Ring*, when Aragorn recites part of it to the Hobbits when Samwise begs for a tale "about Elves" since "the dark seems to press round so close" at Weathertop (*LR* 1.11, 187).

Aragorn complies, noting that "it is a fair tale, though it is sad, as are all the tales of Middle-earth, and yet it may lift your hearts."[1] Indeed, this sad but fair tale of an ancient love and courage that surmounts impossible odds serves as an inspiration to the characters of the *Lord of the Rings* and informs their stories. For instance, Samwise wonders if folk will come to hear "the story of Nine-fingered Frodo and the Ring of Doom" just as he and Frodo had listened to "the tale of Beren One-hand and the Great Jewel" at Rivendell (*LR* 6.4, 929). Beren and Lúthien's tale is a tale that Samwise uses to situate his and Frodo's, since it is a hopelessly impossible quest that, like theirs, succeeds at the brink of failure. In turn, Arwen and Aragorn's romance echoes Lúthien and Beren's.[2] And also in turn, Beren and Lúthien's story is strikingly similar to another great love story, the story of Pyramus and Thisbe, as told in the classical Roman poet Ovid's *Metamorphoses*.

Beren and Lúthien's story was among the first that Tolkien wrote and rewrote for his mythology. There are multiple extant versions in a variety of styles and forms. Verlyn Flieger's description of Tolkien's mythos as "its own complex manuscript tradition of multiple and over-lapping story variants" seems particularly apt for the tales of Beren and Lúthien.[3] Disentangling these variants is difficult, even with aid of the textual labors of Christopher Tolkien. J.R.R. Tolkien wrote the first version in 1917 as "The Tale of Tinúviel"; he later wrote another draft over the original penciled draft.[4] Tolkien rewrote that draft as "The Lay of Leithian" between 1925 and 1931 and then, yet again, as "The Lay of Leithian Recommenced" during the 1950s, after he had completed *The Lord of the Rings*.[5] Tolkien finished neither of the lays, but he did draw up synopses for unwritten parts of the first lay.[6] The prose version in *The Silmarillion* was itself based on both a prose "Sketch of the Mythology" that Tolkien wrote in 1926 and those unfinished lays.[7] The greatest changes occurred between "The Tale of Tinúviel" and "The Lay of Leithian." In the former, Beren and Lúthien still fall in love and set out to get the Silmaril at the demand of her father, but instead of being captured by Sauron and imprisoned in his dungeon, Beren becomes a servant in the halls of Tevildo, Prince of Cats. Beren is an Elf, and Elves are called "gnomes."[8] The sons of Fëanor make no appearance, and neither does their awful Oath. But Huan the Hound does, and he can speak more than three times.

Tolkien's story of Beren and Lúthien, with its blood feuds, oaths taken, magic items, and helper animals, has often been compared to Germanic and Scandinavian epics such as the *Kalevala*, the Finnish national epic that Tolkien first read in translation as a schoolboy.[9] Others, such as Flieger, have compared it to the Arthurian stories of Guinevere and Lancelot and of Tristan and Isolde. Unlike those love affairs, Beren and Lúthien's is "neither forbidden nor illicit."[10] However, those traditions are not the only ingredients in Tolkien's mythological stew. Tolkien also drew upon classical literature and mythology, the backdrop for much of western European literature. Such connections have been noted by several critics. For instance, David Greenman argues that Tolkien used Aeneidic and Odyssean narrative patterns of escape and return in "The Fall of Gondolin" and *The Return of the King*.[11] In turn, Mac Fenwick compares female heroines and monsters from Homeric epics to those in *The Silmarillion*.[12]

However, this "classical" mode of reading has received relatively little attention. There has been far more work done on Tolkien's use of other traditions, especially the before-mentioned Germanic and Scandinavian. Many critics have made the observation that Tolkien seems to have been far more interested in Northern mythology than in classical. For instance, Flieger argues against using classical myth as a mythological model for Tolkien's works "on the grounds that Tolkien had no particular affinity for what he called 'Southern' myth."[13] Flieger instead argues that one should look to Arthurian legends as a model.[14]

More broadly, one may claim, as Michael D.C. Drout and Hilary Wynne do, that arguing that Tolkien used a given story or tradition can be fraught with the peril of careless generalities:

> There is an important epistemic difference between analogy (a similarity that has arisen independently in two different places) and a homology (a similarity that arises due to a shared lineage). Sorting out analogies from homologies can be very difficult work, and too many critics have not followed Shippey's lead, using mere resemblances (and often faint resemblances) to make claims about putative sources.[15]

Drout and Wynne argue that many Tolkien source studies are flawed because their authors argued derivation on the basis of mere likeness. Drout and Wynne also note that, even when one "knows" that Tolkien used a given myth or story to derive his own, that fact still may not tell one very much because "all texts must be interpreted. Finding a source merely defers the problem of interpretation; it cannot eliminate it."[16] In other words, the more interesting question may be, "So what?" So what if Tolkien used the Rapunzel story to derive his story of Lúthien escaping from Thingol's tower down a rope made of her hair?[17] What does it tell us about Lúthien? Or for that matter, what might it tell us about Rapunzel?

Comparing Tolkien's works to classical mythology can illuminate ways in which Tolkien, even if he did prefer Northern myth, was writing within a larger western European, classically derived tradition. Such a comparison also illustrates the ways in which Tolkien's works were different in both substance and spirit from classical mythology and literature. Regardless of whether a given classical story was the "basis" for one of Tolkien's (or whether they both shared a common past source), the similarities and differences between the two stories can tell us much about Tolkien's own mythology.

Tolkien's mythology as a whole may be best seen in *The Silmarillion*. Since Tolkien was unable to complete a "definitive" version of his mythology, *The Silmarillion*, posthumously edited by Christopher Tolkien, is the closest that we have to one. There are a number of similarities between Tolkien's *Silmarillion* and the Roman poet Ovid's *Metamorphoses*. Both works are interwoven collections of stories. Both also depict a historical progression within those stories, starting from the creation of the universe and progressing onward to a relatively modern period (the founding of Rome and the Third Age, respectively). Ovid's tales were derived from a number of sources, including Latin folklore and Homeric epic, while Tolkien's are versions of stories that he had been working and reworking for most of his life.

One particularly striking point of comparison between the two works is Ovid's story of Pyramus and Thisbe and Tolkien's Beren and Lúthien. Although Ovid's tale is a relatively short story within his larger work, it is a key text for western European literature. Essentially, it is the tale of two lovers. Forbidden to marry by their parents, they exchange whispers through a chink in the wall between their families' properties. Finally, they decide to meet secretly outside of the city and run away together. Thisbe shows up first but flees from a lioness. The lioness, which has just been hunting, tears at Thisbe's discarded veil with her bloody mouth. When Pyramus arrives later, he finds the bloody veil. Believing Thisbe to be dead, he kills himself. Some of his blood spurts onto a nearby mulberry tree. It is not necessarily obvious to the reader that the berries were stained with Pyramus's blood. Thisbe comes back and finds Pyramus dying. She then begs that their story be remembered and kills herself. Their deaths result in the berries of the mulberry tree being permanently stained red—hence the metamorphosis.

Ovid apparently based this story on a Near Eastern tale, but his source no longer exists, except perhaps in fragments.[18] Ovid's version has been interpreted and retold throughout the history of Western literature. As Robert Glendinning notes, this story was used as a theme for poetry exercises by students in medieval classrooms, "occup[ying] a privileged place in the curriculum of a number of important schools in France, Germany, and probably England in the decades before and after 1200."[19] Students would rewrite the story along the lines of a given interpretation or would choose to emphasize particular elements from it. Many medieval poets saw the poem as an allegory. In a collection of medieval legends, the *Gesta Romanorum*, Pyramus becomes a representative of Christ who dies for the sake of Thisbe, the human soul, who then chooses to follow him through good works and denial of the body, as apparently symbolized by her suicide.[20] In contrast, Gottfried von Strasburg's thirteenth-century *Tristan and Isolde* celebrates the union of the two lovers' souls and fates.[21] A couple of centuries later, William Shakespeare emphasized the more ridiculous elements in the version performed by the mechanicals of *A Midsummer Night's Dream* and the tragic in *Romeo and Juliet*. Other more modern adaptations include Susan Sontag's "The Very Comical Lament of Pyramus and Thisbe," an allegory of the unification of East and West Germany.

Many literary critics have noted a tension between the absurd and tragic elements of the tale. As Werner Brönnimann puts it, Pyramus's "sacrifice was either utterly tragic or utterly stupid" since he misreads the sign of Thisbe's bloodied veil in a "grotesque" fashion.[22] The moment in which the dying Pyramus sees Thisbe and realizes his error has its own grotesque irony. One reason for the many retellings of this tale throughout Western literature may be its very ambiguity, as critics and writers seek interpretive closure.

This thwarted lovers' tale would have been well known by Tolkien, especially given his classical education.[23] It is quite possible that he read it into his own life—like Pyramus and Thisbe, he and his wife Edith fell in love while adolescents. After Father Francis, Tolkien's guardian, found out about the romance, he forbade Tolkien from pursuing the relationship until he turned twenty-one and attained adulthood because Francis feared that it would distract Tolkien from working for an Oxford scholarship (*Biography*, 40–42). Like Pyramus and Thisbe, Tolkien and Edith wanted to be together, and it wouldn't have been surprising for Tolkien to have rewritten the story behind Pyramus and Thisbe, only with a happier ending. Tolkien and Edith did ultimately marry—perhaps because of, rather than in spite of, Father Francis's prohibition, which very well might have, as Humphrey Carpenter argues, "transform[ed] a boy-and-girl love-affair into a thwarted romance" (*Biography*, 27). In fact, Tolkien based "Beren and Lúthien" at least partly on his own love story, with Lúthien playing the young Edith's role. Tolkien had the names "Beren" and "Lúthien" inscribed on his and his wife's gravestones and, in a letter to Christopher Tolkien about Edith's tombstone, Tolkien writes that "she was (and knew she was) my Lúthien . . . she was the source of the story" (*Letters*, 420).

Tolkien's own version of this story celebrates the sublime rather than the tragicomic elements. His story is set in a high and serious world of oaths and heroic deeds. Instead of focusing on the union of the two lovers' souls, as did *Tristan and Isolde*, Tolkien's version celebrates their union as mortal lovers, both in that they actually get another life on Middle-earth together and in that they created a bridge between Men and the Elder race. We can take it one step further and regard Tolkien's version as an embodiment of his concept of "eucatastrophe," or "joyous 'turn'" ("OFS," 81).

For Tolkien, this joyous turn was the key element of fairy-stories, setting them opposite tragedies with their attendant catastrophes. It is, he explains, "a sudden and miraculous grace: never to be counted on to return" ("OFS," 81). There are several examples of eucatastrophes in Tolkien's works, perhaps the chief being Gollum's fall into the cracks of Mount Doom with the One Ring. Like Frodo and Sam, Lúthien and Beren succeed in their impossible quest. Their story is almost a sublimation of the Pyramus and Thisbe plot. The differences between Tolkien's and Ovid's tales illustrate Tolkien's enactment of this eucatastrophe.[24]

These differences are most immediate in the general plot structure. In both cases, a young man and maiden fall in love with each other, against the wishes of at least one parent. Ovid tells us that for Pyramus and Thisbe "both their hearts were caught in love's snare, and both burned with equal passion."[25] In turn, Lúthien falls in love with Beren—"doom fell upon her, and she loved him" while he has a "fate . . . laid upon him" (*Silm*, 165).

In both cases, the male and female lovers are equally caught in a "snare" or "doom" that binds them. However, unlike Pyramus, Beren has no parents. He is an orphan, and it is only Lúthien's father who is against the match (her mother, Melian, seems to be ambivalent at worst). Both pairs of lovers are kept apart from each other: in Ovid's story the parental prohibition and a wall that separates while simultaneously allowing communication create barriers. In Tolkien's story they are divided, first, by Thingol's insistence that Beren complete a quest and, then, by Thingol's imprisonment of Lúthien in a tree house. However, unlike Pyramus, Beren at least has the possibility of marrying Lúthien, however unlikely. Both pairs of lovers strive to be together. Pyramus and Thisbe arrange to meet outside the wall at night; in turn, Beren embarks on his quest in order to gain Lúthien's hand, and Lúthien flees from Doriath in order to rescue Beren from Sauron's dungeon of Tol-in-Gaurhoth. She then aids him in his quest despite the efforts of both Thingol and Beren himself to prevent her from doing so. While Pyramus and Thisbe only succeed in a kind of posthumous metaphorical union, Beren and Lúthien do ultimately succeed in completing Thingol's impossible quest. Ultimately, both sets of lovers die. Both Pyramus and Beren are the first to die—Pyramus kills himself because he wrongly believes that Thisbe is dead, and Beren is slain by Carcharoth the Wolf. After Pyramus and Beren die, so do their loves—Thisbe kills herself, while Lúthien's spirit "fell down into darkness, and at the last it fled, and her body lay like a flower that is suddenly cut off and lies for a while unwithered in the grass" (*Silm*, 186). While Thisbe pleads that she and Pyramus be buried in a common grave, Lúthien appeals to Mandos to allow their spirits to be together. Both of these requests are successful, but Lúthien's results in a union of spirit rather than in mere mortal ashes. Thisbe also begs the mulberry tree to always bear red berries in memory of their death, an immortality that is also carried through by their story, just as Beren and Lúthien's is carried through the many stories and songs. However, Beren and Lúthien also gain a certain immortality through their descendants that stems from their second life on Middle-earth. Beren and Lúthien's seizing of the Silmaril also ultimately results in Eärendil's voyage to appeal to the Valar to aid the inhabitants of Middle-earth against Morgoth (he uses the Silmaril as light to guide him).

Throughout the plot, these differences are enacted partly through the differing degrees of agency of Thisbe and Lúthien in their respective love affairs. Unlike the majority of Ovid's heroines, Thisbe goes out to meet Pyramus instead of unwillingly being chased by him. Not only is she the object of his love, but she also loves him—his "snare" is her snare.[26] In turn, Lúthien actively goes out to meet Beren. Unlike Thisbe, who was "bold" enough to go out to meet her lover but ran and hid from the lioness,[27] Lúthien successfully faces multiple perils to help and to be united with Beren. For instance, she sets out alone to rescue Beren from Sauron's dungeon and is ultimately successful. Lúthien's agency is also represented by her voice, as when she entrances Morgoth with song or sings her plea to Mandos. In essence, Lúthien's very voice is itself emblematic of her larger scope of agency.[28] Thisbe's voice is also important, but less effective than Lúthien's. She and Pyramus communicate through the chink in the wall with their voices. Thisbe also uses her voice to make her requests of the mulberry tree and their parents. Her pleas touch the gods, and apparently the parents, for both appeals are granted. Although both sets of entreaties are successful, Lúthien's surpasses Thisbe's: both pairs of lovers are immortalized through story, but only Beren and Lúthien are granted another life together—on Middle-earth.

Tolkien also uses the fairy tale of Rapunzel to highlight Lúthien's greater scope of action.[29] Unlike Rapunzel, who passively lets her hair grow and then allows the witch and prince to climb up it into her tower, Lúthien, held prisoner in a tree house by Thingol, uses her magic to grow her hair out. She then cuts it off and climbs down it herself. Whereas Rapunzel is acted upon from without, Lúthien frees herself. Lúthien also actively uses illusion to disguise herself, Huan, and Beren from Sauron and Morgoth. In effect, she uses those illusions and her cloak of blindness to cause Sauron and Morgoth to misread her—she obscures the text. In turn, Thisbe obscures the text by dropping her veil during her flight to the cave. That veil is then stained by the lioness, which results in Pyramus's misreading its text. But while Thisbe's inadvertent textual obscuring results in her own death and the death of Pyramus, Lúthien's results in the success of the quest to gain the Silmaril.

The question of agency is further heightened by the very different roles of "fate" in both stories. Whereas fate, in much of Ovid's stories and in Greek and Roman mythology as a whole, often appears to be something that is beyond humans and inescapable (consider Oedipus), fate appears far less predetermined in Tolkien's universe. Pyramus and Thisbe are trapped by an unlucky turn of events. There is nothing overtly obvious to tell us why the lioness comes when she does with blood on her mouth or why the lovers apparently picked the wrong night to meet. We are not even given overt clues to suggest that they deserved their fate for disobeying their parents' wishes; in fact, their parents apparently later celebrate that love. Rather, they were in the wrong place at the wrong time and "caught in love's snare."[30]

In contrast, Beren and Lúthien are ensnared in a fate that was woven by many. Beren himself is enmeshed in a series of oaths and loyalties. He is given aid by King Finrod Felagund because of an oath that Finrod had made to Beren's father Barahir. This aid in turn forces Finrod to leave his kingdom because of the wrath of the sons of Fëanor, who are bound up in the Oath of Fëanor to regain the Silmarils that results in the Doom of Mandos upon them. The Doom also ensnares Thingol when he gives Beren the quest of bringing back a Silmaril from Morgoth. Thus, although Beren and Lúthien are, to some extent, trapped by circumstances beyond their control, these circumstances were created by choices that were made by the inhabitants of Middle-earth rather than some doom apparently randomly or otherwise distantly handed down by omniscient gods.

And even these circumstances, or fates, are not certain. As Huan advises Beren, "[T]he fate that lies before you [is] hopeless, yet not certain" (*Silm*, 179). Indeed, Beren and Lúthien do succeed in their seemingly impossible task, although not without the collapse of at least one kingdom, the death of King Finrod Felagund and his ten faithful companions, the loss of Beren's hand, the death of Beren, and ultimately, the Elves' loss of Lúthien.

There are several moments in the Beren and Lúthien story in which this uncertain fate is exposed. As opposed to the relentless chain of events in "Pyramus and Thisbe," these are moments in which more than one outcome can be achieved. One comes during Lúthien's quest to rescue Beren from the dungeons of Tol-in-Gaurhoth. She is captured by the hound Huan and becomes the prisoner of Celegorm and Curufin. At this point the story could have easily ended with Lúthien forcibly married to Celegorm and Beren dying in the dungeons. However, Huan grieves at her captivity and helps her escape from the sons and then rescue Beren from the dungeons (*Silm*, 41). Not only does Huan's act result in rectifying the immediate problem of Lúthien's captivity, but it also leads into the larger overthrow of Sauron's fortress and Beren's freedom, which in turn allows the quest to continue.

Another such moment comes when Beren tries to leave Lúthien in Doriath—after his recovery from the dungeons—because he doesn't want her to face further danger. Huan the Hound convinces him to let her come on the grounds that she is already subjected to Beren's doom because of her love: "[F]rom the shadow of death you can no longer save Lúthien, for by her love she is now subject to it" (*Silm*, 173).

Beren had wanted to protect Lúthien by making her choice for her, but he yields and lets her come. Had he not, then he probably would have died at Morgoth's hand, and the quest would have failed. Similarly, Thingol chooses to yield after Beren and Lúthien return to Doriath minus the Silmaril and Beren's hand. After Beren shows him his empty wrist, "Thingol's mood was softened," and he listens to their story and finally "yielded his will" to their "doom" (*Silm*, 184–85).

Up until then, Thingol had been resolute and hardened against Beren because Beren was human, despite Melian's counsel. Thingol's yielding brings reconciliation with his daughter and, ultimately, closer ties between Elves and Men. By giving up the oath that Beren had sworn to him, Thingol steps outside of the system of oaths and obligations that runs throughout the story. Giving up the oath is an act of grace—something freely given.

Grace also comes after the death of Beren when Lúthien chooses to die as well so that she might petition Mandos to let her and Beren be joined. Her song "of the sorrow of the Eldar and the grief of Men" moves Mandos to pity, "who never before was so moved, nor has been since" (*Silm*, 181). He allows them to meet in his Halls and then petitions Manwë to allow them to be together afterward as well. Ultimately, Lúthien is given the choice to be a mortal with Beren, and they are given another life together on Middle-earth. This "joyous turn" not only unites their kindred through their children, but it also accomplishes her release from deathlessness; in fact, the story is also known as "Release from Bondage" among the Elves (*Silm*, 162). The significance of this title may be seen in Tolkien's essay "On Fairy-Stories"—wherein, Tolkien argues that while Men might dream of "Release from Death," so too might Elves dream of release from deathlessness ("OFS," 81). Lúthien's story is almost a "happy ever after" story for Elves. Moreover, the story of Beren and Lúthien's impossible quest offers hope to the free peoples of Middle-earth who come after them.

Ovid's Pyramus and Thisbe also have a certain amount of choice in their story. The lovers do choose to meet outside of the wall and do choose to kill themselves. But in each of the places where they might make a better choice, they do not. Pyramus does not look for the wounded or dead Thisbe after finding the bloodied veil, but almost immediately assumes that she is dead and thrusts his sword into his side, declaring "'Tis I who am to blame: poor girl, it was I who killed you! I told you to come by a night, to a place that was full of danger."[31] Pyramus's statement stands in sharp contrast to the narrator's previous note that earlier "they determined that, at dead of night, they would try to slip past the watchman and steal out of doors."[32] They, the two lovers, had decided on the plan, not Pyramus alone. Unlike Beren, Pyramus denies choice to his lover: rather than acknowledge her as a free agent who chose to meet outside the wall, he makes her a passive follower who is not responsible for her own actions and presumed death. Thisbe, too, when she finds Pyramus's body, does not even stop to consider alternate plans of action but almost immediately starts her appeal to the mulberry tree and to their parents before killing herself. The tragedy (or pathos) of Pyramus and Thisbe may be as much about their lack of conscious choices as it is about Pyramus's misreading.

Tolkien's version of the Pyramus and Thisbe plot did not come about instantly. Rather, the elements were developed slowly over the decades that he wrote and rewrote this story. Beren was originally an Elf in "The Tale of Tinúviel" (*BLT2*, 11). By making him a human, Tolkien gave further reason for the barriers against Beren and Lúthien's union. He also heightened the union between peoples that resulted when Beren and Lúthien did marry. Beren's humanity leads to Lúthien's choice to take his mortal fate as well as the half-Elven descendants that result from their union. Another major addition was Celegorm and Curufin, two of the sons of Fëanor. By incorporating them into the story, Tolkien weaves in more of the Northern world of high oaths and allegiances. He also complicates the role of fate by making it something that was created at least in part by these oaths and allegiances rather than merely by the whim of the gods. The sons of Fëanor and their Oath also bring a graver, more tragic element into the tale. Perhaps they may be Tolkien's version of Ovid's irony, for despite the fact that the sons show the virtues of loyalty to their father by upholding the Oath of Fëanor, that loyalty is destructive. Rather than help Beren regain the jewel, they are angered because they want the jewel themselves. While the Oath might appear to be something that should result in regaining the Silmaril from Morgoth, it only impedes Beren and Lúthien's quest. And in general, the elements that Tolkien introduces in subsequent versions of his tale, especially between "The Tale of Tinúviel" and "The Lay of Leithian," deepen the sense of tragedy and gravity. Beren becomes a prisoner in Sauron's dungeon rather than merely Tevildo's servant, assigned to the kitchens because the cats judge him to be an inept hunter. Tevildo, Prince of Cats, himself was a relatively comic character in comparison to Sauron. Not surprisingly, he cannot bear dogs and enjoys naps.

Thus, Tolkien rewrites the story underlying the Ovidian text to produce a happier ending for his hero and heroine, one that is a eucatastrophe instead of a catastrophe. Rather than using pathetic comedy, as did Ovid, he focuses on the theme of united love in and after death. His plot is longer and far more complicated, making it more permeable to conscious choice on the part of the characters—and this plot is linked to a quest that gives the characters something greater to work for than their own togetherness. Their completion of this impossible quest lifts them into a certain immortality in Middle-earth, offering a glimpse of hope to its inhabitants that Morgoth's, and later Sauron's, plot to conquer Middle-earth could be defeated. In fact, one can consider Morgoth's and Sauron's attempts to conquer Middle-earth as closed narratives. Under their respective rules, there would have been no more choices for the inhabitants of Middle-earth to make, and very little, if anything, would have likely ever happened or changed. Middle-earth would have effectively been in stasis. In the same way, the Pyramus and Thisbe plot and the "impossible quest" plot given to Beren and Lúthien could both be considered closed narratives. However, unlike Pyramus and Thisbe, Beren and Lúthien escape the tragic plot that they could have so easily been trapped by. Beren and Lúthien's escape from their own closed narrative suggests that the rest of Middle-earth can also escape.

Notes

1. Aragorn's recitation appears to be based on the version of the story that is in "The Lay of Leithian." According to Christopher Tolkien's notes, J.R.R. Tolkien didn't start "The Lay of Leithian Recommenced" until after completing the *Lord of the Rings* (Christopher Tolkien, ed., *The Lays of Beleriand,* vol. 3 of *The History of Middle-earth* [London: George Allen and Unwin, 1985], 330).

2. Peter Jackson, who directed the recent films *The Fellowship of the Ring* and *The Two Towers*, endows his Arwen with many of Lúthien's characteristics. Like Lúthien, Jackson's Arwen can weave powerful spells, defies her father (or at least tries to), and rescues people, namely Frodo. By doing so, Jackson effectively collapses the two characters into one (*The Fellowship of the Ring*, dir. Peter Jackson, 179 min., New Line Cinema, 2001) (*The Two Towers*, dir. Peter Jackson, 178 min., New Line Cinema, 2002).

3. Verlyn Flieger, "J.R.R. Tolkien and the Matter of Britain," *Mythlore* 87 (summer/fall 2000), 55.

4. "The Tale of Tinúviel" is included in *Lays of Beleriand.*

5. Tolkien, *Lays of Beleriand*, 150, 330.

6. An example is the outline of Synopsis 2, which includes material that eventually became part of canto 10 of "The Lay of Leithian." A comparison of the outline of Synopsis 2 to canto 10 reveals many striking early changes that Tolkien made in the story, including the addition of Celegorm and Curufin's attack on Beren and Lúthien (Tolkien, *Lays of Beleriand*, 270).

7. Tolkien, *Lays of Beleriand*, 153.

8. Beren was also an Elf in the initial A-text of "The Lay of Leithian" (*Shaping*, 54).

9. Iwan Rhys Morus, "The Tale of Beren and Lúthien," *Mallorn* 20 (September 1983): 21.

10. Flieger, "J.R.R. Tolkien and the Matter of Britain," 53.

11. David Greenman, "Aeneidic and Odyssean Patterns of Escape and Return in Tolkien's 'The Fall of Gondolin' and *The Return of the King*," *Mythlore* no. 68 (spring 1992), 4.

12. Mac Fenwick, "Breastplates of Silk: Homeric Women in *The Lord of the Rings*," *Mythlore* no. 81 (summer 1996): 17–23, 50 (online version, 24 December 2002), www.trentu.ca/~mfenwick/mythlorepaper.htm.

13. Flieger, "J.R.R. Tolkien and the Matter of Britain," 49, 87.

14. Flieger's argument that Beren and Lúthien are themselves a purging of the "gross" from the tales of illicit romance between Lancelot and Guinevere and between Tristan and Isolde is particularly interesting, especially since the story of Tristan and Isolde itself has some ties to that of Pyramus and Thisbe (Flieger, "J.R.R. Tolkien and the Matter of Britain," 53). See Robert Glendinning, "Pyramus and Thisbe in the Medieval Classroom," *Speculum* 61 (June 1986): 75.

15. Michael D.C. Drout and Hilary Wynne, "Tom Shippey's *J.R.R. Tolkien: Author of the Century* and a Look Back at Tolkien Criticism since 1982," *Envoi* 9 (fall 2000): 106.

16. Drout and Wynne, 107.

17. T.A. Shippey notes the connection to the Grimms' Rapunzel in his *Road to Middle-earth* (Boston: Houghton Mifflin, 1983), 193.

18. William S. Anderson, ed., *Ovid's Metamorphoses: Books 1–5* (Norman, Okla.: University of Oklahoma Press, 1997), 418. See Peter E. Knox, "Pyramus and Thisbe in Cyprus," *Harvard Studies in Classical Philology* 92 (1989): 316.

19. Glendinning, 71.

20. Werner Brönnimann, "Susan Sontag's *Pyramus and Thisbe*," *Sh:in:E— Shakespeare in Europe* (University of Basel, Switzerland), 24 December 2002, http://www.unibas.ch/shine/wbroe.htm.

21. Glendinning, 75.

22. Brönnimann.

23. Fenwick, 17–23, 50.

24. I am basing this analysis on the version of "Beren and Lúthien" in *The Silmarillion*, Tolkien's "latest" version of the tale. However, I will refer to earlier versions when appropriate.

25. Ovid, *Metamorphoses*, trans. Mary M. Innes (Baltimore, Md.: Penguin, 1968), 95. All references to Ovid come from this text.

26. Ibid.

27. Ovid, 96.

28. The importance of Lúthien's voice increases between the successive versions of the story. In the initial "Tale of Tinúviel," Lúthien calls for Beren at the palace of Tevildo, Prince of Cats, when she comes to rescue him. In the much later *Silmarillion* version, she actually uses the power of her voice to weave a spell that entrances Sauron.

29. Shippey, *Road to Middle-earth*, 193.

30. Ovid, 95.

31. Ovid, 97.

32. Ovid, 96.

Chapter 8

PROVIDENCE, FATE, AND CHANCE

Boethian Philosophy in
The Lord of the Rings

KATHLEEN E. DUBS

All serious students of J.R.R. Tolkien's fictional writings recognize his scholarly background as a medievalist, and as a result have spent much time analyzing "medieval influences" on elements within his works.[1] What is curious, however, is that no critic (medievalist or modernist) has discussed the "medieval influences" on the larger concepts of providence, fate, chance, or free will—although critics have recognized the significance of these themes.[2] No one has suggested the possible value for Tolkien study of Boethius's *Consolation of Philosophy*, acknowledged by one translator as "one of the most popular and influential books in Western Europe from the time it was written, in 524, until the end of the Renaissance."[3] Surely a medievalist as learned as J.R.R. Tolkien would have known the *Consolation*, if for no other reason than through his study of King Alfred, who translated it into Anglo-Saxon. The attraction for King Alfred was the same as for other thinkers of the Middle Ages—even of our own day: the problematic relationships between providence, fate, chance, and free will. Spacks, Helms, and others have noted these concepts in Tolkien's works, and they agree that the relationships among them are complex, perhaps even contradictory: Spacks discussing free will; Helms, providential control. But such oppositions are only apparent, and if we turn to Boethius's *Consolation of Philosophy*, we will see why.

I suggest Boethius's work not simply because it had to be known to Tolkien. I offer it first because, as students of Tolkien readily admit, he deliberately eschewed any reference to Christianity in his works, unlike C.S. Lewis, for example, who insisted on Christian doctrine as a basis for his imaginative writings. Thus Tolkien would have found Boethius not only more general (less catholic, perhaps), but also more clear-cut with regard to the issues at hand. Christian doctrine is anything but distinct in such matters as predestination and free will. Second, and perhaps more important, Boethius does not depend on the Christian historical perspective. Unlike, for example, Augustine, who depends on the Christian view of history as linked to scripture, Boethius presents the philosophical issues quite apart from any link to Christian history (the Creation, the Fall, the Passion, and so on). For Tolkien, who was creating his own mythos, his own history, such an independent presentation was essential. An examination of Boethian definitions for the concepts at issue, then, can help elucidate episodes in *The Fellowship of the Ring*, the foundation of the trilogy, and direct us toward a clearer vision of Tolkien's providential cosmos.

In Book 4 of the *Consolation of Philosophy* Boethius entreats Lady Philosophy to explain to him the "apparent injustice" of an all-powerful and benevolent God rewarding the wicked, often at the expense of the good. She responds sympathetically to his confusion:

> This problem is such that when one doubt is cleared up many more arise like the heads of the Hydra, and continue to spring up unless they are checked by the most active fire of the mind. Among the many questions raised by this problem are these: the simplicity of Providence, the course of Fate, unforeseeable chance, divine knowledge and predestination, and free will.[4]

Lady Philosophy here admits what students of Tolkien's trilogy also recognize: these concepts cannot be separated easily. However, as a philosopher (indeed as Philosophy herself) she does distinguish them, mainly on the basis of properties:

> It is easy to see that Providence and Fate are different if we consider the power of each. Providence is the divine reason itself which belongs to the most high ruler of all things and which governs all things; Fate, however,

belongs to all mutable things and is the disposition by which Providence joins all things in their own order. For Providence embraces all things equally, however diverse they are, however infinite. Fate, on the other hand, sets particular things in motion once they have been given their own forms, places, and times. Thus Providence is the unfolding of temporal events as this is present to the vision of the divine mind; but this same unfolding of events as it is worked out in time is called Fate. Although the two are different things, one depends upon the other, for the process of Fate derives from the simplicity of Providence. (4 pr.6)

Providence is the divine reason itself, the unfolding of temporal events as this is present to the vision of the divine mind; fate is this same un-folding of events as it is worked out in time, as we perceive it in the temporal world. We as human beings are unable to know providence. All we can know is fate.

"Some things, however, which are subject to Providence are above the force of Fate and ungoverned by it" (4 pr.6). Thus, although some events *seem* discordant or chaotic from our temporal perspective, they are not, because they remain subject to the order which proceeds from providence. It is our limited perception that is incapable of penetrating to the order which lies behind the apparent disorder. "Therefore, when you see something happen here contrary to your ideas of what is right, it is your opinion and expectation which is confused, while the order in things themselves is right" (4 pr.6). All things have a purpose:

The generation of all things, and the whole course of mutable natures and of whatever is in any way subject to change, take their causes, order, and forms from the unchanging mind of God. This divine mind established the manifold rules by which all things are governed while it remained in the secure castle of its own simplicity. (4 pr.6)

Thus providence, which rules all things, also governs fate, which is the earthly manifestation of that rule.

In Book 5, Boethius pursues the other matters Lady Philosophy had originally joined with the distinction between providence and fate. "Your exhortation is a worthy one," Boethius concedes, "but I should like to know whether there is any such thing as chance, and, if so, what it may be" (5 pr.1). Although she regards this as a digression, Lady Philosophy responds:

> If chance is defined as an event produced by random motion and without
> any sequence of causes, then I say that there is no such thing as chance. . . .
> For what room can there be for random events since God keeps all things
> in order. . . . But if anything should happen without a cause, it would
> seem to come from nothing. And if this cannot be, chance as we defined
> it a moment ago is impossible. (5 pr.1)

Chance, defined as random or nonsequential activity, does not exist in a
teleological universe; but "chance" defined "correctly" does. Following her
"true follower" Aristotle,[5] Lady Philosophy correctly defines the concept:

> Whenever anything is done for one reason, but something other than
> what was intended happens on account of other reasons, it is called
> chance. . . . Therefore, we can define chance as an unexpected event
> brought about by a concurrence of causes which had other purposes in
> view. These causes come together because of that order which proceeds
> from inevitable connection of things, the order which flows from the
> source which is Providence and which disposes all things, each in its
> proper time and place. (5 pr.1)

As an example of so-called chance Lady Philosophy describes a farmer
who, digging with the intention of planting, unearths a cache of gold. To
him it seems a lucky chance—as it seems an unlucky chance to the man
who buried it with the intention of later recovering it. Both of these
actions (the diggings) had other purposes in view; but the chance occurred because the order which flows from providence, which disposes
all things—even things unknown to men—brought the events together.
Order and purpose, cause and effect always exist, but when man is ignorant of them, their results seem like chance.

We can see from these few excerpts that Boethius presents a universe created and governed by a benevolent providence, a universe of
order and harmony in which everything—including fate and chance—
has purpose, even if that purpose is beyond the perception of human
understanding. Furthermore, this ordered universe also allows for questions of human will. In Book 5, Boethius asks: "But, within this series of
connected causes, does not will have any freedom, or are the motions of
human souls also bound by the fatal chain?" "There is free will," Philosophy answered, "and no rational nature can exist which does not have

it" (5 pr.2). This is clear enough, but when Boethius asks about the relationship between freedom of will and divine providence he elicits a lengthier response:

> But, you may say, if I can change my mind about doing something, I can frustrate Providence, since by chance I may change something which Providence foresaw. My answer is this: you can indeed alter what you propose to do, but, because the present truth of Providence sees that you can, and whether or not you will, you cannot frustrate the divine knowledge any more than you can escape the eye of someone who is present and watching you, even though you may, by your free will, vary your actions. (5 pr.6)

Thus Boethius allows for freedom of will, for independent action, even though that action is under the watchful eye of the benevolent providence. This universe is precisely the same as Tolkien's.[6]

As we might expect, the foundations of Tolkien's universe, Middle-earth, are laid in the first part of the trilogy, with only passing references to the "order and purpose" of the cosmos in the remaining two.[7] Providence acting in the world is obvious in many episodes, and a recitation of them all would prove tedious. The "fortuitous" appearance of Strider at The Prancing Pony and the "lucky" rescue by Elves who aren't usually seen in those parts but who "just happen" by are but two of the many episodes which illustrate the providential pattern. That characters within the trilogy recognize this providential pattern is clear from their statements. When Frodo "marvels" that he escaped the Riders with only a slight wound, Gandalf replies: "Yes, fortune or fate have helped you, . . . not to mention courage. For your heart was not touched, and only your shoulder was pierced; and that was because you resisted to the last" (*LR* 2.1, 216). The role of "fortune or fate" is here quite clear, as is the idea that "fortune or fate" bears a direct relationship to the independent actions of individuals. Fate helped Frodo because he helped himself. Like Boethius, Tolkien allows for both freedom and fate, and in such a way that each seems to depend upon the other. Furthermore, Elrond hints at the role of providence, in a complementary relationship with chance, when he addresses his Council:

> "You have done well to come," said Elrond. "You will hear today all that you need in order to understand the purposes of the Enemy. There is

naught that you can do, other than to resist, with hope or without it. But you do not stand alone. You will learn that your trouble is but part of the trouble of all the western world. The Ring! What shall we do with the Ring, the least of rings, the trifle that Sauron fancies? That is the doom that we must deem.

"That is the *purpose* for which you are called hither. *Called*, I say, *though I have not called you* to me, strangers from distant lands. You have come and are here met, in this very nick of time, by *chance* as it may seem. Yet it is not so. Believe rather that *it is so ordered* that we, who sit here, and none others, must now find counsel for the peril of the world" (emphasis added; *LR* 2.2, 235–36).

This mingling of ostensibly contradictory terms and concepts seems confusing. Paul H. Kocher has noted a similar "confusion" in the Tom Bombadil episode:

Frodo himself raises the question whether his rescue by Bombadil from Old Man Willow was only happenstance: "Did you hear me calling, Master, or was it just chance that brought you at that moment?" Tom's answer is both yea and nay, but the yea is louder. He did not hear Frodo calling for help, and he was on an errand that afternoon which took him to that part of the Old Forest to gather waterlilies. On the other hand, he had been alerted by Gildor that the hobbits were in need and he was watching the danger spots. In sum, said Tom, "Just chance brought me then, if chance you call it. It was no plan of mine, though I was waiting for you." The incredulous "if chance you call it" tends to deny that the rescue was really chance, however mortals may commonly define the concept. "It was no plan of mine" involves the thought that there was a plan, though it was not his.[8]

Both episodes can be clarified by recalling the distinctions made by Boethius in the passage given above. Everything in the cosmos has a purpose: the Company's is to deem the doom of the Ring; at this particular time, Bombadil's is to rescue the Hobbits. The Company has been called for its purpose (as has Tom) by providence, the shaper and controller of "plans." And they have all met "by chance as it may seem," or "by chance, if chance you call it"—but not chance as they might perceive it: arriving in the "nick of time." It is chance because they met as a result of causes of which they are ignorant, but causes which have none-theless ordered their meeting. Indeed, "it is so ordered that [they] . . . and none others, must now find counsel for the peril of the world"; that "it was no plan of [Tom's], though [he] was waiting for [them]." The order of the universe calls for action by individuals. Tom responded by wait-ing, the Company by meeting; now Frodo must respond to his individual challenge:

> "If I understand aright all that I have learned," [Elrond] said, "I think that this task is appointed for you, Frodo; and that if you do not find a way, no one will. This is the hour of the Shire-folk, when they arise from their quiet fields to shake the towers and counsels of the Great. Who of all the Wise could have foreseen it? Or, if they are wise, why should they expect to know it, until the hour has struck?" (*LR* 2.2, 264)

Elrond suggests that "this task is appointed for" Frodo, referring to the purpose Frodo now assumes; he also concedes that this task was unfore-seen, unknown even to the wise, yet a task ordered by a recognized providence. But even here Elrond is tentative: "*If* I understand aright . . . *I think* that this ask is appointed" (emphasis added). Further, as Kocher has also pointed out:

> Gandalf has said that Bilbo was "meant" to find the Ring in order to pass it on to Frodo as his heir. Frodo was "meant" to bear it from then on. But Gandalf does not assume that Frodo will necessarily do what he was intended to do, though he should. When Frodo, rebelling at first against the duty imposed on him, asks the natural question. "Why was I chosen?" the wizard can only reply that *nobody knows why*; Frodo can be sure only that it was not because of any surpassing merits he has: "But you have been chosen, and you must therefore use such strength and heart and wits as you have." . . . Yet Gandalf carefully goes on to inform Frodo that he is free to accept or reject the choice: ". . . the decision lies with you."[9]

Again we can see that these episodes are consistent with Boethian philosophy. For as Elrond had insisted earlier, we must "believe" that this order persists, and that we are part of it, just as Gandalf believes that we are a part of it even if he does not know why. Frodo has been ap-pointed to the task, yet he must also accept it. Elrond tells him just that:

"I do not lay [this task] on you. But if you take it freely, I will say that your choice is right" (*LR* 2.2, 264). Elrond believes that this is the way things must be, even if he does not know everything fully. So does Gandalf. So does Frodo.

Toward the end of part 2, the Lady Galadriel also acknowledges that a plan exists, and, in her remarks to Frodo following her willing rejection of his "generous" offer of the Ring, seems also to join incompatibly free will and fate: "They stood for a long while in silence. At length the Lady spoke again. 'Let us return!' she said. 'In the morning you must depart, for now we have *chosen*, and the tides of *fate* are flowing'" (emphasis added; *LR* 2.7, 357). These ideas (free will and fate) are not incompatible if we view them in Boethian terms, for free will operates within the order of the universe, fate being merely the earthly manifestation of that order. And here we can see more clearly than before that free will sets that order in motion. Frodo's and the Lady's choices have determined the direction of that order, have set the tides moving. It has not worked in the reverse direction. For "determinism" to be applicable here, it would have to be defined anew.

Finally, by the end of this part of the trilogy, Frodo and even Sam seem to accept the providential control of the universe, and to play their parts in it. Frodo has tried without success to leave Sam behind; at last he gives it up:

> "So all my plan is spoilt!" said Frodo. "It is no good trying to escape you. But I'm glad, Sam. I cannot tell you how glad. Come along! It is plain that we were meant to go together. We will go, and may the others find a safe road! Strider will look after them. I don't suppose we shall see them again."
>
> "Yet we may, Mr. Frodo. We may," said Sam. (*LR* 2.10, 397)

Frodo here admits, albeit lightheartedly, that he and Sam "were meant to go together," yet doubts the eventual success of their and their followers' missions. Sam, apparently, does not. True to the optimistic spirit he consistently displays, he holds out hope that all will be right in the end—as in fact it is.

These examples should serve to document the foundation Tolkien lays. There are other episodes in the later parts: the "choice" of Sam to persist; their sparing of Gollum; and Gandalf's repeated assurances that

Gollum has a part to play, even though he—as well as Sam and Frodo—does not know what it is. All join inextricably the concepts of providence, fate, chance, and often free will. But seeming contradictions can be resolved by following Boethius in distinguishing providence, which orders the universe; fate, the temporal manifestation of that order; chance, that "fate" which occurs not according to our expectations, and for causes of which we are unaware; and, of course, freedom of will, which operates as part of this providential order. It is the fusion of all these concepts that gives complexity to Tolkien's fantasy, and which in large part accounts for its continuing intellectual and imaginative appeal. For the very fusion of the paradoxical elements discussed above gives an impression of authenticity to the work. As readers we, on the one hand, identify with Tolkien's characters, sharing their uncertainty, determination, and courage. We struggle with the problems of Frodo and Sam from their point of view: Why me? What now? On the other hand we follow an omniscient author, and sense his repeated—though often subtle—assurances that in this teleological universe that he has created all will turn out well. Whatever the course of events, the rightness of the Hobbits' mission guarantees their ultimate success. It is this perfect tension between uncertainty and confidence, between knowing and believing, such as Boethius explains, which excites and satisfies Tolkien's audience.

Notes

1. Richard C. West, *Tolkien Criticism: An Annotated Checklist* (Kent, Ohio: Kent State University Press, 1970). For individual studies on various "medieval elements," see W.H. Auden, "The Quest Hero," *The Texas Quarterly* 4 (1962): 81–93, rptd. in *Tolkien and the Critics*, ed. Neil D. Isaacs and Rose A. Zimbardo (Notre Dame, Ind.: Notre Dame Press, 1968), 40–62; David Miller, "Narrative Patterns in *The Fellowship of the Ring*," in *A Tolkien Compass*, ed. Jared Lobdell (LaSalle, Ill.: Open Court Pub. Co., 1975), 95–107; John Tinkler, "Old English in Rohan," in Isaacs and Zimbardo, eds., 164–70; and Richard C. West, "The Interlace Structure of *The Lord of the Rings*," in Lobdell, *A Tolkien Compass*, 77–95.

2. Patricia Meyer Spacks, "Power and Meaning in *The Lord of the Rings*," in Isaacs and Zimbardo, eds., writes: "In *The Lord of the Rings* . . . references to these two themes—freedom of will and order in the universe, in the operation of fate—are so strongly recurrent that it is remarkable that they have not been noted before in discussions of the work" (87). Randel Helms, observing that providential control of the universe was such a dominant theme, established it

as the first of his five internal laws of Middle-earth. The other four are: (2) intention structures results; (3) moral and magical laws have the force of physical law; (4) will and states of mind, both evil and good, can have objective reality and physical energy; and (5) all experience is the realization of proverbial truth (Randel Helms, *Tolkien's World* [Boston: Houghton Mifflin, 1974], 9). C.N. Manlove discusses these themes in *Modern Fantasy: Five Studies* (Cambridge: Cambridge University Press, 1975). Chapter 5, "J.R.R. Tolkien (1892–1973) and *The Lord of the Rings*," 152–207, treats many matters, but 173–78 focus on the points at hand.

3. Boethius, *The Consolation of Philosophy*, trans. Richard Green, The Library of Liberal Arts, no. 86 (New York: Bobbs-Merrill, 1962), ix.

4. Boethius, *The Consolation of Philosophy*, trans. Richard Green, 4 pr.6. All subsequent quotations are from this edition, and the specific location of each passage will be identified in the text by book and prose or meter number.

5. Boethius here refers to Aristotle's *Physics*, 2.4–5, in *The Basic Works of Aristotle*, ed. Richard McKeon (New York: Random House, 1941), 243–46. Green also cites the *Metaphysics*, 5.30, in McKeon, 777.

6. This universe is not reserved for the trilogy alone. As Spacks has also noted, in the last paragraph of *The Hobbit* Tolkien hints, through Gandalf, that the universe is providentially controlled—even though none may understand that control: "Surely you don't disbelieve the prophecies, because you had a hand in bringing them about yourself? You don't really suppose, do you, that all your adventures and escapes were managed by mere luck, just for your sole benefit? You are a very fine person, Mr. Baggins, and I am very fond of you; but you are only quite a little fellow in a wide world after all!" (*H*, 1966, 315). See also Spacks, "Power and Meaning," 86–87. This providential pattern is also quite clearly explicated in *The Silmarillion*, "Quenta Silmarillion," chapter 1, "Of the Beginning of Days."

7. An example that involves recollection occurs in part 4 when Sam remembers past decisions (*LR*, 341); a direct narrative statement to the effect of providential control (in the working out of fortune) occurs when Tolkien uses such a paragraph to open chapter 6: "The Battle of the Pelennor Fields" (*LR*, 1).

8. Paul H. Kocher, *Master of Middle-earth* (Boston: Houghton Mifflin, 1972), 38–39.

9. Kocher, 36–37.

Part III

TOLKIEN AND OLD NORSE

Chapter 9

TOLKIEN AND THE APPEAL OF THE PAGAN

Edda *and* Kalevala

TOM SHIPPEY

Works Rooted and Uprooted

"It is an interesting question: what is this flavour, this atmosphere, this virtue that such *rooted* works have." Tolkien posed the question near the start of his 1953 lecture on *Sir Gawain and the Green Knight* (*Monsters,* 72), but then he confessed that it was not his business to answer it that day—or, alas, any other. Nevertheless it remains an interesting question, not least because Tolkien so clearly devoted much of his lifelong writing effort to attempting to duplicate, or emulate, or counterfeit whatever the secret ingredient was. It may seem that this was wasted effort. If "rootedness" comes from having deep roots in old and half- or more-than-half-forgotten myth, as Tolkien thought was the case with *Sir Gawain* and *Beowulf* and Shakespeare's *King Lear* and *Hamlet*, then no work of fiction individually created by a modern author can hope to match it. It could also be said that a committed Christian author like Tolkien ought not to be rummaging in the depths of mythologies that were evidently pagan, at best misguided, at worst soul-destroying. Tolkien countered the first objection by keeping open the possibility that the quality he admired so much in *Beowulf* was indeed "largely a product of art" ("Beowulf," 247); and he countered the second by his developed theory of "mythopoeia," the right to create, or sub-create.[1] In any case, the whole issue of relations between individual authors and the roots of their tradition may well be a complex one, as the cases to be considered here will show.

In searching for this unknown quality that Tolkien saw and admired, I will examine in particular two works that Tolkien certainly knew and used from an early date: the *Prose Edda* of Snorri Sturluson and the *Kalevala* of Elias Lönnrot. Proving that he knew and used them is now hardly necessary. If there were any doubt left after repeated demonstrations, then the essays of Marjorie Burns, Richard West, and several others in this volume would answer it. The issue I wish to take up here starts by noting that when one writes, as I just have, "the *Prose Edda* of Snorri Sturluson and the *Kalevala* of Elias Lönnrot," the word "of" has two quite distinct meanings.

Snorri Sturluson was an Icelandic writer and politician, born in 1179, murdered by his enemies in 1241. The work we know as the *Prose Edda* is essentially a handbook written by him to instruct poets wishing to continue the complex tradition of Norse skaldic poetry, which Snorri evidently felt was slipping out of cognizance. In order to do this he not only wrote a section on skaldic meters, the *Hattatal*, or "list of meters," but also one on "poetic diction," the *Skáldskaparmál*, which explains the complex allusions to mythic events once part of the skaldic vocabulary. He preceded both of these, however—though the sections now go *Gylfaginning*, *Skáldskaparmál*, *Hattatal*, they may have been written in reverse order[2]—with the *Gylfaginning*, or "Deluding of Gylfi," an extensive and coherent account of the pagan Norse mythology, some twenty thousand words in length, set in the form of a conversation between the deluded Gylfi and three divine or semidivine beings. There is no doubt that Snorri was the author of this work in an entirely modern sense. However, its accepted modern title, the *Prose Edda*, sometimes the *Younger Edda*, indicates a problem, though it may be ours, not Snorri's. It is used to distinguish Snorri's work from the *Elder* or *Poetic Edda*, a collection of poems now found primarily in two manuscripts separate from Snorri's work. It is certain, though, that Snorri knew these poems, and some that are not contained in surviving manuscripts, as he quotes from them freely in what is, after all, a manual on poetry. The mythological stories in the *Prose Edda*, then, are certainly not Snorri's own, nor can one tell how old they are. The word "edda," used previously in the Middle Ages to refer to Snorri's work, could meanwhile mean one of several things: "the book of Oddi" (Snorri was brought up there); "the book of poetry" (from *odr*, "poetry," which is cognate with the name of the god Odin, patron of poets); "great-grandmother" (so, as it were, "tales from long ago"); or just "composition" (from the Latin word *edo*, "I compose").[3] *Edo*, however, also gives us the word "edit," and Snorri can be seen as having in some ways the function of an editor of poetry rather than of a straightforward composer of prose. There is no doubt, then, about the "rootedness" of the *Prose Edda*. It goes back to a pagan age that had been officially terminated in Iceland more than two hundred years before Snorri wrote, and it draws on material that must be, in essence and perhaps in actual wording, even older.

The case of the *Kalevala* is entirely different but even more complex. Briefly, during and after the Napoleonic wars the nations or proto-nations of Europe became engaged in what was almost an "arms race" to provide themselves with national literary traditions that would cement their claim to having always existed, a desire especially strong among nations such as Germany whose claim to existence was in fact shaky or threatened. One early manifestation of this, for instance, was the craze for the works of "Ossian." From 1760 onward a Gaelic-speaking Highlander named James Macpherson—it will be remembered that the rebellion of Bonnie Prince Charlie had been defeated and Highland tradition all but crushed in and after the Battle of Culloden in 1746—created a sensation in England and eventually across Europe with his translations from the Gaelic of fragments, and then of entire epic poems, centered on the hero Ossian, or Oisín. Macpherson, however, despite increasing pressure and skepticism, refused to produce the manuscripts from which he claimed to have drawn, and opinion eventually hardened into a belief that he had never had any. His work, in other words, was a fake, however damaging this might be to Scottish amour propre. Recent opinion has tended to rehabilitate Macpherson slightly and to see him as an improver, compiler, and editor of what was then still a living tradition of Gaelic poetry.[4] But this was not the view of, for instance, Jacob Grimm, the great philologist, author of the *Deutsche Mythologie* or *Teutonic Mythology*, and collector with his brother Wilhelm of *Grimm's Fairy Tales*—another work allegedly "rooted" in antiquity, but one in which the Grimms have been repeatedly accused of going beyond the proper limits of collectors and editors and turning into rewriters. Grimm nevertheless made sharp distinction between what he saw as a genuine work of antiquity like the *Poetic Edda* and a "phony" one like the Ossian cycle. Indeed, prefiguring Tolkien, he saw the distinction as one of basic quality, to be felt by anyone with any sense for authenticity at all. How could one possibly mistake a work like the *Elder Edda*, he asked rhetorically, a work whose plan, style, and substance breathe the remotest antiquity, whose songs lay hold of the heart in a far different way from the extravagantly admired poems of Ossian?[5] The one was rooted, the other a mere modern fad.

Grimm never made any further comparison with Elias Lönnrot's *Kalevala*, but its existence adds a further complication to the whole issue of "edition" as opposed to "composition." Lönnrot, a Finnish doctor working in remote areas of Karelia, took an interest in the traditional songs of the area and made a collection of them. In doing so he did no more than the Grimms, for instance, collecting folktales or Walter Scott collecting ballads. Lönnrot, however, went on to arrange the songs into a connected cycle, or even epic, which he published in twenty-five *runos*, or cantos, in 1835, and expanded to fifty in 1849. In doing this Lönnrot was in line with the contemporary doctrine of *Liedertheorie*, first propounded in 1795 by F.A. Wolf, which held that even the great classical epics of Homer had begun as short, independent, anonymous, nonliterate *Lieder*, or "lays," or "ballads," which had then been, so to speak, stitched together into a connected whole by a single named poet. It was then an entirely appropriate activity for any would-be creator of a national epic to arrange and connect up traditional songs into an epic cycle, just as Homer had, especially if he believed, like Lönnrot, that he was really reassembling something that had once already taken epic shape. Conversely, it became the characteristic activity of critics, especially German critics, to dissect epic poems like *Beowulf* or the *Nibelungenlied* back into their original allegedly separate *Lieder* or ballads. Or one might, like Lord Macaulay, take a familiar Roman historian like Livy and write versions of the ballads his histories might be thought to have been based on: these are Macaulay's *Lays of Ancient Rome*, which Tolkien began his poetic career by imitating.[6] The distinction between the genuine and the phony, which both Grimm and Tolkien were so sure of, accordingly became a matter of inner quality, not to be decided on purely objective criteria, though it deserves to be said here that Lönnrot kept particularly accurate records of what he had collected and what he had himself added or changed. His work has been reedited to the highest scholarly standards in the thirty-three–volume *Suomen Kansan Vanhat Runot*, [The Ancient Runes of the Finnish People].[7]

Meanwhile Lönnrot's *Kalevala* became, as intended, the Finnish national epic, the date of its publication still a national holiday, and it could be argued that Finland owes its current existence as an autonomous and prosperous state to it and to the national spirit it invigorated. Tolkien would unquestionably have wished to do the same for England, a nation whose ancient traditions, he felt, had been even more thoroughly suppressed than those of Macpherson's Scottish Highlands, and whose autonomy had (and has) been subsumed into the United Kingdom of Great Britain and Northern Ireland, to which Tolkien felt little loyalty.[8] But he had nothing like the resources that Lönnrot had to work with or even what was available to Snorri: England had no living native mythical tradition nor any poetic corpus based on it. Nevertheless, the *Prose Edda* and the *Kalevala* had a quality he admired and that he perhaps thought they shared, in spite of the very different circumstances of composition outlined above. In what follows I try to set out what this quality was and how it was created, so that the rest of this essay becomes in large part a critique of *Edda* and *Kalevala* and of their reception, seeking however always to identify the elusive "flavor of rootedness" that Tolkien himself detected.

Norse Tradition and the *Prose Edda*

The exact chronology of the rediscovery of Snorri's *Prose Edda* remains obscure. Unlike *Beowulf*, for instance, it does not seem to have burst upon the learned world all at once, though there was a Latin edition by the Danish scholar Resenius (Peder Resen) as early as 1665, which, however, had limited circulation. Rather, as with the *Elder Edda*, knowledge of it seems to have leaked out in selections and paraphrases. An important step was Paul Henri Mallet's *Introduction à l'histoire de Dannemarc*, with its second volume of translations, *Monumens* [sic] *de la mythologie et de la poésie des Celtes et particulièrement des anciens Scandinaves* (1755–56), translated into English by Thomas Percy (discoverer of the Percy Manuscript, another manuscript whose existence was long in doubt) as *Northern Antiquities* (1770). These and a succession of other mythological guides and handbooks made familiar to the world stories that are now known worldwide, if only at comic-book level: the Chaining of

Fenris-Wolf, Thor's trip to Utgartha-Loki, Thor's fishing for the Midgard-Serpent, and a score of others. By Tolkien's time there were a definitive edition by Finnur Jónsson and English translations by Sir George Dasent (1842) and A.G. Brodeur (1916). A long selection from the *Prose Edda* forms the first item in E.V. Gordon's *Introduction to Old Norse* (1927), compiled at a time when Tolkien and Gordon were close collaborators.

The very familiarity of these stories has, however, overlaid the shock effect that they had on the literary world when they first began to appear in print. They introduced an entirely new mythology, which had been completely forgotten everywhere except in remote outposts like Iceland. To someone brought up on classical epic and Bible story, they further-more introduced an entirely new worldview, or mind-set, or as Tolkien might say, literary "flavour." And yet, on further inspection, English read-ers might start to think it was not so absolutely unfamiliar after all. Snorri's readiness to treat themes of the utmost importance, such as old age and death and the end of the world, with a pervasive humor, while strange to and indeed forbidden by classical literary theory, was just what Shakespeare had been accused of by generations of French critics. Snorri's Old Icelandic still translates very easily into colloquial modern English. Perhaps the worldview had not gone away after all; it had just been dropped by the literary caste, the media people, the teachers and arbiters of literature—people who, as Tolkien would readily have agreed, had consistently rejected any form of native popular culture, whether *Grimm's Fairy-Tales* or Shakespeare or Tolkien himself, coming around only slowly and reluctantly in a whole series of rearguard actions. What, we should ask, were the surprising or shocking novelties in Snorri's matter and method?

One is his remarkable laconicism, a habitual use of understatement. When the Æsir bind Fenris-Wolf, he refuses to allow them to put the fetter Gleipnir on him, fearing treachery, unless the god Tyr will stand with his hand in Fenris's mouth as a guarantee of good faith. Once it is clear that Fenris cannot escape from the fetter, "[all the gods] laughed, except for Tyr. He lost his hand."[9] A little earlier, as Snorri runs through a list of the Norse pantheon, he says of Tyr, "[H]e is one-handed and he is not considered a promoter of settlements between people."[10] This lat-ter statement means that he is the god of war and stirs up fighting. But it is characteristic of all Norse tradition to play down demonstrations of emotion and to speak in terms of opposites. The trait remains perfectly familiar: in some English social groups, including Tolkien's, "not bad at all" is about the highest compliment that can be paid. Tolkien certainly aimed at similar effects from the start of his writing career. See, for instance, his description of the Valar in *The Silmarillion*, which clearly imitates Snorri's account of the pantheon, and of Tulkas in particular, the Vala equivalent of Tyr: "He has little heed for the past and the future, and is of no avail as a counselor" (*Silm*, 29). More strikingly, one might note the end of chapter 2 of the "Quenta Silmarillion," when Yavanna warns Manwë that trees now have protectors (the Ents): "Now let thy children beware! For there shall walk a power in the forests whose wrath they will arouse at their peril." Aulë says only, "Nonetheless they will have need of wood," and goes on with his work (*Silm*, 46). The remark prefigures millennia of conflict leading all the way to Gimli and Treebeard, but no more is said. No more needs to be.

Scenes like this furthermore indicate another element in the *Prose Edda*, and in Norse tradition as a whole, which was early identified as "fatalism." It was rather a strange sort of fatalism, for it was anything but resigned. Norse heroes appeared to be quite sure they were doomed, while making violent efforts to avert that doom. In Snorri, even the gods are constantly under threat—from the giants, from old age (when the giant Thiassi makes off with Idunn's apples of immortality), from death (for Balder is killed and sent down to Hel, and Odin, his father, has no power to rescue him). They are also well aware that at Ragnarök they will be defeated and killed by their enemies, though once again this does not stop Odin from continually recruiting warriors to join his Einheriar, live in Valhalla, and fight with him in the Last Battle. But while this incompatibility may be illogical, it is also both attractive and, in a way, realistic. "Fate often spares the man who is not doomed, as long as his courage holds," says Beowulf at one point (lines 572–73), and while this makes no sense, viewed analytically—could fate spare the man who *was* doomed? Aren't fate and doom much the same thing?—it remains an excellent guide for future conduct. Keep your spirits up, as no one can be sure what is fated: this is advice often given by Gandalf. Tolkien clearly pondered extensively on the whole question of fate, doom, chance, and luck, and the relation of these powers to individual free will, building his answers into the whole structure of *The Lord of the Rings*, and especially into the repeated expansions of the "Tale of Túrin."[11] In doing so he was trying, I believe, to retain the feel or "flavour" of Norse myth, while hinting at the happier ending of Christian myth behind it.

His reason for doing this, I would further suggest, was a wish to retain the heroic quality of his Norse sources. Tolkien made his thoughts on this clear in his famous lecture on *Beowulf*, where he argued, for one thing, that, while ancient English mythology had all but totally vanished, it could not have been very different from Norse—and here he meant predominantly the two *Eddas*, prose and poetic. The striking fact about this shared mythology, he said, was its "theory of courage . . . the great contribution of Northern literature" ("Beowulf," 262). By the "theory of courage" he did not mean that in Norse mythology courage was admired, as it is in all human traditions. He meant that Norse mythology was unique in confronting certain and ultimate defeat, but regarding that neither as an excuse for giving up nor as a logical refutation of one's position. Evil will triumph, but it will still be evil; those killed resisting it, even those killed beyond death like Odin's Einheriar, will still be in the right. This is not a consolation, but it is a fact. Tolkien did not go on to say this, but one might add that it is then not so surprising that the pagan English were converted so readily to a religion of hope; Tolkien did say that as soon as that conversion took place, the old stories, not yet forgotten, were "viewed in a different perspective" ("Beowulf," 263). That is the perspective of the *Beowulf*-poet, writing about pagan times and heroes but a Christian himself; of Snorri Sturluson, in exactly the same position but with both a stronger tradition of paganism and a longer tradition of Christianity; and of Tolkien as well, writing in a society with a far longer history of Christianity, but also one under renewed and different threat.

A last point about the "flavour" of Snorri and of Norse tradition as a whole, and an especially surprising one in view of what has just been said, is its endemic good humor. The world of Snorri's myth is the exact opposite of a *divina commedia*, but Snorri writes habitually as a comedian. Thor repeatedly loses his dignity in his encounters with the giant Skrymir, striking him three times while he is asleep with the lightning-hammer Miollnir, only for Skrymir to wake each time and wonder vaguely if something has fallen on his head—a leaf? an acorn? bird-droppings? "Thor backed away quickly and replied that he had just woken up."[12] There is grotesque farce in the tests of strength that Utgartha-Loki sets for Thor—draining a horn (connected to the sea), picking up a cat (it is really the Midgard-Serpent), wrestling an old crone (she is Elli, Old

Age)—and marked ribaldry in Loki's defeat of the giant contracted to build Asgarth: he entices away the giant's draught stallion in the shape of a mare. The gods laugh as Tyr loses his hand and think it good sport to throw and shoot at Balder, confident in his invulnerability. Strong and fierce amusement runs through the *Poetic Edda* as well, as in the mythological poem *Þrymskviða*, which E.V. Gordon selected for his Norse reader—it tells a story not included in Snorri, of how a giant stole Thor's hammer to ransom it for Freyja, only for Thor to disguise himself as Freyja and turn up for the wedding. It is normal for saga heroes to die with a wisecrack of some kind. The last line of one of the first Norse poems to be translated, the *Krakumál*, or "Death-Song of Ragnar Lödbrog," is *hlæjandi skal ek deyja*, "I shall die laughing."

All this was quite seriously offensive to many educated tastes as Norse became familiar. Not only was laughter itself thought to be vulgar by many eighteenth-century ladies and gentlemen (Ragnar's last line was habitually toned down in translation to a mere smile),[13] there was a strong feeling against mixing laughter with anything serious. It contradicted notions of stylistic decorum. Tragedy was high style and comedy was low style, and the two should be carefully separated (his failure to do this was one of the French arguments against Shakespeare, while later on Dickens remained in the critical wilderness for generations because comedy could not be taken seriously). But Norse writers seemed to have no feeling for decorousness. As mentioned above, Snorri was ready to combine themes of the utmost importance with a pervasive humor. And this too is a part of the heroic temperament and the "theory of courage." Indeed, everything that has been said here about Snorri can be seen as part of a coherent philosophy. The laconism connects to the fatalism: If things are fated, there is no point in talking about them. Both connect further with the cult of "naked will": The hero cannot be defeated, even by fate, if he refuses to give up or yield, while he shows the self-control that is most admired by refusing to speak, or groan, like Gunnar in the snake pit and his brother Högni having his heart cut out. Laughter like Ragnar's, also in a snake pit, shows the ability to rise above mere personal circumstance.

These qualities together not only form a coherent philosophy; they also mark a quite distinctive literary style—one that, I repeat, had been lost to the world. And this perhaps gives us one answer to Tolkien's question about "rootedness." What distinguishes rooted works like

Snorri's *Prose Edda* is the fact that even what may seem accidental or minor qualities, like the pervasive humor, are there because they fit an entire worldview and the mythology it generated, unless, indeed, the mythology generated the worldview. In a "rooted" work one may not be able to separate one from the other, or from the story—so that the story may continue to embody aspects of a mythology and a worldview long dead and thus (in Tolkien's words) compensate for "the inevitable flaws and imperfect adjustments that must appear, when plots, motives, symbols, are rehandled and pressed into the service of the changed minds of a later age" (*Monsters,* 72).

Indeed, those rehandlings themselves may possess their own charm, just because they demonstrate a disjunction between author and material and so open up the sense—Tolkien uses the word "flavour" once again—of "a great abyss of time" ("OFS," 128). A final point to remember about Snorri's *Prose Edda* is that it is basically an epitome. Snorri is not telling stories, but summarizing them for the benefit of apprentice poets, secure in the knowledge that they exist already, often as well-known poems (even if we no longer happen to have them). What is *The Silmarillion* but an epitome? As Christopher Tolkien says, "My father came to conceive *The Silmarillion* as a compilation, a compendious narrative, made long afterwards from sources of great diversity (poems, and annals, and oral tales) that had survived in agelong tradition" (*Silm,* 8). And he goes on to say that to some extent that was how it was actually written, with prose tales from *The Book of Lost Tales* turned into extensive poems in *The Lays of Beleriand,* and then epitomized in their turn in various versions, including annals in different languages.[14] Perhaps another characteristic of a "rooted" work is simply that it can survive as an epitome, for (to quote Tolkien once again) "myth is alive at once and in all its parts" ("Beowulf," 257). The air of summarizing much more extensive knowledge is another feature of Snorri's work that Tolkien spent great effort in trying to recapture, in many versions of *The Silmarillion,* and that was to bear fruit in the continual allusiveness of *The Lord of the Rings.*

Lönnrot and the *Kalevala*

Tolkien's interest in the *Kalevala* is even better recorded than his interest in Snorri's *Edda.* He had discovered W.F. Kirby's translation of it before he left school in 1911 and tried to read it in the original Finnish the following year. In 1914 he began work on "The Story of Kullervo," a retelling of one of the *Kalevala*'s main sections. Though never completed, this was to become the germ of the story of Túrin, one of the Great Tales, as Tolkien called them (*Biography*, 57, 66–67, 81, 104). Nevertheless, though Tolkien's interest is well known, the reasons for it have not been discussed. They deserve consideration, especially as, with Tolkien's normal finickiness over what was authentic and what was not, he might have been expected to show a certain skepticism about its origin. Tolkien was very ready to dismiss other nineteenth-century rewritings of mythical stories, such as Wagner's *Ring*, as Ossian-style fakes. What did he see, and value, in the *Kalevala*?

One very evident answer is its pathos. Old Norse literature is notoriously the most hard-hearted in Europe, its very emblem the heart that is cut from Högni and brought to his brother Gunnar. Gunnar looks at it approvingly—his captors have earlier tried to fool him by bringing a base-born heart and passing it off as Högni's—and recognizes it by its lack of (literal) trepidation:

Here I have the heart of Högni the brave,
Not like the heart of Hjalli the coward.
Little does it tremble as it lies on the plate.
It trembled much the less when it lay in his breast.[15]

There is no room for sentiment in the heroic tradition.

By contrast, the *Kalevala* is strongly marked by pathos—and often by sympathy for the fate of females: the girl Aino who drowns herself rather than face an unwanted marriage, the Maiden of Pohja weeping as she prepares to leave home for an unknown husband, a series of anxious mothers wondering whether their sons will return from expeditions, repeated allusions to wife-beating and rape. Children also come into the story. And here anyone aware of the facts of Tolkien's life would find it hard not to see a personal motive in his selection of "The Tale of Kullervo." This, *runos* 31–36 in Lönnrot's extended version of 1849, is the most easily detachable of the ten or eleven interlinked sections that make up the *Kalevala*. It tells the story of two brothers, who fall out over fishing and grazing. One of them, Untamo, then wipes out the whole family of the other, Kalervo:

> Left of Kalervo's folk only
> But one girl, and she was pregnant.[16]

She gives birth to Kullervo, who is born in slavery. Untamo repeatedly tries to murder him without success but eventually sells him cheaply to Ilmarinen the Smith, in exchange for a few worn-out tools: "For a slave completely worthless."[17] Kullervo is then ill-treated by Ilmarinen's wife, once the Maiden of Pohja. She bakes a stone into his bread, on which his knife-point breaks. Kullervo takes this especially hard:

> Save this knife I'd no companion,
> Nought to love except this iron,
> 'Twas an heirloom from my father.[18]

He revenges himself by sending bears and wolves to kill the wife, after which he escapes into the forest. There—very strangely—he is told that his family are in fact still alive and is reunited with them, but once again spoils matters by his violence and clumsiness, which terminate in a (euphemistically described) rape of his unrecognized sister and her suicide. Kullervo also considers suicide, is dissuaded by his mother, and takes delayed vengeance on Untamo instead. He returns to find his family once more dead, and he eventually kills himself with his own sword on the spot where he met his sister. This last motif, and the motif of the sword replying to him when he asks whether it will kill him, were to remain the ending of Tolkien's "Tale of Túrin" through all revisions.

The faults of this story as a narrative are easy to see, and in some ways Tolkien set himself to cure them, but parts of it must surely have struck a particular chord with him. Tolkien's father had died when he was four, his mother when he was twelve, after which, estranged from other members of his family, he lived in a succession of lodgings, student rooms, camps, barracks, and bedsitters, literally without a home of his own for the following twenty years (*Biography*, 25–114 passim). Kullervo's laments, then, could easily be applied to himself (indeed, they fit Tolkien rather better than they do Kullervo):

> I was small, and lost my father,
> I was weak, and lost my mother,
> Dead is father, dead is mother,
> All my mighty race has perished.[19]

Tolkien must also have felt sympathy with the moral pronounced at the end by "the aged Väinämöinen":

Never, people, in the future,
Rear a child in crooked fashion,
Rocking them in stupid fashion,
Soothing them to sleep like strangers.[20]

Children reared in this way will not get over it.

Tolkien, of course, did very successfully get over the traumas of his childhood and the further traumas of his young maturity, but the pathos of the *Kalevala* may have done more than catch his eye and his sympathies. The whole structure of the *Kalevala* is, in a way, a sad one. The fifty *runos* of the 1849 version are divided, as has been said, into about ten loosely linked sections of two to eight *runos* each, with several connecting themes and characters running through them, but for all the exuberance of the narrative, the thematic trend is downward. The *sampo*, mystic source of prosperity, is forged by Ilmarinen as payment for the Maiden of Pohja; but the Maiden is killed by Kullervo, and when Ilmarinen and his companions recapture the *sampo*, it is broken in the resultant fighting. Väinämöinen regards this as a benefit, for the fragments of the *sampo* will remain in Finland, and he beats off repeated revenge attacks from Pohja; even the theft of the Sun and Moon is canceled out by the relighting of a new Sun and Moon with magic fire. Nevertheless, Väinämöinen is superseded in the end, and he sails away to an unknown country, leaving behind only his harp and his songs as a consolation. The story opens with Väinämöinen trying to find a bride, but he is never successful. Ilmarinen also fails, first in his attempt to make a bride out of gold, then in his attempt to replace his wife by her sister. Lemminkainen too, despite his many exploits and adventures, fails to carry off a bride, while his marriage with Kyllikki founders. There are repeated scencs throughout the *Kalevala* of heroes returning to discover their homes laid waste, as there are of suicide and of aged mothers weeping. All round, one can see why Longfellow, attempting to produce an American national epic (difficult for a country with no Middle Ages), should have picked the *Kalevala* as a model for his epic of dispossession and replacement, *The Song of Hiawatha*. The *Kalevala* ends, finally, with an apology from the imagined poet, which repeats the grief of

Kullervo, "I was small when died my mother," but also presents the poet as an outcast, abused and unwanted:

> Even now do many people,
> Many people I encounter
> Speak to me in angry accents,
> Rudest speeches hurl against me,
> Curses on my tongue they shower.[21]

Tolkien perhaps remembered this self-characterization many years later, when he came to write the poem "Looney," rewritten in *The Adventures of Tom Bombadil* as "The Sea-Bell," where it is also alternatively titled "Frodos Dreme." The self-images scattered through his work show a persistent streak of alienation—Niggle, Ramer, Smith of Wootton Major[22]—while the quietly sad ending of *The Lord of the Rings* echoes the departure into exile of Väinämöinen. But the example of the *Kalevala* may further have allowed Tolkien to see that a national epic need not be triumphalist (though all too often they are). It can be about loss as well as gain, loss of the *sampo*, loss of the Silmarils; it can be about partial success, with Sun and Moon replacing the Light of the Trees in *The Silmarillion* rather as the new Sun and Moon replace the old ones in *Kalevala*; it can confront an ultimate failure.

This last point may have grown to be especially important to Tolkien. In his youth he remarked that "[t]hese mythological ballads are full of that very primitive undergrowth that the literature of Europe has been steadily cutting and reducing for many centuries"[23]; the word "primitive" is surprising, for the *Kalevala*, as said above, is as it stands a work of the nineteenth century and, by Tolkien's standards, modern literature. But one of its remarkable features, for a poem from a country nominally Christian for centuries, is the absence from it of any obvious Christianity. Some characters wear crosses, and there is a supreme deity called Ukko, who, however, rarely intervenes. W.F. Kirby, the translator, wrote in 1907, "The religion of the poem is peculiar; it is a Shamanistic animism, overlaid with Christianity,"[24] but he may have been writing defensively: the overlay is barely visible. Once again this may have given Tolkien a hint, a glimpse of a genuinely pre-Christian atmosphere—one not exactly of gloom, for the heroes and heroines of the *Kalevala* are too boisterous and resourceful for that, but one that accepts ultimate defeat and finds victory only in song, in recreation. This is very much the atmosphere of Middle-earth, both in *The Lord of the Rings* and *The Silmarillion*. Despite all the efforts and successes of the characters, everything is slowly winding down, being lost, heading for extinction. That is the best that human beings or Hobbits can do, without the Divine Redemption from outside of which characters in Middle-earth have only the faintest of inklings.

Conclusion

If Snorri's *Edda* is an epitome, the *Kalevala* is an edited anthology, and its collective origins are betrayed at every turn. Even in paraphrase, as given above, the story of Kullervo does not make good sense. His family is wiped out in *runo* 31, and it is very clear that he is a posthumous child, but they are alive again in *runo* 34, without explanation for the discrepancy. It makes good sense for Kullervo to be surly and violent while carrying out the tasks set for him by his hostile uncle Untamo, but he repeats this behavior when working for his father, against whom he has no apparent grudge. Kullervo's incestuous rape of his sister can be excused, even within the morality of the poem, only by not knowing who she is; but in order for him not to know that, she too has to be separated from her family, in a repeat of the "lost child" motif. Any German *Liedertheorist* of the nineteenth century would have had no hesitation in pointing out the doublings and contradictions and in deducing the multiple authorship that we know at bottom to be the case. Retelling the story as that of Túrin, Tolkien explained away all such problems with great care, keeping the major scenes of bereavement, disobedience, rescue, heartbreak, and suicide, but embedding them in a quite different framing narrative. This too gives his work a kind of "rootedness." One can see Tolkien doing his best to compensate for (repeating his own words) those "inevitable flaws and imperfect adjustments that must appear, when plots, motives, symbols, are rehandled [in this case by Lönnrot] and pressed into the service of the changed minds of a later age" [both Lönnrot and Tolkien]. Even flaws and discrepancies can serve a purpose.

More generally, though, what Snorri's *Edda* and the *Kalevala* did for Tolkien was to give him two quite different but complementary views of a pre-Christian age, both the product of Christians looking back at but still in touch with pagan imaginations. The fierce and uncompromising

Norse mythology gave Tolkien Gandalf, the divine messenger with a short temper, heavy hand, and strong if unpredictable sense of humor. The romantic and mysterious Finnish mythology contributed a sense of grief and loss, together with a powerful foundation in natural beauty and love of the native land. Snorri and Lönnrot must certainly have been among Tolkien's major role models, along with the anonymous poets of *Beowulf* and *Sir Gawain*, the Worcestershire poet Layamon, and the great philologists Grimm and Grundtvig. As for what gives the "flavour," the "atmosphere," the "virtue" of "rootedness," several suggestions have already been made in this essay, but surely the most vital one must be the sense of many minds, not just one, pouring their thought and emotion into the greatest issues of human life—and death. Ramer, one of the characters in "The Notion Club Papers," already mentioned as a particularly likely representative of Tolkien himself, tells his colleagues:

> I don't think you realize, I don't think any of us realize, the force, the daimonic force that the great myths and legends have. From the profundity of the emotions and perceptions that begot them, and from the multiplication of them in many minds—and each mind, mark you, an engine of obscure but unmeasured energy.[25]

Mythologies, like languages, can never be entirely individual productions, not even when (as with Quenya and Sindarin and the myths of Middle-earth) we know quite certainly who invented them, for they are always built on a foundation, in Tolkien's case a foundation of deep philological knowledge. But he would never have done the work to acquire that knowledge if he had not first been stirred by the appeal of works like these, the appeal of the pagan.

Notes

1. For which, see "OFS," cited here as reprinted in J.R.R. Tolkien, *Monsters,* 109–61. Tolkien's discussion of "sub-creation" comes mainly on 139–45. For "mythopoeia," see the poem of that name printed in later editions of Tolkien's *TL.*

2. See Anthony Faulkes, trans., *Snorri Sturluson: Edda* (London: Dent, 1987), xi–xii.

3. The varying theories are summarized in Faulkes, xvi.

4. For an account of the history and current state of opinion, see Fiona Stafford's introduction to Howard Gaskill's edition of James Macpherson, *The*

Poems of Ossian and Related Works (Edinburgh: Edinburgh University Press, 1996), v–xxxi.

5. The quotation here comes from J.S. Stallybrass, trans., *Teutonic Mythology*, 4 vols. (London: George Bell, 1882–88), 3: v–vi, translating Jacob Grimm, *Deutsche Mythologie*, ed. Elard Hugo Meyer, 4th ed., 3 vols. (Berlin: Dümmler, and Gütersloh: Bertelsmann, 1875–78), vol. 2.

6. In his poem "The Battle of the Eastern Field," published in his school magazine, the *King Edward's School Chronicle*, in 1911, when he was 19; see *Biography*, 266. For discussion of Macaulay's relation to *Liedertheorie* and Tolkien's response to it, see Tom Shippey, *J.R.R. Tolkien: Author of the Century* (London: HarperCollins, 2000), 233–36.

7. I owe these remarks to Dr. Osmo Pekonen of the University of Helsinki.

8. See, for instance, *Letters*, 131, 144, 180.

9. See Faulkes, 29.

10. Faulkes, 25.

11. See Shippey, *J.R.R. Tolkien: Author of the Century*, 143–47 and 249–54, respectively. See also chapter 8 this volume, Kathleen E. Dubs's "Providence, Fate, and Chance: Boethian Philosophy in *The Lord of the Rings*."

12. Faulkes, 40.

13. See the examples given in Shippey, "'The Death Song of Ragnar Lödbrog': A Study in Sensibilities," in *Medievalism in the Modern World: Essays in Honour of Leslie Workman,* ed. Richard Utz and Tom Shippey (Turnhout: Brepols, 1999), 155–72.

14. The best account of this remains that by Charles Noad, "On the Construction of 'The Silmarillion,'" in Verlyn Flieger and Carl F. Hostetter, eds., *Tolkien's "Legendarium": Essays on "The History of Middle-earth"* (Westport, Conn.: Greenwood, 2000), 31–68.

15. My translation of lines 2–5 of stanza 25 of the Eddic *Atlakviða*.

16. W.F. Kirby, trans., *Kalevala: The Land of Heroes,* 2 vols. (London: Dent, 1907; New York: Dutton, 1907), 2:40.

17. Kirby, 2:78.

18. Kirby, 2:94.

19. Kirby, 2:102.

20. Kirby, 2:125.

21. Kirby, 2:274.

22. Niggle is the main character of "Leaf," as Smith is of "Smith." Ramer is one of the members of the Notion Club. See "The Notion Club Papers" in J.R.R. Tolkien, *Sauron Defeated: The End of the Third Age, The Notion Club Papers and the Drowning of Anadûné* (London: HarperCollins, 1992; Boston: Houghton Mifflin, 1992), and the discussion of that work in Shippey, *J.R.R. Tolkien: Author of the Century*, 287–88.

23. The only known source for this remark is Carpenter's citation from unpublished papers in *Biography*, 67.

24. Kirby, 1:ix.

25. Tolkien, *Sauron*, 228.

Chapter 10

NORSE AND CHRISTIAN GODS

The Integrative Theology
of J.R.R. Tolkien

MARJORIE J. BURNS

Like others of his time, J.R.R. Tolkien was drawn to literature of the pagan world, particularly the Northern world with its untamed reaches and its restless, adventure-seeking Northern deities, but Tolkien was also a deeply moral and a devoutly religious man, a man committed to the concept of a single, benevolent God. As a scholar, Tolkien had no difficulty studying mythological works and taking them as they were. But as a writer of fiction, as a creator of his own deific beings, Tolkien was doing more than acknowledging the beliefs of the ancients; he was, in a sense, evoking their ghosts, both for himself and for a readership that no longer accepted the concept of multiple gods nor the rougher, less sympathetic morality that is part of their character.[1]

There is no question that Tolkien was well aware of the philosophical contradictions inherent in *The Silmarillion*, his own "cosmogonic myth."[2] In a 1966 transatlantic telephone interview, Tolkien was asked by Henry Resnick to name his favorite books. "Mostly mythology moves me," Tolkien answered, though it "also upsets me because most mythology is distasteful to people." He then went on to say, "[W]e miss something by not having a mythology," but this needs to be a mythology "which we can bring up to our own grade of assessment."[3]

Tolkien was not the first to have had such concerns. Snorri Sturluson, the thirteenth-century redactor of Iceland's mythology, was also well aware that his work needed to be acceptable to a Christian audience. He therefore opens his *Prose Edda* with a prologue that claims these ancient Norse tales came from the misunderstandings of people who had "lost the name of God."[4] Later, in a section entitled "The Poesy of Skalds," Snorri addresses the matter again, this time admonishing his readers to treat these stories with respect but not to believe in them:

> But now one thing must be said to young skalds, to such as yearn to attain to the craft of poesy and to increase their store of figures with traditional metaphors; or to those who crave to acquire the faculty of discerning what is said in hidden phrase: let such an one, then, interpret this book to his instruction and pleasure. Yet one is not to forget or discredit these traditions as to remove from poesy those ancient metaphors with which it has pleased Chief Skalds to be content; nor, on the other hand, ought Christian men to believe in heathen gods, nor in the truth of these tales.[5]

Snorri then begins the tales themselves through a narrative device that further distances him from his material. What we learn about the gods (in a section entitled "The Beguiling of Gylfi," sometimes translated as "The Deluding of Gylfi") was supposedly first recounted to a traveling king. Snorri is therefore merely "recounting" what the king was told.

King Gylfi of Sweden (so the story goes) leaves home "in the likeness of an old man" to make his way to Asgard and seek knowledge from those wiser than he. On his journey he comes at last to a town and then to a hall where "deceptions of the eye" have been prepared in anticipation of his arrival. The hall is unnaturally tall and strangely made, and the king finds "unbelievable many things" that he sees.[6] Calling himself Gangleri, he asks and is given lodging for the night. Now begins a series of questions directed to his hosts—directed, in fact, to a disguised Odin who appears in triune form under the names of Hárr, Jafnhárr, and Thridi (High, Highest, and Third).

"Who is foremost, or oldest, of all the gods?" Gangleri asks.[7] The "Allfather" is the answer (given by Odin,[8] the Allfather, speaking here as Hárr). The Allfather is then listed by twelve other names. Further questions and further answers follow: questions about creation, about the structure of heaven and earth, about the other gods and their halls, and about Ragnarök to come. Bit by bit, through this interrogatory frame, information is relayed and our primary focus is shifted from King Gylfi to the Asgard gods.

Tolkien used the same device when he first described his Valar and their "Guarded Realm" of Valinor. In "The Cottage of Lost Play" (the opening piece for *The Book of Lost Tales, Part One*),[9] we are told the story of Eriol, "a traveller from far countries, a man of great curiosity," who comes to a town as night falls and asks for lodging at what turns out to be a magical cottage, one that is far larger than it first appears (*BLT1*, 13). Like King Gylfi, Eriol does not give his true name, and here, too, a pattern of questions and answers begins, questions and answers that shape the storytelling through the remainder of the book. Three figures (Lindo, an Elf; Vairë, his wife; and Rúmil, a sage)[10] respond to Eriol, and what Eriol learns from their answers teaches us as well:

> "But," said Eriol, "still are there many things that remain dark to me. Indeed I would fain know who be these Valar; are they the Gods?"
>
> "So be they," said Lindo, "though concerning them Men tell many strange and garbled tales that are far from the truth, and many strange names they call them that you will not hear here." (*BLT1*, 45)

And so, in a remarkably similar way, Tolkien opens the earliest versions of his creation story and continues on from there to describe his Valar, their powers, their dwellings, and the destruction that Melkor brings. Like Snorri, Tolkien's interrogatory framework introduces a pantheon (though Tolkien will later deny that the Valar are gods). Like Snorri, he plays on the misperception human ignorance brings.

Once descriptions of the Valar begin, however, differences appear, differences prompted by Tolkien's wish (expressed to Resnick) to "modernize" mythology and make it "credible." Tolkien avoids, for example, the muddled and (from a human point of view) rather unflattering material that clutters the beginning of Norse mythology. Where Norse creation includes fire and ice, the sullen presence of a mysterious and demonic Black Surt, an evil giant who produces a male and female from the sweat of his underarm, a cow that licks a human figure free from salty ice, and a confusing trio of higher beings who carve a man and woman out of driftwood found along the shore, Tolkien gives us instead a single creating god, Eru, "Father-of-All," a god quite compatible with

Christian values and Christian attitudes. Much will change over the years, as Tolkien revises his myth, but not this image of Eru as "The One."

Eru, however, has only a short moment on the cosmological stage. In the published *Silmarillion*, he begins by producing the Ainur as "the offspring of his thought" (*Silm,* 15), a far tidier, far more complimentary creation than what the Norse conceived. Where Eru is "The One," the Ainur are the "Ones," closely related titles suggesting that Eru (or Ilúvatar, as he is called on Earth) has paradoxically added plurality to his own singular state. With this one creative act, Eru/Ilúvatar, for the most part, quietly steps away. We now have the Ainur (some of whom become Valar, the guardians of Earth), and the Ainur in essence are gods.

Gods, however (individual gods in a real pantheon), are a mixed and troubling lot. There is little question that much of what is fairly common behavior for an Asgard god is reprehensible by the standards of today. It is not just slaughter, trickery, deception, and indifference to another's pain that mark most of these Northern deities but *delight* in slaughter, *pride* in trickery or deceit, and such moments as the all-around amusement Asgard enjoys when Tyr, one of their number, sacrifices a hand. To add to this, there are the fertility gods. A man like Tolkien, born in Victorian times, could hardly have been comfortable with Njord, who lies with his own sister and so fathers Freyja and Freyr, or with Freyja herself, who sleeps one night each with four dwarfs to gain a necklace of gold.

Problems of other sorts abound as well, problems that typically arise in the history and configuration of any pantheon. Snorri claims that there are twelve Aesir gods of divine descent, but he then lists thirteen, beginning with Odin. Other individuals not mentioned in Snorri's list appear to be divine as well. And not all of those cited by Snorri are of the Aesir race. Some of those called Aesir are actually Vanir, rival gods who moved over to Asgard in a treaty exchange, and the question of which gods are in fact Vanir is not always clear.[11] Names are easily confused as well. There are places where both Odin and Jörd (likely another name for Frigg, Odin's wife) are referred to as Fjörgynn, but elsewhere Frigg is cited as the daughter of Fjörgynn. And nearly all of the other goddesses, scholars believe, are aspects of Frigg rather than goddesses in their own right.

When it comes to what Georges Dumézil, in *Gods of the Ancient Northmen*, calls "the boundaries of divine specialties,"[12] other difficulties arise. The ever-popular Thor, for example, seems simple enough in personality. He is easily recognized as the Norse thunder-and-fire god, the hammer-wielding, goat-chariot god, the god who overcomes giants, monsters, and larger-than-life obstacles for the love of doing so. But Thor has other, less-well-known attributes, some of which seem antithetical. Thor is a sky god, but Thor is also known as God-of-the-Land (under this title he serves fertility). And in spite of his goat-drawn chariot and its ability to move through the air, he is mostly depicted on foot or wading over streams. He is as well a divine protector of human communities. And though thralls who die in battle are given to him and he is honored for his prowess in single combat, Thor nonetheless is not referred to as a battle god. On the other hand, Tyr and Odin most certainly are, and Tyr and Odin are the two other gods who share the battle dead with Thor.

The entire matter of Norse battle gods is rampant with similar inconsistencies. Tyr, Snorri tells us, has "much authority over victory in battle"[13] and is routinely invoked by warriors on the field (though other deities can be invoked as well). However, Tyr is also a god who maintains law and order and settles human disputes (a quality shared with Forseti, yet another god). Outside the boundaries of the gods themselves, there are the Valkyries, armor-wearing females who ride swiftly through the air on horseback, bestowing victory or defeat and leading the battle dead to the Hall of the Slain. The Valkyries are not deities; yet "no description of the gods of battle can be complete without them," as H.R. Ellis Davidson says.[14] Like the battle gods themselves, the Valkyries also play contradictory roles. Once back at Valhalla, they drop their bloodthirsty manners and wait on the fallen warriors like good serving maids.

Most perplexing, most troubling of all, is Odin, the Allfather of the Norse. More than any of the other gods, Odin is based on a hodgepodge of attributes and specialties—amassed, for the most part, by deity conquest, by his cult snowballing over other gods and gathering up their traits. Through time and accumulation Odin became not only a battle god but a sky god, a poetry god, a psychopompos, a worker of magic and runes, a cargo god, a shape-shifter, a patron of heroes (both living and dead), a god of ravens and wolves, a god who aids or destroys at will, a god who walks through the Norse middle-earth disguised as a bearded old man.

Faced with such an untidy listing of roles and attributes, Tolkien's answer was to pick and choose among the Norse gods for his improved pantheon—downplaying and redistributing certain conventional traits, removing other traits entirely, and now and then adding traits that are lacking or underdeveloped in Norse mythology. In doing so, Tolkien avoids the inconsistencies and unevenness found among Norse gods and gives us instead seven Valar lords, matched and balanced by seven Valar queens. He establishes a fairer distribution of talents or powers as well, and (with the exception of Melkor) he introduces more kindly personalities and a higher moral tone.

First in authority (as listed in the "Valaquenta" of *The Silmarillion*) is Manwë, chief of the Valar, whose "delight is in the winds and the clouds, and in all the regions of the air" (*Silm*, 26). Next is Ulmo, Lord of Waters and King of the Sea; and following Ulmo and Manwë are Aulë, a smith and master of crafts; Oromë, "hunter of monsters and fell beasts" (*Silm*, 29); Tulkas, the Valiant, who "delights in wrestling and contests of strength" (*Silm*, 28–29); and Námo (called Mandos), who is "keeper of the Houses of the Dead" and who is matched with his brother Irmo (called Lórien), "master of visions and dreams" (*Silm*, 28).

At one time there was an eighth Vala who also belonged to the lords. This is Melkor (or Melko in early drafts), the destroyer who becomes Morgoth. But Melkor is no longer counted among the Valar, and his "name is not spoken upon Earth" (*Silm*, 26). In this, Tolkien again imitates Snorri, who removes Loki from his list of gods, allowing that Loki belongs to the Aesir but citing him separately.

First among the queens is Varda, called Elbereth by the Elves and held highest in their "reverence and love" (*Silm*, 26). She is Lady of the Stars, the one who listens to supplications and knows all the regions of the world. Next is Yavanna, who sometimes appears in the form of a tall, stately tree and who is Earth-lady in *The Book of Lost Tales*. Nienna is the lady of pity, the universal mourner. Estë is the "healer of hurts and weariness" (*Silm*, 28). Vairë is the weaver, the one who "weaves all things that have ever been in Time into her storied webs" (*Silm*, 28), and Nessa fulfills the traditional huntress role. The seventh queen is Vána, a figure more decorative than active. She is the Ever-young; where she walks flowers spring and "all birds sing" (*Silm*, 29).

Though the matching of Tolkien's Valar to the Northern gods is by no means exact (there is too much Tolkien would wish to change), it is easy enough to pair certain Valar with certain Asgard gods. Among

Tolkien's queens, gentle Estë is a clear version of Fir, the Norse goddess of healing. Yavanna, giver of fruits, is an easy match for Asgard's Idun, whose apples keep the gods young—though Vána, as the Ever-young, echoes Idun as well. Nienna, the Vala of lamentation, is (at least in later drafts) a more kindly, more genteel version of the weeping goddess figure, one that the Norse represent both in Odin's wife, Frigg, and in Freyja (at those times when Freyja is seen not as a seductress but as a grieving wife shedding tears of gold).

The male Valar are somewhat more complex. Oromë, the destroyer of monsters, shares much with Thor, the god who strides off to Jotunheim or the Edge of the World to test himself against giants or other monstrous beings. But Tolkien splits Thor's role (much as he splits Idun's), creating not only Oromë but the ruddy-fleshed Tulkas, the Vala who is "greatest in strength and deeds," who "rides no steed" (*Silm*, 28–29), and whose anger is intense but short-lived. In coloring and temperament (and in suggestions of the comic that these two qualities bring), Tulkas is very much like the red-bearded, quick-tempered, ready-for-action Thor.

But, of all the gods, Odin remains the most problematic, and Odin makes his way into Tolkien's writing more than any other god. Manwë, the chief of the Valar, is closely linked to Odin through his Allfather title (used predominantly in the *Quenta* manuscripts),[15] his power over birds, his "splendour of poesy" (*BLT1*, 59), his sky-blue robes, and his similar, high-seated throne. In *The Lord of the Rings*, Gandalf (an emissary of Manwë) continues the Odin connection—most obviously by wearing a broad-brimmed hat and carrying a walking staff, as the wandering Odin does, though Gandalf's association with eagles, his enmity with wolves, and his ownership of a nearly supernatural horse add to this as well.[16]

Still, to deserve a place in Tolkien's idealized pantheon, Manwë needs to disown much of his Odin heritage. Where Odin claims for himself by far the largest and most diversified roles among the Northern gods, Manwë is limited primarily to powers over the wind and sky. Where Odin is a violent, terrifying, and untrustworthy god, there is no brutality or unseemliness in Tolkien's Vala king. The closest Manwë comes to Odin in Odin's wrathful mode is when he (in brief imitation of an Old Testament God) justly punishes the errant Númenoreans by drowning their island realm.[17]

Odin's negative traits, however, are not thrown away. They surface in Melkor, who traffics in wolves (as Odin does) and who (like Odin) is a persistent promoter of war. But Melkor, the destroyer and betrayer, also plays an obvious Loki role—and plays it with far more intensity and consistency than does Loki, the trickster god. Like Loki, Melkor is placed in bonds by his fellow "gods"; like Loki, his destruction cannot be contained. And just as Odin's son, Vidar, will fight Fenrir (Loki's wolf son) in Ragnarök, the day will come (so Tolkien wrote in a 1920s draft) when Manwë's son, Fionwë, will fight with Morgoth in Dagor Dagorath, the "Last Battle" of all.

And there is more. *The Book of Lost Tales* has two Valar, Makar and Meássë (from words meaning "battle" and "gore"), who are "spirits of quarrelsome mood" (*BLT1*, 67). Makar, like Odin, is a warrior host, and Meássë, his "fierce sister," is a one-woman representation of the Valkyries. Battle is "waged unceasingly" in their hall, and Meássë moves among the warriors, encouraging them to blows. Respite comes only during feasts, and then "fierce songs of victory, of sack and harrying" are sung (*BLT1*, 77–78). But Makar and Meássë, with all their obvious links to the Norse battle gods, do not long endure in Tolkien's mythology. As Christopher Tolkien writes, the "'Melkor-faction' in Valinor . . . was bound to prove an embarrassment," and the two of them soon disappear (*BLT1*, 89).

Among these Norse-based deities, however, there is one striking omission. Tolkien makes no obvious use of Balder, the wise, the good, the gentle—the one god in the Norse pantheon acceptable as he is. It may be that Balder is too much of an aberration in Tolkien's eyes, that he seems out of place not only in the morally lax world of the Norse gods but also in the energetic world of Tolkien's Valinor. The Valar are, after all, referred to as "the Powers," and their characters are determined by what it is they do. Balder, however, is all beauty and radiance; he is not a god with focus or activity. It may also be that a Vala based on Balder (who dies but will arise again) seemed preemptive of Christ, whose time is yet to come in Tolkien's pre-Christian mythology. And, finally, it may even be that Balder's goodness and beauty do have a presence in Tolkien's pantheon, but one that is shared equally throughout Valinor, where all are "noble" and "fair."

More often the problem is one of positions that Asgard fails to include or covers only insufficiently. The Norse, for example, have more than one god with connections to ships and the sea but no god within the pantheon proper whose focus (like Neptune's or Poseidon's) is fully on water, no god unhappy on solid land. There is indeed Heimdall, who is described as "wet" or "muddy" and who is born of nine mothers (traditionally interpreted to mean the waves of the sea). Heimdall's watery nature is further suggested by his choosing to fight with Loki in the form of a seal. But Heimdall is Asgard's warden god, the one who guards the heaven-spanning Rainbow Bridge, keeping it safe from giants who might try to invade. This is not a role that brings him near the sea.

There is as well Freyr, who possesses a magic ship, one that can hold all the gods and still be folded small enough to be placed within a pouch. But Freyr is a fertility god, and tales about Freyr again place him on land and away from the sea.

Somewhat more satisfying is Freyr's father, Njord, a god of prosperity who has control over winds and water, whose hall, Nóatún, means the place where ships are enclosed, and who appears, somewhat puzzlingly, to dwell both in heaven and near the sea. He is the god who stills fire, and in his water role he gives help to fishermen and to those who travel in ships; but Njord, like other Asgard gods, possesses variable traits. He is also the god called upon by hunters, and together with Freyr and Freyja, he dominates Norse fertility.

Even Thor, the recognized God-of-the-Land, plays a sea role. Because of his connection to thunder, winds, and weather, he too was invoked by those seeking protection on the sea. In fact, according to Davidson, in one way or another, all male gods in Norse belief have an association with the sea "over which they come, and by which they sometimes return when their work is over."[18]

The role of water god is, then, a particularly fragmented and shared one among Norse deities, making it a highly tempting position for Tolkien, the revisionist, to condense and rearrange. Tolkien therefore creates Ulmo, a deep-voiced Vala who "does not love to walk upon land," who dwells alone, "nowhere long," and who "moves as he will in all the deep waters about the Earth or under the Earth." In his arising, Ulmo is "terrible as the mounting wave that strides to the land." He is, then, something of a Neptune figure but only partly so, for Ulmo is also a Vala who "loves both Elves and Men" (*Silm*, 26–27), and he judges them more kindly than other Valar do, making him (in spite of his alarming qualities) a fully appropriate candidate for Tolkien's pantheon.

It might seem that Ulmo is an exception to Tolkien's dependence on the Norse, that Ulmo is essentially a Christianized classical god transplanted north to fill the ranks of Tolkien's Valinor. But Ulmo has no reason to doubt his ancestral purity. The Norse do have a sea figure that Tolkien could have drawn upon, though not within their recognized list of gods. This figure is Aegir, whom Davidson takes to be a "personification of the ocean"[19] and whom scholars believe is an ancient, half-forgotten god. Though Snorri claims Aegir is merely a "man," one "deeply versed in black magic,"[20] Aegir has power over water and waves, and the sea can be called by variations on his name. Moreover, Aegir visits Asgard with the air of a social equal, and the gods in return visit him.

Once again, however, Tolkien spreads his borrowing over more than one character. Serving under Ulmo are two figures who are numbered among the Valar in early accounts but become Maiar (beings of the same order but of less degree) by *The Silmarillion*. These are Ossë, a vassal of Ulmo, and Ossë's spouse, Uinen, the Lady of the Seas. The two together have control over waves, very much as do Aegir and his wife, Ran. Uinen, however (particularly in later drafts), plays a more kindly role than Ran does. Uinen calms the waves to save mariners, while her Eddic ancestress is known for catching "all men who go upon the sea."[21]

Similar models exist for other gaps among the official Norse gods. Tolkien's Aulë is a reinterpretation of the traditional craftsman deity, a figure well known in classical mythology but one that seems to be missing from the Norse pantheon. Asgard does have Thor, the fire god, the hammer-carrying god, but unlike the classical Vulcan (who is also a hammer and fire god), Thor is not a worker of crafts. Only the dwarfs, those misshapen, scheming creators of goddess-ensnaring jewelry and desirable artifacts, serve in craftsman roles, but the dwarfs hardly seem appropriate models for any deity. Nonetheless, the dwarfs of Norse mythology did give Tolkien a basis that he could build upon, and he transfers not only their craftsman skill to Aulë but something of their unreliable nature too. In Tolkien's mythology, in fact, it is Aulë who first created the Dwarves (to here use Tolkien's preferred capitalization and plural). Like these "Children" of his own making (*Silm*, 43–46 passim), Aulë delights in gold, in "gems that lie deep in the Earth," and in "works of skill," fascinations that have a notoriously dangerous side. Pride comes too easily to Aulë (*Silm*, 27). Like Melkor, he desires to make things "that should be new and unthought of by others" (*Silm*, 27). Unlike Melkor, however, Aulë is neither hostile nor envious. He is tempted and errs but submits himself to Eru once again.

Sometimes Tolkien's Norse connections are even more obscure, as they are in Vairë, who weaves "all things" that happen into her "storied webs." Like Ulmo and Aulë, Vairë may again seem more classical than Eddic, as though inspired by the Greek and Roman Fates. But the Norse, too, have their fate-weaving figures, the three powerful Norns.

Even more intriguing is Varda's role as Lady of the Stars, a role that initially seems fully innovative on Tolkien's part, but one that nonetheless is firmly linked to Norse mythology. It is Odin and his brothers who place sparks from the fire realm, Muspell, into the heavens and assign places to each. Some of these "fires" are allowed to wander "free under the heavens," though along a set path, while others are destined to remain where they are.[22] In the published *Silmarillion*, this Eddic inspiration is all but lost. We only know that some of the stars that Varda creates come from the "silver dews" (*Silm*, 48) of the vats of Telperion (one of Valinor's two light-bearing trees), but this seems far removed from Odin working with fire. Earlier, however, in *The Book of Lost Tales*, Varda herself uses sparks, silver sparks that are struck from Aulë's hammer. Moreover, like the wandering or steady stars that Odin and his brothers create, some of Varda's stars move on "mazy courses high above the Earth," while others hang where they are placed and do not move (*BLT1*, 181).[23]

Tolkien also simplifies and greatly softens the Norse image of death. Among the Valar there is no divvying up of the battle-slain as there is among Odin, Tyr, and Thor. (Tolkien does, however, bestow differing forms of death upon Elves, Dwarves, and Men.) And rather than Loki's daughter, Hel (half living woman, half rotting corpse), who takes as her own those who die in sickness and old age, Tolkien has Mandos, a keeper of the dead, wise and good, though a habitual speaker of doom. Mandos and his brother, Lórien (the dream-and-vision Vala), are "masters of spirits" and create a mood that is more melancholy and haunting than horrifying, morbid, or grim. There are as well two female Valar associated with Mandos and Lórien, and they further soften the mood. In *The Silmarillion*, Lórien's spouse is Estë, the healer and giver of rest; and the grieving Nienna is sister to Mandos and Lórien, adding a decorous pathos to the realm of the dead—a far cry from the horror the Norse Hel instills!

And yet, in Tolkien's earliest accounts, Nienna is not so very different from the Norsemen's figure of Hel. There she is often called Fui (a name meaning "darkness" or "night"). "Slaughters and fires, hungers and mishaps, diseases and blows dealt in the dark, cruelty and bitter cold and anguish and their own folly" (*BLT1*, 77) bring the dead to Nienna's hall, a hall roofed with the wings of bats and lit by a single coal (a fitting match for Sleet-cold, the dreary abode of Hel). This hall is named Fui after Nienna's own name, just as the realm of Hel also goes by the name of Hel; and in these early tales, Nienna is the one who decides the fates of dead Men, sending them to various regions and realms, just as Hel in Norse mythology apportions "all abodes" among those sent to her.[24]

Fui Nienna is also known by a variety of other "grievous" names, for "she is Núri who sighs and Heskil who breedeth winter, and all must bow before her as Qalmë-Tári the mistress of death" (*BLT1*, 66). By the time of the published *Silmarillion*, however, all of this nastiness has gone. The Houses of the Dead (having lost their horror) are no longer downward and north in imitation of the *Eddas* but lie more pleasingly "westward in Valinor" (*Silm*, 28), and Nienna is no longer Mandos's death-goddess wife but a sister in sorrow to both Mandos and Lórien.

In many ways the greatest changes come in the area of fertility. Where Norse goddesses are nearly always, in one way or another, connected to procreation (often in reprehensible, selfish ways), female Valar are far more distanced from sexuality and far more restrained. (Male fertility figures have no place at all.) Nonetheless, the forces of fertility do make themselves known within Tolkien's pantheon—always in blameless, fruit-and-flower ways. (Yavanna is the bestower of fruit, and flowers spring up when her sister, Vána, walks by.) Moreover, those female Valar who do not contribute to vegetative forms of increase are, at the very least, guardians, nurturers, preservers—individuals who support life, who focus on the lives of others, and who look to others' needs. In one way or another, then, they find their place in the most traditional female roles.

Even fleet-footed Nessa, a variation on the virgin huntress, is a model of tenderness. Like the Norse Skadi (a giantess who marries a god), Nessa delights in activity and movement and prefers the out-of-doors. She is "swift as an arrow," a phrase that emphasizes her huntress heritage; but where Skadi goes about with bow and arrows and "all weapons of war,"[25] Nessa carries no weapons and never shoots a bow. "Deer she loves," and they "follow her train whenever she goes in the wild" (*Silm*, 29). Unlike Skadi, then (and unlike Diana or Artemis), Nessa is a huntress only in garb and guise.

In fact, with the exception of Melkor, there is no excess, no cruelty, no evil of any kind in Tolkien's final pantheon. Even Oromë, the hunter, lives in peace with Valinor's animals, and the hunting he does occurs only beyond Valinor's sacred plains. Loyalty, dedication, and service now prevail, so much so that attributes possessed by Tolkien's pantheon seem more like occupations or positions than manifestations of natural forces or strengths.

Much has changed since *The Book of Lost Tales*. Bit by bit the Valar of Valinor have been civilized and modernized. Bit by bit, they have been brought up to the "grade of assessment" that Tolkien, in the Resnick interview cited above, claimed he wished to achieve. This was a process that inevitably distanced the Valar from their Eddic past. It was also a process that slowly and steadily weakened their claim to divinity.

In the earliest versions, the Valar are not just gods but "the Gods," spelled with a capital *G*. By 1930, however, the opening of the *Quenta* states that *Valar* means the "Powers," though Men often call them "Gods." But the issue is even more complex and less settled than this. In spite of the *Quenta's* opening statement (a statement implying that Men alone call the Valar "Gods" and do so erroneously), the term "Gods," in reference to the Valar, nonetheless continues to appear and in places where the perception is not that of Men but that of the narrator. "God," in all these early examples, is consistently capitalized.

Slowly this too changes. The suggestion of a Valar godhead is lessened. The capital *G* is dropped. Emphasis on Ilúvatar's creation of the Ainur is increased, as is his role in the generation of their music. The fact that Men called the Valar "gods" (now a small *g*) is no longer at the beginning of the text, weakening their rumored godhead just that much more. The narrative voice now speaks of the Valar as the "Holy Ones."

Along with this, the physicality of the Valar is markedly reduced, and cohabitation among the Valar is no longer described in earthly, familial terms. The word *wife* is dropped. A Valar now has a "spouse"; and "spouse," Tolkien explains, indicates a spiritual unity and not a physical one. In early versions, children had been born to the Valar. By the mid-twentieth century these sons and daughters have become "heralds" and "handmaidens," rather than children of the flesh.

Nonetheless, the fact that Tolkien slowly and slightly brought his Valar more in line with his Christian belief does little to change the reader's perception that those Ainur who become the Valar are a pantheon. Even when we take Ilúvatar fully into account, even when we remember how Tolkien emphasizes Ilúvatar's primary role and the Valar's derivative one, it is hard not to feel that the Valar themselves are at least serving as gods. And Tolkien invites this attitude. It is the Ainur whose music begins the world, but it is Ilúvatar who gives vision to their song, so that we seem to have two sets of divine rule, two coexisting versions of a godhead, both of which are needed to bring the world into being. The balance is not an easy one. Ilúvatar has the ultimate power. This is clearly stated and stated repeatedly, yet Ilúvatar soon fades from the main narrative tale, becoming more a figurehead than a participant, and the Valar—in spite of reassurances to the contrary—now seem in charge.

This is cleverly done. By sharing out the godhead role into two differing forms, Tolkien was able to evoke the ancient world and still satisfy the religious beliefs of the modern one. By focusing primarily on the Valar, he could rely upon a pantheon's dramatic interaction as well as on a pantheon's traditional connection to the world it oversees. Such drama could not occur on the Ilúvatar plane. "The One" by himself does not a story make—and drama does occur. Melkor, now Morgoth, aligns himself with Ungoliant, and the two destroy the light-giving Trees of Valinor. The Elves awake and rebellion will soon begin.

There are, however, certain limitations to the dramatic potential of Tolkien's godlike Valar beings. Given his tastes and preferences, given his determination to place all evil in Melkor alone, much of what holds our interest in Asgard is gone from Valinor. Gone is the joy of giant bashing, gone the good times found in sneaking and trickery, and gone the open pleasure of pre-Christian sex. In Tolkien's twentieth-century descendants of Norse gods, all the blood, fire, lust, and self-seeking behavior have been allotted to villains alone, to Melkor/Morgoth, who loses his right to a Vala title and respectability.

But Melkor, of course, is essential. He too helps Christianize these gods. By serving as the power of negativity, Melkor effectively directs all that is evil or destructive away from Ilúvatar and the Vala pantheon. Though everything that *is* has existed in Ilúvatar from the first and must always be there as well, it is as though Ilúvatar, through the mechanism of Melkor, is freed of any negative taint, any accusation of a shadow side. He has cast it off, and Melkor, consciously and deliberately, has claimed it for his own. Like a self-selected scapegoat (and much like

Loki and Lucifer), he then enters the wilderness—bearing all negation, bearing the stigma of the un-good, a victim of authorial need. What remains for Tolkien's godhead is mere goodness in singular and multiple forms. Much has been gained—unquestionably. But something of the great human muddle and stir has been lost as well.

And so it is for good and ill (and perhaps literally for Good and Ill) that Tolkien finds a balance between his Christian devotion and his attachment to ancient gods.

Notes

1. *The Silmarillion* and *The Lord of the Rings* draw from several world mythologies but most heavily and most consistently from the Celtic and the Norse (the two mythologies that most influenced England's early history). Celtic gods, however, are a freewheeling, individualistic lot; when it came to creating a structured pantheon, Tolkien took inspiration mostly from the Norse.

2. J.R.R. Tolkien, *Morgoth's Ring*, vol. 10 of *The History of Middle-earth*, ed. Christopher Tolkien (Boston: Houghton Mifflin, 1993), 357.

3. J.R.R. Tolkien, "An Interview with Tolkien," interview by Henry Resnick, *Niekas* 18 (late spring 1967): 40.

4. Snorri Sturluson, *The Prose Edda*, trans. Arthur Gilchrist Brodeur (New York: American-Scandinavian Foundation, 1923; London: Humphrey Milford, Oxford University Press, 1923), 13.

5. Snorri Sturluson, 97.

6. Snorri Sturluson, 14.

7. Snorri Sturluson, 15.

8. Where standardized forms exist in English (i.e., Odin, for Oðinn), they will be used instead of the Icelandic.

9. See pages 13 and 45 of *BLT1* for the dating of these unfinished pieces written before 1920.

10. Lindo and his wife disappear from subsequent drafts, though the name "Vairë" is later given to another character in Tolkien's pantheon. Rúmil still plays a part in *The Silmarillion*, as a Deep Elf who is credited for devising the first written characters.

11. The Aesir and the Vanir of the Norse, it should be noticed, are matched by the Ainur and Valar of Tolkien's mythology, an interesting parallel of the initial *A* and *V* and of the final *r*, used by the Scandinavians to indicate plurality and here by Tolkien as well. *Ás* and *Van* (in the Norse) and *Ainu* and *Vala* (in Tolkien) are the singular.

12. Georges Dumézil, *Gods of the Ancient Northmen*, trans. John Lindow, Alan Toth, Francis Charat, and George Gopen, and ed. Einar Haugen (Berkeley, Los Angeles, and London: University of California Press, 1977), 5.

13. Snorri Sturluson, 39.

14. H.R. Ellis Davidson, *Gods and Myths of Northern Europe* (Harmondsworth, Middlesex, Eng.: Penguin, 1964), 61.

15. J.R.R. Tolkien, "The Quenta," in *The Shaping of Middle-earth*, vol. 4 of *The History of Middle-earth*, ed. Christopher Tolkien (Boston: Houghton Mifflin, 1986), passim.

16. See Marjorie Burns, "Gandalf and Odin," in *Tolkien's "Legendarium,"* ed. Verlyn Flieger and Carl F. Hostetter (Westport, Conn.; London: Greenwood Press, 2000), 219–31, for a full account of Manwë's dependence on Odin and Tolkien's acknowledgment of the relationship.

17. The concept of a vast or world-covering deluge (usually as a form of punishment) appears in mythologies around the world. In Norse creation, Bergelmir and his wife use a ship to escape such a flood.

18. Davidson, 107. This concept, which appears in Celtic belief as well, is borrowed by Tolkien for those of his wizards who were sent to Middle-earth and for those of his Elves who came from Valinor.

19. Davidson, 128.

20. Snorri Sturluson, 89.

21. Snorri Sturluson, 144.

22. Snorri Sturluson, 20.

23. Christopher Tolkien speculates that his father was here thinking of a time "when the regular apparent movement of all the heavenly bodies from East to West had not yet begun" (*BLT1*, 200). A simpler explanation, however, is that Tolkien was borrowing closely from the Norse.

24. Snorri Sturluson, 42.

25. Snorri Sturluson, 91.

Chapter 11

THE TWILIGHT OF THE ELVES

RAGNARÖK AND THE END OF THE THIRD AGE

ANDY DIMOND

WHAT OF THE GODS? WHAT OF THE ELVES?
GIANTHOME GROANS THE GODS ARE IN COUNCIL
THE DWARVES GRIEVE BEFORE THEIR DOOR OF STONE,
MASTERS OF WALLS. WELL, WOULD YOU KNOW MORE?
—*Voluspa*, Auden and Taylor translation

In the cosmology of Old Norse religion, even the gods themselves were destined to die. It was believed that this would happen in a final battle between the Aesir (the famous Norse gods of Asgard) and a league of giants, monsters, and rogue gods known as the Destroyers of the World. This confrontation, which became known as Ragnarök, would mark the end of the traditional Norse pantheon headed by Odin and the dawn of a new age. J.R.R. Tolkien, in all his Middle-earth literature and particularly in *The Lord of the Rings*, is influenced by Norse mythology's fatalism and its view of the ephemeral, changing nature of all things. Tolkien's books contain both thematic reflections of and explicit references to the *Voluspa*, which is a part of the collection known as the *Elder*, or *Poetic*, *Edda* and the oldest extant source of the Ragnarök myth. In his work there is more than one echo of the Ragnarök, and the existence and nature of this correspondence have been described with varying degrees of success by the critical community.

Mention has been made quite frequently of Ragnarök in Tolkien studies, but almost always in the form of brief innuendos within essays on Tolkien and Old Norse in general, or on a topic tangentially related, if at all. For instance, Charles Moseley gives a short description of the Eddic cosmology in a biographical section of his book on Tolkien.[1] Moseley immediately moves on to other influences on Tolkien, and while he does assert that the general Norse worldview affected J.R.R. Tolkien's moral and narrative sensibility, he never returns to the subject of Ragnarök to elaborate on its relevance to Tolkien's own "sub-created" world. It is also worth noting that at least one Tolkien critic has referenced Ragnarök in negative terms. Patrick Curry writes, in *Defending Middle-earth*, of its alleged irrelevance to that world.[2]

Some critics have made more substantial contributions to our understanding of the Norse eschatology's influence on *The Lord of the Rings*. Gloriana St. Clair, for example, correctly identifies the Elves as the parallel to the Aesir in terms of Tolkien's own Ragnarök.[3] Yet as perceptive as her passage's treatment of the Ragnarök theme is, it is again only a brief detail in St. Clair's "Overview of the Northern Influences in Tolkien's Works"—as it should be in an essay surveying such a vast and multifaceted subject. Ruth S. Noel, on the other hand, has the luxury of space in her book *The Mythology of Middle-earth*, and she devotes a few helpful paragraphs to the Ragnarök parallels in Tolkien. She notes the Balrog's obvious similarities to Surt[4] and compares its fight with Gandalf on the bridge of Khazad-Dum to Surt's destruction of the bridge Bifröst.[5]

The estimable T.A. Shippey touches upon the legend a few times in his *Road to Middle-earth*, explaining its contribution to the moral shape of Tolkien's story: "[A] major goal of The Lord of the Rings was to dramatise that 'theory of courage' which Tolkien had said in his British Academy lecture was the 'great contribution' to humanity of the old literature of the North. The central pillar of that theory was Ragnarök— the day when gods and men would fight evil and the giants, and inevitably be defeated. Its great statement was that defeat is no refutation. The right side remains right even if it has no ultimate hope at all."[6]

The most extensive treatment of our topic until now would seem to be a *Mythlore* article by J.R. Wytenbroek, entitled "Apocalyptic Vision in *The Lord of the Rings*." Wytenbroek mentions a few superficial comparisons between the War of the Ring and Ragnarök (the sun's disappearance and the evil wolves; the world in decay), adding a single point unnoticed by other critics: that in such a model the White Tree of Gondor "suggests the ash Tree Yggdrasil, the tree of Life" in representing the renewal of the world after the final battle.[7] Unfortunately for our purposes Wytenbroek's interests lie far more in Christian mythology; his essay's introduction states that it is an article focused on both Ragnarök and John's Revelations, but of twenty-eight paragraphs only seven even refer to Norse elements. He ventures off into a stimulating analysis of Aragorn's fit in the role of an apocalyptic Christ figure and neglects to return to the Northern sources, even in his conclusion.

So despite much lip service and a few penetrating paragraphs, as far as I know no critic has devoted an entire article to this subject. In general, critical appreciation of the similarities between these two stories, though common, has remained inadequate because thus far scholars have both unfairly assumed familiarity on the reader's part with a somewhat obscure myth and failed to delve deeper into its influences. The aim of this work is to synthesize these critics' insights and supplement them with my own (hopefully more thorough) inquiry into this question: How exactly did the most important myth from Tolkien's favorite mythology inform the creation of his own?

The specific area I would like to examine, and the richest source of these allusions in Tolkien, is his retelling of the myth in the form of the War of the Ring and the subsequent transition from the Third Age to the Fourth Age, as told in *The Lord of the Rings* trilogy and particularly in *The Return of the King*. Most superficially, Ragnarök's influence is manifest in Tolkien's sampling of some of the Norse iconography[8] and the use of symbols common to Ragnarök and other apocalyptic traditions (e.g., the disappearance or "swallowing" of the sun). In terms of mood, also, he borrows the notion of decline and decay preceding the final battle; he projects a doomed world. On the narrative level, the locus of Ragnarök's influence in *The Lord of the Rings* is the passing of the Elves, translating into the death of the gods. Lastly, and most meaningfully, each tale serves as a mythological bridge from the magical, larger-than-life world of supernatural beings to the "mundane" one characterized by both Christianity and rationalism.

The muddled status of Ragnarök within Tolkien studies can perhaps be partly attributed to an insufficient knowledge of the myth itself on the part of both critics and readers. It therefore may be helpful to offer a brief synopsis of that myth here. The events of Ragnarök begin in the years leading up to what is referred to as the "twilight of the gods."[9] A prophetess, Vala, foretells to Odin a surge of sin, vice, and anarchy, "foul murderers, and perjurers, and them who other's wives seduce to sin."[10] If this were not bad enough, three unbearable winters follow one after another with no intervening summers. Chaos increases: "Brothers slay brothers. . . . Sensual sin grows huge."[11] The end of the world then begins in earnest. Wolves devour the sun and moon; the stars fall from the sky; earthquakes level the mountains and forests; and the ocean rushes over the land. A ship sails over the now flooded world. Called Naglfar, the ship is made of men's fingernails, and its cargo consists of many unsavory monsters and evil gods, led by a fire-demon named Surt. The boat smashes through Bifröst, the Rainbow Bridge that leads from the human world to the gods' home of Asgard. The final battle then begins on a field called Vigrid. Heimdall, god of the rainbow, sounds his horn, and the gods come armed for battle. Thunder god Thor and a monster known as the Midgard-Serpent destroy each other, as do the dog Garm and Tyr, a war- and sky-god considered one of the oldest and most important of the pantheon. Many minor gods also meet their doom. At last, Fenrir the wolf eats Odin, king of the gods, and Odin's mute son Vidar avenges him. Heimdall and the trickster-god Loki also kill each other. The earth is engulfed in flames and then sinks into the sea, to be reborn at a later time.[12]

As I will elaborate in this essay, the apocalypse of Tolkien's Third Age does have certain differences from that of the Icelandic cosmos. The apocalypse is not prophesied, though dark, foreboding rumors circulate in the years leading up to it: the Shire's borders experience a scourge of strange Men and beasts; the Elf and Dwarf populations have begun to scatter or decline. As early as the time of Bilbo's adventures in *The Hobbit*, tales tell of a "Necromancer" gathering forces abroad. Like Fenrir and many of the other Norse monsters, Sauron is a threat long ago subdued but not destroyed, returning to wreak havoc. (While, unlike the Destroyers of the World, he apparently intends only to enslave it, the notion of an inconceivably evil being controlling the Earth is hardly much rosier.) He gathers an equally monstrous menagerie of wraiths, Orcs, Trolls, and wicked Men to do his bidding; as in Norse myth, wolves play a part for evil—Tolkien's intelligent wolflike Wargs, this time, instead of the Old Norse Fenriswulf. The divine powers in Tolkien are represented by the Istari, a race of godlike beings sent to Earth to fight Sauron, but all save Gandalf are lost or corrupted. Gandalf does manage to gather the Free

Peoples of Middle-earth (Elves, Dwarves, Men, and a few Hobbits) to form a coalition against the Dark Lord. As in the *Voluspa*, the evil forces cause the sun to disappear, but it comes back after a day, and the climactic battle takes place on the plain of Cormallen. The good guys win this one, however, and victory is due, not to a coalition of mighty immortals, but in large part to the fortitude of the little Hobbits Frodo Baggins and Samwise Gamgee, who destroy Sauron's great Ring, killing him and scattering or killing his allies.

In his letters J.R.R. Tolkien makes several comments that reveal his close study of the Ragnarök legend. In a letter written as an attempt to convince Milton Waldman of Collins to publish *The Silmarillion*, Tolkien confesses that that book's concluding battle "owes, I suppose, more to the Norse vision of Ragnarök than to anything else, though it is not much like it" (*Letters*, 149). It is not this last battle of the First Age but that of the Third that concerns us here, but this quote does serve to illustrate Tolkien's desire to play with the idea of apocalyptic battles. He also uses the term casually in a letter to his son Christopher to complain about his lifelong pet peeve, industrialization: "If a ragnarök would burn all the slums and gas-works . . . I'd go back to trees" (*Letters*, 96).

Tolkien's lifelong enthusiasm for Norse myth in general and the *Eddas* in particular has been well documented. There is explicit evidence that Tolkien used the *Edda* as inspiration for his literature. In a 1967 letter to W.H. Auden, written to thank him for dedicating his translation of the *Voluspa*[13] to Tolkien, he writes that he will send along in exchange a copy of "a thing I did many years ago when trying to learn the art of alliterative poetry": his own reinterpretation of the part of the *Elder Edda* concerning the Volsungs.[14]

But the *Völsungasaga* was not the only part of the *Edda* that influenced Tolkien. In a letter to a certain Mr. Rang, he reveals that names in both *The Hobbit* and *The Lord of the Rings* trilogy are taken directly from Eddic literature, and specifically that "Mirkwood" Forest, "Gandalf," and nearly all of Tolkien's Dwarf names come from the *Voluspa*.[15] Tolkien also tells of a race of wise immortal beings, "guardians of the world" called the Valar, Vala in the singular. Vala is also the name of the sorceress or Sibyl in the *Voluspa* who foretells the coming of Ragnarök for Odin. The Valar, like Vala herself, are omniscient; in their roles as creators and maintainers of the world they are higher even than the wizards (or Istari), who would be more closely analogous to the gods of Asgard.

Tolkien helped to found an Old Norse reading group called the Kolbítar, which over the years met to read all the chief sagas, with the *Elder Edda* as the concluding work. The membership of this small group consisted of other professors, including C.S. Lewis, whose own *The Last Battle* also contains many themes drawn from both Ragnarök and the Christian understanding of the Apocalypse. Tolkien directed the readings, being the most experienced student of Norse literature in the group, and the fact that he left the *Edda* for the final reading might indicate not only its eschatological nature but also perhaps a special fondness for the work. As a college student in the mid-1910s he had studied Old Norse as a special subject under W.A. Craigie; during this period the young Tolkien first came upon the *Voluspa* and the rest of the *Elder Edda* (*Biography*, 63). Humphrey Carpenter describes the significance of this discovery in his Tolkien biography: "The most remarkable of all Germanic mythological poems, it dates from the very end of Norse heathendom, when Christianity was taking the place of the old gods; yet it imparts a sense of living myth, a feeling of awe and mystery, in its representation of a pagan cosmos. It had a profound appeal to Tolkien's imagination" (*Biography*, 65).

This points to an aspect of Ragnarök myth that is crucial in light of Tolkien's work—its anticipation of the Christian era. Though there is much evidence suggesting that the myth itself had circulated orally among Norsemen for centuries before, the written account in the *Voluspa* only dates to A.D. 1000, 230 years after the first Christian missionaries came to Iceland. The author of the earlier of the two versions of the *Elder Edda*, known as the *Codex Regius*, is believed to be a monk. And both the author of the later version of the *Elder Edda* and Snorri Sturluson, writer of the *Younger*, or *Prose*, *Edda*, were certainly Christians. Therefore, Ragnarök as we have it in these written sources can be seen as an interpretation of the original myth filtered through Christian sensibilities, neither entirely pagan nor completely Christian.

The relevance of Christianity within the myth comes in what happens after Ragnarök: the regeneration, or rebirth, of the world. Though many of the same supernatural beings of the pagan era survive in this new age, the later of the two surviving *Edda* manuscripts, the *Hauksbok*, foreshadows the coming of Christ as the result of Ragnarök: "Then comes a ruler / to keep dominion, a mighty lord / majestic over all."[16] A later edition of this same *Hauksbok*, the *Voluspa hin Skamma*, goes a step further, saying: "Then comes one / who is greater than all / though never his name / do I dare to name; few now see / in the future further than the moment Odin / is to meet the Wolf," and "Rule he orders / and rights he fixes, Laws he ordains / that ever shall live."[17] These veiled references are nowadays considered dubious parts of the *Voluspa*, perhaps added later, and scholars argue over the text's integrity, but whether or not the original author (whatever that means in mythology) intended to refer to Christ's coming is irrelevant here. What *is* important is that the version Tolkien would have read almost ninety years ago did contain these lines.

In addition, many of the interpretative texts on the subject up to Tolkien's time were written from a religious perspective, and their authors did everything possible to legitimize Norse paganism as a subject for good Christians to study. Rasmus Bjorn Anderson's *Norse Mythology* was one of the more prominent of these, a self-described "first complete and systematic presentation of the Norse mythology in the English language," published in the late nineteenth century after Wagner's operas made fashionable all things Teutonic. Anderson presents Ragnarök as an allegory of the literal death of paganism and the conversion of Iceland. It is not stated in any available source if Tolkien ever read this particular book, but given his keen interest and its wide publication it is quite likely, and in any case Anderson's book is representative of a whole slew of similar tracts of the time. Christian faith permeates this work, but it is nonetheless very reverent of the old gods, and Anderson (like the Icelandic bards before him and Tolkien after) tries to reconcile the one God he is supposed to believe in with the many clashing, heroic ones who obviously excite him far more.

It is easy to see how this perspective on Ragnarök must have interested the deeply Catholic Tolkien when he created his own mythology. Tolkien had much the same dilemma as that of Anderson and the monk who transcribed the *Edda*: to tell stories about magical beings whose powers hailed from other sources than the God of his own Christian faith, without openly contradicting myths. Needing to satisfy both his love for the discarded legends of the past and his own deeply held beliefs, Tolkien took a cue from those, like Anderson, who had postulated a pagan-Christian transition and set his own stories in a mythological pre-Christian era: that is, his First, Second, and, most prominently, Third Ages of our "Middle-"earth. The Fourth Age is when Middle-earth becomes the limited, nonmagical world characterized by both Christianity and modern secularism. But the place of Jesus in Tolkien, as in the *Voluspa*, is by implication and anticipation only.

In Iceland and its native myths, the transition in belief, and meta-phorical transfer of power, from Odin and his comrades to the Holy Trinity is paralleled in Tolkien not by the coming of Christianity specifi-cally, but by the rise of Mankind. During the Third Age, Elves, the old-est race of fallen beings, represented the most accomplished and powerful civilization in Middle-earth. At the time represented by *The Lord of the Rings* books, the Elves' decline is already underway, and by the end of the story they are on their way out. In contrast to the Norse gods slaugh-tered at the battle of Ragnarök, most Elves take their leave of Middle-earth voluntarily. Galadriel and Elrond lead the Elves and a select few from other species from the Grey Havens across the Sea to Valinor, leav-ing Man to become the dominant power. As Gandalf says to Aragorn at the end of *The Return of the King*:

> This is your realm, and the heart of the greater realm that shall be. The Third Age of the world is ended, and the new age is begun; and it is your task to order its beginning and to preserve what may be preserved. For though much has been saved, much must now pass away; and the power of the Three Rings also is ended. And all the lands that you see, and those that lie round about them, shall be dwellings of Men. For the time comes of the Dominion of Men, and the Elder Kindred shall fade or depart. (*LR* 6.5, 949–50.)

It is interesting to note that in neither the Regeneration nor the Fourth Age does the new order totally replace the old. In each case some crea-tures survive the mass extinction of fantasy, preserved like enchanted coelacanths as relics of a strange primordial era. Tolkien writes that Hobbits "have become rare and shy . . . [and can] disappear quietly and quickly when large stupid folk like you and me come blundering along" (*H*, 12). There are also, according to both stories, still Dwarves among us. In Tolkien they exist in isolated subterranean pockets or become no-madic, their populations having been decimated by Elves, dragons, and Men, and according to the *Voluspa*, many reside in a golden hall in the Nida Mountains.[18] The Norse giants party eternally in the drinking hall of Brimer,[19] while Tolkien's tree-like Ents linger in Fangorn Forest. Nei-ther the Norse tradition nor Tolkien seems to be able to let go of their magical creatures, each maintaining that a few still exist in our world, hidden either by their own choice or by our unwillingness to believe in them.

By exiling his Elves and other fairy-tale races, Tolkien helps fill in the historical holes between his mythical world and our own modern one, making it a more convincing and thus more absorbing "sub-creation." He also opens up themes of transience, impermanence, destiny, and progress. In the unused epilogue to *The Lord of the Rings* printed in *Sauron Defeated*, Sam Gamgee's daughter says, "Still I think it was very sad when Master Elrond left Rivendell and the Lady left Lórien"; to which Sam replies, "Elves are sad; and that's what makes them so beautiful, and why we can't see much of them."[20] Their sadness comes from their intelligence, their closeness to and yet separation from the higher powers. The Valar have told them of the imminent passing of their earthly civilization; one imagines the Norse gods experiencing a similar fatalistic sorrow when the Vala forecast their destruction.

In their general debt to the myths of the North and specific allusions to the *Voluspa*, their apocalyptic air and not-quite-final clash between good and evil, and their melancholy fin de siècle mood heralding the change to a "new world order," Tolkien's tales of the end of the Third Age of Middle-earth echo the stories of the Norse Ragnarök. An appreciation of this influence on *The Lord of the Rings* adds yet another layer of meaning to the many facets of these exciting and complex works of mythmaking.

Notes

1. "The *Voluspa* and the *Elder Edda* [*sic*] . . . record a cosmology and a theogony in which these ancient people—ancestors of the English—once believed: and like the humans, the gods too are caught in a net of fate, and the end will be the death of the gods in Ragnarök, the Last Battle and the triumph of the Giants." Charles Moseley, *J.R.R. Tolkien* (Plymouth, Eng.: Northcote House Publishers, 1997), 15.

2. "I would like to point out that there is simply no Wagnerian '*Götterdammerung*' in *The Lord of the Rings*; 'Victory neither restores an earthly Paradise nor ushers in New Jerusalem.' . . . Interestingly, Ragnarök was a relatively late aspect of Germano-Scandinavian mythology that never caught on in the pagan Anglo-Saxon England that so influenced Tolkien. Even then, it was, apparently, un-English in its melodrama." See Patrick Curry, *Defending Middle-earth: Tolkien, Myth, and Modernity* (Edinburgh: Floris Books, 1997), 48. This

is a rather pat dismissal; while Tolkien was always (a bit too?) eager to deny all Wagnerian influence on his work, he was familiar, and undeniably enamored with, the composer's same source material, as proven below. Nor is a Ragnarök model excluded because Middle-earth does not become Paradise; the Norse idea of Regeneration, as we shall see, does not necessarily imply the "New Jerusalem" of the end of the Christian era but, in some sense, that era's beginning.

3. "The fate of the immortals is [like Men's] bleak. In Norse mythology, the old gods . . . battled against the monsters at Ragnarök and were slain. In *The Lord of the Rings*, the Elves flee from Middle-earth taking with them their high artistic, aesthetic, and scientific aspects. . . . The verb doomed summarizes the situation: the world will be less lovely, less enchanting, less exciting, yet man's fate is to remain in it." Gloriana St. Clair, "An Overview of the Northern Influences on Tolkien's Works" in *Proceedings of the J.R.R. Tolkien Centenary Conference 1992*, ed. Patricia Reynolds and Glen H. GoodKnight (Milton Keynes, Eng.: Mythopoeic Press, 1995), 66.

4. Ruth S. Noel, *The Mythology of Middle-earth* (Boston: Houghton Mifflin, 1977), 101.

5. "The Balrog's conflict with Gandalf, producing earthquakes and storms among the mountains, reflects the elemental combat of Ragnarök. The outcome is similar as well, with the powerful wizard destroyed in overthrowing his enemy, but returned to life in a higher form" (Noel, *Mythology of Middle-earth*, 147). Interestingly, and in contrast with the mainstream of Old Norse/Tolkien criticism exemplified by Marjorie Burns's "Gandalf and Odin" essay (in *Tolkien's "Legendarium": Essays on "The History of Middle-earth,"* edited by Verlyn Flieger and Carl F. Hostetter [Westport, Conn., and London: Greenwood Press, 2000], 219–31), Noel identifies the chief god of the Norse religion with Tolkien's Dark Lord: "It may seem ironic that . . . Sauron and the Nazgul . . . resemble the god Odin and his faithful emissaries. However, by the time of the final battle of Ragnarök, Odin, like Sauron, was doomed, and the gods themselves had become corrupt and violent" (Noel, *Mythology of Middle-earth*, 147).

It is true that Sauron, like Odin, was the fearsome commander of the losing side, but whether the Aesir had been in decline or not, no one would dare to claim that Surt and Loki's Destroyers of the World take on a heroic role the way the members of the Fellowship of the Ring do. It may be that the discrepancy between Tolkien's Christian morality and his tale's pagan trappings dictates this difference: he requires at least an approximation of "good versus evil" as opposed to the Vikings' world-weary "bad versus worse" ethic (expressed also in the bleak, hopeless scenarios of their heroic sagas). However, the Ragnarök story as we have it today can hardly be said to be purely "pagan," and just like Tolkien's War of the Ring, the Norse eschatology paves the way for a brighter "new world order."

6. Several times throughout his book (*The Road to Middle-earth* [Boston: Houghton Mifflin, 1983]), Shippey cites a strain of the Germanic temperament he calls the "Ragnarök spirit," which it turns out is not entirely admirable: "In

1936 Tolkien had warned the British Academy that the Ragnarök spirit had survived Thórr and Óthinn, could 'revive even in our own times . . . martial heroism as its own end.' He was quite literally correct in this" (147). Shippey, and presumably Tolkien, refers here to Adolf Hitler's rise to power and subsequent suicidal war making. As we shall see, however, Tolkien's myths redeem this "never die" spirit by infusing it with an ethic of Christian humility.

7. J.R. Wytenbroek, "Apocalyptic Vision in *The Lord of the Rings*," *Mythlore* 54 (summer 1988), 7–12, here, 11.

8. For instance, the recurring appearance of evil, monstrous wolves.

9. This is another popular theme in eschatological myth, one apt example being the Hindu notion of the terrible "Kali Yuga" age (which is, of course, our own era).

10. From the *Edda*, trans. by Rasmus Bjorn Anderson, in *Norse Mythology* (Chicago: S.C. Griggs, 1879; London: Trubner, 1879), 416.

11. Anderson, 417.

12. Anderson, 416–27.

13. *The Song of the Sibyl*, in the collection *Norse Poems*, trans. W.H. Auden and P.B. Taylor; available online at http://www.asatru.org/voluspa.html.

14. Auden and Taylor, 379.

15. Auden and Taylor, 383; William H. Green, *"The Hobbit" and Other Fiction by J.R.R Tolkien* (Ann Arbor, Mich.: University Microfilms, 1970), 46–51.

16. Brian Branston, *Gods of the North* (New York: Vanguard Press, 1955), 289.

17. Branston, 289–91.

18. Anderson, 430.

19. Anderson, 434.

20. J.R.R. Tolkien, *Sauron*, 115.

Chapter 12

GATHERED ROUND NORTHERN FIRES

The Imaginative Impact of the Kolbítar

ANDREW LAZO

In order to trace the origins of J.R.R. Tolkien's achievement in *The Lord of the Rings*, we must trace back what Carl F. Hostetter and Arden R. Smith have rightly called "a mythology for England,"[1] back past the books themselves and their concomitant histories, past Tolkien's extraordinary devotion and diligence in crafting the tales, all the way back to the foundations that not only allowed such mythmaking but also in some ways forced Tolkien to create the legends of Middle-earth. To accurately map out these origins, we must look past even the Inklings and explore the importance of the Kolbítar, the Old Norse reading group that Tolkien founded in 1926 and that devoted itself to translating the *Eddas* and the sagas. In Old Norse, "Kolbítar" (literally, "Coalbiters") were men who gathered close enough to the fire to bite the coals as they told over the old tales. How did this group come about? Who were its members? And what effect did both the myths and the men of the Kolbítar come to have on the most important mythopoeia of the twentieth century? In this essay I shall examine how Norse myth came to play such an important role in Tolkien's creation and how these legends led Tolkien and C.S. Lewis into a friendship that fundamentally altered and shaped both the lives of these two Oxford medievalists and their immeasurably popular and influential imaginative writings. In order to do so, I shall look briefly at the question of language before turning to the process by which the Kolbítar inevitably formed. Finally, I shall draw some conclusions about the dynamics and accomplishments of the group, making a claim that I find as certain as it is absent from much of the current discourse regarding Tolkien's creation.

Today, little doubt can remain concerning the importance of Old Norse language and literature to the fiction of J.R.R. Tolkien and, to a lesser extent, C.S. Lewis. Rather than trod over ground already well covered, I defer to the published and varied work of my betters to defend the claim that a love of "Northerness" played a vital role in Tolkien's creation of Middle-earth.[2]

However, I shall briefly pause to explore such a claim in Lewis's Narnia books. While Lewis shows an almost gleeful indiscrimination in drawing from mythological and fairy-story elements in peopling his imaginative world, I suggest that a love of things Norse informs many elements of Lewis's stories.

Perhaps the most obviously linguistic reference to Old Norse appears in *Out of the Silent Planet*, the first of Lewis's "Interplanetary Romances." In the novel, Lewis's hero, philologist Elwyn Ransom, finds himself kidnapped and taken to Mars, known to its inhabitants as "Malacandra." Ransom there meets three races of beings, having the most contact with a seven-foot-tall creature who later identifies himself as a "hross," one of the "hrossa."[3] According to Eric V. Gordon, *hross* means "horse,"[4] a word Lewis would doubtless have known by the time he wrote his book, which he finished in September 1937,[5] just four years after the dissolution of the Kolbítar. In comparison, Tolkien finished writing *The Hobbit* a year earlier, in 1936. One may safely assume that the legacy of all the Norse literature both men had read still lingered fresh in their minds.

To more fully perceive the effect of Norse myth on Lewis's fiction though, we must turn to the Narnian books, which Lewis wrote from about the end of 1948 to 1953, including a remarkably creative period from the summer of 1948 to the spring of 1951 during which he wrote five of the seven *Chronicles*.[6] While Lewis drew on a wide range of mythologies in creating his tales, Norse myth in particular features prominently in several passages, as it does in Tolkien's work. Lewis, however, took an approach quite dissimilar from that of Tolkien, an approach at once much more inclusive and much less deliberate. While Tolkien's work highlights the product of his years of carefully compiling the histories, genealogies, and philologies of his imaginary world, Lewis's creation originated instead from a relatively short burst of inspiration from a mind full of ideas he wanted to include.

Among those ideas, "Northerness" featured prominently. While many have rightly pointed to elements of Christian myth in the Narniad, fewer acknowledge the important role of Greek and Roman myths. Nearly no one, however, has looked carefully and in depth at the prevalence of Norse myth in the *Chronicles*. This I find extremely puzzling, given the weight Lewis assigned in his writings to the old Germanic tales. Indeed, one might quite profitably set aside the rather obvious Christian elements in favor of the others in light of the claim Lewis made regarding the various myths: "If Christianity is only a mythology, then I find the mythology I believe in is not the one I like best. I like Greek mythology much better: Irish better still: Norse best of all."[7] Because Narnia serves in some ways as home to such a variety of myth and fairy tale, we might well expect to find Norse myth significantly present there. And, in fact, we do.

As Paul Ford has insightfully suggested, Lewis appears to have created a kind of opposition of mythologies, turning to Norse and Celtic sources for many of his evil characters, while looking to the Greek and Christian myths for the forces of good.[8] One, of course, must proceed upon this generalization keeping fully in mind Lewis's consistent practice of treating groups of creatures as distinct members with individual consciences, to whom Lewis invariably offers many opportunities to come right.

Chief among these evil Narnians directly imported from Norse myth is Fenris Ulf, "a huge gray wolf, captain of the White Witch's secret police."[9] Obviously, Lewis refers to the wolf Fenriswulf (or "Fenrir"), whom Loki begot on the giantess Angrboda.[10] Of the wolf, Snorri Sturluson says, "[I]t howls horribly and saliva runs from its mouth."[11] Lewis, too, focuses on the wolf's "great red mouth,"[12] which he uses for "snapping and snarling" and from which he issues a "howl of anger" when attacked.[13] Orknies, which Ford defines merely as "monsters," also take their place among the White Witch's ghastly army, but Ford suggests a link with "Ogres" and helpfully points us to Tolkien's Orcs, lest we had missed that connection.[14] We also find Ettins among the ranks, creatures Ford claims are giants that Lewis employs to "evoke the flavor of ancient times in England and Northern Europe."[15]

We might do well not to pass over this reference to ancient England. Although we must not expand this forum to explore the intriguing ways both Tolkien and Lewis made use of legends from Old English, certainly we might briefly mention *Beowulf*, whose influence on both men I have touched on elsewhere.[16] The poem had a sufficiently lasting effect on Lewis and Tolkien to merit an article in itself. For our purposes, we shall examine only one line from the poem as an earnest of future exploration. Without a doubt, the setting of the poem in medieval Scandinavia merits its inclusion, however brief.

Line 112 makes up a list of nefarious creatures, "eotenas ond ylfe ond orcneas," which Seamus Heaney translates as "ogres and elves and evil phantoms,"[17] while H.R. Ellis Davidson prefers "trolls and elves and monsters."[18] Certainly, these three monsters in *Beowulf* become at least one source—perhaps even the source from which he transliterated—for Lewis's Ettins and Orknies; they also relate at least in part to Tolkien's Elves and Orcs.

Where and when did Tolkien and Lewis's mutual interest in Norse myth begin? Let us consider the former first. One can trace the development of Tolkien's interest in "Northerness" with little difficulty, for it evidenced itself in four aspects. Tolkien's devotion to Northern legends and their language began in childhood, continued as a schoolboy, and in time developed into a scholarly concern. Norse language and myth also provided inspiration for Tolkien's early creative efforts.

As a child, Tolkien's mother, Mabel, proved a key factor in promoting this early interest. She kept him supplied with storybooks, including Andrew Lang's multicolored books of fairy tales. Tolkien first encountered the story of the dragon Fafnir's slaying at the hands of Sigurd, "the best story he ever read," in the *Red Fairy Book* (*Biography*, 22). About this time (age six or seven), Tolkien began to write a story about a "green great dragon," a phrase his mother inexplicably corrected to "a great green dragon" (*Letters*, 214, 221). Tolkien "from early days" found himself deeply affected by Scandinavian and Germanic legends (*Letters*, 144), and here too his mother provided genuine help, giving Tolkien his first lessons in German, and fostering in him an interest in etymology and Germanic languages (*Letters*, 344).

Apart from Mabel's language training and Lang's fairy tales, another author proved of signal importance to Tolkien's developing taste for tales from the North. After discovering the story of Sigurd and Fafnir in the pages of Lang's *Red Fairy Book*, Tolkien went on to explore the story further in William Morris's translation of the *Völsungasaga*. Indeed, that translation, along with Morris's romance *The House of the*

Wolfings, was among the few books Tolkien purchased with money from the Skeat Prize for English he won in the spring of 1914, while at King Edward's School, Birmingham (*Biography*, 69). Morris certainly made a deep impression on the teenaged Tolkien, for later that same year in a letter to his future wife, Edith Bratt, Tolkien describes his plans to write "a short story somewhat on the lines of Morris's romances" (*Letters*, 14). In his article about the Old Norse and Old English elements in Tolkien's work, Jonathan Evans asserts that Tolkien "no doubt means in general *The Roots of the Mountains*, *The House of the Wolfings*, and *The Story of the Glittering Plain*."[19] Evans goes on to trace carefully the lineage of the Sigurd story from Lang, through Morris's 1876 *Volsung* translation, and back to the original twelfth-century written version of the saga, a lineage Tolkien soon followed for himself.[20]

Almost a half-century after buying the Morris books with his prize money, Tolkien, not known for crediting other authors as sources for his own stories, confesses his debt to *The Roots of the Mountains* and *The House of the Wolfings* as his inspiration for the Dead Marshes in *The Lord of the Rings* (*Letters*, 303).

With his childhood discovery of the Sigurd legend in the *Red Fairy Book* and his later explorations into Morris's works, Tolkien's enthusiasm blossomed, and he continued to pursue his interests in things Northern as a schoolboy in Birmingham. While at King Edward's School in his midteens, Tolkien turned to Anglo-Saxon to learn about the roots of English. This led in turn to his early scholarly forays into still older languages, and Humphrey Carpenter records that during his school days in Birmingham Tolkien "taught himself the Norse language and began to read the myths and sagas in their original words."[21]

Not content merely to enjoy his devotion to Norse legend in private, Tolkien soon began to share his discoveries with his friends, recounting "horrific episodes from the Norse *Völsungasaga*" (*Biography*, 46) to the recently founded T.C.B.S., a small tea-drinking society composed of Tolkien and a few friends, to which we shall return. This informal retelling soon gave way to a more scholarly approach, for in 1911 Tolkien "read a paper to the school Literary Society on Norse sagas, illustrating it with readings in the original language" (*Biography*, 49), an event that unmistakably anticipates the advent of the Kolbítar as well as that of the Inklings.

Tolkien's commitment to the language and legend of the dragon stories that had captivated him in childhood and during his school days not only followed him to his undergraduate years at Oxford; they nearly cost him his opportunity to study there. He later reminisced to a correspondent that he was "interested in traditional tales (especially those concerning dragons); and writing (not reading) verse and metrical devices. These things began to flow together when I was an undergraduate to the despair of my tutors and near-wrecking of my career" (*Letters*, 345). Indeed, indulging his passion for languages (besides of course Old Icelandic, Tolkien's "special subject," and English) cost him a first-class degree, for he was able only to rise to a second in Honour Moderations. Moving into a course of study of English language and literature allowed him to indulge his tastes more, and he later took a first-class degree in that subject (*Biography*, 62–63, 77).

Following his military service, in 1918 Tolkien joined the staff of the *New English Dictionary* and became a reader in English literature at Leeds in 1920 (*Biography*, 98–102). Both these tasks allowed him to pursue his now scholarly interests in Old Norse (among other languages), and they introduced to Tolkien men soon to feature prominently in his study of Icelandic. When he arrived at the offices of the dictionary, Tolkien joined C.T. Onions, who had been working there since 1895.[22] At Leeds, he began working with George S. Gordon, professor of English at that school since 1913.[23] After Tolkien had been at Leeds for two years, E.V. Gordon joined him on staff in 1922, and sometime around 1924 the two founded the Viking Club, which I shall discuss in greater detail in the section on clubs (*Biography*, 104, 105). Clearly, though, for most of his life into his late twenties, Tolkien cultivated a profound taste for reading and writing Norse legends, while beginning to develop a circle of fellow enthusiasts in the subject.

Like Tolkien, C.S. Lewis had an early and growing passion for Northerness, and like Tolkien, we can trace the development of this passion from childhood, through his schoolboy days, and into early scholarship, noting also a creative component relating to Norse myth. Indeed, in some ways Lewis makes the case a good deal easier for us in his spiritual autobiography *Surprised by Joy*, wherein he devotes several pages to the impact the legends had upon him. We find another great help in his *Collected Letters*. Volume 1 covers the years from 1905 to 1931 and serves as a bibliographic trace of the breadth and extent of Lewis's reading as a boy and as a young man. Unfortunately, these two sources give us only scattered hints about his early childhood, although at age seventeen he did indicate that he had read Lang with great pleasure, remarking that he found him "always charming whatever he does."[24] One can assume this included at least some of Lang's work on fairy tales.

References in Lewis's early letters to the books he read prove unusually helpful in tracing many interests, among them his early excursions into the realm of Northern myth. Lewis came from an extraordinarily bookish household, and in one memorable passage in his autobiography he claimed, "I had always the same certainty of finding a book that was new to me as a man who walks into a field has of finding a new blade of grass."[25]

He certainly took advantage of this field of books, presumably as a child and certainly as a schoolboy. At age eight or nine, sometime around 1907, Lewis discovered two poems that crashed into his imagination with immense force. Longfellow's *Saga of King Olaf* he encountered first, and the story greatly pleased him,[26] but when he discovered Longfellow's translation of Esias Tegner's *Drapa*—especially in the lament "Balder the Beautiful / Is dead, is dead!"—Lewis found himself "instantly . . . uplifted into huge regions of northern sky, [desiring] with almost sickening intensity something never to be described (except that it is cold, spacious, severe, pale, and remote)."[27]

The experience plunged Lewis into what he would later term his "Norse Complex," which included "Old Icelandic, [Richard] Wagner's *Ring* . . . and [William] Morris."[28] Parallel to the way in which Tolkien's early interest was primarily linguistic and grew along those lines, Lewis's fascination with the mythic aspect of Norse legend similarly developed throughout his childhood and during his days at school.

After Tegner and Longfellow, Lewis first came to the story of Siegfried through Arthur Rackham's illustrations of Wagner's *Ring* cycle. When he was about thirteen, Lewis chanced to see an advertisement for Wagner's *Siegfried and the Twilight of the Gods*, and although he did not know who Siegfried or even Wagner was, Lewis found himself engulfed by "pure Northerness."[29] Synopses of Wagner's Ring cycle from a gramophone catalog thrust Lewis into the world of Wagnerian music and Norse myth, and, just as Tolkien had done, Lewis responded to his reading with a creative effort of his own, beginning to write "a heroic poem on the Wagnerian version of the Niblung story."[30] He intended *Loki Bound* as an opera, and before he abandoned it Lewis had filled thirty-two notebook pages with the poem and written a libretto of the work for an opera he envisioned his friend Arthur Greeves composing.[31] Greeves was an important partner for Lewis, for their shared passion for Norse myth defined much of their early friendship.

While at Oxford in 1920, Lewis reminisced that in those days of his early teens, "everything to do with Norse lore was honey to me."[32] Greeves not only shared this taste but also provided for Lewis a lasting model of friendship, as Lewis would later describe it in *The Four Loves*.[33] Lewis's ideas about and experience of friendship very much consisted in finding someone else with whom to share one's great passions. When one discovers another with such similar interests, Lewis claimed, this revelatory experience leads to a feeling that after friends meet and identify each other "they stand together in an immense solitude."[34] Lewis identifies this sense of friendship with Greeves—as they huddled over a copy of *Myths of the Norsemen*—as the astonishing discovery of one's first friend,[35] and his experience with Greeves became a model for his later friendship with Tolkien, gathered around a text full of Northern myths that both men loved. The Kolbítar provided both means and grounds for this friendship of shared passion to grow strong between the two.

While Tolkien and Lewis disagreed concerning the value of Wagner as a transmitter of Norse legend, they certainly both held Morris in high regard. Perhaps because language interested him more than myth, Tolkien denied much influence by Wagner, "whose interpretation of the myths he held in contempt" (*Biography*, 46). However, regarding the power of Old Icelandic and Morris, the other two elements in Lewis's "complex," Tolkien and Lewis found themselves in complete accord.

In 1914, Lewis ordered a copy of Morris's lyric poem *Sigurd the Volsung*, and this seems to have opened a floodgate of interest in Morris's work, for over the next three years, Lewis read "nearly all of Morris," including his translation of the *Laxdœla* saga.[36] Lewis also delighted in *The Roots of the Mountains*, which, as we have seen, was also an early Tolkien favorite.[37] The Norse element of Morris's romances appealed to the schoolboy Lewis, and as he began to read Morris's source for the book, the *Laxdœla* saga itself, he admitted he found that "the primitive type is far better than Morris's reproduction."[38] By stating this preference, Lewis shows how his childhood and schoolboy interest in Northerness began to lead him to its sources and to Old Norse language, much as it had for Tolkien. Although as a schoolboy he exulted in "the merely intellectual satisfaction of getting to know the Eddaic universe," he goes on to note, "[I]f I could at this time have found anyone to teach me Old Norse I believe I would have worked at it very hard."[39] About ten years later, Lewis found just such a teacher in Tolkien, and he evidently did indeed work very hard at the language as he prepared for the Kolbítar.

Soon Lewis's "first delight in Valhalla and Valkyries began to turn itself . . . into a scholar's interest in them."[40] As I have mentioned, for Lewis such interests often formed the center of lasting friendships, and their shared interest in Old Norse served to prepare Lewis for his friendship with Tolkien a few years later, which, to a large extent, developed and grew within the context of the Kolbítar. The formation of this group seems inevitable, given their shared interest and their long history of founding and participating in a variety of literary and intellectual clubs and societies. The timing appears particularly appropriate in the professional lives of Tolkien and Lewis. Both men had seen their love for things Norse mature into a scholarly interest. Both men also, thanks to the deliberate assistance of future Coalbiter George S. Gordon, had recently acquired the academic positions that would define the early part of their careers, would provide the intellectual environment for their important early scholarly work, and would foster a creative climate, the Inklings, wherein their most famous works would find their first critically accepting audience. But before the Inklings became the club that in many ways characterized the careers of Tolkien and Lewis, both men had involved themselves with a large number of such clubs and societies, activities that would lead directly to their participation in the Coalbiters.

Several elements in most of the clubs to which Tolkien belonged, both as a student at King Edward School and as an undergraduate at Oxford, point directly toward the Kolbítar and its successor, the Inklings. We can trace Tolkien's interests in writing, language, and Norse myth in much of his club involvement. While a schoolboy, Tolkien presented a paper on the sagas to the Literary Society (*Biography*, 49), and he amazed his classmates in the Debate Society by holding debates or making presentations alternately in Latin, Greek, Old English, and even Gothic (*Biography*, 48). In his school days, Tolkien certainly chose clubs that allowed him to indulge his several interests.

He continued this pattern of social involvement while an undergraduate at Oxford, participating in the Essay Club (along with future Inkling Hugo Dyson and future Inkling and Kolbítar Nevill Coghill), the Dialectical Society, and Stapeldon, the college debating society. He also founded his first club, the Apolausticks, whose members devoted themselves to papers, discussions, and debates (*Biography*, 53). Here again we see the element of the Kolbítar and the later Inklings taking form, especially in the Apolausticks. In this group we find Tolkien as the central figure in a little society with composition as its object, elements that would appear later in the clubs with which Tolkien involved himself.

Beginning a club of his own and participating in several other societies certainly prepared Tolkien for founding, along with E. V. Gordon, the Viking Club not long after arriving at Leeds. Club members engaged in reading sagas and singing comic songs (*Biography*, 105). Again, in the Viking Club Tolkien brought together many elements common to both the Kolbítar and the Inklings. In the Viking Club also we note the dynamic pattern of membership that continued to develop, ultimately reaching a final stage in the Inklings. In some sense, with one exception we may see the clubs that Tolkien founded or joined as precursors for both the Apolausticks and the Viking Club, which in turn themselves provided models for their successors, the Kolbítar and the Inklings.

While all of these various groups represented Tolkien's scholarly interests, one of the first clubs to which Tolkien belonged had a far deeper impact emotionally and creatively. While at King Edward's School in 1911, Tolkien and friends Christopher Wiseman and Rob Gilson formed the Tea Club, Barrovian Society (T.C.B.S.), later adding Geoffrey Smith to their number. Originally made up of four schoolboys taking their tea together, the club became the source of one of Tolkien's most enduring friendships, that with Christopher Wiseman. Tolkien also received from the T.C.B.S. the kind of encouragement he depended on throughout his career in order to confidently pursue and complete his own imaginative writing. Of all Tolkien's clubs, the T.C.B.S. occupied an extraordinary place for him personally and spiritually. What made the T.C.B.S. so unique? I believe two elements in the Society had particular effect on Tolkien's later experience with his own writing and with groups, and that the Kolbítar's lack of these two elements provided an impetus for the founding of the Inklings, Tolkien's last real club.

First, the T.C.B.S. centered itself around deep friendships rather than around literary interests. While a literary element eventually became important to the group, those letters of encouragement between members that survive describe heartfelt concern for each other and contain the ardent, almost desperate passion that the deepest of friends often carry for one another. We find evidence of this kind of love in the relationship between Tolkien and Wiseman. Tolkien named his son Christopher after Wiseman (*Letters*, 395), and in Tolkien's last published letter to Wiseman, written in May of 1973, some four months before his death, Tolkien recalls their days in the club more than sixty years earlier, signing the letter with the initials "TCBS." under his signature (*Letters*, 429). At the very end of his last published letter, written four days before his death, Tolkien speaks to his daughter of his desire to visit Wiseman (*Letters*, 432). Thus the T.C.B.S. provided for Tolkien his longest-standing friendship. I believe that during their years together first as Coalbiters and then as Inklings, Tolkien sought from C.S. Lewis a closeness such as he had prized so highly from the members of the T.C.B.S.

Second, the T.C.B.S. provided for Tolkien a sense of high vocation along with the solid encouragement on which Tolkien always depended in approaching his own writing. Just before all four members of the society began their military service, the T.C.B.S. met for its final time at Wiseman's home in London during one December weekend in 1914. In some ways, the sense of mission and purpose regarding his creative work that endured for the rest of his life stems from these few days spent with his old friends. During the "Council of London," the group decided that Tolkien should definitely pursue his poetry in order to achieve the "greatness" for which the members of the T.C.B.S. felt themselves destined (*Letters*, 9). Tolkien emerged from the weekend feeling as though he had found his calling, a vocation charged with aspirations to great accomplishment. Nearly two years later, upon hearing the news that Rob Gilson had died in battle, Tolkien reflected to Geoffrey Smith that, even in light of that devastating loss:

> I cannot abandon yet the hope and ambitions (inchoate and cloudy I know) that first became conscious at the Council of London. That Council was . . . followed in my own case with my finding a voice for all kinds of pent up things and a tremendous opening up of everything for me: I have always laid that to the credit of the inspiration that even a few hours with the four always brought to all of us. (*Letters*, 10)

Tolkien not only found his voice within the context of the T.C.B.S.; he also gained from it a sense of high purpose and mission, even of religious vision, that would later come to characterize C.S. Lewis's work much more than it would Tolkien's. Earlier in the same letter, he remarked that he believed that the members of the group were called or destined to a "greatness." Tolkien explained to Smith:

> The greatness I meant was that of a great instrument in God's hands—a mover, a doer, even an achiever of great things, a beginner at the very least of large things. . . . I meant . . . that the T.C.B.S. had been granted some spark of fire—certainly as a body if not singly—that was destined to kindle a new light, or what is the same thing, to rekindle an old light in the world; that the T.C.B.S. was destined to testify for God and Truth in a more direct way than even by laying down its several lives in the war. (*Letters*, 9, 10)

I believe that this astounding and even evangelistic sense of calling informed the rest of Tolkien's life and certainly underlies his creative work, submerged to the point of near invisibility though it might be. Nevertheless, the T.C.B.S. impressed upon Tolkien the importance of deep friendships and a sense that a holy vocation pervaded life and his writing. This context immeasurably helps us to understand Tolkien's claim that in writing *The Lord of the Rings* he was creating "of course a fundamentally religious and Catholic work; unconsciously so at first, but consciously in the revision" (*Letters*, 172). While his religious purposiveness may appear anomalous to the popular image of Tolkien the fantasist, such a religious vocation certainly makes sense if we view Tolkien as the literary light bearer of the T.C.B.S. In many ways we find in the T.C.B.S. a kind of fervor usually reserved for missionary societies, and, as we shall later observe, Tolkien did indeed "do the work of an evangelist" in offering Lewis a tenable and mythopoeic perspective on Christianity that led directly to the latter's conversion. This event, I believe, singularly shaped the later careers of both men, and the Kolbítar provided the grounds for the development of their far-reaching friendship, within which Tolkien and Lewis communicated to each other ideas essential to both men's thought and work.

In contrast to Tolkien, Lewis had virtually no experiences with clubs and societies as a schoolboy. While Tolkien seemed to fit quite well into the social structure of the King Edward School, Lewis had quite a different experience with the English public school system. His biographer and close friend, George Sayer, has remarked that Lewis "was quite un-suited to the stifling atmosphere of his boarding schools."[41] Three fac-tors lent themselves to this unsuitability. Lewis himself points to the first of these: "I was big for my age, a great lout of a boy . . . [and] useless at games."[42] Part of this uselessness stemmed from a physical impairment he shared with both his brother and his father: although they all appar-ently had the main joint in their thumbs, it would not bend.[43] This clum-siness, along with his admitted great loutishness, made Lewis a poor choice for games, on which so much of the social success in the English public school system depended. Lewis relished his role of a skeptic and an outspoken outsider and at this point proved himself a skillful mocker of those boys most in the center of school society. An old schoolmate remembered Lewis as "a bit of a rebel" and an accomplished mimic, characteristics that contributed to Lewis's being "an abnormal boy" out-side the social structure—and which, along with his bitter wit, made Lewis "riotously amusing."[44] In contrast, Tolkien found it far easier to make friends while at school, in part because of his participation in sports, having been a house-captain of the rugby team one year and gaining his colors the next (*Letters*, 22). Lewis had neither the inclination nor the determination for such achievements.

Second, Lewis's extraordinary intellectual abilities worked to set him apart from the crowd, and until he came to Oxford, he had found the kind of intellectual community that best suited him among his elders rather than with his classmates. Recognizing the failure of the public school, Lewis's father withdrew him and sent him for three years to prepare for Oxford with a private tutor, W.T. Kirkpatrick, who proved to be precisely the rational and learned mentor that suited Lewis best, and under whose rigorous tutelage Lewis flourished.[45] Kirkpatrick, recog-nizing astounding abilities in his charge, commended the young Lewis to his father, Albert, for his "maturity," his "originality," and his "unerr-ing instinct" for literary quality.[46] Kirkpatrick also praised Lewis for his facility with Latin and Greek, comparing his extraordinary classical abili-ties with those of Joseph Addison and Thomas Macaulay, saying, "[T]hese are people we read of, but I have never met any."[47] Such talents isolated Lewis, throwing him into circles of older and more serious men, in whose company he thrived. Small wonder, then, that when Tolkien formed the Kolbítar Lewis would be such an ideal member because of the group's composition as well as its subject matter.

Finally, perhaps because he set himself outside whatever clubbable society he found available to him in his school days, Lewis came to regard inner rings with intense suspicion. In *Transposition and Other Addresses*, he published an essay defining and decrying an "Inner Ring," and later he memorably portrayed their sinister qualities in the N.I.C.E. (National Institute for Co-ordinated Experiments) of *That Hideous Strength*.[48] Indeed, throughout his fiction, many of the most villainous characters are or were schoolboy brutes from inner rings. The main purpose of such groups seems to be to allay "the terror of being outside" and to support "the lust for the esoteric."[49] Lewis had no use for such cliques, preferring instead to draw a circle of enthusiasts or amateurs around their favorite subjects, subjects that were inevitably literary for Lewis. He goes so far as to define friendship itself as a group where "we three or four or five are all travelers on the same quest, have all a common vision," and would gladly welcome others of like mind.[50] While Lewis's more Arthurian description lacks the overtly religious charge of Tolkien's T.C.B.S., there nevertheless appears to both men a preference for friendship in small groups charged with a high calling and a noble purpose. Once Lewis arrived at Oxford, he began to discover societies that suited him exactly and plunged into the new opportunities Oxford gave him. Three clubs in particular deserve special notice: the Martlets, the Mermaid Club, and the Michaelmas Club.

Lewis joined the Martlets in January 1919, not long after returning from military service.[51] This exclusive club consisted of twelve undergraduate members who read papers to the group and also invited others in to read. One such guest was Edward Tangye Lean, original founder of the Inklings. Lewis threw himself into the club, becoming its secretary within a month of his admission and serving as the club's president from 15 October 1919 to 13 June 1921.[52] Small wonder that once Lewis found an inner ring both intellectual and inviting, he quickly became a central figure.

Lewis had also accepted in June of 1926 an invitation to join the Mermaid Club.[53] Here, too, little time passed before Lewis began to take a very active role in the group, which began in 1902 and was devoted to reading Elizabethan and post-Elizabethan drama.[54] He became president of the club in December of 1927, perhaps more out of a sense of obligation than anything else, for he found the undergraduate members distasteful in the extreme and reserved for them privately an unusual ration of vituperation. In diary entries for February 1927, he called them "vulgar and strident . . . a mere collection of barbarians . . . swine . . . rabble . . . sons of Belial."[55] He concluded that "they are nothing but a drinking, guffawing cry of barbarians with hardly any taste among them, and I wish I hadn't joined them: but I don't see my way out now."[56] Perhaps he found three ways out: first, by taking over the presidency of the Mermaids; second, by founding his own club of undergraduates; and third, by joining the society of the Kolbítar and later the Inklings, thus surrounding himself, as he was so fond of doing, with men of similar intellectual ability and taste. Thus, in all his several and varied involvements, we see Lewis, like Tolkien, beginning to assume increasingly important positions in intellectual societies and clubs.

I believe that, among other motivations, Lewis's frustration with the constituency of some of his clubs along with his inclination toward taking a central role in a society of devotees to literature prompted him late in 1928 to form the Michaelmas Club. Lewis and Magdalen history don Bruce McFarlane, also a Kolbítar, founded a club where undergraduates read papers to each other, very much in the spirit of Tolkien's Apolausticks and, eventually, in the spirit of the Inklings. Much like Tolkien's Viking Club, the Michaelmas Club focused primarily on undergraduates and provided for Lewis the opportunity to take a central role in founding a literary society. Lewis and McFarlane found this task all the more difficult, however, because such societies had been prohibited at Magdalen College until a few years earlier by the previous president, Sir Thomas Herbert Warren.[57] However, under the presidency from 1928 to 1942 of George S. Gordon, the intellectual climate at Magdalen College began to better suit Lewis.

So we find Tolkien and Lewis taking increasingly central roles in clubs and choosing for their memberships men with whom they had much in common in terms of literary taste, intellectual abilities, and, certainly, manners. This social climate led Tolkien to form the Kolbítar and to choose as its members a fascinating blend of both his contemporaries and his immediate superiors. I believe that the promise of a gathering that combined friendship with intellectual exploration of a much-loved subject as inexorably drew Tolkien to found the Kolbítar as it drew Lewis to join it.

Membership in the Kolbítar represented a wide range of Oxford scholarship; it was evenly divided between older members, some of whom had filled key mentorship roles for Tolkien and Lewis, and younger members, closer contemporaries to Tolkien and Lewis (see Appendix B: "Kolbítar Roster"). Of the ten members, five were professors and the other five dons or readers; about half could read Old Norse, while the others stumbled their way through. Humphrey Carpenter describes a typical meeting this way:

> Tolkien, who was of course expert in the language and knew the text well, would improvise a perfect translation of perhaps a dozen pages. Then Dawkins and others who had a working knowledge of Icelandic would translate perhaps a page each. Then the beginners—Lewis, Coghill, Bryson and the others—would work their way through no more than a paragraph or two, and might have to call on Tolkien for help in a difficult passage.[58]

In this description, however, Carpenter fails to mention the two senior members of the Kolbítar who, I believe, exhibited two vital, albeit very different kinds of influence on Tolkien and Lewis. For several reasons, one must not overlook the roles that C.T. Onions and George S. Gordon played in the lives of both men. Specifically, Gordon repeatedly acted behind the scenes to secure academic positions for both Tolkien and Lewis, while Onions served as an intellectual light to them.

George S. Gordon often appeared on the scene at crucial moments for both Tolkien and Lewis. More "an organizer than a scholar" (*Biography*, 102), Gordon proved extremely solicitous of Tolkien, who called Gordon "the very master of men" (*Letters*, 56). Tolkien credits Gordon's "far-sighted policy" in his role as head of the English department at Leeds for his post, his relatively high salary, and the free hand Gordon afforded him as reader in English literature (*Letters*, 56–57). One may easily assume that Gordon took an active interest in the selection of Tolkien as his successor when he left Leeds to return to Oxford to become Merton Professor of English Literature in 1922. Gordon certainly made his influence felt three years later by supporting Tolkien's 1925 election to the Rawlinson and Bosworth Chair in Anglo-Saxon.[59]

He also exerted no small influence on Lewis's early career. Lewis began attending Gordon's "capital" lectures on Shakespeare late in 1922,[60] later claiming to "like everything about this man."[61] Early in 1923, Lewis began his participation in Gordon's discussion class, a gathering initiated by Sir Walter Raleigh, Gordon's predecessor as Merton Professor of English Literature.[62] Less than a month into the class, Lewis met future Kolbítar and Inkling Nevill Coghill, "an enthusiastic sensible man, without nonsense, and a gentleman, much more attractive than the majority."[63] Lewis therefore found in Gordon's class not only a lasting friend in Coghill; he also discovered in Gordon an important advocate and benefactor in the political machinations of academic life at Oxford. Two years after beginning his participation in Gordon's class, Lewis, in a letter to his father, records that he had enlisted a testimonial from Gordon as one of his "strongest supports" for his election to a fellowship in English at Magdalen.[64] Gordon's response tells much about his power and his belief in Lewis: at first Gordon replied that he was "exceedingly sorry," having already given his support to Coghill and previously being unaware of Lewis's interest. When he discovered that Coghill had accepted a fellowship from Exeter, Gordon immediately contacted Lewis, promising to back him personally for the Magdalen position. Gordon wrote Lewis after the interview, telling the latter he had put his money on Lewis and that he thought Lewis's chances "good."[65] Although opposed by John Bryson, another future Kolbítar, Gordon was as good as his (apparently quite effective) word, and Lewis won the Magdalen fellowship, a post he would occupy for the following twenty-nine years. Gordon followed Lewis to Magdalen, becoming that college's president from 1928 until his death in 1942, during which years Lewis "saw a great deal" of Gordon.[66] Carpenter aptly describes Gordon as "a great intriguer and campaigner";[67] he certainly campaigned effectively for Tolkien and Lewis. His inclusion in the Kolbítar suggests that Gordon shared intellectual interests with his two protégés for whom he had shown political support.

If Gordon served as an invaluable sponsor and advocate for Lewis and Tolkien early in their academic careers immediately prior to the founding of the Kolbítar, C.T. Onions occupied an equally important place as intellectual mentor to both men during the same period. In a letter to his son following Onions's death in 1965, Tolkien recalled his former editor at the *New English Dictionary* as "one of those people who *were* English at Oxford and at large" when Tolkien began his career (*Letters*, 353). Carpenter records that Tolkien "liked his colleagues" at the dictionary offices, "especially the accomplished C.T. Onions" (*Biography*, 101). Onions surely shared and likely furthered Tolkien's philological interests, and although more than five years passed between Tolkien's leaving the dictionary and his founding of the Kolbítar, Onions obviously remained an eminently appropriate choice as a founding member of the Old Norse society.

Onions also played a crucial and inspirational role in Lewis's early career. While Lewis was preparing his landmark *The Allegory of Love*, Onions, "who knows more than anyone else about the English" of the medieval period,[68] vetted Lewis's translations of Old French into modern English, which gained the former's approval, much to Lewis's relief. Lewis had sat for Onions's lectures on Middle English in 1922–23 and found them "delightful," commending in particular Onions's ability to recite verse from memory, a skill of which Lewis himself was no small master.[69] Upon Lewis's election to the English fellowship at Magdalen (where Onions was also a fellow) and after Lewis joined the Kolbítar, the two became friendly enough to tease each other during a chance meeting.[70] Nonetheless, Lewis shared Tolkien's respect for Onions, naming him as one of the "five great Magdalen men who enlarged my very idea of what a learned life should be."[71]

I argue, then, that the inclusion in the Kolbítar of George S. Gordon and C.T. Onions represented for Tolkien and Lewis a kind of gathering of the leading lights, practically and intellectually, of their early careers. In some ways, Gordon and Onions were the last of Tolkien's and Lewis's schoolmasters. I believe that Lewis's recalling the transition in his relationship with Onions from superior to colleague serves as a model for what happened during the course of the Kolbítar. Tolkien carefully selected his superiors as well as his contemporaries for the Old Norse group, a composition Tolkien's club involvement never thereafter repeated. By the time they finished reading the sagas, I believe that both Tolkien and Lewis found themselves ready to leave their mentors behind and to embark fully upon their own careers, careers during which, to varying degrees, they themselves would begin to mentor others. I suggest that we see the Kolbítar as a kind of finishing school for the impressive academic training of both men. Nearly all their contributions to scholarly and imaginative literature follow the ending of the Kolbítar and the founding of the Inklings, be it Lewis's *The Allegory of Love* (1936) or Tolkien's "Beowulf: The Monsters and the Critics" (1936) and *The Hobbit* (1937), to say nothing of their work in the mid-1940s to early 1950s during and after the height of the Inklings, a period that produced Tolkien's *The Lord of the Rings* and Lewis's Space Trilogy, *Chronicles of Narnia*, and volume 3 of the *Oxford History of English Literature*. I contend that the writing of such works was possible only after the two men had created a climate in which they themselves had become their own leading lights. The Kolbítar provided the very grounds for effecting this vital transition.

I also suggest that the Kolbítar served as the site of three other transitions, all of which proved indispensable to the intellectual, spiritual, and vocational development of Tolkien and Lewis; that in fact the Inklings, the crucible wherein nearly all of both men's most important works were made, could never have existed without the Kolbítar as precedent.

First of all, during the seven years of the Kolbítar, Tolkien effectively fulfilled his mission as a member of the T.C.B.S. "to kindle a new light, or what is the same thing, to rekindle an old light in the world," at the very least in the world of C.S. Lewis. The members of the T.C.B.S. felt that they were "destined to testify for God and Truth"; Tolkien certainly took advantage of the common interest he shared with Lewis in things Northern in order to bear just such testimony. In a December 1929 letter, Lewis records one evening's visit during which he talked far into the night with Tolkien: "I was up till 2.30 . . . talking to . . . Tolkien who . . . sat discoursing of the gods & giants & Asgard for three hours" before departing into the night. "Who c[oul]d turn him out, for the fire was bright and the talk good?"[72] One can imagine many such discussions between the two men, conversations during which they almost certainly debated their views of the role of myth. Lewis, though a great lover of mythology in all its forms, nevertheless called such tales "lies breathed through silver" and rejected them. Their discussions continued until eventually Tolkien was able to show Lewis that the stories were far more than lies, and that such stories might well prove to be "wisdom from the only Wise,"[73] that is, containing truth put into them by God.

One climactic night proved a real turning point for Lewis. Their conversations about such matters, sparked, no doubt, by Tolkien's evangelistic approach to "God and Truth" and fed by the mythology they read together fortnightly during meetings of the Kolbítar, led to the "long night talk" of 19 September 1931, a key turning point in Lewis's life. Although by the Trinity term of 1929 Lewis had completed a long and thoughtful journey from atheism to belief in some kind of God,[74] he still

wrestled with Christianity. As Tolkien and Lewis (along with future Inkling Hugo Dyson) walked round and round Addison's Walk that windy
night, they enjoyed "a good long satisfying talk" on Christianity during
which Lewis "learned a great deal."[75] Specifically, Tolkien and Dyson
challenged Lewis, showing him that he was "prepared to feel . . . myth
as profound and suggestive of meanings beyond [his] grasp . . . provided
[he] met it anywhere *except* in the Gospels." They convinced Lewis that
"the story of Christ is simply a true myth: a myth working on us in the
same way as the others, but with the tremendous difference that *it really
happened*."[76]

The idea worked powerfully upon Lewis, and once he acceded to it,
he "passed from believing in God to definitely believing in Christ—in
Christianity,"[77] a belief he held that deepened for the rest of his life.
Although Lewis continued to expand his extraordinary intellectual
growth, once he accepted Tolkien's view of Christianity as true myth,
Lewis remained of that mind-set for the rest of his life. In fact, Lewis
soon began defending and proclaiming this truth with all the fervor of a
member of the T.C.B.S., much to the consternation of some of his colleagues at Oxford. I suggest that books like *Miracles*, *Mere Christianity*,
and the *Problem of Pain*, all of which staunchly defend and promote
traditional orthodox Christianity, found their origins in the sense of mission that Tolkien shared with Lewis during the course of the Kolbítar.
Indeed, one might not stray too far afield to see Tolkien as in some ways
the author of Lewis's later sense of spiritual vocation. I see the Kolbítar
as the site within which Tolkien effectively communicated to Lewis his
spiritual understanding, and in so doing, Tolkien fulfilled his mission to
be "a beginner at the very least of large things." I further suggest that one
of the large things that Tolkien began was his communication of an evangelistic approach toward "God and Truth" to Lewis, who within ten years
began to transition into being the more visible of the two men as an
active advocate of Christianity.

A second crucial transition that took place within the context of the
Kolbítar is far more practical. As we have seen, both Tolkien and Lewis
had played important roles in founding and leading clubs. The Kolbítar
was the last of these clubs in which Tolkien occupied the most central
position. In much the same way that the end of the Kolbítar brought an
end of the need for Tolkien and Lewis to include their mentors like Gordon and Onions, so also the Old Norse reading group signaled the end of

Tolkien's role as the group's central figure. Between the end of the Kolbítar and the beginning of the Inklings, Lewis transitioned into the leadership position, a role that Tolkien never thereafter occupied. By the time the Kolbítar had ended, Lewis found himself firmly ensconced as the center around which the Inklings gathered.

Finally, I suggest that the end of the Kolbítar and the beginning of the Inklings signaled a more equitable relationship between Tolkien and Lewis. In contrast to the Kolbítar, in which Tolkien acted as an expert in Old Norse, the Inklings offered its members a far more democratic foundation. This, in turn, allowed the friendship between Tolkien and Lewis to flourish. The summer after Lewis's death on 22 November 1963, Tolkien reflected that Lewis "was my closest friend from about 1927 to 1940, and remained very dear to me" (*Letters*, 349). I suggest two things concerning their friendship. First, I argue the Kolbítar as that space wherein friendship between the two sprung up, initially due to their shared interest in myth, but after that because of the whole world of sympathies they shared as practicing Christians. Without Tolkien's influence, Lewis may never have reached these conclusions, which in turned shaped the rest of his life and his work. The friendship between Tolkien and Lewis, which formed the core of the Inklings, first found its home in the Kolbítar. Second, we can hardly overstate the importance of this relationship to the two men. Tolkien himself claimed that he and Lewis "owed each a great debt to the other, and that tie, with the deep affection it begot, remains" even after Lewis's death and after years of some estrangement between the two (*Letters*, 341). I contend that the Kolbítar represents a transition for Tolkien and Lewis from being colleagues to being deep friends, and that this deep friendship, made sure during the Old Norse reading group, became the foundation for much of the most important work of both men.

All of these transitions allude to the transition from the Kolbítar to the Inklings, which follows a direct line. As I have mentioned, Tolkien, Lewis, and Nevill Coghill all were members of the Kolbítar who became founding members of the Inklings. In its construction, I see the Inklings as a group consciously following some examples of the Kolbítar while avoiding other elements with equal deliberateness. Similarities include, of course, a membership of friends and colleagues. Also similar to the Kolbítar, the Inklings gathered with the purpose of indulging in a passion deeply held and delightfully shared by its members. And, like the Kolbítar, the Inklings formed around one central member, although membership was of its very nature more democratic. In the Inklings, Lewis's jocular personality contributed much to his role, much as Tolkien's linguistic expertise had made him the natural leader of the Kolbítar.

The differences between the two groups reveal even more about how Tolkien and Lewis had at last selected a nearly perfect society for themselves. First of all, rather than gathering to read the works of authors long dead in an ancient language as did the Kolbítar, the Inklings met to read unpublished works by current members of the group. Next, members of the group were contemporaries. When they invited guests to join the group, these men invariably were of the same age, with the notable exceptions of Tolkien's son Christopher and Lewis's former pupil, the poet John Wain. Also, members came from both within and without the immediate academic community. While Kolbítar members all held posts in the humanities at Oxford, Inklings represented disciplines as disparate as law, publishing, medicine, the army, and the navy.[78] This circle of "undetermined and unelected friends" (*Letters*, 388) provided for Tolkien and Lewis just the sort of society they liked best as an audience for one of their favorite activities, reading aloud their own writings. Having completed the last of their education in the Kolbítar, the Inklings soon provided the site within which both Tolkien and Lewis began their careers in earnest.

How and when did this club originate? Tolkien recalls the Inklings as a group originally founded by University College undergraduate Edward Tangye Lean, who, as we have seen, knew Lewis from their mutual participation in the Martlets. Lean founded the group sometime around 1931 for the purpose of allowing its members to read their original works to each other (*Biography*, 149), and, as is the nature of such societies, it folded after a year or two. About 1933, after Lean left Oxford, Tolkien and Lewis appropriated the name and purpose of the club (*Letters*, 387–88). Their version of the club enjoyed a much longer and more prodigious life, for they continued to meet on Thursday evenings (and often on Tuesday mornings) from 1933 until 20 October 1947. Warren Lewis's diary, the best and most consistent record of the attendance and proceedings of Inklings meetings, contains on the following Thursday, 22 October 1947, the notation "No one turned up after dinner," a tiny epitaph to the end of the meetings.[79] While they lasted, however, meetings of the Inklings provided for Tolkien, Lewis, and their friends a fertile ground for them to sow the seeds of their ideas, seeds that would bloom into some of the most enduringly popular books of the mid-twentieth century.

I believe that the Inklings inexorably took shape out of the remnants of the Kolbítar for two reasons. First, Tolkien and Lewis had for all purposes only just entered into the deepest part of their friendship with Lewis's adoption of Tolkien's myth-view and subsequent conversion in 1931. Second, if as I have suggested the two had not only just completed the last of their informal education in the Old Norse reading group but had also, with Lewis's conversion, quite recently come to agree about their central worldview, they needed more appropriate grounds to explore their friendship. What better means to accomplish this than within a group that at once provided both of them a place to read their writings to each other and to discuss in depth and in comfortable camaraderie such issues as those writings inspired? How much better still if all the members of the group themselves had deep sympathies with Christianity and myth? I further suggest that upon the conclusion of the Kolbítar, Tolkien and Lewis were both quite ready to embark on their significant careers as writers, and that in each other they found an indispensable sounding board for their work.

Within the context of the Inklings as the Kolbítar's immediate and inevitable successor, both men produced the most important scholarship of their early careers. Tolkien's 1936 Gollancz lecture, "Beowulf: The Monsters and the Critics," and Lewis's equally memorable *The Allegory of Love*, published the same year, represent the scholarly work of each man at that time. We can conjecture that the subjects of both works came up at meetings of the Inklings, if not passages themselves.

There is, however, evidence that both men read aloud to meetings of the Inklings from their groundbreaking early fiction. Tolkien found one of his first audiences for *The Hobbit* of 1937 during gatherings with Lewis and friends. In a letter to his publisher dated June 1938, Tolkien mentions that both his own *Hobbit* and Lewis's *Out of the Silent Planet* had been read aloud to the Inklings, the latter passing the "rather difficult test" of finding approval from the group, once Lewis had made some changes (*Letters*, 36, 29). We also know of the unique role that Lewis played in the creation of *The Lord of the Rings*. Called "the new Hobbit" by members of the Inklings,[80] the editors of Warren Lewis's diaries state that "it was to the audience of the Inklings that J.R.R. Tolkien's *The Lord of the Rings* (1954, 1955), Charles Williams's *All Hallows Eve* (1945), and Jack Lewis's *Perelandra* (1943) were first read."[81] The Inklings thus provided for both men a circle of sympathetic yet critical friends.

Perhaps the most sympathetic and critical, however, in his reading of *The Lord of the Rings* was Lewis. Tolkien makes extraordinary statements about the importance of Lewis's support. "But for the encouragement of C.S.L.," Tolkien asserts, "I do not think that I should ever have completed or offered for publication the *Lord of the Rings*" (*Letters*, 366). Tolkien goes on to acknowledge "the unpayable debt" for "sheer encouragement" that he owed to Lewis: "[Lewis] was for long my only audience. Only from him did I get the idea that my 'stuff' could be more than a private hobby" (*Letters*, 362). Not only did Lewis inspire Tolkien to publish his "private hobby"; he also proved instrumental in pushing Tolkien to complete the work. Earlier, in a letter to his publisher, Tolkien acknowledged, "[O]nly by [Lewis's] support and friendship did I ever struggle to the end of the labour" (*Letters*, 184). Despite Tolkien's fabled "contrasistency,"[82] one must conclude from the sheer bulk of Tolkien's attributions of credit to Lewis that the friendship between the two men played a major part—indeed, became the deciding factor in—Tolkien's starting, continuing, and completing his most memorable work.

Although Tolkien lamented the fact that "'Narnia' and all that part of C.S.L's work should remain outside the range of [his] sympathy" (*Letters*, 352), Tolkien in at least one crucially important way inspired Lewis's imaginative land. By convincing Lewis that fairy-stories were in fact "refracted light . . . splintered from a single White" (*TL*, 98), that Christianity was indeed myth, and that myth could and, in fact, had become fact in the biblical story, Tolkien, within the context of the Kolbítar, provided Lewis with the central principle for all of his fiction. Although Tolkien objected to the hasty jumble of mythologies that filled Lewis's imaginative worlds, especially Narnia, we cannot fail to see the traces of Tolkien's thoughts sponsoring and informing Lewis as he created a world where all mythologies and fairy-stories could come to life. When Lewis's narrator in the first of his Narnian stories claims, concerning Father Christmas, that "though you see people of his sort only in Narnia, you see pictures of them and hear them talked about even in our world—the world on this side of the wardrobe door,"[83] we cannot help but hear, if not Tolkien's voice directly, at least Lewis's version of Tolkien's ideas.

For surely it was Tolkien who brought to Lewis the idea that mythic stories could contain essential truth. I argue that, had Tolkien not succeeded in bringing this "evangelium" to Lewis in the latter days of the Kolbítar, Lewis might never have arrived at the imaginative landscape that allowed him in the late 1940s to begin writing the Narnia books.

This leads me to two conclusions. In the first place, I contend that the only responsible way for anyone to seriously consider the work of either Tolkien or Lewis is to consider systematically and carefully the thoughts of the other. The two men met by custom several times a week for perhaps a dozen years, relishing each other's company and prizing each other's opinions, however critical. Because their two minds so dwelt in the same formative space for so long, I assert that the first resource one should consult in producing any work on Tolkien, apart from Tolkien's own writings (and those of his son and editor Christopher), is the work and thought of C.S. Lewis. And of course, this dictum works the other way round. Tolkien clearly authored the crucial part of Lewis's ontological and creative landscape. By offering Lewis the last answers to his spiritual and imaginative questions, Tolkien provided him with the foundation upon which all Lewis's creative work stands.

And if Tolkien is in a way the father of Lewis's imaginative world, then Lewis acted as a kind of midwife for Tolkien in the creation of Tolkien's epic fantasy. Certainly, Tolkien himself heaped credit upon Lewis's efforts to push Tolkien forward in not only the creation but also the completion of the latter's monumental task. In terms of their most significant work, one must ineluctably consider Tolkien and Lewis immanently together.

In the second place, I cannot see any way in which the two men could have developed such trust and like-mindedness as friends had they not met regularly and for years to discuss those myths nearest to their hearts. Without the Kolbítar, there would probably have been no Inklings, no friendship, and, in all likelihood, no Middle-earth or Narnia. One must not underestimate the transitional dynamic that took place in the Kolbítar nor the way in which it provided for both men the grounds to begin and to complete their most important work, both academic and imaginative.[84] To use a metallurgic metaphor, I believe that as these two Coalbiters forged their finished artworks, while their friendship served as a catalyst and the Inklings acted as a crucible, the sheer heat that enabled the two to craft their work blazed forth from Northern fires.

Appendix A

Kolbítar Chronology

Abbreviations (Kolbítar members in bold)

GEKB	G.E.K. Braunholtz
JB	John Norman Bryson
NC	Nevill Henry Kendal Aylmer Coghill
RMD	Richard MacGillivray Dawkins
EVG	Eric Valentine Gordon
GG	George Stuart Gordon
CSL	Clive Staples Lewis
BMc	Kenneth Bruce McFarlane
CTO	Charles Talbut Onions
JRRT	John Ronald Reuel Tolkien
TCBS	Tea Club, Barrovian Society (Tolkien's earliest society of friends)
NED	*New English Dictionary*

For all colleges and wherever not specified, understand **Oxford University**.

Oxford University School Terms

Michaelmas	October to mid-December
Hilary	January to mid-March
Trinity	April to mid-June

Year	Date/Term	Event
1871	24 October	**RMD** born
1873	10 September	**CTO** born
1881	1 February	**GG** born
1892	3 January	**JRRT** born
	(no date)	**CTO** takes London BA (Mason College, Birmingham)
1895	September	**CTO** joins *NED* staff
1896	15 February	Arthur Tolkien dies
	(no date)	**JB** born

Year	Date/Term	Event
1898	(no date)	**RMD** matriculates Emmanuel College (Cambridge)
	29 November	**CSL** born
1899	19 April	**NC** born
1900–1902	(?)	**GG** studies under Sir Walter Raleigh (Glasgow University)
1900	(no date)	Mabel Tolkien converts and begins instructing sons in Catholicism
1902	(no date)	**GG** matriculates Oriel College
1903	(no date)	**BMc** born
1904	14 November	Mabel Tolkien dies
1906	(no date)	**GG** takes 1st in Greats.
1907	(no date)	**GG** becomes first fellow in English at Magdalen College
1908	23 August	Flora Lewis dies
1911	*Michaelmas*	**JRRT** matriculates Exeter
	(no date)	TCBS formed
1913	(no date)	**JRRT** takes 2nd in Honour Mods
	(no date)	**GG** becomes professor of English (Leeds)
1914–18		World War I; **JRRT, CSL, NC, GG,** and **CTO** all serve
1914	December	"Council of London" of the TCBS
1915	(no date)	**JRRT** takes 1st in English, begins military service
1916	22 March	**JRRT** marries Edith Bratt
1917	*Trinity*	**CSL** matriculates University College
	(no date)	**CSL** begins military service
1918	(no date)	**CTO** works in naval intelligence
	11 November	Armistice ends World War I
	November	**JRRT** joins *NED* staff
1919	*Hilary*	**NC** matriculates at Exeter
1920	*Hilary*	**CSL** takes 1st in Honour Mods
	Michaelmas	**JRRT** becomes reader in English (Leeds)
	(no date)	**CTO** becomes lecturer in English

Year	Date/Term	Event
1922	August	**CSL** takes 1st in Greats, **JB** takes degree(?)
	Michaelmas	EVG joins staff at Leeds and begins work with **JRRT**
		RMD takes Oxford Byzantine and Modern Greek Professorship
		GG elected Merton Professor of English Literature (succeeding Raleigh)
1923	2 February	**CSL** meets **NC** in **GG**'s discussion class
	July	**CSL** and **NC** take 1sts in English
	(no date)	**JB** becomes lecturer, Balliol College; **CTO** elected fellow, Magdalen College
1924	*Michaelmas*	**JRRT** succeeds **GG** as professor of English (Leeds)
	(no date)	**JRRT** founds Viking Club with EVG (?)
		NC elected research fellow, Exeter College
1925	21 May	**CSL** elected English fellow, Magdalen College (**JB** also candidate)
	July	**JRRT** elected Oxford Professor of Anglo-Saxon
	Michaelmas	**NC** elected fellow/librarian, Exeter College
		CSL, JRRT, and **NC** begin new posts
1926	*Hilary*	**JRRT** founds Kolbítar
	11 May	**JRRT** and **CSL** meet
	Michaelmas	**JRRT** invites **CSL** to join Kolbítar
	December	**CSL** begins preparing for Kolbítar
1927	January	**CSL** continues preparing for Kolbítar
	18 February	**CSL** attends Kolbítar for 2nd (?) time
	Hilary, Trinity	Kolbítar, meeting fortnightly on Wednesdays, reads *Younger Edda*, *Völsungasaga*

Year	Date/Term	Event
	9 July	**CSL** working on *Elder (?) Edda*
	Michaelmas	Kolbítar plans to read *Laxdæla* saga
	29 (?) November	**CSL** reports Kolbítar meeting fortnightly
	12 December	**CSL** reports Kolbítar meeting fortnightly on Tuesdays
	(no date)	**CTO** becomes reader in English philology
1928	(no date)	**GG** becomes president of Magdalen
	Michaelmas	**CSL** and **BMc** found Michaelmas Club
1929	*Trinity*	**CSL** converts to theism
	3 December	**CSL** records Kolbítar meeting of 27 November 1929
1930	28 or 29 January	Kolbítar meets
	(no date)	**JRRT** begins and then abandons *The Hobbit*
	15 September	**CSL** mentions still learning Icelandic
1931	19 September	**CSL** and **JRRT** have "long night talk"
	22 September	**CSL** in private correspondence characterizes **JRRT** and **BMc** as "friends of the second class"
	28 September	**CSL** converts to Christianity
1933	(no date)	Kolbítar, having read the sagas and *Eddas*, ceases to meet
		Shorter *NED* and Supplement to *NED* published (ed. **CTO**)
		GG elected professor of poetry

Appendix B

Kolbítar Roster

* indicates a founding member of the Kolbítar
(i) indicates a founding member of the Inklings

Abbreviations (Kolbítar members in **bold**)

NC	Nevill Henry Kendal Aylmer Coghill
CSL	Clive Staples Lewis
JRRT	John Ronald Reuel Tolkien
NED	*New English Dictionary*

For all colleges and wherever not specified, understand **Oxford University**.

NAME	POSITION	Additional Information
J.R.R. Tolkien* (i)	Professor of Anglo-Saxon	Later Merton Professor of English Language and Literature
R.M. Dawkins*	Professor of Byzantine and Modern Greek literature	Published medieval Cypriot *Chronical of Makhairas* in 1932.
G.E.K. Braunholtz*	Professor of comparative philology	
John Fraser*	Professor of Celtic	
George S. Gordon	Professor of English	**JRRT**'s predecessor as professor of English at Leeds, influential in securing posts for **JRRT** and **CSL**, led discussion class wherein **CSL** met **NC**. Later professor of poetry, president of Magdalen.

NAME	POSITION	Additional Information
C.T. Onions*	Reader, lecturer in English, *O.E.D.* editor	**JRRT**'s superior at *NED* and **CSL**'s colleague at Magdalen.
C.S. Lewis (i)	Fellow of English, Magdalen College	Later professor of medieval and Renaissance literature, Cambridge
Nevill Coghill* (i)	Fellow of English and librarian, Exeter College	Member, **GG**'s discussion class, translated *The Canterbury Tales*, later Merton Professor of English, produced plays for Oxford University Dramatic Society, directed Richard Burton and Elizabeth Taylor in 1966 production and 1967 film of *Dr. Faustus*.
John Bryson	Fellow of English, Balliol College	Later librarian of Balliol College.
Bruce McFarlane	Fellow of history, Magdalen College	Friend of **CSL** and cofounder with **CSL** of the Michaelmas Club.

Notes

1. See Carl F. Hostetter, and Arden R. Smith, "A Mythology for England," in *Proceedings of the J.R.R. Tolkien Centenary Conference, Keble College, Oxford, 1992*, ed. Patricia Reynolds and Glen GoodKnight, *Mythlore* 80 and *Mallorn* 30, in one volume (Milton Keynes, England: Tolkien Society; Altadena, Calif.: Mythopoeic Press, 1995), 281. I take the phrase "a mythology for England" most immediately from Hostetter and Smith, although as early as 1979 Jane Chance used it as the subtitle for her book *Tolkien's Art: A Mythology for England* (London: Macmillan, 1979; New York: St. Martin's Press, 1979), and she found it in Carpenter's *Biography,* 89. Carpenter had in mind Tolkien's own comments in his letter to Milton Waldman wherein he laments England's poverty of legends such as those one finds in Greek, Celtic, Finnish, and other traditions (*Letters* 144). For a further discussion, see the revised edition of Chance's *Tolkien's Art: A Mythology for England,* especially vii–ix and 2–3.

2. See, for example, Marjorie Burns, "J.R.R. Tolkien, The British and the Norse In Tension," in *Pacific Coast Philology*, 25.2 (1990): 49–58; Jonathan Evans, "The Dragon-Lore of Middle-earth: Tolkien and Old English and Old Norse Tradition," in *J.R.R. Tolkien and His Literary Resonances: Views of Middle-earth*, ed. George Clark and Daniel Patrick Timmons (Westport, Conn.: Greenwood, 2000), 21–38; Fredrik Heinemann, "Tolkien and Old Icelandic Literature," in *Scholarship and Fantasy: Proceedings of the Tolkien Phenomenon, May 1992, Turku, Finland.* ed. Keith J. Battarbee, Anglicana Turkuensia 12 (Turku: University of Turku, 1993), 99–110; Gloriana St. Clair, "An Overview of the Northern Influences on Tolkien's Works," in *Proceedings of the J.R.R. Tolkien Centenary Conference,* Reynolds and GoodKnight, ed. 63–67, and T.A. Shippey's masterful *J.R.R. Tolkien: Author of the Century* (London: HarperCOllins, 2000; Boston: Houghton Mifflin, 2001).

3. C.S. Lewis, *Out of the Silent Planet* (London: John Lane The Bodley Head, 1938), 58, 60.

4. E.V. Gordon, *An Introduction to Old Norse*, 2nd ed., ed. A.R. Taylor (Oxford and New York: Oxford Univ. Press, 1981), 356.

5. C.S. Lewis, *Letters of C.S. Lewis: Edited and with a Memoir by W.H. Lewis*, 2nd ed., rev. and enlarged by Walter Hooper (San Diego, New York, and London: Harcourt Brace, 1994), 315.

6. For an extensive and informed discussion of the creation of the Narniad, see Hooper's benchmark study *C.S. Lewis: A Companion and Guide* (San Francisco: HarperSanFrancisco, 1996), 397–456, esp. 401–5. See also Paul F. Ford's indispensable *Companion to Narnia* (New York: HarperCollins, 1994), 451, and xxxii–iii n 12, and the interactive timeline at ~*Welcome to NARNIA*~, Ed. Walden Media and HarperCollins, 26 April 2003, http://www.narnia.com/chronicles/cslewis/creation.htm.

7. C.S. Lewis, *They Asked for a Paper: Papers and Addresses* (London: Bles, 1962), 152.

8. Ford, 296.

9. Ford, 189.

10. H.R. Ellis Davidson, *Gods and Myths of Northern Europe* (London: Everyman, 1990), 31.

11. Snorri Sturluson, *Edda*, trans. Anthony Faulkes (London: Everyman, 1995), 29.

12. C.S. Lewis, *The Lion, the Witch, and the Wardrobe* (New York: HarperTrophy, 2000), 98.

13. C.S. Lewis, *Lion*, 131.

14. Ford, 306.

15. Ford, 172.

16. Andrew Lazo, "A Kind of Mid-wife: J.R.R. Tolkien and C.S. Lewis— Sharing Influence," in *Tolkien the Medievalist*, ed. Jane Chance (London and New York: Routledge, 2003), 36–49, 44–45.

17. *Beowulf: A New Verse Translation*, trans. Seamus Heaney (New York: W.W. Norton, 2000), 8–9.

18. Davidson, 3.

19. Jonathan Evans, 24.

20. Ibid.

21. Humphrey Carpenter, *The Inklings: C.S. Lewis, J.R.R. Tolkien, Charles Williams, and Their Friends* (Boston: Houghton Mifflin, 1979), 29.

22. C.S. Lewis, *C.S. Lewis: Collected Letters. Vol. 1: Family Letters, 1905–1931*, ed. Walter Hooper, (London: HarperCollins, 2000), 780 n 74.

23. C.S. Lewis, *Collected Letters*, 643 n 8.

24. C.S. Lewis, *Collected Letters*, 157.

25. C.S. Lewis, *Surprised by Joy: The Shape of My Early Life* (New York: Harcourt Brace, 1956), 10.

26. C.S. Lewis, *Surprised by Joy*, 17.

27. Ibid.; and Hooper, 5.

28. Hooper, 375.

29. C.S. Lewis, *Surprised by Joy*, 72.

30. Ibid.

31. C.S. Lewis, *They Stand Together: The Letters of C.S. Lewis to Arthur Greeves (1914–1963)*, ed. Walter Hooper (New York: Macmillan, 1979), 50–54.

32. C.S. Lewis, *Collected Letters*, 483.

33. C.S. Lewis, *The Four Loves* (New York: Harcourt Brace, 1960), 87–127, esp. 91–92 and 96–98.

34. Ibid., 97.

35. C.S. Lewis, *Surprised by Joy*, 131.

36. C.S. Lewis, *Surprised by Joy*, 147.

37. C.S. Lewis, *Collected Letters*, 119.

38. C.S. Lewis, *Collected Letters*, 122.

39. C.S. Lewis, *Surprised by Joy*, 78.

40. C.S. Lewis, *Surprised by Joy*, 165.

41. George Sayer, *Jack: C.S. Lewis and His Times* (San Francisco: Harper and Row, 1988), 23.

42. C.S. Lewis, *Surprised by Joy*, 94.

43. C.S. Lewis, *Surprised by Joy,* 12.

44. Quoted in Sayer, 42–43.

45. Hooper, 8.

46. Quoted in Sayer, 49.

47. Quoted in C.S. Lewis, *Collected Letters*, 178.

48. See C.S. Lewis, "The Inner Ring," in *Transposition and Other Addresses* (London: Bles, 1949), 55–66, esp. 58 and 61 wherein Lewis describes the dominance of "the desire to be inside the local [Inner] Ring and the terror of being left outside." See also C.S. Lewis, *That Hideous Strength: A Modern Fairy-Tale for Grown-Ups* (New York: Macmillan, 1946), chapter 1, 1–26, esp. 6, wherein the narrator comments regarding protagonist Mark Studdock that, "[y]ou would never have guessed . . . what intense pleasure he derived from [inner ring member] Curry's use of the pronoun 'we.' So very recently he had been an outsider . . . [n]ow he was inside and 'Curry and his gang' had become 'we'. . . It had all happened quite suddenly and was still sweet in his mouth." See also chapter 4, 76–100, esp. 84, wherein it becomes obvious to Studdock that "the real work of the N.I.C.E. [the National Institute of Co-ordinated Experiments, a nefarious group entirely unsuited to its acronym] must go on somewhere else." This is a group into whose "Inner Ring" Studdock hopes to soon find himself.

49. C.S. Lewis, "The Inner Ring," 57, 60.

50. C.S. Lewis, *The Four Loves*, 67.

51. Hooper, 775.

52. C.S. Lewis, *Collected Letters*, 511 n 83.

53. C.S. Lewis, *All My Road before Me: The Diary of C.S. Lewis, 1922–1927*, ed. Walter Hooper (San Diego, New York, and London: Harcourt Brace, 1991), 409.

54. C.S. Lewis, *Collected Letters*, 735 n 96.

55. C.S. Lewis, *All My Road before Me*, 445, 456–57.

56. C.S. Lewis, *All My Road before Me*, 456.

57. C.S. Lewis, *Collected Letters*, 778.

58. Carpenter, *Inklings*, 27–28.

59. Carpenter, *Inklings*, 27.

60. C.S. Lewis, *All My Road before Me*, 138–39, 139.

61. C.S. Lewis, *All My Road before Me*, 147.

62. C.S. Lewis, *All My Road before Me*, 181.

63. C.S. Lewis, *All My Road before Me*, 189.

64. C.S. Lewis, *Collected Letters*, 642–43.

65. Ibid.

66. C.S. Lewis, *Collected Letters*, 643.

67. Carpenter, *Inklings*, 27.

68. C.S. Lewis, *Collected Letters*, 779–80.

69. Onions, C.S. Lewis mentions, quoted "inimitably." C.S. Lewis, *All My Road before Me*, 184. On Lewis's own prodigious memory, see Derek Brewer, "The Tutor: A Portrait," in *C.S. Lewis at the Breakfast Table and Other Reminis-*

cences (New York: Macmillan, 1979), 47, where Brewer recalls that Lewis "had an astonishing memory and could repeat whole passages of prose to illustrate a point . . . . Given any line in *Paradise Lost*, he could continue with the following lines." See also drama critic Kenneth Tynan's recollection of occasionally playing an astonishing game with Lewis in which Tynan would select a book at random from Lewis's library and read a line. Lewis would then, "always identify [the line]—not only by identifying the book, but [Lewis] was also usually able to quote the rest of the page." Quoted in Hooper, 42.

70. C.S. Lewis, *All My Road before Me*, 423.

71. C.S. Lewis, *Surprised by Joy*, 216.

72. C.S. Lewis, *Collected Letters*, 838.

73. See "Mythopoeia," the poem Tolkien wrote to Lewis before the latter's conversion, in *Tree and Leaf*, 2nd ed. (London: Grafton, 1992), 97–101, esp. 97–98.

74. C.S. Lewis, *Surprised by Joy*, 228.

75. C.S. Lewis, *They Stand Together*, 421.

76. C.S. Lewis, *They Stand Together*, 427.

77. C.S. Lewis, *They Stand Together*, 425.

78. Carpenter, *Inklings*, 255–59.

79. Warren Hamilton Lewis, *Brothers and Friends: The Diaries of Major Warren Hamilton Lewis*, ed. Clyde S. Kilby and Majorie Lamp Mead (San Francisco: Harper and Row, 1982), 230.

80. C.S. Lewis, *Letters,* 328.

81. W.H. Lewis, 182 n 202.

82. Tolkien, especially in his letters, often proves notoriously unreliable in his statements to the point that we can count on him to contradict what he has said. Among many examples, see *Letters*, 365, where he claims that he and Lewis never called each other by their Christian names, and page 125, where he affectionately does just that.

83. C.S. Lewis, *Lion*, 107.

84. While many have paid attention to its existence, few, if any, have stressed the real importance of the Kolbítar, which I claim to be the watershed for all that followed. Norman Cantor in his study *Inventing the Middle Ages: The Lives, Works, and Ideas of the Great Medievalists of the Twentieth Century* (New York: Quill, 1991), 205–44, misses this point altogether, although he does blandly assert that "Lewis and Tolkien were good and important for each other," (Cantor, 208). He either dismisses or is not even aware of the fact that two of the key medievalists of the twentieth century spent seven years meeting regularly to pore over medieval and largely mythic texts in their original languages, preferring instead to fill much of his account of Lewis and Tolkien with invective, misinformation, and plain error. Others, including those mentioned in note 2 above, have traced the importance of Old Norse, but not of the means by which Tolkien read the literature, namely, the Kolbítar. Although Colin Duriez rightly notes in his forthcoming volume on Tolkien's and Lewis's friendship that within the context of the Coalbiters, "Tolkien's and Lewis's evolving friendship was of

great significance to both men" (Colin Duriez, *Tolkien and C.S. Lewis: The Gift of Friendship* [Mahwah, N.J.: Hidden Spring, 2003]), nevertheless, he too fails to describe the central importance of the Old Norse reading group to the subsequent lives and work of both men.

Part IV

TOLKIEN AND OLD ENGLISH

Chapter 13

A MYTHOLOGY FOR
ANGLO-SAXON ENGLAND

MICHAEL D.C. DROUT

The phrase "a mythology for England" has been so closely associated with J.R.R. Tolkien's fiction (even though Tolkien never actually used these exact words)[1] that by now it is a foregone conclusion that Tolkien intended for his literary works to create:

> a body of more or less connected legend, ranging from the large and cosmogonic, to the level of the romantic fairy-story—the larger founded on the lesser in contact with the earth, the lesser drawing splendour from vast backcloths—which I would dedicate simply to: to England; to my country. . . . I would draw some of the great tales in fullness, and leave many only placed in the scheme, and sketched. The cycles should be linked to a majestic whole, and yet leave scope for other minds and hands, wielding paint and music and drama. (*Letters*, 144–45)

The critical consensus seems to be that Tolkien succeeded in this project, although there is no consensus as to the definition of "mythology."[2] But if Tolkien did create a "mythology for England," then by necessity he would have had to create a mythology for Anglo-Saxon England as well, a prehistory for the Anglo-Saxons that described their (otherwise unrecorded, though archeologically reconstructed) doings before the fifth-century migration of the Angles, Saxons, and Jutes from the continent to England. In creating this mythology for Anglo-Saxon England Tolkien did not merely develop a speculative history of the

Anglo-Saxon past but also indulged in the imaginative creation of pseudohistory that Tolkien himself did not believe to be factually true. But because this mythological history solved a number of historical and literary puzzles and was in itself aesthetically pleasing, Tolkien found it difficult to eschew it entirely. Therefore, while he explicitly and overtly severed the connections between real European history and Middle-earth, there remains a structural substratum of story-structure, names, and parallels that links early Anglo-Saxon and Germanic culture to Tolkien's imaginative creation.[3] This desire to separate his historical deductions from his creations explains Tolkien's forceful and perhaps disingenuous denials that the Rohirrim represented Anglo-Saxons, and his construction of the framing device of the Red Book of Westmarch and the somewhat labored and rather unconvincing linguistic explications of the end of appendix F in the *Lord of the Rings*.

Although it might seem logical to begin with the Rohirrim and their use of Anglo-Saxon and then work backwards, I instead want to start my analysis with the oldest stratum of Tolkien's *legendarium*, the materials in *The Book of Lost Tales, Part 1* and *The Book of Lost Tales, Part 2*. Here we meet the enigmatic figure of Ælfwine or Eriol, an Anglo-Saxon mariner who travels to the Elvish lands of the West.[4] Verlyn Flieger has already shown how Ælfwine operates as an intermediary through whom Tolkien can transmit his mythology. She notes that Ælfwine allows Tolkien to present the legends as if he is discovering them, rather than as if he (Tolkien) is making them up, linking the "outside" reader to the "inside" culture that generates the myths. Ælfwine is thus analogous to Gangleri in *Gylfaginning*, a figure whom Snorri Sturluson uses to report on the "history" of the Norse gods without creating the impression that Snorri himself (who was a Christian) actually believed in the divine nature of the Norse pantheon.[5]

Ælfwine serves as a bridge between Anglo-Saxon history and Tolkien's mythology. At the early stage of the composition of the *Book of Lost Tales* material, Ælfwine was named Eriol (a name invented by Tolkien) and also "Ottor, who called himself Wǽfre." Ottor is equivalent to the Old English name Ohthere.[6] Ohthere appears in *Beowulf*,[7] where he is the son of Ongentheow, the king of Sweden and the father of the Swedish princes Eadgils and Eanmund.[8] More significantly for the purposes of this argument, Ohthere is also the name of one of the voyagers (Wulfstan is the other) who arrives at the court of King Alfred and provides the Anglo-Saxon king with information about the lands and peoples surrounding the North Sea. The description of Ohthere's voyages was interpolated into the Old English translation of Orosius's *Historiae adversum paganos*, a text translated anonymously during the reign of Alfred.[9] Ohthere is thus a great voyager and mariner, attributes also held by Tolkien's Ælfwine/Eriol/Ottar.

In Tolkien's conception, Ottor Wæfre's father is named Eoh, which means "horse" in Old English. Ottor marries Cwén (Old English for "queen" or "woman") and has two sons, Hengest and Horsa (both names mean "horse" in Old English, a point that we will examine in more detail below). Ottor ends up leaving Heligoland in the North Sea, where he has settled, and goes off to Tol Eressëa (the Lonely Isle of the Elves), where he weds Naimi, who is also called Eadgifu (an Anglo-Saxon name meaning "bliss-gift" and also the antecedent of Modern English Edith). Among the sons of Ottor and Eadgifu is one named Heorrenda (*BLT1*, 21–25; *BLT2*, 290–91). Eriol also adopted the name of Angol, which "refers to the ancient homeland of the 'English' before their migration across the North Sea" (*BLT2*, 291).

This somewhat bewildering collection of names can be disambiguated and related to what is known of ancient English history, creating a coherent narrative that, while not in the slightest way supported by historical evidence, does make logical sense. The Venerable Bede claimed that England was colonized by three Germanic tribes, the Angles, Saxons, and Jutes. These tribes were led by two brothers, Hengest and Horsa.[10] In Tolkien's conception, then, the father of the leaders of the Anglo-Saxon migration was Ælfwine, who therefore must have originally come from the ancestral homeland of the Anglo-Saxons on the continent (in Tolkien's conception, from northern Germany/southern Denmark between the Flensburg fjord and the river Schlie).[11] Ælfwine would have left the continent for Heligoland in the North Sea (where Tolkien says he settled), then from there traveled to the Elvish lands in the West, while his sons would have returned to the continent to lead their people into England (*BLT2*, 290).

Ælfwine's first wife Cwén, the mother of Hengest and Horsa, may also have links to the voyages of Ohthere and Wulfstan. Ohthere described a tribe of northern Sweden called the Cwenas, who at times carried their ships overland to large lakes and then harried the Northmen on these lakes. R.W. Chambers thought that the kind of fighting on lakes between the Cwenas and the Northmen was analogous to the fighting between the Geatas and Swedes in *Beowulf*.[12] In any event, Cwén may represent the union of the ancestors of the Anglo-Saxons with another tribe and would explain the presence of the culture of the farther North in a tribe from southern Denmark/northern Germany.

But the figure of Hengest—the son of Cwén and Ælfwine—is particularly significant to our understanding of the interrelationship of Tolkien's imagined mythology and his Anglo-Saxon scholarship. Tolkien had developed a very complex argument as to the identity of Hengest (who appears in both *Beowulf* and the Finnsburg Fragment). The literary Hengest was, Tolkien believed, the same person as the historical Hengest who led the migration to England, and Hengest and his brother Horsa were the leaders of the Jutish third of the Anglo-Saxon migration.[13] Thus the founder of the Jutish regions of England had also been a major participant in the heroic episode that Tolkien called the "Freswæl" (Frisian slaughter) and appeared in *Beowulf*. Identifying the Hengest of *Beowulf* with the Hengest of the Freswæl creates a variety of literary effects, the most significant of which is to tie the legendary and mythical materials of *Beowulf* to the world of Anglo-Saxon historical culture. Tolkien believed that *Beowulf* preserved to some degree memories of "a tradition concerning moving *historical* events, the arising of Denmark and the wars in the islands."[14] By making the Hengest in *Beowulf* historical, Tolkien also brought the story of *Beowulf* from Geatland to England.

Other connections between history and myth may explain some of the genesis of the Rohirrim. Tolkien notes that both Hengest and Horsa seem to be related to place names in England, including (Ferry) Hinksey, which may be derived from "Hengestes + ig" (Hengest's island).[15] This connection of the word "horse" to English history and place names may provide an explanation for why Tolkien grafted the love of horses onto Anglo-Saxon culture. As Shippey notes, the one aspect of the Rohirrim's culture that does not match the historical culture of the Anglo-Saxons is the centrality of horses in Rohan.[16] It is worth noting that Tolkien first invented the *concept* of the "Horse Kings" and only later endowed the Rohirrim with Anglo-Saxon language and culture (*Shadow*, 422, 434 n. 22). Because Tolkien had already, in his scholarship, linked Hengest ("horse") both to *Beowulf* and to early English history, the further link between horses and Anglo-Saxon may have occurred to him at the point where he decided to bring the "Horse Kings" into his Middle-earth narrative. There is some additional evidence, discussed below, for the connection of horse use to the Anglo-Saxons and to *Beowulf*, but unfortunately these deductions are unprovable. Nevertheless, the three-way link in the person of Hengest (Hengest to *Beowulf*, Hengest to the migration, Hengest to the Ælfwine mythology) provides another bridge-point between Tolkien's invented mythology and his view of early English history.

There are additional links between invented mythology and Anglo-Saxon culture in the figure of Heorrenda, Ælfwine's son by Eadgifu and the half-brother of Hengest and Horsa (in Tolkien's schema). Heorrenda is not a historical Anglo-Saxon, but his name is known to scholars of Old English literature. The poem "Deor," found in the Exeter Book, is the story of an Old English poet, or scop, named Deor who has fallen on hard times. Once Deor had the love and respect of his king, but now a new bard named Heorrenda has usurped his place.[17] Tolkien interpreted this story as suggesting that Heorrenda was a better poet than Deor, and he gave to him the knowledge of all the stories of the Elves, which he recorded in "The Golden Book of Heorrenda":[18] "using those writings that my father Wǣfre (whom the Gnomes name after the regions of his home Angol) did make in his sojourn in the holy isle in the days of the Elves" (*BLT2*, 290–91).

Thus far we have reconstructed a prehistory of the Anglo-Saxons not very different from that described by Christopher Tolkien (*BLT1*, 21–24; *BLT2*, 292–94, 300–312) and analyzed by Shippey.[19] But this rehearsal and clarification is necessary in order to advance to the next step of the argument. With the character of Heorrenda we are able to move from the (now linked) dyad of Tolkien's imaginative creation and the history of the Anglo-Saxons to the more vexed questions of Old English literature. For Tolkien's imaginative reconstruction has an additional layer of connections that, while dismissed by Christopher Tolkien, can be interpreted to show that he was bringing his mythology in line not only with early English history, but with Old English literature—and its cruces. Christopher states that "when lecturing on *Beowulf* at Oxford [J.R.R. Tolkien] sometimes gave the unknown poet a name, calling him *Heorrenda*."[20] If we link this datum to the rest of the mythology sketched above, we note that *Beowulf*, the greatest poem in Anglo-Saxon, would thus be connected to the *legendarium* though the character of Heorrenda (this link would not be obvious in any of Tolkien's published materials).

This link shows how Tolkien's imaginative creation might be connected to his scholarly pursuits in ways more thoroughgoing than the mere borrowing of names. Tolkien's mythology for Anglo-Saxon England would serve, in fact, to explicate one of the great problems of *Beowulf* criticism: the identity of Beowulf's tribe.[21]

Explaining this connection will require a short excursus into *Beowulf* scholarship. Beowulf, the hero of the poem, belongs to the Geatas, a tribe whose identity has been a vexed question for well over a century.[22] Etymologically "Geatas" is equivalent to Old Norse "Gautr," which becomes the modern "Götar," a tribe from southern Sweden. This is the simplest explanation for the name and many scholars are satisfied with this equivalence. But there are some problems that are not solved by identifying the Geatas as the Gautr. Most significantly: why do we have a poem about Danes and Swedes written in Old English and copied sometime in the tenth century? The problem of the presence of Danes in the poem is perhaps the inverse of the problem of the identity of the Geatas. There are a number of plausible reasons why an Old English poet might choose to make Danes an important part of his poem, and their elucidation is beyond the scope of this paper. But the presence of Swedes is another problem entirely. There is no particularly close relationship between the English and the Gautr, and Geatas as a tribe of Sweden are not found elsewhere in the Old English corpus. Furthermore, some of the things said of the Geatas appear to contradict what little historical knowledge we have of the Gautr. A simple explanation for the first of these problems (why an Old English poet would write about Swedes) would be that the poet inherited the story from someone else and just stuck with the Swedish hero—and this explanation is also accepted by many critics who see no need to speculate further. But for some scholars, particularly those of the nineteenth and early twentieth centuries, this explanation was not enough to account for the tribal affiliation of Beowulf and Hygelac.

Part of that better explanation might be found in one of the Old English translations of the Venerable Bede's *Ecclesiastical History*. There the word "Iutarum" is translated with "Geata," so it seems that at least one translator thought that the Geatas were the Jutes.[23] This is significant because, as noted above, the Jutes were one of the three tribes that settled England along with the Angles and the Saxons. Thus if the Geatas were Jutes, then the Geatas of *Beowulf* would be among the ancestors of the English and this relationship could explain why an English poet chose to make the hero of Beowulf a Geat—he would have been writing about his own Jutish ancestors.

But there are problems with this superficially appealing argument. The word "Iutarum" appears one other time in Bede, and there it is translated "Eoten, Ytena." "Jutes" is translated in the *Anglo-Saxon Chronicle* with these Old English words as well. Likewise the actual Old English words for Jutes were "Yte" and "Ytan," not "Geata."[24] Furthermore, the personal names of Geatas in *Beowulf*, Beowulf himself, Hygelac, and Hrethel, among others, never show up in the Kentish genealogies, where scholars would expect to find them if stories about these characters, recognized as Jutes, had circulated in Anglo-Saxon England[25] (because according to Bede the Jutes settled Kent, Hampshire, and the Isle of Wight). This particular absence of evidence is additionally significant because names similar to those in *Beowulf do* appear in the West Saxon genealogies.[26] For R.W. Chambers (whose work Tolkien greatly admired) and many other scholars, these points invalidated the one appearance of "Geata" in Bede and, coupled with the etymological evidence, showed that the Geats were the Gautr.[27] The so-called Jutish hypothesis, advanced by Elis Wadstein, among others, required special pleading, including the idea that the word had been passed through Frisian intermediaries.[28] Tolkien himself rejected this hypothesis at various times and for various reasons. In *Finn and Hengest* he argues that the Geatas and Jutes began to be confused with each other "as soon as knowledge of Scandinavian kings became remote in time or place, and at least as soon as the earliest attempts to put English tradition on record in writing (at the earliest in the seventh century)."[29] This confusion may have arisen because "Jutes on the one side and Geatas on the other were clearly in early times the nearest natural enemies (as neighbors) of the Danes."[30] In *Beowulf and the Critics* he states that:

> the Jutish case is really founded upon the notion that *Beowulf* being in Old English must be a "national epic" and must relate the glories of Jutes not Swedes. But this is a primitive and quite erroneous conception and with its dismissal the Jutish-case, with all its special pleading fails. It should never have been brought forward. If *Beowulf* is a national epic it is an epic of a peculiar kind which includes both Gautr and Jutes.[31]

I think it is fair to say that even though not all of Tolkien's deductions in *Finn and Hengest* have been accepted (Shippey describes the posthumously published book as having "no academic impact at all"),[32] the critical consensus is in fact that the Geatas are not the Jutes. But the Gautr hypothesis still does not explain the big question of why an English poet decided to write about a Swedish hero from an obscure tribe. It is at this point that Tolkien began to weave his mythological web.

We begin in Rohan. Tolkien denied that the Rohirrim were to be equated to the Anglo-Saxons except "in a general way due to their circumstances: a simpler and more primitive people living in contact with a higher and more venerable culture, and occupying lands that had once been part of its domain,"[33] but as Shippey has noted, this denial is hard to accept given the many and detailed parallels between the real culture and Tolkien's invention.[34] The Rohirrim speak Anglo-Saxon—actually, as Shippey has shown, Old Mercian[35]—and follow many Anglo-Saxon customs.[36] If, for the sake of argument, we put aside Tolkien's assertion that the Anglo-Saxons are not the Rohirrim, we can begin this section of our analysis with a simple equation: Rohan = Anglo-Saxon England.

The names of the kings of Rohan are nearly all Anglo-Saxon words or epithets for "king," except for the first king of Rohan, whose name, Eorl, can be translated as "earl, nobleman." Eorl's father is Leod, a name which means "man, leader of a people" (*LR* Appendix A.2, 1038–40). One might even interpret the names of the kings of Rohan as a kind of inside joke—the kings are all named "King," except for the first two, who have not yet come to Rohan and are thus not fully kings. But Tolkien extended the joke, if joke it was, back even further and turned it from lighthearted fancy to rather serious historical speculation by giving the ancestors of the Rohirrim Gothic names (with Latinized spellings). Leod's ancestors, as we learn in appendix A, include one Vidugavia, who called himself King of Rhovanion. Vidugavia's daughter is Vidumavi. She married the Gondorian King Valacar, and their son, Eldacar, was originally named Vinitharya (*LR* Appendix A.1.iv, 1022). In *Unfinished Tales* we learn that the Northmen who settled in the Vales of Anduin are gathered by Marhwini, son of Marhari. "This was the beginning of the Éothéod" (*UT*, 289). The Éothéod is the name of the ancestors of the Rohirrim. Christopher Tolkien notes that these names—Vidugavia, Vidumavi, Vinitharya, Marhiwini, Marhari—are Gothic in form, in contrast to the Old English names of the descendants. He explains this change (from Gothic to Old English) by noting that "since, as is explained in

Appendix F (II), the language of Rohan was 'made to resemble ancient English,' the names of the ancestors of the Rohirrim are cast into the forms of the earliest recorded Germanic language" (*UT*, 311, n. 6). This is, of course, consistent with Tolkien's elaborate "translation" explanation in appendix F, but I think that for the sake of argument it is worth suspending our belief in Tolkien's explanation and reading the history implied by the names. If, as we established above, the Anglo-Saxons = the Rohirrim, then the ancestors of the Rohirrim, who have Gothic names, would be the ancestors of the Anglo-Saxons. That is, the ancestors of the Anglo-Saxons would be Goths. A Gothic ancestry for Anglo-Saxons would have important implications for *Beowulf*, particularly for the question of the identity of the Geatas. For if the ancestors of the Anglo-Saxons were Goths, and the Geatas were Goths, then the hero of *Beowulf* is in fact one of the ancestors of the Anglo-Saxons because he is a Goth. Obviously the rub comes in the assertion that the Geatas were Goths. One cannot make this equivalence from Tolkien's published works, which do not take up this particular element of the question of the identity of the Geatas. But in fact Tolkien did, at least at one point early in his career, identify the Geatas as Goths. In his verse translation of *Beowulf*, which dates from Tolkien's years at Leeds University, Tolkien translated "Geatas" with "Goths."[37]

Now a possible link between Geatas and Goths has long been suggested—and mostly rejected—by scholars of Anglo-Saxon. The detail of the argument is both tedious and beyond the scope of this essay, but one main argument is that the putative historical events of the poem, particularly Hygelac's failed raid, would have occurred too *late* for the Geatas to be Goths.[38] R.W. Chambers states (in a footnote) that "there is certainly a primitive connection between the names of the Geatas (Gautr) and of the Goths: but they are quite distinct peoples: we should not be justified in speaking of the Geatas as identical with the Goths."[39] In other words, with little positive evidence to support an equivalence of Geatas and Goths, the default position is that the Geatas are the Gautr.

What would it mean if the Geatas *were* Goths? The historical Goths were one of the great barbarian peoples of early Europe.[40] They ruled a huge empire until they were defeated by the Huns. Gothic is the oldest Germanic language. But Gothic is not a direct ancestor of Anglo-Saxon; it is an East Germanic language, while Anglo-Saxon is West Germanic. Thus it is very unlikely that the actual cultural and genetic ancestors of the Anglo-Saxons spoke Gothic as we have it recorded. Rather, they would have spoken proto-Germanic, the hypothesized language that would later, but long before any written texts were created, diverge into East, West, and North Germanic languages. But Tolkien loved the Gothic language, which he said "took him by storm,"[41] and he was acutely aware of the historical relationship of Gothic and Anglo-Saxon. Having the Geatas be Goths, and the Goths be ancestors of the Anglo-Saxons, would explain why one of the Anglo-Saxons would write a poem that celebrated a Geat: that Geat was actually a Goth and thus one of the ancestors of the Anglo-Saxon poet (in this schema).

The equation of Geatas and Goths would thus tap into what could be called the synthesizing impulse of myth, and no one was better at imitating this process than Tolkien. The great synthesizing works of Jakob and Wilhelm Grimm in German, Elias Lönnrot in Finnish, and N.F.S. Grundtvig in Danish were all well known to Tolkien. *Beowulf and the Critics* shows us that Tolkien admired Grundtvig greatly; he is, as Shippey deduced, the "very old voice" in the Babel-allegory in "Beowulf: The Monsters and the Critics," who says that *Beowulf* is "a mythical allegory."[42] By making the Geatas Goths, Tolkien ties together many irritating loose ends and thus creates an aesthetically pleasing story.

But Tolkien was a great scholar. Moreover he was a very hard-nosed scholar. While having Geatas = Goths and Goths = ancestors of Anglo-Saxons solves some critical problems, there is, unfortunately, not much chance of these equivalences being factually true. The "Jutish hypothesis" solved one problem only by relying on special pleading and the necessity of accepting one piece of supporting evidence while ignoring other, contradictory evidence. The Geatas = Goths hypothesis founders on historical fact and lack of evidence. In Tolkien's later prose translation of *Beowulf*, which dates from the late 1920s to 1930s when Tolkien was at Oxford, Tolkien eschews the entire Geatas/Goths equivalence and simply translates Geatas as Geats. It seems reasonable to conclude that Tolkien either did not continue to believe that the Geatas/Goths equivalence was accurate, or he did believe that it was true but did not believe that it could withstand critical scrutiny, and he therefore abandoned it in his scholarly work.

It is not unreasonable to suppose that this particular solution of the Geatas problem would have influenced Tolkien in his mythology and his imaginative construction of an early English pseudohistory, a construction that took place years after the *Beowulf* translations were completed. Note that Rohan as the home of the "Horse Kings" is first conceived some time after August 1939 and thus almost certainly *after* the prose *Beowulf* translations (with its avoidance of the Geats = Goths claim) (*Shadow*, 369–70, 409, 422, 434 n. 22). Furthermore, as Shippey has noted, the Goths were recognized by nineteenth- and twentieth-century scholarship as the "horse-folk" par excellence, the *equitatus Gothorum*, "the cavalry of the Goths."[43] Thus we might see the development of Tolkien's thought to run something like this. His pre-1939 conception would be that if the Goths were horse people, and the Geatas were Goths, then the Geatas would be horse people. And if the Geatas were the ancestors of the Anglo-Saxons, then the ancestors of the Anglo-Saxons would have been horse people. That the ancestors of the Anglo-Saxons were horse people might explain why their legendary leaders in the migration, Hengest and Horsa, were named "horse." After 1939, when he had invented the Rohirrim, Tolkien split off the idea that the ancestors of the Anglo-Saxons were horse people from the idea that the Geatas were the Goths. He therefore, for the purposes of this scholarship, abandoned the Geatas/Goths equivalence while at the same time in his fiction radically expanded upon his invented link between the horse people and the ancestors of the Anglo-Saxons. If we tie together all these various strands of historical speculation and recognize that the process of building mythology in fiction is different than historical scholarship, we can, I think, see another way in which Tolkien's mind worked: in his fiction he had found a way to have his cake and eat it too, to preserve the rigorous, uncompromising logic of philological and historical deduction while at the same time building a pseudohistorical mythology that was intellectually and aesthetically appealing.

Let us then summarize the pseudohistory or mythology that Tolkien had created in his fiction: The original settlers of Anglo-Saxon England were the sons and descendants of Ælfwine, the Elf-friend who had sailed across the sea to the Holy Isle of the Elves. The prehistory of the descendants of Ælfwine was Tolkien's invented mythology of Arda, but it also included the story of *Beowulf*, a depiction of the exploits of some others of their ancestors. The early history of Anglo-Saxon England was generated when the half-brothers of Heorrenda, Hengest, and Horsa, led the migration of the Jutes from the continent to England. Heorrenda himself composed *Beowulf* and compiled the legends of Arda in the "Golden

Book of Heorrenda." Hengest is a character in *Beowulf* and in "Finnsburg." The hero of *Beowulf* is a Geat, which equals a Goth, one of the continental ancestors of the Anglo-Saxons, before Hengest and Horsa led them over the sea to England. It all fits nicely together even though it is probably not true (and Tolkien knew this).

The question remains, then, why Tolkien would pursue such a project when he could easily have avoided the initial cross-contamination of invention and deduction. There are, in fact, two useful precedents for this kind of cultural work, and Tolkien almost certainly would have been aware of them: the Roman historian Livy and John Milton.[44]

Livy writes:

> Events before Rome was born or thought of have come to us in old tales with more of the charms of poetry than of a sound historical record, and such traditions I propose neither to affirm nor refute. There is no reason, I feel, to object when antiquity draws no hard line between the human and the supernatural: it adds dignity to the past, and, if any nation deserves the privilege of claiming a divine ancestry, that nation is our own; and so great is the glory won by the Roman people in their wars that, when they declare Mars himself was their first parent, and father of the man who founded their city, all nations of the world might well allow the claim as readily as they accept imperial dominion.[45]

Milton writes:

> What ever might be the reason, this we find, that of *British affairs*, from the first peopling of the Iland to the coming of *Julius Cæsar*, nothing certain, either by Tradition, History, or Ancient Fame hath thereto bin left us. That which we have of oldest seeming, hath by the greater part of judicious Antiquaries bin long rejected for a modern Fable.
>
> Nevertheless there being others besides the first suppos'd Author, men not unread, nor unlerned in Aintiquitie, who admit that for approved story, which the former explode for fiction, and seeing that oft-times relations heretofore accounted fabulous have bin after found to contain in them many footsteps, and reliques of something true, as we read in Poets of the Flood, and Giants little beleev'd, til undoubted witnesses taught us, that all was not fain'd; I have thefore determin'd to bestow the telling over ev'n of these reputed Tales; be it for nothing else but in favour of our

English Poets, and Rhetoricians, who by their Art will know, how to use them judiciously.[46]

It is likely that Tolkien would have known both quotations. Livy had been and remains a standard text in classics, and Tolkien would have studied *The Early History of Rome* both at King Edward's school and in his undergraduate work during his first years at Oxford. Milton's *History of Britain* was not a school text, but it is highly probable that Tolkien would have examined it, given Milton's detailed discussions of Anglo-Saxon history.[47] Both Milton's and Livy's statements have much in common with Tolkien's remarks about the creation of a mythology for England. While Tolkien's comments are not as aggressive and martial as Livy's, we do know that he loved England fiercely and felt as if his country deserved a mythology of its own.[48] Likewise the comment that Tolkien wished other artists to develop his mythology in various media (quoted above) can be analogized to Milton's invocation of other poets who will use the material in *The History of Britain* to further their art.[49] We can therefore take Tolkien's comment (quoted at the beginning of this chapter) seriously because he in fact endeavored to do exactly what he said: create a mythology and a pseudohistory that had an interface with the actual history of England. Without this interface, he would have merely created stories; with the connections engendered by the correspondences in names and events, the stories become mythology.

We can extend this analysis further by noting that, when Tolkien recognized that his creation and its apparent interconnections with actual history and scholarship were about to be published, he then extended and developed his interface so as to obscure exactly the same connections that he had so laboriously built, developing the convoluted and unconvincing argument of appendix F that the common speech and the speech of the Rohirrim are not in fact Modern English and Old English but other, unreported languages that are mapped onto Modern English and Old English. Simple inspection of the *History of the Lord of the Rings* volumes shows that Tolkien in no way composed the names in this manner; Old English names were present from the beginning of the period of composition.

In *The Peoples of Middle-earth* Christopher Tolkien notes that there is a contradiction that he is unable to explain between Tolkien's words in *Foreword: Concerning Hobbits*, where he says that Hobbits spoke a language "very similar" to Modern English, and the assertions of appendix F.[50] Because this contradiction arises between the time in which *The Lord of the Rings* was finished and the time in which Tolkien knew it would be published (appendix F was apparently written immediately after the last chapter of the *Lord of the Rings* in 1948),[51] it seems reasonable to infer that the elaborate, two-tier frame structure (The Red Book of Westmarch and the conceit of the linguistic mapping) was created for the purpose of deliberately separating the invented legends from Tolkien's historical scholarship. And yet the connections, deeply buried and even denied by the author, remain for those who can find them. After all, Tolkien, the past master of invented names and histories, could easily have avoided any linkage at all between his creation and English and Germanic history. But he did not.

We must therefore be skeptical about appendix F and not be completely convinced by the author's protestations that his work on Middle-earth did not have some created connection to English history. We should also recognize that Tolkien had come to embody the very processes that, in "Beowulf: The Monsters and the Critics," he showed were such an important part of the creation of *Beowulf*: He had made medieval myth relevant because it was no longer only myth, but was bound up in the constitution of history and valued literature. And, finally, we can recognize, as Tolkien did, that myth is often so neat and so beautiful that it *should* be true, even when it is not.

Notes

This paper was first presented at the "Tolkien's Modern Middle Ages" conference at Bucknell University. I would like to thank Alf Siewers for organizing the conference, inviting me, and providing much helpful feedback. I am also grateful to my fellow panelists, Jane Chance and Ted Sherman, for their suggestions. Respondent John Hunter made a number of significant contributions to this paper. Gergely Nagy's criticism has improved the argument enormously. Thanks also to Douglas A. Anderson.

1. Anders Stenström, "A Mythology? For England?" in *Proceedings of the J.R.R. Tolkien Centenary Conference 1992*, ed. Patricia Reynolds and Glen H. GoodKnight, *Mythlore* 80 / *Mallorn* 30 (Milton Keynes: Tolkien Society, 1995; Altadena, Calif.: Mythopoeic Press, 1995), 310–14.

2. The idea of Tolkien's mythology for England was first substantively developed by Jane Chance in *Tolkien's Art: A Mythology for England* (London: Macmillan, 1979) and revised in the book's reissue by the University Press of Kentucky, 2001. The "mythology for England" approach has subsequently be-

come a commonplace of Tolkien criticism; see, for example, Tom Shippey, *The Road to Middle-earth,* rev. ed. (London: Harper Collins, 1992), 268–72. For a summary of other critical approaches to the "mythology for England" idea, see Michael D.C. Drout and Hilary Wynne, "Tom Shippey's *J.R.R. Tolkien: Author of the Century* and a Look Back at Tolkien Criticism since 1982," *Envoi* 9, no. 2 (2000): 111–13.

3. With the exception of the Rohirrim's speaking Old English, the links between Middle-earth and historical culture are relatively well hidden in the materials published during Tolkien's lifetime. Only through the combination of the appendices of *LR* and the posthumously published material is it possible to reconstruct fully the mythology for Anglo-Saxon England.

4. It seems that at some points in Tolkien's composition of the stories, Eriol and Ælfwine were two different characters. At other times they were two different names for the same character. Thus, as Christopher Tolkien notes, it is not incorrect to "treat the two names as indicative of different narrative projections— 'the Eriol story' and 'the Ælfwine story'"; *BLT1*, 300–301. For the purposes of my argument, however, it is not necessary to disambiguate this exceptionally tangled matter. For further discussion see Verlyn Flieger, *A Question of Time: J.R.R. Tolkien's Road to Faërie* (Kent, Ohio: Kent State University Press, 1997), 64–67, and Verlyn Flieger, "The Footsteps of Ælfwine," in *Tolkien's "Legendarium": Essays on "The History of Middle-earth,"* ed. Verlyn Flieger and Carl F. Hostetter (Westport, Conn.: Greenwood, 2000), 186–91 and 195–97.

5. Flieger, "Footsteps," 185–90.

6. As Tom Shippey notes, Ottar would definitely be Old Norse; Ohthere would definitely be Old English; but Ottor could be either. Tom Shippey, "Tolkien and Iceland: The Philology of Envy," http://www.nordals.hi.is/shippey.html.

7. Lines 2380, 2394, 2612, 2928, 2932. Fr. Klaeber, ed. *Beowulf and the Fight at Finnsburg*, 3rd ed. (Boston, Mass.: D.C. Heath, 1950).

8. Chambers notes that the name Ottar in the *Ynglinga tal* "is certainly the Ohthere of *Beowulf.*" R.W. Chambers, *Beowulf: An Introduction to the Study of the Poem with a Discussion of the Stories of Offa and Finn*, 3rd ed. (Cambridge: Cambridge University Press, 1963), 343.

9. Janet Bately, "The Nature of Old English Prose," in *The Cambridge Companion to Old English Literature*, ed. Malcolm Godden and Michael Lapidge (Cambridge: Cambridge University Press, 1991), 72. For an edition of the Old English *Orosius*, see Janet Bately, ed., *The Old English Orosius*, EETS vol. 6, 2nd Ser. (London: Oxford University Press, 1980). Every Anglo-Saxonist knows of the *Voyages of Ohthere* and *Wulfstan*, and Tolkien was certainly no exception, but he would have had additional reasons to be familiar with the text: the *Voyages* include the mention of the Old English word for "walrus" (horshwæl), a word that Tolkien defined for the *Oxford English Dictionary*. See Peter M. Gilliver, "At the Wordface: J.R.R. Tolkien's Work on the *Oxford English Dictionary*," in *Proceedings of the J.R.R. Tolkien Centenary Conference*, ed. Reynolds and GoodKnight, 182.

10. Bede, *Ecclesiastical History,* 1.15; *Ecclesiastical History of the English Nation*, trans. J. Stevens, Everyman's Library (London: Dent, 1910 [repr. 1978]), 62–63. For a discussion of the ways that stories of the Anglo-Saxon migration may be more mythical than historical, see Nicholas Howe, *Migration and Mythmaking in Anglo-Saxon England* (New Haven: Yale University Press, 1989), and Allen J. Frantzen, *Desire for Origins: New Language, Old English, and Teaching the Tradition* (New Brunswick, N.J.: Rutgers University Press, 1990). Tom Shippey discusses the parallels between Hengest and Horsa and the leaders of the Hobbit migration, Marco and Blanco (both names can also be translated as "horse"). He notes Tolkien's explanation that Hobbits came from the "Angle" between the Hoarwell and Loudwater rivers, an obvious parallel to the "angle" between Flensburg fjord and the river Schlie; see *The Road to Middle-earth*, 92–93.

11. *BLT1*, 24. Bede notes that Hengest and Horsa were the sons of Wictgils, the son of Witta, the son of Wecta, the son of Woden; Stevens, trans., 63. Tolkien does not use these names (i.e., he does not make Wictgils = Ælfwine), but he does link his mythological construction to Woden by connecting this name (the Old English form of Oðínn) to Manweg (Manwë) of the Valar, though note that only the Elves make this connection; *BLT2*, 290.

12. Chambers, 403.

13. J.R.R Tolkien, *Finn and Hengest: The Fragment and the Episode*, ed. Alan Bliss (Boston: Houghton Mifflin, 1983), 66–69.

14. J.R.R. Tolkien, *Beowulf and the Critics*, ed. Michael D.C. Drout, MRTS vol. 248 (Tempe, Ariz.: Arizona Center for Medieval and Renaissance Studies, 2002), 54, 197; Tolkien, *Finn and Hengest*, 12–16.

15. Tolkien, *Finn and Hengest*, 6 n. 65.

16. Shippey, *Road to Middle-earth*, 112–13.

17. G.P. Krapp and E. van K. Dobbie, *eds., The Exeter Book*, vol. 3, *The Anglo-Saxon Poetic Records* (New York: Columbia University Press, 1936), 178–79. At an earlier stage of Tolkien's composition, Deor was the name of Ælfwine's father, thus possibly complicating the reading I am developing. See *BLT2*, 313.

18. *BLT2*, 290, 324. The authorship of the "Golden Book" is an exceptionally complicated issue that is beyond the scope of this paper. At times the book was authored by Eriol, at others by Rúmil or Pengolod. For the purposes of my argument it is sufficient that the book was, at various times, said to be authored by Heorrenda.

19. Shippey, *Road to Middle-earth*, 268–72.

20. *BLT2*, 323. Christopher Tolkien's comment is substantiated by some of Tolkien's unpublished *Beowulf* commentaries. See, for example, Oxford, Bodleian Library, MS Tolkien A28 C, fol. 6v.

21. And if indeed Heorrenda were the author of *Beowulf*, then the appearance of Heorrenda in *Deor* would be the only clear reference to *Beowulf* in Anglo-Saxon literature.

22. For a summary of the arguments relating to the identity of the Geatas, see Chambers, 8–10.

23. Discussed by Tolkien in *Finn and Hengest*, 61; see also Chambers, 8–9.

24. Chambers, 8–10.

25. Chambers, 343.

26. Tolkien, *Finn and Hengest*, 56; see also Chambers, 343–44. For further discussion of the genealogies, see Kenneth Sisam, "Anglo-Saxon Royal Genealogies," *Proceedings of the British Academy* 39 (1953): 287–346; David N. Dumville, "Kingship, Genealogies, and Regnal Lists," in *Early Medieval Kingship*, ed. P.H. Sawyer and Ian N. Wood (Leeds: School of History, University of Leeds, 1977 [repr. 1979]), 72–104; and Craig R. Davis, "Cultural Assimilation in the Anglo-Saxon Royal Genealogies," *Anglo-Saxon England* 21 (1992): 23–36.

27. "There is nothing peculiar, then, in the fact that *Beowulf* celebrates heroes who were not of Anglian birth. . . . It is repeatedly objected that the Götar are remote from the Anglo-Saxons. . . . Possibly: but remoteness did not prevent the Anglo-Saxons from being interested in heroes of the Huns or Goths or Burgundians or Langobards, who were much more distant. And the absence of any direct connection between the history of the Geatas and the historic Anglo-Saxon records, affords a strong presumption that the Geatas *were* a somewhat alien people. If the people of Beowulf, Hygelac, and Hrethel were the same people as the Jutes who colonized Kent and Hampshire, why do we never, in the Kentish royal genealogies or elsewhere, find any claim to such connection? The Mercians did not so forget their connection with the old Offa of Angle, although a much greater space of time had intervened. The fact that we have no mention among the ancestors of Beowulf and Hygelac of any names which we can connect with the Jutish genealogy affords, therefore, a strong presumption that they belonged to some other tribe" (Chambers, 343–43).

28. Elis Wadstein, "The *Beowulf* Poem as an English National Epos," *Acta Philologica Scandinavica* 8 (1925): 273–91.

29. Tolkien, *Finn and Hengest*, 47.

30. Tolkien, *Finn and Hengest*, 59; see also Oxford, Bodleian Library MS Tolkien A 31 fol. 126: here Tolkien says that Getis is a common confusion for Gothi (Goths), which can also be a confusion for Götar, Gautr.

31. Tolkien, *Beowulf and the Critics*, 84 n. 2. In Oxford, Bodleian Library, MS Tolkien A 31 fol. 122 Tolkien rejects the Jutish hypothesis completely. The Geatas in *Beowulf* are the Gautr of Gautland.

32. Tom Shippey, *J.R.R. Tolkien: Author of the Century* (London: HarperCollins, 2000; Boston: Houghton Mifflin, 2001), 267.

33. *RK*, 414; and see also Tolkien's unpublished response to Burton Raffel, Oxford, Bodleian Library MS Tolkien A 30, section C.

34. Shippey, *Road to Middle-earth*, 112.

35. Ibid.

36. The first published detailed discussion of the Old English affinities of the Rohirrim is John Tinkler, "Old English in Rohan," in *Tolkien and the Critics*, ed. Neil D. Isaacs and Rose A. Zimbardo (Notre Dame, Ind.: University of Notre Dame Press, 1968), 164–69.

37. Oxford, Bodleian Library, MS Tolkien A 29.

38. In the "Moseley" Chronicle Roll, a genealogy of the West Saxon Kings, there is a marginal note that lists "Saxones, Angli, Iuthi, Daci, Norwagences, Gothi, Wandali, Geathi et Fresi" among the descendants of Boerinus (Chambers, 201–4). This evidence suggests that the Geatas were identified as being separate from the Goths. Tolkien cites the Chronicle Roll (in another context) in *Finn and Hengest*, 47 n. 32. Hygelac in *Beowulf* was first identified as the Chlochilaicus of Gregory of Tours's *Historia Francorum* by N.F.S. Grundtvig. See Gregory of Tours, *Historia Francorum*, in *Opera*, ed. W. Arndt and Br. Krusch, vol. 1 of 2 vols., Monumenta Germaniae Historica, Scriptores Rerum Merovingicarum 1 (Hanover: Bibliopolius Hahnianus, 1884), 110–11; N.F.S. Grundtvig, *Bjowulfs Drape. Et Gothisk Helte-Digt fra forrige Aar-Tusinde af Angel-Saxisk paa Danske Riim* (Copenhagen: A. Seidelin, 1820).

39. Chambers, 23 n. 4. It is worth noting that this footnote comes after a discussion of the possible identity of the Heathobards. Chambers argues that the Heathobeardan of *Beowulf* are not the Langobards, "but a separate portion of the people, which had been left behind on the shores of the Baltic, when the main body went south." In *The Lost Road* the name of one of Tolkien's main characters, Alboin, is Langobardic. Alboin is linked to the Goths via the accounts (by Jordanes and by Ammianus Marcelinus) of the destruction of Eormenric's Gothic kingdom by the Huns. "Again, the story of the death of Alboin, as told by Paul the Deacon, *may* contain legendary elements: but it certainly represents Alboin's nationality correctly" (Chambers, 444).

40. The Goths are also mentioned in *Widsith*, line 18; Krapp and Dobbie, *Exeter Book*, 149–53.

41. J.R.R. Tolkien, "English and Welsh," in *Angles and Britons: The O'Donnell Lectures* (Cardiff: University of Wales Press, 1963), 38; reprinted in J.R.R. Tolkien, *"The Monsters and the Critics" and Other Essays*, ed. Christopher Tolkien (London: Allen and Unwin, 1983), 162–97.

42. Shippey, *Road to Middle-earth*, 299; J.R.R. Tolkien, "Beowulf: The Monsters and the Critics," *Proceedings of the British Academy* 22 (1936), 13; Tolkien, *Beowulf and the Critics*, 43, 98–99.

43. T.A. Shippey, "Goths and Huns: The Rediscovery of the Northern Cultures in the Nineteenth Century," in *The Medieval Legacy: A Symposium*, ed. Andreas Haarder, et al. (Odense: Odense University Press, 1982), 53.

44. I am exceedingly grateful to John Hunter, Professor of Comparative Humanities at Bucknell University, for these suggestions.

45. Livy, *The Early History of Rome (Books I–V)*, trans. Aubrey de Sélincourt (Baltimore: Penguin, 1960), 17–18.

46. John Milton, *Complete Prose Works of John Milton,* vol. 5: *1648?–1671*, ed. French Fogle (New Haven: Yale University Press, 1971), 2–3.

47. The evidence for knowledge of Milton is more circumstantial. First, Tolkien cites Milton in "Beowulf: The Monsters and the Critics," 12. Second, Geoffrey of Monmouth's *History* was of interest to Tolkien, as shown by *The Notion Club Papers* (see *Sauron*, 192 and 216) and *Finn and Hengest*, 69 n. 69.

Geoffrey of Monmouth is also an important source for Milton, and it seems reasonable to speculate that Tolkien would have been interested in what use Milton made of Geoffrey. Finally, Milton was very interested in *Brut*, and we know that Tolkien was as well: see Tolkien, *Beowulf and the Critics*, 15 and 97.

48. For a discussion see Chance, *Tolkien's Art*, 1–8. For the discussion of England's impoverished mythology, see Letter 131, *Letters*, 143–61.

49. Both Livy and Milton are intensely ideological writers who promote a specific, partisan view of history and its development. Such an ideological analysis of Tolkien's mythology is beyond the scope of this paper, which has been concerned primarily to reconstruct Tolkien's implied history and mythology for Anglo-Saxon England. Nevertheless, a fair ideological analysis of Tolkien's mythology (unlike the tendentious work of, for example, Mick Otty or Hal Colebatch), one that takes into account the entire *Legendarium* as well as *LR*, is an obvious desideratum for Tolkien scholarship. See Mick Otty, "A Structuralist Guide to Middle-earth," in *J.R.R. Tolkien: This Far Land,* ed. Robert Giddings (London: Vision, 1983), and Hal Colebatch, *Return of the Heroes: "The Lord of the Rings," "Star Wars," and Contemporary Culture* (Perth: Australian Institute, 1990).

50. J.R.R. Tolkien, *The Peoples of Middle-earth*, ed. Christopher Tolkien (Boston: Houghton Mifflin, 1996), 27; *FR*, 10–17.

51. Tolkien, *The Peoples of Middle-earth*, vii–viii.

Chapter 14

OATHS AND OATH BREAKING

Analogues of Old English Comitatus in Tolkien's Myth

JOHN R. HOLMES

What was once incompletely understood is now a commonplace in Tolkien criticism: that the works of this most popular of fantasy authors began as philological experiments. The creation of his fantasy world began with the creation of imaginary languages, and only then followed the creation of cultures informing and informed by those languages. Thus, on paper, if not in Middle-earth, Elvish existed before the Elves.

Much has been written about Tolkien's linguistic background to his fantasy, of course, but the overwhelming majority of it falls into two categories: guides to his invented languages such as those of Ruth S. Noel or Jim Allan[1] and studies of the influence of the ancient languages Tolkien studied and taught at Oxford, such as T.A. Shippey's two books on Tolkien.[2] Somewhere in between is the study of the interplay of philology and theology in Tolkien's fiction by Verlyn Flieger.[3] But relatively little attention has been paid to the semantic interplay of ancient and modern in Tolkien's language, particularly a phenomenon known as "semantic displacement."

Semantic displacement is the ability of language to express things that are not present—either because they have no objective reality, or because they are simply in another place or time. The temporal displacement could be into the past (thus history is semantic displacement) or the future (thus, so is prophecy). Lies are a form of displacement, for by lying we say what is not. But so are promises, for by promising we say what is not *yet*.

In fact, it is the promise type of semantic displacement, which this essay will explore, that provides one of the many unconscious marks of antiquity in Tolkien's fiction—unconscious, that is, to the reader, though painstakingly intentional on the part of the author. T.A. Shippey has successfully extinguished the critical *ignis fatuus* of Tolkien's supposed "archaic diction." Archaisms in the dialogue of *The Lord of the Rings* are always precisely appropriate when they appear; those archaisms aside, the language of the Third Age in Middle-earth is much more "natural" (if that word has any precise critical meaning when applied to dialogue, which I doubt) and modern than Tolkien's more carping critics will allow. As Shippey demonstrates, Tolkien creates a sense of antiquity more often by subtleties of word order and rhythm than by diction.[4] Yet what I hope to demonstrate is that it is the attitudes of Tolkien's characters toward one particular use of language—the promise or oath—that marks them as old-fashioned. More so, it marks them as a vanishing breed even in the Third Age, for the tonal center of Tolkien's fiction is the elegiac mood that he found in Old English literature, the passing from a golden age of heroes to a lesser age of all-too-human, life-sized, base-metal (or Styrofoam, perhaps) people. The heroic age was populated by keepers of great oaths; to those who came after, oaths were just words.

No reader of *Beowulf* needs to be convinced of the centrality of the oath in Old English culture, though in a moment we will glance at the preeminence of oath in *Beowulf*. Nor do we need a nod to the ultimate source of the theme in Germanic culture at large—the discussion of *comitatus* in Tacitus's *Germania*—though we shall visit that as well. Rather, to demonstrate how vital the oath is to Old English culture—and how integral is that Old English sense of the passing of the heroic age—we can turn to a single, rare, and curious word for oath breaking in a famous sermon, *Sermo Lupi ad Anglos* [Sermon to the English by Wulfstan], given by Archbishop Wulfstan of Ely in A.D. 1014. In heroic epics like *Beowulf* (if it *is* an epic; Tolkien questioned the categorization—see *Monsters,* 13) or even heroic poetry about historical battles, like *Brunanburh* or *Maldon*, we expect to find elements central to the heroic code, as I argue oath making to be. But finding those elements in a sermon, the genre whose job it is to apply the gospel to everyday life, suggests that, to the Old English mind, or at least to Wulfstan's eleventh-century Old English mind, the making (and breaking) of oaths is an everyday moral concern not limited to the heroic age.

Or perhaps, like the heroic poem, the sermon, at least the sermon of the jeremiad type, like Wulfstan's *Sermo Lupi*, also in its essence contrasts the fallen nature of the present to the glorious deeds (spiritually heroic) of the past. It may be that Tolkien himself connected Old English heroic poetry and the Old English sermon: Hrothgar's lengthy speech to Beowulf sketching moral guidelines for a potential king (lines 1758–84) is called by the *Beowulf* poet a *giedd*, which Tolkien translates as "sermon" (*Monsters,* 37). In Wulfstan's famous *giedd*—and *only* there—appears a fascinating word: *āðbrice*. Its interest stems not merely from its being a *hapax legomenon*, a nonce word, a word that appears once and once only in all the records of a dead language. It is also interesting because of the litany in which the word appears, giving it a rhetorical prominence to which only a culture founded on the oath would give it, for *āðbrice* means, simply, "oath breach," or "oath breaking."

Perhaps it is only half true that *āðbrice* is a nonce word. Both roots in this compound word are high-frequency, well-known words (*āð* appears 23 times in the Old English poetic corpus and *brecan* 105 times), and compounding was a nearly universal phenomenon in Old English. Compounding is still fairly common in modern English, as evidenced by the fact that the most popular cartoon of the new century is named by a double compound: *Sponge-Bob Square-Pants*. Tolkien translates the compound directly in modern English in *The Lord of the Rings* when Aragorn hails the "Sleeping Dead" of Erech as "Oathbreakers" (*LR* 5.2, 772). We will look at the context in Tolkien in a moment, but first I would like to look at the context of *āðbrice* in Wulfstan's sermon. One of the most arresting things about the word to the twenty-first–century mind—or at least to my twenty-first–century mind—is how deadly seriously the eleventh century looked at oath breaking. Wulfstan is listing the most horrible sins that the English people have committed in recent years, for which God has punished them by sending the Danish marauders. We have been guilty, Wulfstan says, of greed, theft, pillaging, selling of men, attacks on kinsmen, manslaughter, adultery—and it is only in culmination of this list that he adds oath breaking.[5] It strikes the modern ear almost as a comic non sequitur, though Wulfstan is quite serious.

What kind of culture is it that would rank oath breaking with pillaging and murder? The example of *Beowulf* and the earliest written record of Germanic culture, Tacitus's *Germania*, suggest that the oath is the very foundation of Germanic society. The political relationship between thegn and lord, to which Tacitus gives the Latin name *comitatus*, is essentially an oath sworn in the mead hall—for the lord to share his treasures with his thegns, and for the thegn to defend his lord to the death.[6] The Old English version of Prince Hal's "once more unto the *āðbrice*" in *Beowulf*, in *The Battle of Maldon*, and in *The Battle of Brunanburh* is an earl on the battlefield reminding his men of the oaths they swore and that now is the time to redeem those pledges. It is this same heroic code that Tolkien tries to capture in *The Lord of the Rings*, and we'll look at a few direct references to *āðbrice* in Tolkien's trilogy.

The first oath breaker mentioned in *The Lord of the Rings* is the last person one would suspect: Gandalf himself. It might be objected that what Gandalf breaks is not exactly an oath, and it was extraordinary circumstances, and not a lack of integrity, that prevented Gandalf from keeping his word. I have split this hair with all four of my sons as they were growing up, each one construing an offhand suggestion that *maybe* we could stop at the video arcade as a solemn oath sworn on the Precious that we *would*, come hell or high water. But it is precisely the casualness of Gandalf's promise, and the supernatural intensity of the forces that prevent him from honoring it—literally *both* hell *and* high water—that make it so extraordinary that Gandalf feels he must apologize to a mere Hobbit. The word Gandalf uses is not the Old English *āð* but the Norse word *tryst*. It is at the end of Gandalf's long résumé to the Council of Elrond of his narrow escape from the tower of Saruman, imprisonment which had kept him from meeting Frodo and company in Bree as planned. He asks forgiveness: "But such a thing has not happened before, that Gandalf broke tryst and did not come when he promised. An account to the Ring-bearer of so strange an event was required, I think" (*LR* 2.2, 258).

Thus the first broken oath in *The Lord of the Rings* is not a moral fault, and it introduces the notion that there are permissible limits to oaths. The Elvenking Elrond implies just that when he sends off the newly formed Fellowship of the Ring, by refusing to bind them to an oath whose consequences and price they cannot see. "The further you go," Elrond tells the Fellowship, "the less easy will it be to withdraw; yet no oath or bond is laid on you to go further than you will. For you do not yet know the strength of your hearts, and you cannot foresee what each may meet upon the road" (*LR* 2.3, 274). Consider, for a moment, the implication for the ethics of the oath in Elrond's words. He is making provisions for two loopholes that might invalidate the oath of a fellow sworn to defend the ringbearer. First, the strength of his heart may prove too little—he may lose courage. Second, he might meet a danger he hadn't reckoned on—"you cannot foresee what each may meet." It would seem that Elrond is setting the bar rather low.

And yet Aragorn gives almost exactly the same break to the untried recruits just before the final battle with Sauron, that is, just before the opening of the Black Gate. He allows them to go home. "Go!" says Aragorn. "But keep what honour you may, and do not run! And there is a task which you may attempt and so be not wholly shamed. Take your way south-west till you come to Cair Andros, and if that is still held by enemies, as I think, then re-take it, if you can; and hold it to the last in defence of Gondor and Rohan" (*LR* 5.10, 868). Like Elrond, Aragorn recognizes that the task to which *he* and his best warriors are turning might be beyond these lesser conscripts, and so, like Elrond, he releases them from their oath. Not very heroic. But that is just the point. Aragorn understands that these youths and farmers are not called to the *comitatus* oath, and it would not be fair to send a boy to do a thegn's job. It is very reminiscent of the opening scene in the Old English poem *The Battle of Maldon*, the original of Tolkien's "Homecoming of Beorhtnoth Beorhthelm's Son." Beorhtnoth's (or as *The Battle of Maldon* spells it, Byrhtnoth's) advice to the conscripts in the trenches is basic: just don't embarrass us. But then he joins his *hearðwerod*, his hearth-companions, and to *them* he invokes the mead-hall oaths. For Aragorn, as for Beorhtnoth, the oath is still the measure of the heroic culture—it is just that not everyone is a hero. Yet the nine hearth-companions of the Fellowship of the Ring include the last of the ancient kings, Aragorn, and the Elf Legolas—surely Elrond should have expected them worthy of an oath without escape clauses.

I think the solution to this dilemma is what leads us to our next example of an oath release. Elrond's limits on the oath were doubtless directed toward the four Hobbits in the Fellowship—or perhaps were a premonition of the treachery of Boromir. Elrond admires the unusual bravery the Hobbits have shown so far, but he does not, like Gandalf, know the hidden depths of their courage. Even when two human kings bind Hobbits to *comitatus* oaths—Pippin to Denethor, steward of Gondor, and Merry to Théoden, king of Rohan—it is more ceremonial than serious. Merry and Pippin are no doubt thought of as mascots rather than as thegns. Yet when Théoden attempts to release Merry from his oath and Denethor releases Pippin (*LR* 5.3, 784; *LR* 5.4, 807), just as Elrond and Aragorn did in the previous examples, both Hobbits reveal that they honor the oath more than either king does. Of the two kings, Théoden comes closer to comprehending the courage of Hobbits, and he does allow Merry to ride with him part of the way toward the battle. But Denethor's release is absolute, because he has released himself as well—from his duty to fight evil and from hope itself.

> "Farewell, Peregrin, son of Paladin! Your service has been short, and now it is drawing to an end. I release you from the little that remains."
>
> . . . "I will take your leave, sir," [Pippin] said; "for I want to see Gandalf very much indeed. But he is no fool; and I will not think of dying until he despairs of life. But from my word and your service I do not wish to be released while you live." (*LR* 5.4, 807)

Thus, Pippin and Merry honor the *comitatus* oath even when they were not expected to. Long after the death of Denethor, after being himself crowned king of Gondor, Aragorn considers Pippin's oath still in effect: "For do not forget, Peregrin Took, that you are a knight of Gondor, and I do not release you from your service" (*LR* 6.6, 960).

We started the subject of oath breaking with the one character *least* likely to break an oath, and so it's appropriate that we turn now to the character *most* likely: Gollum. And because we have been taking the references to oath breach more or less in the order they appear in the book, it may be that Tolkien intended the progression. In fact, it is the very treacherousness of Gollum, his very unaptness for any sort of oath, that points all the more strongly to the centrality of oaths in the heroic world of Middle-earth. Because, once bound by the oath, Gollum does not, in fact, strive to break it, but instead he performs mental contortions to find a way to destroy Sam and Frodo without violating his oath not to harm them. Nor does Gollum raise the objection that is obvious to Tolkien's modern readers: that in fact it is Sméagol who swears, and it is Gollum who breaks the oath. Gollum relies not on the mutability of identity but on a semantic shift between signifier and signified to wriggle out of a linguistic trap.

As T.A. Shippey has pointed out, this "surprising" virtuousness on Gollum's part in observing the ethics of oath swearing is perhaps surprising only to the modern reader. In the ethos of Old English heroic literature, as well as in that of Tolkien, the monsters (if not the critics) "are moral beings, with an underlying morality much the same as ours."[7] Perhaps in the end it is not Gollum at all but the Precious who precipitates his *āðbrice*, as Frodo observes when he bids Gollum swear on the Ring: "Would you commit your promise to that, Sméagol? It will hold you. But it is more treacherous than you are. It may twist your words. Beware" (*LR* 4.1, 604). Whether it is the Precious or he who does the twisting, Gollum offers two very different justifications for an oath breach. The first is a quibble between Sméagol and Gollum over the scope of the signifier "master." Sméagol speaks first, speaking of himself in the third person:

> "Sméagol promised to help the master."
> "Yes, yes, to help the master: the master of the Precious. But if we was master, then we could help ourselfs, yes, and still keep promises." (*LR* 4.2, 618)

But then as they draw close to Mordor, to Shelob's lair, Gollum discovers another loophole in the oath: "Thou shalt not kill" apparently does not mean that thou canst not hire a hit man or, in this case, a hit spider. "O yes," slavers Gollum, while he pictures the giant arachnid devouring the Hobbits, "Shelob will get him, not Sméagol: he promised; he won't hurt Master at all" (*LR* 4.9, 709). As I said, what is remarkable in both of Gollum's evasions is that he does *not* deny the validity of the oath, but rather he attempts to feign a fidelity to it.

Yet if the world at the end of the Third Age is not yet so corrupt that even a gangrel creature like Gollum would be squeamish about oath breaking, it is clear in *The Lord of the Rings* that things were headed in that decadent direction. Just as *āðbrice* climaxes Wulfstan's list of vices, a number of characters endure any insult except the doubting of their word. At the outskirts of Lothlórien, Gimli refuses to wear a mask to hide from him the location of the Elvish land. "I will go forward free," he said, "or I will go back and seek my own land, where I am known to be true of my word, though I perish alone in the wilderness" (*LR* 2.6, 338). Boromir makes almost the same protest after looking in the Mirror of Galadriel, though in his case he seems to protest too much. "I should have said that she was tempting us, and offering what she pretended to have the power to give. It need not be said that I refused to listen. The Men of Minas Tirith are true to their word" (*LR* 2.7, 349). It seems to me that things that need not be said *need not be said*. Even as he is trying to take the Ring from Frodo, Boromir is offended that Frodo will not take his word: "Why are you so unfriendly?" asks Boromir. "I am a true man, neither thief nor tracker. I need your Ring: that you know now; but I give you my word that I do not desire to keep it. Will you not at least let me make trial of my plan? Lend me the Ring!" (*LR* 2.10, 390).

But even the most virtuous men sometimes need to be reminded of their given word. Aragorn knows, as does Gandalf, that the proper course for Théoden as Sauron's army approaches is to meet it in a frontal attack they will not expect. Yet Théoden King (as Tolkien calls him) insists on retreating to Helm's Deep, playing into Sauron's plan. What Gandalf does next is one of the most beautiful affirmations of free will in *The Lord of the Rings*, a renunciation of the will to power as profound as Frodo's destruction of the Ring. A wizard as powerful as Gandalf could certainly bend Théoden King to his will. But then he would just become another Sauron or Grima Wormtongue. So he allows the king to make a mistake. And Aragorn, who knows his military skill would be optimally exercised at the front, meeting the Orcish army, is sworn as a Ranger to defend the Mark—among other places. Gandalf has to remind him of this oath, unmentioned elsewhere in the novel. "Your next journey," Gandalf tells Strider, "is marked by your given word. You must go to Edoras and seek out Théoden in his hall. For you are needed" (*LR* 3.5, 489). When the cavalry of Théoden are reminded of their own version of this mutual defense treaty—a league with Gondor—the oath is realized not by words but by a concrete emblem of those words: a red arrow, which the Gondorian Hirgon delivers to the riders of Mark, along with a more noble version of Boromir's paradox of saying what "need not be said." "My lord does not issue any command to you," Hirgon announces, "he begs you only to remember old friendship and oaths long spoken, and for your own good to do all that you may" (*LR* 5.3, 782).

A consideration of the role of Fangorn/Treebeard in promise break- ing sheds some light on Elrond's apparent slighting of the oath for the Hobbits, offering an alternative explanation no doubt more obvious than the one I offered above. For Treebeard anticipates and dismisses any criticism that may come to him for deliberately ignoring his promise to guard the defeated Saruman. "Now do not tell me, Gandalf, that I promised to keep him safe; for I know it. But things have changed since then. And I kept him until he was safe, safe from doing any more harm. You should know that above all I hate the caging of live things, and I will not keep even such creatures as these caged beyond great need. A snake without fangs may crawl where he will" (*LR* 6.6, 958). Treebeard's interpretations of the ethics of the promise sound just as waffling as Elrond's at the start of the Fellowship, yet both are in reality equally high-minded. The apparent waffling could be construed to be as treacherous as Gollum's: first he rationalizes the promise to "keep him safe" into "keep him *until* he is safe." Then he seems to rationalize about the conditions of the oath: "things have changed since then." This familiar oath breaker's plea echoes Elrond's reluctance to bind the Hobbits when "things may change." But finally he moves the argument to another level altogether, one which again echoes Elrond's oath release. This time what invalidates the oath is not what Treebeard says, but who he is, his place in the hierarchy of being.

Now, I want to take care not to be misunderstood here, because we are beginning to touch on the Christian analogue to the *comitatus* oath, which hovers behind the oath-trope both in Old English poetry and in Tolkien's fiction. It is a theme that runs through Old and New Testaments from the rainbow to the Resurrection: the theology of the covenant. I do not mean to imply that Treebeard and Elrond, because they are of a higher order than Hobbits and "big people," can play fast and loose with an oath. One of the remarkable features of Jewish and Christian covenant theology is that covenants between Jahweh and his chosen people are just as binding on Jahweh as they are on his children. Yet this does not imply a legal "hold" or leverage that mere humans have on God: not to be true to the covenant is not to be God. The "must" is not compulsion or obedience to another potency but simply fulfilling God's nature. Similarly, to cage a creature (and even Saruman is a creature) is against Treebeard's nature. When Elrond circumscribes the Fellowship oath for the Hobbits, he is surely thinking of the dread fact of their mortality. That is precisely what Treebeard is thinking of a half-dozen paragraphs before his promise waffling, when he mitigates a potential promise from King Aragorn. Aragorn thanks Treebeard for the help of the Ents: "Never shall it be forgotten in Minas Tirith or in Edoras." Treebeard's answer reminds Aragorn that he is mortal: "*Never* is too long a word even for me. . . . Not while your kingdoms last, you mean; but they will have to last long indeed to seem long to Ents" (*LR* 6.6, 957).

Treebeard's ambivalence toward a promise to Gandalf points to the problem in moral philosophy of the rash or compromised promise. As a motif in myth and folktale, the "rash promise" story usually implies that promises are immutable, and that the oath binds the swearer to the letter rather than to the intent of the oath. Thus in Greek mythology, when Hera swore that no land "touched by the sun" can give birth to Apollo, she uses the phrase to be all-inclusive, that is, all the lands of the world. But the island of Delos, because it was under the sea at the time of Hera's proclamation, was exempt because it was technically, by the letter, not touched by the sun. In Christian moral teaching, however, promises that violate a greater law can be invalid, even in moral theologies that reject the notion of "proportionalism," or intentionally doing evil for a greater good. For the reader of Tolkien, of course, neither Christian nor classical (nor Norse) manifestations of the rash promise resonate so clearly as that of Tolkien's own mythology. The *locus classicus* for oath breaking in Tolkien's myth is the so-called Oath of the Sons of Fëanor in chapter 9 of *The Silmarillion*. Fëanor, angry at the theft of the Silmarils, which he created, commands his sons to swear an oath to avenge any theft of the jewels. As the oath is sworn, Tolkien's narrator sides with other ancient myths, and against Christian teaching, on the issue of oath release: "Many quailed to hear the dread words. For so sworn, good or evil, an oath may not be broken, and it shall pursue oathkeeper and oathbreaker to the world's end" (*Silm*, 83).

I have not yet touched on a large category of oaths in the Old English tradition—the boasting speech—partly because the category is so large that it would require a separate study, and partly because it is not immediately self-evident that the Old English *bēot* is in fact a form of oath, though I believe it is. Nor am I alone in that belief: in a performance-oriented study on the Old English boast, Dwight Conquergood presents the *bēot* as a communal activity, in which the audience of the boast acts "as a witness in the boasting contract."[8] Beowulf in *Beowulf* and Byrhtnoth in *The Battle of Maldon* both seem to consider the *bēot* a down payment on deeds to be delivered—that is, not a boast in the modern sense, but a promise. C.M. Adderly has identified a distinction in the Old English nomenclature of boasting, with bragging in the modern sense of vainglorious self-congratulation always associated with *bēot*, and the heroic boast in the sense of a virtuous promise indicated by the verb *gylpan*.[9]

Tolkien's version of this distinction can be seen in the pointed contrast between Boromir and Aragorn, part of which has already been cited: Boromir's vainglorious *bēot* "It need not be said that I refused to listen." There is a parallel opportunity for Aragorn to boast, and in fact it is an opportunity sprung from the goading of Boromir. T.A. Shippey has briefly explicated this very subtle interchange between the two heroes, and has even connected it with the Old English boasting tradition.[10] I have spoken of Boromir's vainglory. It is only a relative vainglory, if I may speak so, for there is a great deal of heroism about him. It's just that the heroism is compromised. This vainglory is seen not only in his boasts about himself but also in his needling of Aragorn. The *miles gloriosus* sees "glory," like the Homeric κυδος or the Old English *lof*, as a zero-sum game: the braggart gains more of this prized commodity either by building up himself or by tearing down another. Still, it is not just the braggart who seeks *lof* in Old English heroic poetry. As Tolkien observes, the last word of *Beowulf* describes the eponymous hero as *lofgeornost*, "most eager for glory" (*Monsters*, 36).

Thus Boromir snipes at Aragorn in a passive-aggressive manner, bating his barbs in polite speech. "Mayhap the Sword-that-was-Broken may still stem the tide," he says, and then he pauses—the mere dash in Tolkien's text is the border between the feigned praise of Aragorn and the thinly veiled taunt that follows: "if the hand that wields it has inherited not an heirloom only, but the sinews of the Kings of Men" (*LR* 2.2, 261). The "if" here is the opening for Aragorn's boast: if Aragorn were another Boromir he would take the bait and make a *bēot*: "Of *course* my hand is the hand of the Kings of Men!" But that is just what Aragorn does not say. His reply, as Shippey points out, is an Old English heroic commonplace: "Who can tell? . . . But we will put it to the test one day" (*LR* 2.2, 261). Aragorn's refusal to resort to the *bēot* here is in fact a sort of implicit *gylp*, the "non-bragging boast" with which Beowulf, in a similar situation, answers Unferth.

With all of these deadly serious examples of *āðbrice*, I almost hesitate to mention the last one that appears in the novel, a comic version that is also a parody of the oaths of courtly love. Tolkien has a dual reason for ridiculing this particular trope of courtly love, because it is (a)

Renaissance rather than medieval and (b) continental rather than English. The lovesick would-be gallant extols his lady's beauty by offering to duel anyone who does not agree publicly that his lady is the most beautiful in the world. Gimli, who had called her the Witch of the Forest before he saw her, now swears he must fight Éomer if he does not agree that Galadriel is the fairest of all women. This impasse leads to the only laudable oath breach in the novel:

> "You shall judge," said Éomer. "For there are certain rash words concerning the Lady in the Golden Wood that lie still between us. And now I have seen her with my eyes."
>
> "Well, lord," said Gimli, "and what say you now?"
>
> "Alas!" said Éomer. "I will not say that she is the fairest lady that lives."
>
> "Then I must go for my axe," said Gimli.
>
> "But first I will plead this excuse," said Éomer. "Had I seen her in other company, I would have said all that you could wish. But now I will put my Queen Arwen Evenstar first, and I am ready to do battle on my own part with any who deny me. Shall I call for my sword?"
>
> Then Gimli bowed low. "Nay, you are excused for my part, lord," he said. "You have chosen the Evening; but my love is given to the Morning. And my heart forebodes that soon it will pass away forever." (*LR* 6.6, 953)

Rather than end on the most frivolous example of oath breaking, my final observation on that particular semantic displacement that I call *āðbrice* will be this: the core of *The Lord of the Rings* could be thought of as a kind of *comitatus* oath—the "Fellowship" of the Ring. But I do not want to follow this line of thought too far, because it involves that most sordid (Sauronic?) of oaths—a business contract. Etymologically, a "fellow" in any enterprise is a *fēolaga*, one who lays down a fee. The financial stake represents the fellow's commitment to the success of the venture. The Latin cognate for fee is *pecus*, but another legal term for the price of a share in a fellowship is the Latin cognate for the word "price." The noun form, *pretium*, is, as Tolkien points out, related to our modern word "praise," the heroic Old English *lof* (*Monsters*, 37). But the adjectival form—*pretiosum*—gives us a favorite word of the breakers of fellowship: "Precious."

Notes

1. Ruth S. Noel, *The Languages of Tolkien's Middle-earth* (Boston: Houghton Mifflin, 1980); Jim Allan, et al., *An Introduction to Elvish and to Other Tongues, Proper Names, and Writing Systems of the Third Age of the Western Lands of Middle-earth as Set Down in the Published Writings of John Ronald Reuel Tolkien* (Frome, Somerset, Eng.: Bran's Head Books, 1978).

2. T.A. Shippey, *The Road to Middle-earth* (1982; rev. ed. London: HarperCollins, 1992); T.A. Shippey, *J.R.R. Tolkien: Author of the Century* (Boston: Houghton Mifflin, 2001).

3. Verlyn Flieger, *Splintered Light: Logos and Language in Tolkien's World* (Grand Rapids, Mich.: William B. Eerdmans, 1983; rev. ed. Kent, Ohio: Kent State University Press, 2002).

4. Shippey, *J.R.R. Tolkien: Author of the Century*, 68–77.

5. Dorothy Whitelock, *Sermo Lupi ad Anglos*, 3rd edition (London: Methuen, 1966), 60–61. I have exaggerated the climactic position of *āðbrice* in this paraphrase, but even if the word is demoted to merely another word on this list, the point still holds: being in such serious company makes oath breaking a very foul deed.

6. Tacitus, *Germania* 13, in *Tacitus in Five Volumes*, trans. by M. Hutton, revised by E.H. Warmington, Loeb Classical Library (Cambridge, Mass.: Harvard University Press, 1970), 150–53.

7. Tom Shippey, "Orcs, Wraiths, Wights: Tolkien's Images of Evil," in *J.R.R. Tolkien and His Literary Resonances: Views of Middle-earth*, ed. George Clark and Daniel Timmons (Westport, Conn.: Greenwood Press, 2000), 184.

8. Dwight Conquergood, "Boasting in Anglo-Saxon England: Performance and the Heroic Ethos," *Literature in Performance: A Journal of Literary and Performing Art* 1 (1981): 30. I am grateful to C.M. Adderly for drawing my attention to this study, and for sharing his own essay, "To Bēot or Not to Bēot: Boasting in *Beowulf*," currently in manuscript, which he read at the International Medieval Congress in Kalamazoo, Michigan, on 8 May 2003.

9. Adderly, 2–3.

10. Shippey, *J.R.R. Tolkien: Author of the Century*, 73.

Chapter 15

"ON THE BORDERS OF OLD STORIES"

Enacting the Past in Beowulf *and* The Lord of the Rings

ALEXANDRA BOLINTINEANU

Only a year after the publication of *The Hobbit*, readers of J.R.R. Tolkien began drawing parallels between his fiction and the Anglo-Saxon epic *Beowulf*: in January 1938, the *Observer* published a letter inquiring, among other things, whether "the hobbit's stealing of the dragon's cup [was] based on the cup-stealing episode in *Beowulf*."[1] While Tolkien answered that the "episode of the theft arose naturally (and almost inevitably) from the circumstances" of the story and that the parallel episode from *Beowulf* had not been "consciously present to the mind in the process of writing," he nevertheless called *Beowulf* one of his most valued sources (*Letters*, 31).

That Tolkien's academic preoccupation with *Beowulf*, especially as it appears in his famous essay "Beowulf: The Monsters and the Critics," shaped his own stories is amply illustrated in Jane Chance's study *Tolkien's Art: A Mythology for England*. The study traces the thematic concerns of Tolkien's scholarly writing as they appear in his fictional work, thus offering a reading of Tolkien's stories through the perspective provided by his own analysis of other literature.[2] Interestingly, the recently published edition of Tolkien's *Beowulf and the Critics* reverses the perspective: Michael Drout discusses Tolkien's essay not only in the context of *Beowulf* scholarship but in the context of Tolkien's own fiction, using the latter to illuminate the imagery of the former.[3]

The influence of *Beowulf* on Tolkien's fiction is not simply a matter of borrowed incidents, like the theft of the cup from the dragon's hoard in *The Hobbit*. Chance draws structural parallels between the narrative of *The Hobbit* and that of the Anglo-Saxon epic,[4] while Diana Wynne Jones, discussing Tolkien's narrative technique in *The Lord of the Rings*, traces his use of the legendary past of his fictional world to *Beowulf*. Jones observes that Tolkien "took over the idea of the inset histories and legends from the Anglo-Saxon poem *Beowulf*, in which each inset vaguely echoes the action in the poem's present and each is progressively more doom-laden."[5] Gergely Nagy, in his essay "The Great Chain of Reading: (Inter-)Textual Relations and the Technique of Mythopoesis in the Túrin Story," persuasively traces, using *Beowulf* and Malory as models, how these inset narratives, along with other allusions to events or people in the legendary past, produce relationships between texts that mimic those of "real-world mythological corpora" and thus create the mythological quality of Tolkien's fiction.[6]

Instead of exploring Tolkien's mythopoeic techniques, I would like to examine how both *Beowulf* and *The Lord of the Rings* use the content, rather than the form, of these inset narratives. In both texts, numerous episodes from the legendary past resurface in the present, either through narratorial allusion or in a character's voice, often echoing the situation in the fictional present. In *The Lord of the Rings*, this connection between past and present is perhaps most striking when Frodo enters the land of Lothlórien, and the legendary past appears not simply as an inset narrative but as actual reality: "As soon as he set foot upon the far bank of Silverlode a strange feeling had come upon him, and it deepened as he walked on into the Naith: it seemed to him that he had stepped over a bridge of time into a corner of the Elder Days, and was now walking in a world that was no more" (*LR* 2.6, 340). In her discussion of Tolkien's treatment of time, Verlyn Flieger remarks that Lothlórien is a manifestation of "that high and far-off mythic time 'in the beginning.'" She proceeds to explore the nature of this "mythic time," pointing out connections with Mircea Eliade's theory of mythical time and with J.W. Dunne's theories of "time as a static field rather than linear progression."[7]

In this essay, I am interested in a different aspect of that "mythic time," not so much in its nature as in the implications of the act of narrating it. Here, too, Eliade furnishes a useful theoretical concept. By retelling the myths, he writes, "one emerges from profane, chronological time and enters a time that is of a different quality, a 'sacred' Time at once primordial and indefinitely recoverable . . . one re-enacts fabulous, exalting, significant events. . . . What is involved is not a commemoration of mythical events but a reiteration of them."[8] In *Beowulf* and *The Lord of the Rings*, the relationship between legendary past and present is less obvious. The past is not actually summoned back by recitation; in fact, the recitations themselves lament its irrecoverability. In *Beowulf*, King Hrothgar "feorran rehte" [recount{s} tales of long ago], intermingling his narrative with laments for his lost youth:

> Hwilum eft ongan,   eldo gebunden,
> Gomel guðwiga   gioguðe cwiðan,
> Hildestrengo. . . .

> [At times again the old warrior, fettered by age, began to lament his youth, his strength in battle.][9]

The inset narratives of *The Lord of the Rings* suggest a similar sense of loss. The brief snippet of *The Fall of Gil-galad* emphasizes from the very first stanza that Gil-galad and the glory of his kingship are gone beyond recovery:

> Gil-galad was an Elven-king.
> Of him the harpers sadly sing:
> the last whose realm was fair and free
> between the Mountains and the Sea. (*LR* 1.11, 181)

Nevertheless, though retelling legends does not literally bring back the past, still, the legendary past is both active and enacted in the present: the events of the fictional present intertwine with the legendary narratives as the characters of both texts create legend, guide themselves by it, and echo it in their lives. Most prosaically, the characters enact legends by performing in the fictional present deeds that will provide legendary material for future generations. Both texts dwell on the process through which significant moments of the central narrative are transmuted into legend and recur in narrative episodes.

It is not an infallible transmutation. Both texts sometimes offer competing versions of past events (one authoritative, the other suspect), showing that the legendary past can be distorted in the telling, from conscious desire or ignorance. In the Anglo-Saxon epic, Unferth, who envies Beowulf and wishes to discredit him, retells a twisted version of Beowulf's legendary contest with Breca. Beowulf fights back with the same weapon—a narrative of the past. He offers his own version of the contest with Breca, more believable both because Beowulf is a hero and because he is an eye-witness to the contest:

> Soð ic talige,
> þæt ic merestrengo   maran ahte,
> earfeþo on yþum,   þonne ænig oþer man.

[Truly I maintain, that I had more sea-strength, {more} hardships in the waves, than any other man.] (*Beowulf*, lines 532–84)

In the course of the narrative, Beowulf scuttles Unferth's moral authority as a narrator by reminding the audience that Unferth is not only drunk ("beore drunken," line 531) but also a hell-bound fratricide:

> Þeah ðu þinum broðrum   to banan wurde,
> heafodmægum   þæs þu in helle scealt
> werhþo dreogan.

[However, you became the slayer of your brother, your close kinsman; because of that you will suffer damnation in hell.] (*Beowulf*, lines 587–89)

In *The Lord of the Rings*, unreliable narratives deal with events already "witnessed" by the readers. The Hobbits' journey into Mordor, for instance, assumes exaggerated proportions when retold by the ignorant: "Why, cousin, one of them [the Hobbits] went with only his esquire into the Black Country and fought with the Dark Lord all by himself, and set fire to his Tower" (*LR* 6.5, 945). Interestingly, the Hobbits as featured in this account assume more stereotypically heroic proportions. The Hobbits' endurance and courage become feats of physical derring-do (fighting Sauron in person and burning down his tower); their reliance on Gollum's antiheroic help is edited out (Frodo was accompanied "*only* by his esquire"); and the relationship between Frodo and Sam takes on chivalric overtones (Sam becomes Frodo's "esquire" instead of what he actually is—his gardener). In retelling, the truth stretches to fill out the conventions of legendary narrative.

Such inaccuracies not only render the legendary narratives more authentic as such; they also emphasize the fact that, even when they suffer from faults of interpretation, legends are based, however loosely, on actual events. This becomes more evident when the legendary narratives are actually reliable. In *Beowulf*, for instance, Grendel becomes a legend in his own lifetime; stories of his depredations in Heorot travel accurately as far as the Geatish court (*Beowulf*, lines 409–15). In *The Lord of the Rings*, when one of Éomer's men challenges him, Aragorn delivers to the Riders of Rohan a timely reminder that legend and reality—both past and present reality—are anything but mutually exclusive; that, in fact, the present is the material of future legend, which in turn means that legends can be founded on past reality and useful knowledge.

> "Halflings!" laughed the Rider that stood beside Éomer. "Halflings! But they are only a little people in old songs and children's tales out of the North. Do we walk in legends or on the green earth in the daylight?"
>
> "A man may do both," said Aragorn. "For not we but those who come after will make the legends of our time. The green earth, say you? That is a mighty matter of legend, though you tread it under the light of day!"
> (*LR* 3.2, 424)

And the Hobbits, climbing the stairs of Cirith Ungol, imagine themselves as the characters of a story "told by the fireside, or read out of a great big book with red and black letters, years and years afterwards" (*LR* 4.8, 697). To comfort themselves, they picture their present ordeals not just as past but as formally narrated past, as historical text. It is an inversion of Eliade's theory of myth. Eliade, as mentioned above, claims that, through mythical narrative, one emerges from mundane time and comes to reenact mythical events. The Hobbits are painfully enacting legend; they use the notion of legendary narrative in an effort to reenter, however briefly, their ordinary world.

As the characters of the two texts shape future legend, so their lives are shaped by legendary narratives of the past. In both *Beowulf* and *The Lord of the Rings*, characters use the episodes as exempla to serve their moral or emotional needs. Contemplating the similarity between legendary situations and their own, they determine what they will do in the present based on the desirability or undesirability of fully reenacting the past in their own lives.

In *Beowulf*, the exempla are mostly negative. In his sermon to Beowulf, Hrothgar refers to the story of Heremod (*Beowulf*, lines 901–15). In his youth, Heremod had seemed a courageous protector for the Danes, but afterwards he proved bloodthirsty, avaricious, and ultimately self-destructive. The target of the allusion is clearly Beowulf. Having just slain the two monsters, he is in the same position as was the young Heremod. Hrothgar warns him not to act out the rest of Heremod's story in his own life.

In *The Lord of the Rings*, the explicit exempla are mostly positive. Perhaps this is because the characters' chances of success are so small, and the consequences of failure so devastating, that they cannot afford to dwell too much on the possibility of defeat. Instead, they use legendary narrative as a source of positive inspiration. Sam, for instance, encourages Frodo and himself by remembering the successes of past heroes: "Beren now, he never thought he was going to get that Silmaril from the Iron Crown in Thangorodrim, and yet he did, and that was a worse place and a blacker danger than ours" (*LR* 4.8, 696). Because of its resemblance to the present, the past becomes a positive example, a model and a comforter; legendary narrative appears morally and emotionally relevant to the present. Retelling it, the characters invite it into their lives, invite themselves to enact it.

Even when the characters do not consciously use legendary narrative as a guide for present actions, they enact it nevertheless. In both texts "history" repeats itself, as present actions fulfill the same universal patterns of fratricide or heroic sacrifice or transience that inform the legendary episodes. Such echoes integrate the events of the main story into the thematic currents traversing each text.

Examples of this device abound in *Beowulf*. Perhaps the most moving instance occurs as Beowulf prepares for his attack on the dragon. At this point in the poem he is an old man, doomed to die in the battle ahead:

> Him wæs geomor sefa,
> Wæfre ond wælfus,   wyrd ungemete neah,
> Se ðone gomelan   gretan sceolde,

Secean sawle hord,   sundur gedælan
Lif wið lice;   no þon lange wæs
Feorh æþelinges   flæsce bewunden.

[His spirit was mournful, restless, and ready for death, the fate unmeasurably near {which should} come upon the old one, seek out the soul's hoard, divide the life from the body; the prince's life was not enclosed in flesh for long.] (*Beowulf*, lines 2419–24)

It is at this point, and in this mood, that Beowulf chooses to recount a collection of sad stories about feuds and royal families. Of these, no fewer than three episodes echo his situation. The first is the despair and eventual death of the old King Hrethel, bereft of his eldest son through an accidental fratricide and unable to take revenge because his son's killer is also his own son (*Beowulf*, lines 2430–43). This is closely followed by the analogous predicament of an old man left childless because his son "swing[s] young on the gallows" (*Beowulf*, lines 2446–59). Like Hrethel, this old man is also unable to console himself through revenge. And last, Beowulf recounts the death in battle of the "gomela" (aged) Scylfing King Ongentheow, simultaneously assailed by two younger warriors (*Beowulf*, lines 2487–89). The plights of these three figures echo that of Beowulf: they are all old men, two of them kings, two of them tragically bereft of their sons even as Beowulf is childless, all of them overwhelmed by events. They also echo—though more remotely—Hrothgar's situation: his age and his powerlessness against the monster slaughtering his retainers, against the usurpation of his son's legacy, and against the eventual destruction of Heorot. In itself, Beowulf's last battle is moving: it is a great hero's fall before an enemy worthy of his strength and courage. But the echoing episodes all show old men powerless against implacable circumstance. They give Beowulf's last battle a wider significance, more moving because more universal: even for heroes and kings, there comes one enemy at the end of his life—be it heartbreak or human enemy, man-eating monster or fire-breathing dragon—whom he may struggle against but not survive. Beowulf's battle with the dragon becomes instance and incarnation of the battle of all humankind with desolation and mortality—in Tolkien's words, "man at war with the hostile world, and his inevitable overthrow in Time" ("Beowulf," 18).

The problem of mortality and temporality is a central motif in *The Lord of the Rings*. As Tolkien writes in a letter to a reader, "The real theme for me is about something much more permanent and difficult [than power and domination]: Death and Immortality" (*Letters*, 246). As C.S. Lewis points out, the text is full of "the memory of vanished civilizations and lost splendour."[10] The great watchtower on Weathertop "was burned and broken. . . . Yet once it was tall and fair" (*LR* 1.11, 181). The poetry of the Rohirrim laments the passage of the years (*LR* 3.6, 497). The Ents feel the world closing in around them and sense themselves doomed to slow but fairly certain extinction (*LR* 3.4, 457–58). The history of Gondor, as told both by Elrond and Faramir, is essentially the story of a long decline (*LR* 2.2, 237–38, *LR* 4.5, 662–63). And at the very end, as has been foretold throughout the text, the Elves must pass into the West and leave the mortal world behind (*LR* 2.7, 356). The elegiac mood permeates history and legend.

Complementary to the transience of all good and great things is the resilience of evil. "Always after a defeat and respite," says Gandalf, "the Shadow takes another shape and grows again" (*LR* 1.2, 50). Elrond describes past wars against evil as "many defeats, and many fruitless victories" (*LR* 2.2, 237); Galadriel, referring to her and Celeborn's stand against evil, says that "together through ages of the world we have fought the long defeat" (*LR* 2.7, 348). The pattern of things that these remarks evoke seems to be that which Tolkien perceives in *Beowulf* and in Norse myth: "The monsters had been the foes of the gods, the captains of men, and within Time the monsters would win" ("Beowulf," 22). But in *The Lord of the Rings* it is not true. Victories against evil are achieved, and though they are neither impervious to the passage of time nor altogether free from bitterness, they are nonetheless of great worth.

This thematic pattern is developed through the correspondence between the main story and the episodes echoing it. In the main story, the pattern occurs in its entirety. The Ring is destroyed, and a great evil is banished from the world. The victory is neither permanent nor complete: much that is good and beautiful, not the least being the kingdom of Lothlórien, passes away with the destruction of the Rings of Power, and to some of the world's troubles, like the plight of the Ents, the victory over Sauron brings no cure. But, though the achievement is alloyed with sorrow, its essential goodness abides.

Three episodes in particular echo the main story: that of the Last

Alliance, that of Eärendil, and that of Beren and Lúthien. The first involves the lure of the Ring: Isildur succumbs to it, just as Gollum, Boromir, and at last even Frodo do in the main story. The failure of even a legendary hero to resist the temptation of the Ring shows the Ring to be a truly threatening temptation. In turn, this makes Frodo's long resistance to it more meritorious. It also renders his final lapse more widely significant: the precedent set by Isildur makes this failure at the last moment not just an instance of individual weakness under pressure but an element of the universal pattern of things, a demonstration of "human" fallibility.[11] Besides this, the first war of the Ring resembles the second in that neither victory is achieved without great and irrevocable loss to the world. In the main story, the chief loss is perhaps the departure of the Elves; in the episode, it is the deaths of the great heroes who fall in the battle against Sauron, deaths that mark the beginning of the end for the Elves' dominion.

The plot of the Eärendil episode is more difficult to make out because the episode is told in fairly cryptic verse. But even without reading the prose version in *The Silmarillion,* resemblances to the main story are clearly discernible. Like Frodo, Eärendil carries a jewel of great significance. Like Frodo, he undertakes a hard and dangerous quest. But most importantly, once he has accomplished his task, Eärendil cannot return to his homeland and must indeed renounce the mortal world altogether. It is a foreshadowing of Frodo's realization as he prepares for his departure into the West at the end of the story: "I tried to save the Shire, and it has been saved, but not for me. It must often be so, Sam, when things are in danger: some one has to give them up, lose them, so that others may keep them" (*LR* 6.9, 1006).

The episode of Beren and Lúthien has its parallels to Frodo's quest, too. As Tolkien points out, "Here we meet, among other things, the first example of the motive (to become dominant in Hobbits) that the great policies of world history, 'the wheels of the world,' are often turned not by the Lords and Governors, even gods, but by the seemingly unknown and weak. . . . It is Beren the outlawed mortal who succeeds (with the help of Lúthien, a mere maiden even if an elf of royalty) where all armies and warriors have failed" (*Letters,* 149). Like Frodo's journey into Mordor, the quest of Beren and Lúthien involves a precious magical jewel, a struggle against all odds with the incarnate power of evil in its own domain, and a victory seasoned with grief. This last point of resemblance suggests yet another parallel. The love of Beren and Lúthien mirrors that of another couple in which one of the lovers is mortal and the other immortal, namely Aragorn and Arwen. This parallel is drawn by Arwen herself: "I shall not go with him [Elrond] now when he departs to the Havens; for mine is the choice of Lúthien, and as she so have I chosen, both the sweet and the bitter" (*LR* 6.6, 952). She is not self-pityingly explicit about her predicament, and from a storytelling point of view she does not need to be. The story of Beren and Lúthien develops the implications of her words: by choosing a mortal lover, she has chosen not only loss but also mortality for herself (*LR* 1.11, 189). Nevertheless, though eventually—on or off stage—mortality does overcome Frodo, Aragorn and Arwen, and Beren and Lúthien, it does not render their courage worthless, nor does it overpower the splendor of their heroism or their love. This poignant tension between the precariousness of all mortal achievement and its enduring worth and power is maintained through the tone of the narration. This is how Aragorn describes the Beren and Lúthien episodes: "a fair tale, though it is sad, as are all the tales of Middle-earth, and yet it may lift up your hearts" (*LR* 1.11, 187). The comment, with its twofold "but," applies to the entire story of *The Lord of the Rings* itself as well as to the episodes that echo it and lend its thematic pattern scope and universality.

In *Beowulf* and *The Lord of the Rings,* present events and legendary narrative are more reciprocally connected than Eliade's description of the mythical past suggests. He suggests that the present is transfigured and exalted by the invasion of legendary narrative, but in *Beowulf* and *The Lord of the Rings*, the constant interplay between legend and main story serves to validate and exalt each in terms of the other. When the present appears as prospective legendary material, its stature is enhanced, for it is shown to be as magnificent, as consequential, and as deserving of long remembrance and fame as all the other legends. When the legends appear as a guide for the present, they are shown to be morally and factually reliable, relevant to present-day reality. When legend and principal narrative run in parallel, they explain each other and enrich each other's significance. Eliade's language suggests theatrical metaphor: it invites us to imagine legendary narrative as the script of a play, given flesh to and enacted in the present. The use of legendary narrative in *Beowulf* and *The Lord of the Rings* suggests rather a conversation. Like voices in talk, legendary narrative and current events echo or contradict each other, question or build on each other's arguments, enrich and complete one another.

Notes

1. The original letter, containing the query, was published in the *Observer* on 16 January 1938, while Tolkien's answer was published on 20 February 1938. Quoted in *Letters,* 30.

2. Jane Chance, *Tolkien's Art: A Mythology for England* (Lexington, Ky.: University Press of Kentucky, 2001). My thanks go to Professor Chance, who generously made this book electronically available to me.

3. Michael Drout, introduction to *Beowulf and the Critics,* by J.R.R. Tolkien, ed. Drout (Tempe, Ariz.: Arizona Center for Medieval and Renaissance Studies, 2002), 10–11.

4. Chance, *Tolkien's Art,* 50–52.

5. Diana Wynne Jones, "The Shape of the Narrative in *The Lord of the Rings,*" in *J.R.R. Tolkien: This Far Land,* ed. Robert Giddings (London: Vision Press, 1983; Totowa, N.J.: Barnes and Noble Books, 1984), 94. See also T.A. Shippey's remark on Tolkien's use of the past: "[T]he sense is there that Middle-earth has many lives and many stories besides the ones that have come momentarily into focus. The trick is an old one, and Tolkien learned it like so much else from his ancient sources, *Beowulf* and the poem of *Sir Gawain,* but it continues to work." T.A. Shippey, *J.R.R. Tolkien: Author of the Century* (London: Harper Collins Publishers, 2000), 49.

6. Gergely Nagy, "The Great Chain of Reading: (Inter-)Textual Relations and the Technique of Mythopoesis in the Túrin Story," in *Tolkien the Medievalist,* ed. Jane Chance (London and New York: Routledge, 2002), 423–56. My thanks to Gergely Nagy, who kindly made an electronic copy of his essay available to me.

7. Verlyn Flieger, *A Question of Time: J.R.R. Tolkien's Road to Faërie* (Kent, Ohio, and London, Eng.: Kent State University Press, 1997), 91–92.

8. Mircea Eliade, *Myth and Reality,* trans. William R. Trask (New York and Evanston: Harper and Row, Publishers, 1963), 18–19.

9. *"Beowulf": A Student Edition,* ed. George Jack (Oxford: Clarendon Press, 1995), lines 2111–13. The translations from the Old English are my own. Subsequent references to this work will include line numbers in parentheses within the text.

10. C.S. Lewis, "Tolkien's *The Lord of the Rings,*" in *On Stories and Other Essays on Literature,* ed. Walter Hooper (London: Harcourt Brace Jovanovich, 1982), 86.

11. I use "human" very loosely here, to encompass all the rational, humanlike races of Middle-earth.

Part V

TOLKIEN AND FINNISH

Chapter 16

A MYTHOLOGY FOR FINLAND

Tolkien and Lönnrot as Mythmakers

VERLYN FLIEGER

J.R.R. Tolkien's stated ambition to dedicate a mythology to England is now generally accepted as the original and primary motive behind his fiction. The motive behind the ambition, however, has not been interrogated as to its rationale. England had survived for many centuries without a mythology. What impulse, at a particular point in history, made Tolkien suddenly decide it needed one? What besides his own literary ambition might have impelled a young, unpublished writer to attempt such an enormous undertaking? In at least partial answer, I offer two quotes. First:

> Why has not England a great mythology? Our folklore has never advanced beyond daintiness, and the greater melodies about our countryside have all issued through the pipes of Greece. Deep and true as the native imagination can be, it seems to have failed here. It has stopped with the witches and the fairies. It cannot vivify one fraction of a summer field, or give names to half a dozen stars. England still waits for the supreme moment of her literature—for the great poet who shall voice her, or, better still, for the thousand little poets whose voices shall pass into our common talk.[1]

And second:

> I was from early days grieved by the poverty of my own beloved country: it had no stories of its own (bound up with its tongue and soil), not of the

quality that I sought, and found (as an ingredient) in legends of other
lands. There was Greek, and Celtic, and Romance, Germanic, Scandinavian, and Finnish (which greatly affected me); but nothing English, save
impoverished chap-book stuff. . . . I had in mind to make a body of more
or less connected legend . . . which I could dedicate simply to: to
England. (*Letters*, 144)

The second quote seems to be so clearly both a paraphrase of and a
response to the first that it is next to impossible to read the two in conjunction without hearing the same voice in both, or imagining at least an
ongoing conversation between like-minded individuals. "Witches and
fairies" (from quote number one) could certainly qualify as "impoverished chap-book stuff" (from quote number two), and the plea of the
first that "England still waits for . . . the great poet who shall voice her"
is answered in the second by the stated intent to make "a body of more
or less connected legend" and dedicate it to England.

Similar as these sentiments appear, they were expressed by two very
different writers at two widely separated times. The first quote is from
E.M. Forster's *Howards End*, first published in 1910, in which Forster
put the sentiments in the mouth of Margaret Schlegel, an English woman
of Germanic heritage who is trying to find a home. The second is from
J.R.R. Tolkien's 1951 letter to Milton Waldman of Collins Publishing
explaining the rationale behind his mythology. That they are so close in
expression of national sentiment and desire for cultural heritage is for
one good reason. Both were responding to the same stimulus, and the
same climate of thought.

This stimulating climate was the folklore movement, the great surge
of collecting and cataloguing of myth and folklore that swept western
Europe in the nineteenth and early twentieth centuries. National mythologies were being discovered or rediscovered at an astounding
rate, and studies of their languages and lore were the focus of new scholarship. In this movement Finland was, and remained for many years, the
leader. This was largely because of the impact on the Finns in particular
and on the emerging European nationalistic spirit in general of the newly
formulated Finnish national epic, *Kalevala*. Francis Magoun, who translated *Kalevala* into English in 1963, states that:

Appearing at a time when there was little or no truly bellelettristic
Finnish Literature, the *Kalevala* unquestionably—and most understand-

ably—became a source of great satisfaction and pride to the national consciousness then fast developing among the Finns, who had been growing restive under their [then] Russian masters. To some extent the *Kalevala* became a rallying point for these feelings, and permitted and in a measure justified such exultant statements as "Finland can [now] say for itself: I, too, have a history!"[2]

More specifically and more personally, the Finns themselves said of Elias Lönnrot, the man who compiled and published *Kalevala*, "A single man, by scurrying about, has created a heritage for us."[3]

Lönnrot in effect gave Finland its own myth and mythic identity equal to that of Greece or Scandinavia. He gave it its own prehistory and its own cultural individuality apart from the overlordship of Russia and Sweden, both of which had annexed Finland at one time or another. *Kalevala* became an extended rallying cry in Finland's struggle for nationhood, a struggle that culminated in its declaration of independence in December 1917.

The work's effect on Finnish art and culture was equally profound. It became the instant inspiration for all kinds of artistic expression. In music it inspired Finnish composer Jan Sibelius to first write the nationalistic *Finlandia*, and then to interpret a number of stories from *Kalevala*. His *Lemmenkäinen* suite, the *Tapiola* suite, the *Kullervo* symphony, the *Swan of Tuonela*, all owe their inspiration to *Kalevala*, as does the *Aino* symphony of Sibelius's contemporary Robert Kajanus. As part of the same Finnish arts movement, painter Akseli Gallen-Kallela executed a series of powerful pieces illustrating scenes from *Kalevala*, which gave a new energy to Finnish visual art.

How did this affect Forster and inspire Tolkien? It gave them both an example. A simple sequence of dates will show a clear temporal, if not necessarily causal, sequence leading from *Kalevala* to the Forster passage and thence to Tolkien's burgeoning ambition to provide a mythology for England. In 1907 the earliest Finnish-English translation of *Kalevala*, W.F. Kirby's Everyman edition, was published. In 1910 Forster's *Howards End*, with Margaret Schlegel's lament for an English mythology, appeared and was widely read. In 1914 Tolkien's first effort at intentional mythmaking, "The Voyage of Eärendel," was written. Until more of his correspondence with the members of his earliest literary circle, the T.C.B.S., becomes available, we have no way of ascertaining if Tolkien had read *Howards End*, although the striking similarity in the paragraphs quoted above certainly encourages such an assumption. We do know, however, that he had read *Kalevala*, at that time the most recent and most visible evidence of the value of myth to a society in need of a voice.

Tolkien's published letters make it clear that his interest in *Kalevala* dates back to the period in his life outlined by 1910 to 1914. Recall his statement quoted above that Finnish "greatly affected" him. Similar comments in less mythically descriptive letters specifically attribute much of his immediate inspiration to *Kalevala*. In October 1914 he wrote to his wife, Edith, that he was trying to turn one of the stories of *Kalevala* "into a short story somewhat on the lines of Morris' romances with chunks of poetry in between" (*Letters*, 7). In 1944 he wrote to his son Christopher that "Finnish nearly ruined my Hon. Mods. and was the original germ of the Silmarillion" (*Letters*, 87). In 1955 he wrote to W.H. Auden that *Kalevala* "set the rocket off in story," and that his *legendarium* was "an attempt to reorganize some of the Kalevala, especially the tale of Kullervo the hapless, into a form of my own" (*Letters*, 214).

Although he was not yet published in any scholarly or artistic field when he launched his dream in 1914, Tolkien's knowledge of mythology, especially the mythologies of northern Europe and the British Isles, was both deep and wide. He was familiar with the Icelandic *Eddas* and sagas; the Germanic history-cum-myth of the Huns and Burgundians; the Irish hero tales; the Welsh *Mabinogion*; and the complex and comprehensive Arthurian "Matter of Britain." With such an array of national stories to draw on, what was it about this mythology for Finland that spurred him first to imitate it, and then to invent one of his own for England? I suggest that as much or more than the stories themselves, the specific example of *Kalevala*'s compiler, Elias Lönnrot, was what inspired Tolkien.

What had Lönnrot done? He had "scurried about," roaming over the backwoods and rural areas of Finland and the Russo-Finnish Karelian border collecting and transcribing from unlettered peasants their *runos*, their orally performed songs. His project stretched over twenty years and resulted first in his university thesis on Väinämöinen in 1827, published as the Proto-Kalevala in 1928; then the *Old Kalevala*, the name given to the 1835 edition after publication of the much longer version of 1849, which is the *Kalevala* as we have it today. Lönnrot compiled, selected, and put into narrative order songs of creation and heroism, incantations and shamanism, and the vagaries of ordinary human life. In so doing he gave Finland, for two hundred years the fief alternately of Sweden and Russia, its own mythic and literary heritage—its own national identity. He reconstructed for Finland a world of magic and mystery, a heroic age of story that may never have existed in precisely the form he gave it, but nevertheless fired Finland with a sense of its own independent worth.

I propose that Tolkien envisioned himself doing exactly that, constructing a world of magic and mystery, creating a heroic age that, although it might never have existed, would give England a storial sense of its own mythic identity. But with this difference—that his work, unlike Lönnrot's, would be a fictive construct. Unlike Lönnrot, Tolkien would not be "scurrying about." He was a writer, not a collector. He would invent, and by connecting his invented myths to England's extant history he would interweave a whole tapestry where only disconnected scraps of information had been before. He would be, in Forster's words, both the "great poet" who would give England her voice, and the "thousand little poets" whose voices would "pass into our common talk." Tolkien would follow the Lönnrot model in having an auditor (ultimately a series of auditors) who heard, transcribed, and passed on the songs of his fictive race of Elves, but he would be at once the singer and the compiler, the performer and the audience.

Several factors related only tangentially to *Kalevala* added impetus to Tolkien's developing ambition. As a student at King Edward's School in Birmingham, he had added excursions into Old English to his growing store of languages, reading the sparse remnants of early English mythic poetry, among them the *Crist*, *Beowulf*, and *Sir Gawain and the Green Knight*. Each in its separate way fired his imagination—the *Crist* which gave him the name Eärendel, which he co-opted and wove into his own myth; *Beowulf*, whose tragedy gave him a model for heroic struggle; *Sir Gawain*, whose combination of myth and chivalry with a flawed hero intrigued him. Nevertheless, while these were certainly mythic, and certainly in English, they were not what Tolkien wanted as a mythology for England. None could be England's *Kalevala*. The *Crist* is overtly Christian, which he found too explicit for an invented myth; *Beowulf* is an English poem but not an English myth, having as its subject matter the exploits of a northern Scandinavian who goes to Denmark; and *Sir Gawain and the Green Knight* is directly connected to Arthur and his court, therefore Celtic or British rather than English.

Growing out of this as a related factor may have been Tolkien's perception of the deleterious effect of the Norman Conquest on English language and culture, an event in English history which he regarded as an unmitigated catastrophe and which he heartily condemned. At some time in the school year of 1909–10 the eighteen-year-old Tolkien made a speech to the school debating society on the motion—"probably," says his biographer Humphrey Carpenter, "of his own devising"—"That this house deplores the occurrence of the Norman Conquest." Here he attacked "the influx of polysyllabic barbarities which ousted the more honest if humbler native words" (*Biography*, 40).

It seems safe to suppose that in addition to the ouster of language in the wake of the Conquest, Tolkien might also have mourned the ouster of a presumed pre-Conquest mythology for which the Old English language, now suppressed by "the influx of polysyllabic barbarities," had been the vehicle. Nor is it unreasonable to speculate that his imagination could make an analogy between the plight of Finnish lore and language overrun by the Swedes and Russians and that of Old English lore and language overrun by the Normans. In restoring or newly creating his mythology dedicated to England, he created as well a language to be its vehicle, Quenya, which he called "Elven-latin" and which he intended to be a language of lore, whose phonology is directly and intentionally modeled on the phonology of Finnish.

A further comment by Tolkien in his description of his projected mythology invites another comparison with *Kalevala*. He wrote that "[t]he cycles should be linked to a majestic whole and yet leave scope for other minds and hands, wielding paint and music and drama" (*Letters*, 145). We need look no further than the paintings of Akseli Gallen-Kallela and the music of Jan Sibelius to see what inspired that statement, nor is it a great stretch of imagination to speculate that Tolkien might have hoped for artists of that caliber to continue and elaborate his own work.

In fact, although not necessarily always of that caliber, and perhaps not quite in the arenas he would have wanted, he has been granted his wish. Operas and concert pieces inspired if not by *The Silmarillion* at least by *The Lord of the Rings* abound, while pseudo-folk music settings of the poems from that book, chiefly on guitar, are legion. Painting has also taken Tolkien's work for inspiration. Tolkien calendars and illustrated volumes of all his works continue to appear, not a few of them by reputable and able artists such as Ted Nasmith, Alan Lee, and Michael Hague. As for drama, there have been several BBC radio productions of *The Hobbit* and *The Lord of the Rings* as well as any number of amateur productions. In addition, there have been to date three attempts to translate his books into film. Whether Tolkien would have approved of any of the results remains a matter for speculation and debate.

What, finally, can we conclude from this concatenation of mythic impulses? Did Tolkien answer Forster's call? Did he succeed, like Lönnrot, in giving England a mythology all its own? While the answer to the first question is "yes," the answer to the second must be, "no, he did not succeed," not, at least, in any nationalistic sense. Neither *The Silmarillion* nor its offshoot, *The Lord of the Rings*, will ever inspire patriotic emotion in the English breast, or culturally distinguish any English person from the rest of the world. But he did give England—and the rest of the world—a work of mythic quality and mythic proportions and, we may safely suppose by this time, a kind of mythic endurance. And for that, our thanks must go in large measure to Elias Lönnrot.

Notes

1. E.M. Forster, *Howards End* (New York: Everyman, 1991), 279.
2. *The Kalevala*, compiled by Elias Lönnrot, prose translation by Francis Peabody Magoun Jr. (Cambridge, Mass. and London, England: Harvard University Press, 1963), xiv.
3. *Kalevala,* 343. The reference is to A.W. Linsén's cartoon of 1847 of Lönnrot on a field trip, with an inscription adapted from Ennius's Annals, xii, fr. l. v. 1 as reproduced on 343.

Chapter 17

SETTING THE ROCKET OFF IN STORY

The Kalevala *as the Germ of Tolkien's* Legendarium

RICHARD C. WEST

"[T]his strange people and these new gods, this race of unhypocritical low-brow scandalous heroes," wrote the young man about a book he had recently devoured, "the more I read of it, the more I felt at home and enjoyed myself" (*Biography*, 49). J.R.R. Tolkien was referring to the Finnish *Kalevala,* which he discovered in about 1910 or 1911, late in his tenure at King Edward's School in Birmingham—in the translation by W.F. Kirby published in the Everyman series in 1907. It proved to be a seminal moment in both his linguistic and his literary career.

He was later to remark many times that Finnish had almost ruined his career, for example, in rueful but jocular missives to his son Christopher in 1944 (*Letters*, 87), to W.H. Auden in 1955 (*Letters*, 214) and to Christopher Bretherton in 1964 (*Letters*, 345). Reading Kirby's poetic translation had whetted his appetite to read the work in its original language, a natural desire in a polyglot who had demonstrated at King Edward's that he was already well along in his studies of Latin, Greek, Gothic, Anglo-Saxon, and Old Norse. In 1912, while he was an exhibition student at Oxford University, he found C.N.E. Eliot's *A Finnish Grammar* in the library at Exeter College, and he felt impelled to study the language and try to read in the original Finnish what a year or two before he had enjoyed in English translation. Since he was at the same time also preparing for Classical Honour Moderations, the time and en-

285

ergy demanded by this side interest took its toll. He ended up being awarded a Second Class in 1913, when it was as clear to him as to his tutors that he had been capable of getting a First, and he considered himself fortunate that he did not lose the partial scholarship that enabled him to attend Oxford (*Letters*, 214). He applied himself, and went on to graduate with honors, serve in the First World War, and have a distinguished academic career. But throughout his life he also continued to devote considerable time and energy to his many interests, fortunately for those of us who enjoy his writings outside of his major discipline.

He described that discipline late in life by saying: "I am primarily a scientific philologist. My interests were, and remain, largely scientific. . . . " (*Letters*, 345). While this is true, he also spoke of "the acute aesthetic pleasure derived from a language for its own sake" (*Letters*, 213), and this aesthetic pleasure in language he had throughout his life was thoroughly intertwined with his scientific studies of language. It was entirely Tolkienesque for him to declare about finding that *Finnish Grammar* that "It was like discovering a complete wine-cellar filled with bottles of an amazing wine of a kind and flavour never tasted before. It quite intoxicated me. . . ." (*Letters,* 214). As a result, he said that his own series of invented languages "became heavily Finnicized in phonetic pattern and structure" (*Letters,* 214).

This influence is particularly strong on Quenya, the classical or "high" language of Tolkien's Elves. (The "everyday" Elven language is Sindarin, which shows more the influence of the Celtic tongues, especially Welsh, which Tolkien also loved). Linguistic scholars like Thomas DuBois, Scott Mellor, and Helena Rautala have discussed how Quenya sometimes seems to have loan-words from Finnish (e.g., *tie* means "road" in Finnish and "path" in Quenya),[1] and, even more basically, that the two tongues share many similar grammatical features (e.g., both Finnish and Quenya are rich in multiple suffixes that can be attached to nouns and verbs to alter their meaning, enabling a speaker to compress a great deal of nuance into a single word). While Tolkien did not rely solely on the model of any single language, and indeed each of his invented tongues draws from a great many linguistic sources, Finnish was clearly one of his chief inspirations. Taum Santoski summarized by observing that Tolkien's "languages are a rethought, recast, and reforged amalgam of most European languages. Influences on his languages may be found from German, Old Icelandic, Finnish, Welsh, Danish, Old Norse, Russian, the Slavic language area, Latin, Italian, Greek, Hvestan and Farsi, and even Gothic and Old Irish." He also averred that it was the *Kalevala*, "the epic stories of Finland, and Finnish which really opened up Tolkien's inventive abilities."[2]

Tolkien referred to his invented languages as "games" and "a secret vice." While this is true enough, it should be noted that there was also a very serious side to them related to his scientific study. Just as his writing down the baby talk of his children deepened his understanding of how the human mind learned and used language,[3] so his constructing Quenya and Sindarin and other tongues following known philological rules helped him grasp how historical languages grew and evolved. It was play, but learned play.

He was modest in his assessment of his knowledge of the language of the *Kalevala*. "I never learned Finnish well enough to do more than plod through a bit of the original, like a schoolboy with Ovid," he wrote to W.H. Auden in 1955 (*Letters*, 214). But eleven years earlier in a letter to his son Christopher he wrote a light-hearted account of poem 20, in which beer is fermented for the first time and the heroes get very drunk, noting that "Kirby's translation is funnier than the original" (*Letters*, 87). He evidently thought he grasped the language well enough to judge this. Tolkien had some proficiency in so many languages that it can be difficult to assess how fluent he was in any of them other than those that were his primary study, particularly since most of us are far less linguistically gifted than he, but it would not be wise to underestimate him.[4] It is clear that the *Kalevala* made a deep impression, both in its "queer language" and in its "glimpse of an entirely different mythological world" (*Letters*, 87, 345).

If "Finnish nearly ruined my Hon. Mods," as he wrote to his son Christopher, it was also "the original germ of the Silmarillion" (*Letters*, 87). It was Finnish, he wrote to his former student W.H. Auden, "that set the rocket off in story" (*Letters*, 214). We can trace this perhaps as far back as 1912, when Tolkien was in his first year at Oxford's Exeter College and presented a paper to a college society on the *Kalevala*, in which he expressed the wish that there were more of the same sort of "primitive undergrowth" of mythology surviving, particularly in England (*Biography*, 59). And certainly it can be traced at least to October 1914, the approximate date of a letter (itself undated) that he wrote to his future wife, Edith Bratt. In talking to her of the *Kalevala*, he says: "Amongst other work I am trying to turn one of the stories—which is really a very great story and most tragic—into a short story somewhat on the lines of Morris' romances with chunks of poetry in between" (*Letters*, 7).

Thus the *Kalevala* provided literary as well as linguistic stimulus to the young Tolkien. Whatever survives of that initial attempt has not been published. Humphrey Carpenter says it was "little more than a pastiche" (*Biography*, 73) of William Morris, the avowed model, and was never finished. This in itself tells us a good deal. Tolkien worked on so many and disparate projects throughout his life that it was unavoidable that he would leave a good number of them unfinished, and this early period was one in which he was so busy (with Honour Mods, for one thing) that it is hardly surprising that he would have to set his little story aside. But it is interesting to speculate why he did not come back to it. One of the central facts about Tolkien is so obvious that we may overlook its significance: he was a writer. He wrote in almost every spare moment: he wrote voluminously; he revised incessantly. An image he often used about himself was that a pen was to him as a beak was to a hen: he was always pecking away (e.g., *Letters*, 335). He left us thousands of pages of manuscripts. More of his works have been published since his death than were during his lifetime, since during his lifetime nothing was finished to his exacting standards. He had many writing projects that he worked on intermittently over decades. Turning a fairly self-contained section of the *Kalevala* into a short story (or even a long story) in the manner of William Morris does not appear to be too ambitious a plan for a born writer. Had this really been something central to Tolkien's deepest interests, he would probably either have finished it eventually, or, at least, he would certainly have written more of it. It could not have been just that the Great War intervened: Tolkien observed that the war quickened his philological and literary interests, and anyway William Morris was extremely popular among the soldiers in the trenches.[5] Rather I think we see here an early example of something Tolkien later said was characteristic of him: that his typical response to reading an old work of literature was to write something in the same vein.[6] I suggest that we will find that both the *Kalevala* and the prose romances of William Morris were absorbed into his imagination and inform his *legendarium*, not as imitation or pastiche, but as a natural part of his mind-set.

Consider the story of Kullervo that he selected to work on, which occupies *runos* or poems 31 through 36 in the *Kalevala* and involves that staple of heroic literature, a family feud. Untamo, with his retainers, attacks and kills his brother, Kalervo, and all his household save one woman, spared apparently because she is with child. But the father is the slain Kalervo, and Untamo fears that the boy who is born shortly, and named Kullervo, will grow up to take vengeance. Even as a baby Kullervo is capable of Herculean feats of strength that frustrate the attempts of his uncle to kill him. Eventually he is sold as a slave to one of the major characters in the *Kalevala*, Ilmarinen the Smith, but his awesome strength makes all his work turn out awry as it had when he was laboring for Untamo. When he feels ready to return as an avenger (and perhaps get out of the way of Ilmarinen, whose wife he has slain), he is dissuaded by receiving news that his parents and siblings are somehow still alive and well and living in Lapland.

He then joins his father and mother and a sister, but finds that a brother is dead and another sister has disappeared. Again everything he works at turns out badly, since his heroic strength results in such things as pulling apart fishing nets instead of hauling in fish. While traveling by sledge he on three occasions passes comely maidens and each time tries to entice them to accept a ride. They all prudently decline, but the third time he forces the young woman into the sledge. Only afterward do they discover that she is his missing sister, and she immediately drowns herself in remorse for their unwitting incest.

Now the distraught Kullervo does take his long-delayed revenge and slaughters his uncle Untamo and his household. But when he returns he finds both his parents and his other sister (and a brother who somehow had not died previously after all) are now really dead. Only his hunting dog survives, to lead him to the spot where he met and seduced his sister. He asks his sword if it will slay him, and it magically speaks, agreeing to do so. Thus dies Kullervo the hapless, running onto his own sword.

I apologize if this summary[7] occasionally seems facetious, but I trust it shows both that the story touches powerful archetypes while also having some real problems with artistic unity. The poems meander through disparate traditions about the main character so they are not completely consistent one with another, and it should be mentioned that they are at least as interested in charms relating to herding cattle or warding off bears and suchlike as in developing a narrative. Keith Bosley notes that Elias Lönnrot, in compiling the *Kalevala*, "virtually invented" this character of Kullervo "by combining poems about an orphan child of Herculean strength . . . about a departing warrior . . . about incest . . . and about reacting to news of death . . . ; the main characters of these poems have various names, including Kullervo, while the incestuous brother is sometimes Lemminkäinen,"[8] one of the other major figures of the Finnish epic.

The inconsistencies in the *Kalevala* account may not bother a reader being swept along by the ballad, but they must have caused problems for someone trying to write a coherent short story. It would be necessary to make changes, so perhaps it came to seem easier, rather than to retell the story of Kullervo, to introduce a new protagonist who would have vicissitudes like those of Kullervo but which could be more consistently developed: who would speak, not Finnish, but Tolkien's own language, or a tongue of his invention.

However it came about, Tolkien did soon turn to a new protagonist whom he came to call Túrin, son of Húrin, whose story he developed and expanded and revised beginning in the teens of the twentieth century, returning to it again and again for decades. The shape of the final story (or as final as the author left it) is full of incident (*Silm*, 198–226).

Túrin is not exactly orphaned, but he does lose his father after the great Battle of Unnumbered Tears when a vast army of Elves and Men is annihilated and Morgoth, Tolkien's version of Satan, takes Húrin the Steadfast prisoner and lays a curse on his family. With Túrin's homeland of Dor-lómin now depleted of its warrior defenders and overrun by invaders, his mother Morwen sends her son to the safety of the Elvish kingdom of Doriath to be fostered by King Thingol and his consort, Melian (a Vala or angelic being whose power protects Doriath). But Morwen retains custody of her daughter Nienor, an infant too young to travel, and so Túrin does not see her again until she is a fair young maiden.

Túrin grows into a redoubtable warrior, but a quarrel that results in the death of an Elf sends him into self-imposed exile from Doriath. Though his comrade-in-arms Beleg seeks him out to tell him he has been pardoned by King Thingol, Túrin is too proud to return and stays with the band of outlaws he has joined. He and Beleg turn the band into a guerrilla force against Morgoth's Orcs, but they are eventually betrayed, the band is wiped out, and Túrin is led away into captivity. Beleg comes to his rescue in the dead of night, but Túrin mistakes what is happening and kills his best friend by mistake. He is then led to the

Elvish kingdom of Nargothrond, where he becomes a great war leader, rallying its forces against Morgoth for a considerable time, but the ultimate result is that Nargothrond is overwhelmed by an army of Orcs led by the dragon Glaurung. The dragon tricks Túrin into returning to his homeland in search of his mother and sister, so that the Elf maid Finduilas, who was in love with him, is killed before he can rescue her. His return to Dor-lómin is also ill-fated, resulting in many deaths, including that of his aunt Aerin, and much trouble for his people. Having learned that Morwen and Nienor had gone to Doriath where they should be safe, and being still unwilling to return to Thingol's court, Túrin instead takes up with the Men of Brethil and is soon leading them into battle against marauding Orcs. His sister comes in search of him, but encounters Glaurung and has her memory taken away by the dragon's magic. Túrin finds her wandering in the wild, but they do not know each other, and eventually they marry. Glaurung comes against Brethil, and Túrin slays him in a heroic battle, but the dying dragon reveals the incestuous union. Nienor is much more fully characterized than her rather sparsely drawn prototype in the *Kalevala*, but she also ends by drowning herself in remorse. In words that echo Kullervo's, Túrin asks his great sword, which has slain so many during his long career, if it will also drink his blood, and it magically speaks its agreement.

This rather bare-bones outline will serve to show that we have gotten pretty far afield from the story in the *Kalevala*, though some elements survive from the original source. Tolkien frequently refers to Kullervo as "hapless," and this element is certainly retained in Túrin, but the story that Tolkien called "most tragic" has had the tragedy intensified. Túrin, with the best intentions, wreaks a good deal more havoc wherever he goes than even Kullervo managed, and, unlike Kullervo, not by being a somewhat dim-witted hero who does not know his own strength. Túrin's story has become entwined with the other stories of the Silmarils that Tolkien was developing at the same time, and other archetypes and motifs have been subsumed into it. The family curse, like that on the House of Atreus. The outlaw band, like Robin Hood. The mistaken killing, like Sohrab of his son Rustum or Balin of his brother Balan. The dragon lore that always so fascinated Tolkien. Throughout, as I have argued elsewhere (West, "Túrin's *Ofermod*"), Tolkien uses the character of Túrin to examine the theme of heroic excess, a hero who is the embodiment of a critique of heroism.

The element of incest and its ghastly outcome is retained, but, if Tolkien had not told us, I am not sure we would recognize this as having its particular source in the *Kalevala* account rather than in many other analogues. As Tolkien wrote to Milton Waldman, Túrin is "a figure that might be said (by people who like that sort of thing, though it is not very useful) to be derived from elements in Sigurd the Volsung, Oedipus, and the Finnish Kullervo" (*Letters*, 150). It could be added that the incest taboo is widely used in tales, occurring also, for example, in legends of King Arthur and of Charlemagne. Tracing influence is a slippery proposition, for plausible sources are usually multiple, and even the author may not know what was growing in his unconscious mind. But I believe we can see it in the talking sword that agrees to take the despairing hero's life, something which, to the best of my knowledge, happens only in the stories of Kullervo and of Túrin, and is a powerful scene in both.

Much of the influence of the Finnish epic is simply that it pervaded Tolkien's imagination. Both Randel Helms[9] and Jonathan Himes,[10] for example, argue that the Sampo, an object of mystery and power throughout the *Kalevala*, is a source for Tolkien's Silmarils, or Jewels of Power. Quests for objects of power are common in legend and literature, but the Finnish Sampo was part of the compost in Tolkien's mind.

Yet I think there is at least one other scene in Tolkien's fiction that has its source in the *Kalevala*. The singing match in poem 3 between Väinämöinen and Joukahainen, in which the latter (a young upstart) challenges the old wizard but ends up being sunk in a swamp by the magic of song and having to ransom his life, seems to me to have an echo in another of Tolkien's favorite stories, that of Beren and Lúthien (as has also been noticed by Paul Kocher).[11] When Beren sets out on his quest to recover a Silmaril, he receives aid from King Finrod Felagund and a small company of Elves. They are disguised as Orcs by the magic of Finrod, but Sauron is suspicious of the unknown band as they pass his citadel and has them brought before him. "Then befell the contest of Sauron and Felagund which is renowned. For Felagund strove with Sauron in songs of power, and the power of the King was very great; but Sauron had the mastery. . . ." (*Silm*, 170–71). It is left to another powerful singer, Lúthien herself, to rescue her lover, Beren, from the dungeons of Sauron and achieve their quest even to the stronghold of the Satanic Morgoth.

It is in this use of word and song and story, I think, that we can see what specially drew Tolkien to the Finnish epic. As Albert B. Lord observes: ". . . the key to an understanding of the *Kalevala* is the power of the word, the power of incantations and of the story that brings power. Its heroes are word-masters and wonder-workers."[12] The same thing could be said of Tolkien's mythos, and often is. Luigi de Anna, for example, speaks of "the magic of words,"[13] the eloquent essay by Dwayne Thorpe[14] of the spell Tolkien weaves around his readers, and the wide-ranging books by Jane Chance[15] and Verlyn Flieger[16] of Tolkien's artistic use of wordcraft and powerful archetypes. Ultimately, then, the budding young philologist found a kindred spirit in the ostensibly alien world of the Finns. And perhaps, as Tolkien contemplated the achievement of Elias Lönnrot in compiling the old tales of his people into a mythology for Finland that was accepted as such by his compatriots, he was encouraged in his own efforts to make a "mythology for England" that might be acceptable to his own countrymen. We can be grateful to the *Kalevela* for "set[ting] the rocket off in story."

Notes

1. Thomas DuBois and Scott Mellor, "The Nordic Roots of Tolkien's Middle-earth," *Scandinavian Review* 90, no. 1 (summer 2002): 38.

2. Taum Santoski, "Introduction to the Study of Elvish," preface to Nancy Martsch, *Basic Quenya: Quenya Language Lessons, with Elvish-English Vocabulary*, 2nd ed. (Sherman Oaks, Calif.: "Beyond Bree" Publication, 1992), i.

3. Michael Tolkien, "J.R.R. Tolkien—The Wizard Father," *Sunday Telegraph*, 7 September 1973, 654.

4. Note, however, that when he felt he knew the language into which his works were being translated well enough to take exception to choices of words or phrasing, his translators did not always agree that he understood the nuances. See Luigi de Anna, "The Magic of Words: J.R.R. Tolkien and Finland," in *Scholarship and Fantasy: Proceedings of the Tolkien Phenomenon, May 1992, Turku, Finland* (special issue), ed. K.J. Battarbee, 10–11, Anglicana Turkuensia, no. 12 (Turku: University of Turku, 1995).

5. Paul Fussell, *The Great War and Modern Memory* (Oxford and New York: Oxford University Press, 1975), 135–37.

6. Richard C. West, "The Interlace Structure of *The Lord of the Rings*," in *A Tolkien Compass*, ed. Jared Lobdell (LaSalle, Ill.: Open Court, 1975), 80.

7. Following Richard C. West, "Túrin's *Ofermod*: An Old English Theme in the Development of the Story of Túrin," in *Tolkien's "Legendarium": Essays on "The History of Middle-earth,"* ed. Verlyn Flieger and Carl F. Hostetter, 237–38, *Contributions to the Study of Science Fiction and Fantasy*, no. 86 (Westport, Conn. and London: Greenwood Press, 2000).

8. Keith Bosley, ed. and trans. *The "Kalevala," an Epic Poem after Oral Tradition by Elias Lönnrot* (Oxford and New York: Oxford University Press, 1989), xxxii.

9. Randel Helms, *Tolkien and the Silmarils* (Boston: Houghton Mifflin Company, 1981), 42–44.

10. Jonathan Himes, "What J.R.R. Tolkien Really Did with the Sampo," *Mythlore* 22, no. 86, (spring 2000), 69–85.

11. Paul H. Kocher, *A Reader's Guide to "The Silmarillion"* (Boston: Houghton Mifflin, 1980), 130–32.

12. Cited in Bosley, vii.

13. Luigi de Anna, "The Magic of Words: J.R.R. Tolkien and Finland," in *Scholarship and Fantasy: Proceedings of the Tolkien Phenomenon, May 1992, Turku, Finland* (special issue), ed. K.J. Battarbee, 7–19, Anglicana Turkuensia, no. 12 (Turku: University of Turku, 1993).

14. Dwayne Thorpe, "Tolkien's Elvish Craft," in *Proceedings of the J.R.R. Tolkien Centenary Conference, Keble College, Oxford, 1992*, ed. Patricia Reynolds and Glen H. GoodKnight, 315–21, published as special issues of *Mythlore* 80 / *Mallorn* 30 (1995).

15. Jane Chance, *Tolkien's Art: A Mythology for England* (1979; rev. ed., Lexington, Ky.: University Press of Kentucky, 2001).

16. Verlyn Flieger, *Splintered Light: Logos and Language in Tolkien's World* (1983; rev. ed., Kent, Ohio: Kent State University Press, 2002).

Chapter 18

J.R.R. TOLKIEN AND THE KALEVALA

Some Thoughts on the Finnish Origins of Tom Bombadil and Treebeard

DAVID ELTON GAY

As a scholar of the *Kalevala* I have long been fascinated with questions of its composition and influence: What was it that Lönnrot did to Finnish epic and mythology, and why was his version of the epics and mythology so influential outside of Finland? What do non-Finnish readers make of Lönnrot's highly romanticized vision of Finnish mythology? Did non-Finnish writers draw from it in their works, and if so, what parts of the story did they use?[1] J.R.R. Tolkien's love of the Finnish language and of the *Kalevala* is well known, which makes Tolkien one of the obvious writers to turn to when examining issues of the influence and reception of the *Kalevala*. Tolkien himself highlights the importance of the *Kalevala* as a source for his *legendarium*: its origin was, in part, an effort to rewrite the Kullervo story of the *Kalevala*.[2] The influence of the *Kalevala* and the Finnish language on *The Silmarillion* and on Tolkien's creation of languages, notably Elvish and Entish, is the most widely known and discussed influence of Lönnrot's work on Tolkien's. What I want to examine here, however, is the influence of the *Kalevala* on Tolkien's published works, especially *The Lord of the Rings*.

It is not clear how much Tolkien knew about the composition of the *Kalevala*. Tom Shippey writes that "Tolkien . . . admired the *Kalevala* as

295

a product of exactly the kind of literary rescue-project which he would have liked to see in England," which suggests that Tolkien was aware of the distance between the *Kalevala* and Finnish folk tradition. But Tolkien also seems to have shared some of the common misconceptions about the nature of Lönnrot's epic and its sources.[3] In a letter to Edith Bratt, for instance, he writes that he has introduced a friend to the *Kalevala*, but he refers to its poems as ballads rather than the epic texts they in fact are (*Letters*, 7). Because the relationship of the 1849 *Kalevala* to Finnish tradition is often misunderstood by scholars in Tolkien studies, as it may have been by Tolkien himself, it seems appropriate to begin with a description of just what the *Kalevala* is and where it came from.[4] It is best to state from the outset that the *Kalevala* is Elias Lönnrot's creation, his vision of what a Finnish national epic and mythology should be, not a text from Finnish folk tradition. The sources of the *Kalevala* are in Finnish tradition, but its creation was a product of the national aspirations of Finnish intellectuals in the eighteenth and early nineteenth centuries. It was in this period that a growing national awareness led Finnish intellectuals to notice the epic and mythological traditions of the Finnish-speaking peasantry. By the early decades of the nineteenth century this interest had expanded into the desire to discover or reconstruct a Finnish national epic. In the 1820s the newly established Finnish Literature Society commissioned Elias Lönnrot to collect traditional epic texts with the goal of creating from them a single coherent Finnish national epic.[5] His first creative effort was the 1834 *Runokokous Väinämöisesta* (a collection of poems about Väinämöinen), but this version was not published in his lifetime. Instead, he rewrote his *Runokokous Väinämöisesta* and published it as the *Kalevala* (usually called the *Old Kalevala*) in 1835. The *Kalevala* was quickly accepted both as an authentic Finnish folk epic and as the desired national epic. Lönnrot's vision of the epic, however, continued to develop, and he extensively revised and expanded this 1835 version in the mid-1840s, publishing a new version of the *Kalevala* (often called the *New Kalevala*), one far more literary in style, and far more his own creation, in 1849. It is the 1849 version that has been widely accepted as the canonical version of the epic and the one that Tolkien himself knew, first through Kirby's translation, and then, once he had learned some Finnish, through his own reading of the Finnish text.

For the student of the *Kalevala*, *The Lord of the Rings* is perhaps the most disappointing part of Tolkien's *legendarium* to study for influences from the *Kalevala* and Finnish language. There are a few obvious places where one might look for the connections, such as in the Elvish and Entish languages, but even here the Finnish element in the book is reduced because the Elvish language most encountered in *The Lord of the Rings* is Sindarin, the Welsh-based version of Elvish. This is not to say, however, that the *Kalevala* is absent as an influence in *The Lord of the Rings*. Some scenes in *The Lord of the Rings* draw from Kalevalaic imagery, and Tom Bombadil's ancestry includes Väinämöinen, the great singer of Lönnrot's epic, as does that of Treebeard and the Ents.

There can be no doubt that Väinämöinen is the most enigmatic character both in traditional Finnish mythology and epic and in Lönnrot's *Kalevala*. He has been variously explained as a wizard, shaman, and nature god, without any explanation ever gaining full acceptance.[6] His temperament can show the good nature of a being living at peace in his world and his fury at threats to his well-being. Slow to anger, but terrible in his rage, Väinämöinen is the great singer who was present at the creation (though he is not the creator), whose words can heal but also destroy, depending on his mood. In the second poem of the *Kalevala* he begins to bring order to nature through the cutting of trees, the clearing of land, and the planting of crops. In the third poem his peace is disturbed by Joukahainen, who is jealous of Väinämöinen, and who travels to Väinämöinen's home to challenge him to a contest of knowledge. Joukahainen fails in his challenge—Väinämöinen is far more powerful than he is, and his knowledge is far deeper—and Joukahainen succeeds only in provoking Väinämöinen into a rage. The third poem ends with Joukahainen promising Väinämöinen his sister as a way of escaping the great singer's anger. Even in such a brief synopsis of Väinämöinen's role in the first poems of the *Kalevala*, the contradictions of his character stand out, as do the connections that he has to Tom Bombadil and Treebeard.

Certain general similarities come immediately to mind when comparing Väinämöinen, Tom Bombadil, and Treebeard: for instance, they are ancient beings who live in small largely forested countries that they control through their great power, though they do not own the countries; they have an extraordinary closeness to their world; and they are fearless because of their power.[7] The Elves certainly recognize Bombadil's power.[8] Glorfindel remarks, for instance, when the suggestion is made that the Ring be sent to Bombadil for safekeeping, that Sauron will then simply turn his strength upon Tom Bombadil, and he questions whether or not Bombadil is powerful enough to defy Sauron on his own. His answer is that, "if all else is conquered, Bombadil will fall, Last as he was First" (*LR* 2.2, 259). As someone whose power enables him to resist Sauron until he is the last free being, Bombadil's strength is among the greatest in Middle-earth, as Väinämöinen's is in Kaleva. The peculiar closeness of Bombadil and Väinämöinen to their countries, their "naturalness," as Shippey calls it, comes from the fact that they are the most ancient creatures in their particular world: Tom and Väinämöinen are, as Tom says, "oldest." They are, in fact, immortal. And Treebeard is the oldest of mortal creatures. As Elrond says of Bombadil in "The Council of Elrond," with words that could easily apply to Väinämöinen, and perhaps also to Treebeard: "I had forgotten Bombadil, if indeed this is still the same that walked the woods and hills long ago, and even then was older than the old. . . . Iarwain Ben-adar we called him, oldest and fatherless" (*LR* 2.2, 258).

For both Väinämöinen and Tom Bombadil power comes from their command of song and lore rather than from ownership and domination. Väinämöinen spends his time in endless singing, not singing songs of power, however, but rather songs of knowledge. Indeed, it would appear that he, like Tom Bombadil, sings for the simple pleasure of singing. As Lönnrot writes:

> Väinämöinen, old and steadfast
> Passed the days of his existence
> Where lie Vainola's sweet meadows,
> Kalevala's extended heathlands:
> There he sang of sweetness,
> Sang his songs and proved his wisdom.
> Day by day he sang unwearied,
> Night by night discoursed unceasing,
> Sang the songs of by-gone ages,
> Hidden words of ancient wisdom,
> Songs which all the children sing not,
> All beyond men's comprehension,
> In these days of misfortune,
> When the race is near its ending.[9]

As has been often noted, much of what Tom says is, in fact, sung. As with Väinämöinen's singing, Tom's has power, and the power of his singing is clearly similar to Väinämöinen's. When we first meet Tom he saves Merry and Pippin from Old Man Willow through the threat of his singing: as he says to Frodo and Sam, "I'll sing his roots off. I'll sing a wind up and blow leaf and branch away" (*LR* 1.6, 117). Goldberry later tells Frodo that Tom is master of his land. And, as Tom's conversations with the Hobbits make apparent, his mastery of his land, like Väinämöinen's, is through knowledge and experience rather than ownership.

If, as I propose, Tom Bombadil is based in part on Väinämöinen, then Tom's control of his world through knowledge expressed in song is to be expected: To have power over something in the mythology of the *Kalevala* one must know its origins and be able to sing the appropriate songs and incantations concerning these origins. Great power in the world of the *Kalevala* requires great age and great knowledge, and Väinämöinen has both. A large part of his power comes from the fact that as the oldest of all living things he saw the creation of things, heard their names, and knows the songs of their origins, and it was his works that helped give shape to the land. The same is clearly true of Tom Bombadil. Tom says to Frodo, when asked who he is:

> I am old. Eldest, that's what I am. . . . Tom was here before the river and the trees; Tom remembers the first raindrop and the first acorn. He made paths before the Big People, and saw the Little People arriving. He was there before the Kings and the graves and the Barrow-wights. When the Elves passed westward, Tom was here already, before the seas were bent. He knew the dark under the stars when it was fearless—before the Dark Lord came from outside. (*LR* 1.7, 129)

Tom's choice of the adjectives "old" and "eldest" to describe himself links him to Väinämöinen, for throughout the whole of the *Kalevala* epos, from Lönnrot's early drafts through to the 1849 edition of the epic, Väinämöinen is "steadfast old Väinämöinen" (*vaka vanha Väinämöinen*). Indeed, one of the important contrasts between Väinämöinen and his enemy Joukahainen is that Väinämöinen is old, whereas Joukahainen is young, a contrast that we are constantly reminded of by the repetition of the formulas *vaka vanha Väinämöinen* and *nuori Joukahainen* (young

Joukahainen). In *The Adventures of Tom Bombadil*, too, Tom is consistently given the epithet "old" (*TR*, 189–251).

The events Tom describes are events that occurred in the First Age of Middle-earth: the creation of the world, the new world lit by starlight when no evil had yet entered Middle-earth, the first passing of the Elves westward to Elvenhome, and the arrival of Morgoth from the West. Some of the Elves—Glorfindel, Cirdan, Elrond, and Galadriel, for example—certainly know of the First Age, but not even their great knowledge and memory goes as far back as Tom's. Tom's description of himself could easily be taken for Väinämöinen's describing his own experience at the creation of Kaleva in this passage from the third poem of the *Kalevala*, when Väinämöinen dismisses Joukahainen's claim to have seen the creation of the world:

> You at least were never present
> When the ocean was first furrowed,
> And the ocean depths were hollowed,
> And the caves dug for fishes,
> And the deep abysses sunken,
> And the lakes first created,
> When the hills were heaped together,
> And the rocky mountains fashioned.
>
> No one ever yet had seen you,
> None had seen you, none had heard you,
> When the earth was first created,
> And the air above expanded,
> When the posts of heaven were planted,
> And the arch of heaven exalted,
> When the moon was shown his pathway,
> And the sun was taught to journey,
> When the Bear was fixed in heaven,
> And the stars in heaven were scattered.[10]

Väinämöinen can say this to Joukahainen because Väinämöinen was at the creation and Joukahainen was not. Though Lönnrot phrases Väinämöinen's speech in a negative way, the similarity to Bombadil's speech is obvious.

The *Kalevala* has something of a reputation for its imagery of Finnish forests and lakes, though it is not this aspect of the epic that most influences *The Lord of the Rings*. Rather, its imagery appears in two scenes of extreme destruction, where the violence verges on the apocalyptic: the destruction of Isengard in *The Two Towers* and of Mordor in *The Return of the King*. Both draw something from a brief passage in the third poem of the 1849 *Kalevala*, where Väinämöinen's rage at Joukahainen's arrogance causes an apocalyptic upheaval. When Väinämöinen began to sing:

> Lakes swelled up, the earth was shaken,
> And the coppery mountains trembled,
> And the mighty rock resounded,
> And the mighty mountains clove asunder;
> On the shore the stones were shivered.[11]

What Lönnrot is describing here is the result not of Väinämöinen's singing of incantations or other magical songs but rather of the sound of Väinämöinen's voice when it is raised in such ferocious anger: the sound alone has the power to rip apart the seams of the world.

Though Treebeard does not have the supernatural power of Väinämöinen, he is similar in significant ways, and further, he and the Ents turn out to be dangerous in a way that is reminiscent of Väinämöinen. There are hints of Treebeard's great power and that of the other Ents and of their relationship to Väinämöinen: Legolas, for instance, the only other member of the Fellowship who knows of the Ents, and of their possibilities, is stunned when Gandalf tells Aragorn, Legolas, and Gimli that, for the first time since the First Age, the Ents are angry enough to wake up and discover their strength (*LR* 3.5, 488). Unlike Väinämöinen's power, however, Treebeard's power is tempered by the Ent's deliberateness and control over himself and his emotions, which makes him seem rather more amusing at first glance than dangerous. Though Treebeard does not like to lose control, the depredations of Saruman and his Orcs against his trees have aroused his anger; with the arrival of Merry and Pippin and their news of Saruman's treachery, his anger breaks into rage, which ignites that of the other Ents as well. There is something of the power of Väinämöinen's rage in Treebeard and the Ents when they destroy Isengard:

> They roared and boomed and trumpeted, until stones began to crack and
> fall at the mere noise of them. . . . [T]he Ents went striding and storming
> like a howling gale, breaking pillars, hurling avalanches of boulders
> down the shafts, tossing huge slabs of stone into the air like leaves. The
> tower was in the middle of a spinning whirlwind. (*LR* 3.9, 554)

As with Väinämöinen's voice raised in fury, the sound of the Ents' voices
shatters stone, and their fury after the death of Beechbone, like that of
Väinämöinen at Joukahainen's arrogance, is like a cataclysmic natural
disaster. They do not have the power of Väinämöinen to create a truly
apocalyptic event, but they can certainly, on a smaller scale, inflict upon
Saruman the equivalent. In the midst of this fury, Treebeard maintains
his calm and his control of the other Ents, and he is able to stop them
before they hurt themselves. As with Väinämöinen, Treebeard's power
comes from his great age, the wisdom that has come with that age, and
his closeness to his land.

The cataclysm in Mordor after the Ring is destroyed is also similar
to that caused by Väinämöinen's rage:

> Towers fell and mountains slid; walls crumbled and melted, crashing
> down; vast pires of smoke and spouting steams went billowing up, up
> until they toppled like an overwhelming wave, and its wild crest curled
> and came foaming down upon the land. (*LR* 6.3, 925–26).

The sudden release of Sauron's power with the destruction of the Ring
brings on, with a violence equal in its shattering effect to that of
Väinämöinen's rage, both the collapse of the things that he has built and
a convulsion of the land that he has so long dominated.

As I noted above, even if the influence of the *Kalevala* on *The Lord
of the Rings* is limited, it is nonetheless important, as it is to the whole
of Tolkien's *legendarium*. Though few characters and incidents in
Tolkien's work are based directly on the *Kalevala*, the importance of
Lönnrot's epic for Tolkien should be considered not only in this regard. Lönnrot's *Kalevala* was important as a source of ideas and images, but its role as a model for an invented world was even more
crucial (as the other essays in this section testify). While Tolkien's
work is indeed very different from Lönnrot's, Tolkien's encounter with
the invented world of the *Kalevala* encouraged his creation of Middle-

earth. In this way, a marvelous act of sub-creation from the nineteenth century helped inspire an even more extraordinary one in the twentieth, *The Lord of the Rings*.

Notes

1. I have examined these issues in several essays: for instance, "The Creation of the *Kalevala*, 1834–1849," *Jahrbuch für Volksliedforschung* 42 (1997): 63–77; and "Renewing Old Poems: The 1849 *Kalevala* as Finnish Tradition in the English-Speaking World," in *The "Kalevala" and the World's Traditional Epics*, ed. Lauri Honko (Helsinki: Finnish Literature Society, 2002), 54–63.

2. Tolkien to W.H. Auden in his *Letters*, 211–17; see especially 214.

3. Tom Shippey, *J.R.R. Tolkien: Author of the Century* (Boston: Houghton Mifflin, 2001), 244. See too xv and xxxiv.

4. Surveys of the background of the *Kalevala* can be found in, among others, Juha Pentikäinen, *Kalevala Mythology*, trans. Ritva Poom (Bloomington: Indiana University Press, 1989); Thomas DuBois, *Finnish Folk Poetry and the "Kalevala"* (New York: Garland, 1995); and Lauri Honko, ed., *Religion, Myth, and Folklore in the World's Epics: The "Kalevala" and Its Predecessors* (Berlin: Mouton de Gruyter, 1990). There are also useful materials, including Lönnrot's prefaces to his various editions, in F.P. Magoun's translations *The Old "Kalevala" and Certain Antecedents* (Cambridge: Harvard University Press, 1969) and *The "Kalevala," or Poems of the Kaleva District* (Cambridge: Harvard University Press, 1963). I am assuming an English-reading audience for this essay and thus limit my citations here, and elsewhere, mostly to works in English. Those able to read Finnish will find the relevant Finnish language bibliographical references in the works by Pentikäinen, DuBois, and Honko.

5. Shippey is in error when he states that because "Lönnrot . . . wrote, rewrote, and interpolated . . . you cannot tell what is by him and what is 'authentic'" (Shippey, *J.R.R. Tolkien: Author of the Century*, xxxiv). The difference is knowable, and I have explored exactly that issue in my "The Creation of the *Kalevala*" and in my 1995 Ph.D. dissertation, *"Revising Tradition: Folklore and the Making of European Literary Epic"* (Indiana University, Bloomington), 28–70, in regard to the poem "Kilpalaulanta" ("The singing match"; the source for poem 3 of the 1849 *Kalevala*), as has DuBois with regard to the Marjatta poem and others in his *Finnish Folk Poetry and the "Kalevala."* The key work for tracing the poems of Lönnrot's 1849 *Kalevala* back to their sources—thus determining what is his and what is traditional—is Väinö Kaukonen's *Elias Lönnrotin Kalevalan toinen painos* (Helsinki: SKS, 1956).

6. Though problematic in some ways, Martti Haavio's *Väinämöinen, Eternal Sage*, trans. Helen Goldthwait-Väänänen, Folklore Fellows Communications, 144 (1952; reprint, Helsinki: Suomalainen Tiedeakatemia, 1991), remains the best monograph on Väinämöinen in Finnish tradition.

7. In *The Road to Middle-earth* (1982; rev. ed., London: HarperCollins,

1992), 94–100, esp. 96–97, Tom Shippey suggests that two of Tom Bombadil's main features are "fearlessness" and "naturalness," both of which tie him even more strongly to Väinämöinen and, combined with his obvious power, increase, I think, the likelihood that Tom is one the Maiar of Middle-earth, rather than, as Shippey suggests, "a *lusus naturae*, a one-member category."

8. Just who Tom Bombadil is, and what his meaning is for the story, are perennial topics for discussion. See, for instance, Shippey, *The Road to Middle-earth*, 95–99; Håkan Arvidssson "The Ring: An Essay on Tolkien's Mythology," *Mallorn* 40 (November 2002): 45–51, esp. 49–50; Michael Stanton, *Hobbits, Elves, and Wizards* (New York: St. Martin's Press, 2001), 29–30; and Jane Chance, *The Lord of the Rings: The Mythology of Power*, rev. ed. (Lexington, Ky.: University Press of Kentucky, 2001), 40–45.

9. W.F. Kirby, trans., *Kalevala, The Land of the Heroes* (London: Athlone Press, 1985), 22.

10. Kirby, 28–29.

11. Kirby, 30.

Bibliography

Primary Works by J.R.R. Tolkien

———, and E.V. Gordon, eds. *Sir Gawain and the Green Knight*. London: Oxford UniversityPress/Humphrey Milford, 1925; 2nd ed. revised by Norman Davis, Oxford: Clarendon Press, 1967.

———. "Beowulf: The Monsters and the Critics." *Proceedings of the British Academy* 22 (1936): 245–95. Reprinted in *An Anthology of Beowulf Criticism*, edited by Lewis E. Nicholson, 51–104. Notre Dame, Ind.: University of Notre Dame Press, 1963; and *The Monsters and the Critics and Other Essays*, edited by Christopher Tolkien, 5–34.

———. *The Hobbit; or There and Back Again*. London: George Allen and Unwin, 1937, 2nd ed., 1951; Boston: Houghton Mifflin, 1938, 2nd ed., 1958; New York: Ballantine, 1965, reprinted 1974; New York: Ballantine, 1966; London: George Allen and Unwin, 1978.

———. "On Fairy-Stories." In *Essays Presented to Charles Williams*, edited by C.S. Lewis, 38–89. London: Oxford University Press, 1947. Reprint, Grand Rapids, Mich.: William B. Eerdmans, 1966. Revised and reprinted in *Tree and Leaf*; and in *The Tolkien Reader*.

———. "English and Welsh." In vol. 1 of *Angles and Britons: The O'Donnell Lectures*. Cardiff: University of Wales Press, 1963, 1–41; Mystic, Conn.: Verry, Lawrence, 1963. Reprinted in *"The Monsters and the Critics,"* edited by Christopher Tolkien, 162–97.

———. *The Fellowship of the Ring*. New York: Ballantine, 1965; Boston: Houghton Mifflin, 1982, 1987.

———. *The Two Towers*. New York: Ballantine, 1965; Boston: Houghton Mifflin, 1982, 1987.

———. *The Return of the King*. New York: Ballantine, 1965; Boston: Houghton Mifflin, 1982, 1987.

———. *The Lord of the Rings*. 3 vols.: *The Fellowship of the Ring, The Two Towers*, and *The Return of the King*. 2nd ed. London: George Allen and Unwin, 1966; Boston: Houghton Mifflin, 1967. First published in a single vol. 1968; London: HarperCollins, 1993. Reset ed., HarperCollins, 1994; Boston: Houghton Mifflin, 1994.

———. *The Tolkien Reader*. New York: Ballantine, 1966.

———. "The Adventures of Tom Bombadil." In *The Tolkien Reader*, 11–23.

———. "An Interview with Tolkien." Interview by Henry Resnick. *Niekas* 18 (1967): 37–43.

———. "Guide to the Names in *The Lord of the Rings.*" In Lobdell, *A Tolkien Compass,* 153–57.

———. *The Silmarillion.* Edited by Christopher Tolkien. London: George Allen and Unwin, 1977; Boston: Houghton Mifflin, 1977.

———. *Unfinished Tales.* Edited by Christopher Tolkien. London: George Allen and Unwin, 1980; Boston: Houghton Mifflin, 1980.

———. *The Letters of J.R.R. Tolkien.* Edited by Humphrey Carpenter with assistance from Christopher Tolkien. London: George Allen and Unwin, 1981; Boston: Houghton Mifflin, 1981; London: HarperCollins, 1995.

———. *Finn and Hengest: The Fragment and the Episode.* Edited by Alan Bliss. London: George Allen and Unwin, 1982; Boston: Houghton Mifflin, 1983.

———. *The Monsters and the Critics and Other Essays.* Edited by Christopher Tolkien. London: George Allen and Unwin, 1983; Boston: Houghton Mifflin, 1984.

———. "A Secret Vice." In *The Monsters and the Critics and Other Essays,* edited by Christopher Tolkien, 198–223.

———. *The History of Middle-earth.* Edited by Christopher Tolkien. 12 vols. London: George Allen and Unwin, 1983–95; Boston: Houghton Mifflin, 1984–96.

———. *The Book of Lost Tales, Part 1.* Vol. 1 of *The History of Middle-earth.* Edited by Christopher Tolkien. London: George Allen and Unwin, 1983; Boston: Houghton Mifflin, 1984; New York: Ballantine, 1992.

———. *The Book of Lost Tales, Part 2.* Vol. 2 of *The History of Middle-earth.* Edited by Christopher Tolkien. London: George Allen and Unwin, 1984; Boston: Houghton Mifflin, 1984; New York: Ballantine, 1992.

———. *The Lays of Beleriand.* Vol. 3 of *The History of Middle-earth.* Edited by Christopher Tolkien. London: George Allen and Unwin, 1985; Boston: Houghton Mifflin, 1985.

———. *The Shaping of Middle-earth: The Quenta, the Ambarkanta and the Annals.* Vol. 4 of *The History of Middle-earth.* Edited by Christopher Tolkien. London: George Allen and Unwin, 1986; Boston: Houghton Mifflin, 1986; New York: Ballantine, 1995.

———. *The Lost Road and Other Writings.* Vol. 5 of *The History of Middle-earth.* Edited by Christopher Tolkien. London: Unwin Hyman, 1987; Boston: Houghton Mifflin, 1987; New York: Ballantine, 1987, reprint, 1996.

———. *The Return of the Shadow [Part 1 of "The History of The Lord of the Rings"].* Vol. 6 of *The History of Middle-earth.* Edited by Christopher Tolkien. London: Unwin Hyman, 1988; Boston: Houghton Mifflin, 1988.

———. *The Treason of Isengard [Part 2 of "The History of The Lord of the*

Rings"]. Vol. 7 of *The History of Middle-earth*. Edited by Christopher Tolkien. London: George Allen and Unwin, 1988; Boston: Haughton Mifflin, 1989.

———. *Tree and Leaf Including the Poem Mythopoeia*. London: Unwin Hyman, 1988; Boston: Houghton Mifflin, 1989.

———. *Sauron Defeated: The End of the Third Age, The Notion Club Papers and The Drowning of Anadûné [Part 4 of "The History of The Lord of the Rings"]*. Vol. 9 of *The History of Middle-earth*. Edited by Christopher Tolkien. London: HarperCollins, 1992; Boston: Houghton Mifflin, 1992.

———. "Athrabeth Finrod Ah Andreth." In *Morgoth's Ring: The Later Silmarillion, Part One*. Vol. 10 of *The History of Middle-earth*, edited by Christopher Tolkien, 303–66. London: HarperCollins, 1993; Boston: Houghton Mifflin, 1993.

———. *The Peoples of Middle-earth*. Vol. 12 of *The History of Middle-earth*. Edited by Christopher Tolkien. London: HarperCollins, 1996; Boston: Houghton Mifflin, 1996.

———. *Beowulf and the Critics*. Edited by Michael D.C. Drout. Medieval and Renaissance Texts and Studies, vol. 248. Tempe, Ariz.: Arizona Center for Medieval and Renaissance Studies, 2002.

Primary and Secondary Works by Others

Adderly, C.M. "To Bēot or Not to Bēot: Boasting in *Beowulf*." Paper presented at the International Medieval Congress, Kalamazoo, Mich., 8 May 2003.

Allan, Jim, et al. *An Introduction to Elvish and to Other Tongues, Proper Names, and Writing Systems of the Third Age of the Western Lands of Middle-earth as Set Down in the Published Writings of John Ronald Reuel Tolkien*. Frome, Somerset, Eng: Bran's Head Books, 1978.

Althusser, Louis. "Ideological State Apparatuses." In *Lenin and Philosophy, and Other Essays*. Translated from the French by Ben Brewster, 123–73. London: New Left Books, 1971; New York: Monthly Review Press, 1972.

Amsler, Mark. *Etymology and Grammatical Discourse in Late Antiquity and the Early Middle Ages*. Studies in the History of the Language Sciences, vol. 44. Amsterdam: John Benjamins, 1988.

Anderson, Douglas A. E-mail to Jane Chance. Summer 2002.

Anderson, Rasmus Bjorn. *Norse Mythology*. Chicago: S.C. Griggs, 1879; London: Trubner, 1879.

Annas, Julia. "Plato's Myths of Judgement." *Phronesis* 27, no. 2 (1982): 119–43.

Ansen, David. "A 'Ring' to Rule the Screen." *Newsweek*, 10 December 2001.

Aristotle. *The Basic Works of Aristotle*. Edited by Richard McKeon. New York: Random House, 1941.

Arthur, Ross G. *Medieval Sign Theory and "Sir Gawain and the Green Knight."* Toronto: University of Toronto Press, 1987.

Arvidsson, Håkan. "The Ring: An Essay on Tolkien's Mythology." *Mallorn* 40 (November 2002): 45–51.

Auden, W.H., and P.B. Taylor, trans. *Norse Poems*. London: Athlone Press, 1981; http://asatru.org/voluspa.html.

Barber, Dorothy. "The Meaning of *The Lord of the Rings*." *Mankato State College Studies* 2 (1967): 38–45.

Barfield, Owen. *Poetic Diction*. London: Faber and Faber, 1964.

———. *Saving the Appearances: A Study in Idolatry.* London: Faber and Faber, 1965.

Bately, Janet. "The Nature of Old English Prose." In *The Cambridge Companion to Old English Literature*, edited by Malcolm Godden and Michael Lapidge, 71–87. Cambridge: Cambridge University Press, 1991.

———, ed. *The Old English Orosius*. Early English Text Society, 2nd ser., vol. 6. London: Oxford University Press, 1980.

Battarbee, K.J., ed. *Scholarship and Fantasy: Proceedings of the Tolkien Phenomenon, May 1992, Turku, Finland* (special issue). Anglicana Turkuensia, no. 12. Turku: University of Turku, 1993.

Bede, Venerable. *Ecclesiastical History of the English Nation*. Translated by J. Stevens. Everyman's Library. London: Dent, 1910. Reprint 1978.

Bell, Judy Winn. "The Language of J.R.R. Tolkien in *The Lord of the Rings*." In *Mythcon I: Proceedings of the Mythopoeic Society*, edited by Glen GoodKnight, 35–40. Los Angeles: Mythopoeic Soc., 1971.

Bliss, Alan. See J.R.R. Tolkien, *Finn and Hengest: The Fragment and the Episode,* edited by Alan Bliss.

Blockley, R.C. "Roman-Barbarian Marriages in the Late Empire." *Florilegium* 4 (1982): 63–77.

Boethius. *The Consolation of Philosophy*. Translated by Richard Green. Library of Liberal Arts, no. 86. New York: Bobbs-Merrill, 1962.

Boler, John F. "Isomorphism: Reflections on Similitude and Form in Medieval Sign Theory." *Livstegn: Journal of the Norwegian Association for Semiotic Studies* 7, no. 2 (1989): 72–90.

Bosley, Keith, ed. and trans. *The "Kalevala," an Epic Poem after Oral Tradition by Elias Lönnrot*. Translated from the Finnish with an introduction and notes by Keith Bosley and a foreword by Albert B. Lord. World's Classics series. Oxford and New York: Oxford University Press, 1989.

Branston, Brian. *Gods of the North*. New York: Vanguard Press, 1955.

Bratman, David. "The Literary Value of *The History of Middle-earth*." In Flieger and Hostetter, 69–91.

Brewer, Derek. "The Tutor: A Portrait." In *C.S. Lewis at the Breakfast Table and Other Reminiscences*. New York: Macmillan, 1979.

Brisson, Luc. *Plato, Myth Maker*. Translated by Gerard Naddaf. Chicago and London: University of Chicago Press, 1998.

Brönnimann, Werner. "Susan Sontag's *Pyramus and Thisbe*." *Sh:in:E—*

Shakespeare in Europe. University of Basel, Switzerland. 24 December 2002. http://www.unibas.ch/shine/wbroe.htm.

Bryce, Lynn. "The Influence of Scandinavian Mythology on the Works of J.R.R. Tolkien." *Edda: Nordisk Tidsskrift for Literaturforskning* 2 (1983): 113–19.

Burnet, John, ed. *Platonis opera*. Oxford Classical Texts. 5 vols. Oxford: Oxford University Press, 1899–1906.

Burns, Marjorie. "Gandalf and Odin." In Flieger and Hostetter, eds., 219–31.

Cantor, Norman. *Inventing the Middle Ages: The Lives, Works, and Ideas of the Great Medievalists of the Twentieth Century*. New York: Quill, 1991.

Caplan, Harry. "Rhetorical Invention in Some Medieval Tractates on Preaching." In *Of Eloquence: Studies in Ancient and Medieval Rhetoric*, edited by A. King and H. North, 79–92. Ithaca: Cornell University Press, 1970.

Carpenter, Humphrey. *The Inklings: C.S. Lewis, J.R.R. Tolkien, Charles Williams, and Their Friends*. Boston: Houghton Mifflin, 1979.

———. *J.R.R. Tolkien: A Biography*. London: George Allen and Unwin; Boston: Houghton Mifflin, 1977.

Carter, Lin. *Tolkien: A Look Behind "The Lord of the Rings."* New York: Ballantine, 1969.

Cassiodorus. Letter on Amalasuntha. http://freespace.virgin.net/angus.graham/Cass-V10.htm.

Cassirer, Ernst. *Language and Myth*. Translated by Susanne K. Langer. New York: Harper, 1946.

———. *The Philosophy of Symbolic Forms*. Vol. 1, *Language*. Translated by Ralph Manheim. New Haven: Yale University Press, 1953.

Chambers, R.W. *Beowulf: An Introduction to the Study of the Poem with a Discussion of the Stories of Offa and Finn*. 3rd ed. Cambridge: Cambridge University Press, 1963.

Chance, Jane [Nitzsche]. *Tolkien's Art: A Mythology for England*. London: Macmillan Press, 1979; New York: St. Martin's Press, 1979. Rev. ed. Lexington: University Press of Kentucky, 2001.

———. *The Lord of the Rings: The Mythology of Power*. New York: Twayne/MacMillan, 1992. Rev. ed. Lexington, Ky: The University Press of Kentucky, 2001.

———, ed. *Tolkien the Medievalist*. Routledge Studies in Medieval Culture and Religion, no. 3. London and New York: Routledge, 2002, 2003.

Clare, P.G.W, ed. *Oxford Classical Dictionary*. Oxford: Clarendon Press, 1973.

Clark, George, and Daniel Timmons, eds. *J.R.R. Tolkien and His Litereary Resonances: Views of Middle-earth*. Westport, Conn.: Grenwood Press, 2000.

Clarke, W. Norris. "The Problem of the Reality and Multiplicity of Divine Ideas in Christian Neoplatonism." In *Neoplatonism and Christian Thought*, edited by Dominic J. O'Meara. Studies in Neoplatonism: Ancient and Modern, no. 3. Albany: State University of New York Press, 1982.

Colebatch, Hal K. *Return of the Heroes: "The Lord of the Rings," "Star Wars," and Contemporary Culture.* Perth: Australian Institute for Public Policy, 1990.

Colish, Marcia L. *The Mirror of Language: A Study in the Medieval Theory of Knowledge.* Lincoln: University of Nebraska Press, 1968.

Conquergood, Dwight. "Boasting in Anglo-Saxon England: Performance and the Heroic Ethos." *Literature in Performance: A Journal of Literary and Performing Art* 1 (1981): 24–35.

Coplestone, Frederick. *A History of Philosophy.* Vol. 2, *Augustine to Scotus.* New York: Doubleday, 1985.

Cox, John. "Tolkien's Platonic Fantasy." *Seven* 5 (1984): 53–69.

Curry, Patrick. *Defending Middle-earth: Tolkien, Myth, and Modernity.* Edinburgh: Floris Books, 1997.

———. "Tolkien and His Critics: A Critique." In *Root and Branch: Approaches towards Understanding Tolkien*, edited by Thomas Honegger, 81–148. Zurich and Bern: Walking Tree Publishers, 1999.

Dante, Alighieri. *The Divine Comedy.* 3 vols. Edited and translated by John Sinclair. New York: Oxford University Press, 1948.

Davidson, H.R. Ellis. *Gods and Myths of Northern Europe.* Harmondsworth, Middlesex: Penguin, 1964; London: Everyman, 1990.

Davis, Craig R. "Cultural Assimilation in the Anglo-Saxon Royal Genealogies." *Anglo-Saxon England* 21 (1992): 23–36.

De Anna, Luigi. "The Magic of Words: J.R.R. Tolkien and Finland." In Battarbee, ed., 7–19.

de Armas, Frederick A. "Gyges' Ring: Invisibility in Plato, Tolkien, and Lope de Vega." *Journal of the Fantastic in the Arts* 3, no. 4 (1994): 120–38.

Donaldson, E. Talbot, trans. *Beowulf: A New Prose Translation.* New York: Norton, 1966.

Dorson, Richard M. *The British Folklorists: A History.* Chicago: University of Chicago Press, 1968.

Drout, Michael D.C. "Introduction: Soil, Seeds, and Northern Sky." In Tolkien, *Beowulf and the Critics*, 1–29.

Drout, Michael D.C., and Hilary Wynne. "Tom Shippey's *J.R.R. Tolkien: Author of the Century* and a Look Back at Tolkien Criticism since 1982." *Envoi* 9, no. 2 (fall 2000): 101–67.

DuBois, Thomas. *Finnish Folk Poetry and the "Kalevala."* New York: Garland, 1995.

———, and Scott Mellor. "The Nordic Roots of Tolkien's Middle-earth." *Scandinavian Review* 90, no. 1 (summer 2002): 35–40.

Dumézil, Georges. *Gods of the Ancient Northmen.* Translated by John Lindow, Alan Toth, Francis Charat, and George Gopen. Edited by Einar Haugen. Berkeley, Los Angeles, and London: University of California Press, 1977.

Dumville, David N. "Kingship, Genealogies, and Regnal Lists." In *Early Medieval Kingship*, edited by P.H. Sawyer and Ian N. Wood, 72–104. Leeds: School of History, University of Leeds, 1977. Reprint 1979.

Durbin, Karen. "Propaganda and 'Lord of the Rings.'" *New York Times*, 15 December 2002.

Duriez, Colin. *Tolkien and Lewis: The Gift of Friendship.* Mahwah, N.J.: Hidden Spring, 2003.

———. *The Tolkien and Middle-earth Handbook.* Tunbridge Wells, Eng.: Monarch, 1992.

Eliade, Mircea. *Myth and Reality.* Translated by William R. Trask. New York and Evanston, Ill.: Harper and Row, 1963.

Evans, Jonathan. "The Anthropology of Arda." In Chance, ed., *Tolkien the Medievalist*, 194–224.

———. "The Dragon-Lore of Middle-earth: Tolkien and Old English and Old Norse Tradition." In *J.R.R. Tolkien and His Literary Resonances: Views of Middle-earth*, edited by George Clark and Daniel Timmons, 21–38. Westport, Conn.: Greenwood Press, 2000.

Evans, Robley. *J.R.R. Tolkien.* New York: Warner, 1972.

The Fellowship of the Ring. Directed by Peter Jackson. New Line Cinema, New Zealand, 2001.

Fenwick, Mac. "Breastplates of Silk: Homeric Women in *The Lord of the Rings.*" *Mythlore* no. 81 (1996), 17–23, 50.

Ferrari, G.R.F. *Listening to the Cicadas: A Study of Plato's "Phaedrus."* Cambridge: Cambridge University Press, 1987.

Flieger, Verlyn. "The Footsteps of Ælfwine." In Flieger and Hostetter, eds., 186–97.

———. "J.R.R. Tolkien and the Matter of Britain." *Mythlore* 87 (summer/fall 2000), 47–59.

———. Lecture on "Splintered Light: Logos and Language in Tolkien's World." In a course on "J.R.R. Tolkien: A Mythology for England." University of Maryland, College Park. 1 October 2002.

———. "Naming the Unnameable: The Neoplatonic 'One' in Tolkien's *Silmarillion.*" In *Diakonia: Studies in Honor of Robert T. Meyer*, edited by Thomas Halton and Joseph P. Williman, 127–33. Washington D.C.: Catholic University of America Press, 1986.

———. *A Question of Time: J.R.R. Tolkien's Road to Faërie.* Kent, Ohio, and London, Eng.: Kent State University Press, 1997.

———. *Splintered Light: Logos and Language in Tolkien's World.* Grand Rapids, Mich.: Wm. B. Eerdmans, 1983. Rev. ed. Kent, Ohio: Kent State University Press, 2002.

Flieger, Verlyn, and Carl F. Hostetter, eds. *Contributions to the Study of Science Fiction and Fantasy.* Westport, Conn. and London: Greenwood Press, 2000.

———. *Tolkien's "Legendarium": Essays on "The History of Middle-earth."* Westport, Conn. and London: Greenwood Press, 2000.

Ford, Paul F. *Companion to Narnia.* New York: HarperCollins, 1994.

Forster, E.M. *Howards End.* New York: Everyman, 1991.

Foster, Robert. *A Guide to Middle-earth.* New York: Ballantine Books, 1974.

Frantzen, Allen J. *Desire for Origins: New Language, Old English, and Teaching the Tradition.* New Brunswick: Rutgers University Press, 1990.

Frazer, James George. *The Golden Bough: A Study in Magic and Religion.* New York: Macmillan, 1934.

Freccero, John. "Dante's Medusa: Allegory and Autobiography." In *By Things Seen: Reference and Recognition in Medieval Thought*, edited by David Lyle Jeffrey, 33–46. Ottawa: University of Ottawa Press, 1979.

Fussell, Paul. *The Great War and Modern Memory.* Oxford and New York: Oxford University Press, 1975.

Gay, David E[lton]. "The Creation of the *Kalevala*, 1834–1849." *Jahrbuch für Volksliedforschung* 42 (1997): 63–77.

———. "Renewing Old Poems: The 1849 *Kalevala* as Finnish Tradition in the English-Speaking World." In *The "Kalevala" and the World's Traditional Epics*, edited by Lauri Honko, 54–63. Helsinki: Finnish Literature Society, 2002.

———. "Revising Tradition: Folklore and the Making of European Literary Epic." Ph.D. diss., Indiana University-Bloomington, 1995.

Giddings, Robert, ed. *J.R.R. Tolkien: This Far Land.* London: Vision Press, 1983; Totowa, N.J.: Barnes and Noble Books, 1984.

Gilliver, Peter M. "At the Wordface: J.R.R. Tolkien's Work on the *Oxford English Dictionary*." In Reynolds and GoodKnight, eds., 173–86.

Glendinning, Robert. "Pyramus and Thisbe in the Medieval Classroom." *Speculum* 61 (1986): 51–78.

Godden, Malcolm, and Michael Lapidge, eds. *The Cambridge Companion to Old English Literature.* Cambridge: Cambridge University Press, 1991.

Goffart, Walter. *The Narrators of Barbarian History (A.D. 55–800): Jordanes, Gregory of Tours, Bede, and Paul the Deacon.* Princeton: Princeton University Press, 1988.

Gordon, E.V. *An Introduction to Old Norse.* 2nd ed. edited by A.R. Taylor. Oxford and New York: Oxford University Press, 1981.

Grant, Patrick. *Six Modern Authors and Problems of Belief.* London: Macmillan, 1979.

———. "Tolkien: Archetype and Word." *Cross Currents* (1973): 365–79.

Green, William Howard. *"The Hobbit" and Other Fiction by J.R.R. Tolkien.* Ann Arbor, Mich.: University Microfilms, 1970.

Greenman, David. "Aeneidic and Odyssean Patterns of Escape and Return in Tolkien's 'The Fall of Gondolin' and *The Return of the King*." *Mythlore* no. 68 (1992), 4–9.

———. "*The Silmarillion* as Aristotelian Epic-Tragedy." *Mythlore* 14, no. 3 (1988), 20–25.

Gregory of Tours. *Historia Francorum.* In *Opera*, edited by W. Arndt and Br. Krusch. Vol. 1 of 2 vols. Monumenta Germaniae Historica, Scriptores Rerum Merovingicarum, 1. Hanover: Bibliopolius Hahnianus, 1884.

Griffin, William. *Clive Staples Lewis: A Dramatic Life*. San Francisco: Harper and Row, 1986.

Grimm, Jacob. *Teutonic Mythology*. Translated from the 4th ed. [1875] with notes and appendix by James Steven Stallybrass. 4 vols. London, 1883. Gloucester, Mass.: Peter Smith, 1976.

Grundtvig, N.F.S. *Bjowulfs Drape. Et Gothisk Helte-Digt fra forrige Aar-Tusinde af Angel-Saxisk paa Danske Riim*. Copenhagen: A. Seidelin, 1820.

Gutkind, Eric. *The Body of God: First Steps toward an Anti-Theology*. New York: Horizon, 1969.

Haavio, Martti. *Väinämöinen, Eternal Sage*. Translated by Helen Goldthwait-Väänänen. Folklore Fellows Communications, 144. 1952. Reprint, Helsinki: Suomalainen Tiedeakatemia, 1991.

Haddon, Alfred C. *Magic and Fetishism*. London: Constable, 1921.

Havelock, Eric A. *Preface to Plato*. Cambridge: Cambridge University Press, 1963.

Heaney, Seamus, trans. *Beowulf: A New Verse Translation*. New York: Norton, 2000.

Helms, Randel. *Tolkien and the Silmarils*. Boston: Houghton Mifflin, 1981.

———. *Tolkien's World*. Boston: Houghton Mifflin, 1974.

Herder, Johann Gottfried von. *Ideen zur Philosophie der Geschichte der Menschheit*. Leipzig: Johann Friedrich Hartknoch, 1821.

Hertlzer, Joyce O. *A Sociology of Language*. New York: Random House, 1965.

Himes, Jonathan. "What J.R.R. Tolkien Really Did with the Sampo." *Mythlore* 22, no. 86 (spring 2000): 69–85.

Holmberg, Annika. "J.R.R. Tolkien, Kalevala och det finska språket." *Kulturtidskriften-Horisont* 33 (1986): 73–74.

Homer. *The Odyssey*. Edited and translated by A.T. Murray. Revised by George E. Dimock. Loeb Classical Library Series. Cambridge, Mass.: Harvard University Press, 1995.

Honko, Lauri, ed. *The "Kalevala" and the World's Traditional Epics*. Helsinki: Finnish Literature Society, 2002.

———, ed. *Religion, Myth, and Folklore in the World's Epics: The "Kalevala" and Its Predecessors*. Berlin and New York: Mouton de Gruyter, 1990.

Hooper, Walter. *C.S. Lewis: Companion and Guide*. San Francisco: Harper, 1996.

Houghton, John William. "Augustine in the Cottage of Lost Play: The *Ainulindalë* as Asterisk Cosmogony." In Chance, ed. *Tolkien the Medievalist*, 171–82.

———. "Commedia as Fairy-Story: Eucatastrophe in the Loss of Virgil." *Mythlore* 17, no. 2 (1990): 29–32.

Howe, Nicholas. *Migration and Mythmaking in Anglo-Saxon England*. New Haven: Yale University Press, 1989.

Isaacs, Neil D., and Rose Zimbardo, eds. *Tolkien and the Critics*. Notre Dame, Ind.: Notre Dame Press, 1968.

Jack, George, ed. *"Beowulf": A Student Edition*. Oxford: Clarendon Press, 1995.

Jones, Diana Wynne. "The Shape of the Narrative in *The Lord of the Rings*." In Giddings, ed., 87–109.

Jordanes. *Getica.* http://www.thelatinlibrary.com/iordanes.html#XIV and http://www.thelatinlibrary.com/iordanes.html#LX.

Kaukonen, Väinö. *Elias Lönnrotin Kalevalan toinen painos* (The second edition of Elias Lönnrot's *Kalevala*). Helsinki: SKS, 1956.

Keith, A.M. "Etymological Wordplay in Ovid's 'Pyramus and Thisbe' (*Met.* 4.55–166)." *Classical Quarterly* 51 (2001): 309–13.

Kienpointner, M. *Historisches Wörterbuch der Rhetorik,* edited by Gert Ueding, et al. Vol. 45 (Hu–Kl). Tübingen: Max Niemeyer, 1998.

Kilby, Clyde S. *Tolkien and "The Silmarillion."* Wheaton, Ill.: Harold Shaw Publishers, 1976.

Kirby, W.F., trans. *Kalevala, The Land of the Heroes.* 2 vols. London: Dent, 1907. New York: Dutton, 1907. Reprint, London: Athlone Press, 1985.

Klaeber, Fr., ed. *"Beowulf" and The Fight at Finnsburg.* 3rd ed. Boston: D.C. Heath, 1950.

Knapp, Bettina. "A Jungian Reading of *The Kalevala*, 500–1300? Finnish Shamanism—The Patriarchal Senex Figure, Part I: Introduction." *Mythlore* 29 (autumn 1981), 25–28.

———. "A Jungian Reading of *The Kalevala*, 500–1300? Finnish Shamanism—The Patriarchal Senex Figure, Part II: The Archetypal Shaman/Hero." *Mythlore* 30 (winter 1982), 33–36.

———. "A Jungian Reading of *The Kalevala*, 500–1300? Finnish Shamanism—The Patriarchal Senex Figure, Part III: The Anima Archetype," *Mythlore* 31–32 (spring–summer 1982), 35–36.

Knox, Peter E. "Pyramus and Thisbe in Cyprus." *Harvard Studies in Classical Philology* 92 (1989): 315–28.

Kocher, Paul. *Master of Middle-earth: The Fiction of J.R.R. Tolkien.* Boston: Houghton Mifflin, 1972. New York: Ballantine, 1977.

———. *A Reader's Guide to "The Silmarillion."* Boston: Houghton Mifflin, 1980.

Krapp, George P., and Elliot van Kirk Dobbie, eds. *The Anglo-Saxon Poetic Records.* 6 vols. New York: Columbia University Press, 1931–42.

Lane, Anthony. "The Hobbit Habit: Reading *The Lord of the Rings*." *New Yorker,* 10 December 2001, 98–105.

Lazo, Andrew. "A Kind of Mid-Wife: J.R.R. Tolkien and C.S. Lewis—Sharing Influence." In Chance, ed., *Tolkien the Medievalist,* 36–49.

Lewis, C.S. *All My Road before Me: The Diary of C.S. Lewis, 1922–1927,* edited by Walter Hooper. San Diego, New York, and London: Harcourt Brace, 1991.

———. *C.S. Lewis: Collected Letters.* Edited by Walter Hooper. Vol. 1, *Family Letters, 1905–1931.* London: HarperCollins, 2000.

———. *The Four Loves.* New York: Harcourt, Brace and Company, 1960.

————. "The Inner Ring." In *Transpositions and Other Addresses*, 55–66. London: Bles, 1949.

————. *Letters of C.S. Lewis: Edited and with a Memoir by W.H. Lewis*. 2nd ed. by Walter Hooper. San Diego, New York, and London: Harcourt Brace, 1994.

————. *The Lion, the Witch, and the Wardrobe*. New York: HarperTrophy, 2000.

————. *Out of the Silent Planet*. London: John Lane The Bodley Head, 1938.

————. *Surprised by Joy: The Shape of My Early Life*. New York: Harcourt Brace and Company, 1956.

————. *That Hideous Strength: A Modern Fairy-Tale for Grown-Ups*. New York: Macmillan, 1946.

————. *They Asked for a Paper: Papers and Addresses*. London: Bles, 1962.

————. *They Stand Together: The Letters of C.S. Lewis to Arthur Greeves (1914–1963)*, edited by Walter Hooper. New York: Macmillan, 1979.

————. "Tolkien's *The Lord of the Rings*." In *On Stories and Other Essays on Literature*, edited by Walter Hooper, 83–90. London: Harcourt Brace Jovanovich, 1982.

Lewis, Warren Hamilton. *Brothers and Friends: The Diaries of Major Warren Hamilton Lewis*. Edited by Clyde S. Kilby and Marjorie Lamp Mead. San Francisco: Harper and Row, 1982.

Livy. *The Early History of Rome (Books I–V)*. Translated by Aubrey de Sélincourt. Baltimore: Penguin, 1960.

Lobdell, Jared. *England and Always: Tolkien's World of the Rings*. Grand Rapids, Mich.: Eerdmans, 1981.

————, ed. *A Tolkien Compass*. La Salle, Ill.: Open Court, 1975.

Lönnrot, Elias, comp. *"The Kalevala," or Poems From the Kaleva District*. Translated by Francis Peabody Magoun Jr. Cambridge, Mass., and London: Harvard University Press, 1963.

Lyttkens, Hampus. *The Analogy between God and the World: An Investigation of Its Background and Interpretation of Its Use by Thomas of Aquino*. Uppsala, Sweden: Almqvist and Wiksells, 1952.

Magoun, F.P., trans. *"The Kalevala," or Poems of the Kaleva District*. Cambridge: Harvard University Press, 1963.

————, trans. *The Old "Kalevala" and Certain Antecedents*. Cambridge: Harvard University Press, 1969.

Manlove, C.N. *Modern Fantasy: Five Studies*. Cambridge: Cambridge University Press, 1975.

Milton, John. *Complete Prose Works of John Milton*. Vol. 5, *1648–1671*. Edited by French Fogle. New Haven: Yale University Press, 1971.

Moors, Kent F. *Platonic Myth: An Introduction*. Washington: University Press of America, 1982.

Morgan, Kathryn A. *Myth and Philosophy from the Pre-Socratics to Plato*. Cambridge: Cambridge University Press, 2000.

Morse, Donald E. *Evocation of Virgil in Tolkien's Art: Geritol for the Classics.* Oak Park, Ill: Bolchazy-Carducci, 1986.

Morse, Robert E. "Rings of Power in Plato and Tolkien." *Mythlore* 7, no. 25 (1980), 38.

Mortensen, Viggo. Interview by Charlie Rose. *Charlie Rose Show.* PBS-TV, 3 December 2002.

Morus, Iwan Rhys. "The Tale of Beren and Lúthien." *Mallorn* 20 (September 1983): 19–22.

———. "'Uprooting the Golden Bough': J.R.R. Tolkien's Response to Nineteenth Century Folklore and Comparative Mythology." *Mallorn* 27 (1990): 5, 8.

Moseley, Charles. *J.R.R. Tolkien.* Plymouth, Eng.: Northcote House, 1997.

Murphy, James J. *Rhetoric in the Middle Ages: A History of Rhetorical Theory from St. Augustine to the Renaissance.* Berkeley, Los Angeles, and London: University of California Press, 1974.

Murray, Penelope. "Inspiration and Mimesis in Plato." In *The Language of the Cave*, edited by Andrew Barker and Martin Warner. *Apeiron* 25, no. 4 (1992), 27–46.

Nagy, Gergely. "The Great Chain of Reading: (Inter-)textual Relations and the Technique of Mythopoesis in the Túrin Story." In Chance, ed., *Tolkien the Medievalist*, 239–58.

Nagy, Gregory. *Homeric Questions.* Austin, Texas: University of Texas Press, 1996.

Nitzsche, Jane Chance. See Chance, Jane.

Noad, Charles E. "On the Construction of 'The Simarillion.'" In Flieger and Hostetter, eds., 31–68.

Noel, Ruth S. *The Languages of Tolkien's Middle-earth.* Boston: Houghton Mifflin, 1980.

———. *The Mythology of Middle-earth.* Boston: Houghton Mifflin, 1977.

Obertino, James. "Moria and Hades: Underworld Journeys in Tolkien and Virgil." *Comparative Literature Studies* 30, no. 2 (1993): 153–69.

Ong, Walter J. *Orality and Literacy: The Technologizing of the Word.* London and New York: Methuen, 1982.

Otty, Mick. "A Structuralist Guide to Middle-earth." In Giddings, ed., 154–78.

Ovid. *Metamorphoses.* Translated by Mary M. Innes. Baltimore: Penguin, 1968.

———. *Ovid's "Metamorphoses": Books 1–5.* Edited by William S. Anderson. Norman: University of Oklahoma Press, 1997.

The Oxford English Dictionary. 13 vols. Oxford: Clarendon Press, 1933.

Page, R.I. *Norse Myths.* Avon, Eng.: Bath Press, 1990.

Pentikäinen, Juha. *Kalevala Mythology.* Translated by Ritva Poom. Bloomington: Indiana University Press, 1989.

Petty, Anne C. *One Ring to Bind Them All: Tolkien's Mythology.* University: University of Alabama Press, 1979.

Powys, John Cowper. *A Philosophy of Solitude.* New York: Simon and Schuster, 1933.

Price, Simon. *Religions of the Ancient Greeks.* Cambridge: Cambridge University Press, 1999.

Rautala, Helena. "Familiarity and Distance: Quenya's Relation to Finnish." In Battarbee, ed., 21–32.

Read, Carveth. *Man and His Superstitions.* Cambridge: Cambridge University Press, 1925.

Reilly, R.J. *Romantic Religions: A Study of Barfield, Lewis, Williams, and Tolkien.* Athens: University of Georgia Press, 1971.

Reynolds, James, and Fiona Stewart. "Lord of the Rings Labelled Racist." *Scotsman,* 14 December 2002.

Reynolds, Patricia, and Glen H. GoodKnight, eds. *Proceedings of the J.R.R. Tolkien Centenary Conference, Keble College, Oxford, 1992. Mythlore* 80 / *Mallorn* 30. Milton Keynes, England: Tolkien Society, 1995; Altadena, Calif.: Mythopoeic Press, 1995.

Rose, Mary Carman. "The Christian Platonism of C.S. Lewis, J.R.R. Tolkien, and Charles Williams." In *Neoplatonism and Christian Thought,* edited by Dominic J. O'Meara, 203–12. Norfolk: International Society for Neoplatonic Studies, 1981.

Ryan, J.S. "German Mythology Applied—The Extension of the Ritual Folk Memory." *Folklore* 77 (1966): 45–57.

Santoski, Taum. "Introduction to the Study of Elvish." Preface to Nancy Martsch, *Basic Quenya: Quenya Language Lessons, with Elvish-English Vocabulary.* 2nd ed. Sherman Oaks, Calif.: "Beyond Bree" Publication, 1992.

Sayer, George. *Jack: C.S. Lewis and His Times.* San Francisco: Harper and Row, 1988.

Shippey, T[homas] A. "'The Death Song of Ragnar Lödbrog': A Study in Sensibilities." In *Medievalism in the Modern World: Essays in Honour of Leslie Workman,* edited by Richard Utz and Tom Shippey, 155–72. Turnhout: Brepols, 1999.

———. "Goths and Huns: The Rediscovery of the Northern Cultures in the Nineteenth Century." In *The Medieval Legacy: A Symposium,* edited by Andreas Haarder, Iorn Pio, Reinhold Schroder, and Preben Meulengracht Sorensen, 51–69. Odense: Odense University Press, 1982.

———. *J.R.R. Tolkien: Author of the Century.* London: HarperCollins, 2000; Boston: Houghton Mifflin, 2001.

———. "Orcs, Wraiths, Wights: Tolkien's Images of Evil." In Clark and Timmons, 183–98.

———. *The Road to Middle-earth.* London: Allen and Unwin, 1982. Boston: Houghton Mifflin, 1983. 2nd ed., London: Grafton, 1992. Rev. ed., London: HarperCollins, 1992.

———. "Tolkien and Iceland: The Philology of Envy." http://www.nordals.hi.is/ shippey.html. The Sigurður Nordal Institute, Reykjavík, Iceland. (Director: Úlfar Bragason.)

Sisam, Kenneth. "Anglo-Saxon Royal Genealogies." *Proceedings of the British Academy* 39 (1953): 287–346.

Smith, Janet E. "Plato's Myths as 'Likely Accounts, Worthy of Belief.'" *Apeiron* 19, no. 1 (1985): 24–42.

Snorri Sturluson. *Edda*. Translated by Anthony Faulkes. London: Dent, 1987. London: Everyman, 1995.

———. *The Prose Edda*. Translated by Arthur Gilchrist Brodeur. New York: American-Scandinavian Foundation; London: Humphrey Milford, Oxford University Press, 1923.

———. *The Prose Edda*. Translated by Jean I. Young. Berkeley: University of California Press, 1954.

Sontag, Susan. "The Very Comical Lament of Pyramus and Thisbe (An Interlude)." In *Where the Stress Falls*, 290–93. New York: Farrar, Straus and Giroux, 2001.

Spacks, Patricia. "Ethical Pattern in *The Lord of the Rings*." *Critique* 3 (1959): 30–42.

———. "Power and Meaning in *The Lord of the Rings*." In Isaacs and Zimbardo, eds., 81–99.

Spelling, Ian. "For Viggo Mortensen, The War of the Rings Gets Serious." *Inside Sci-Fi and Fantasy*. New York Times Syndicate, 15 December 2002. http://www.allbiehn.com/telcontar/interviews/spelling121302.html.

Stanton, Michael. *Hobbits, Elves, and Wizards*. New York: St. Martin's Press, 2001.

St. Clair, Gloriana. "An Overview of the Northern Influences on Tolkien's Work." In Reynolds and GoodKnight, eds., 63–67.

Stenstrøm, Anders. "A Mythology? For England?" In Reynolds and GoodKnight, eds., 310–14.

Stevens, J., trans. *Ecclesiastical History of the English Nation*. London: Dent, 1910. Reprint, 1978.

Tacitus, P. Cornelius. *Germania*. In *Tacitus in Five Volumes*, translated by M. Hutton and revised by E.H. Warmington, Loeb Classical Library. Cambridge, Mass.: Harvard University Press, 1970.

———. *Tacitus on Britain and Germany*. Translated by H. Mattingly. Harmondsworth, Eng.: Penguin, 1960.

Tinkler, John. "Old English in Rohan." In Isaacs and Zimbardo, eds.,164–69.

Tjeder, David. "Tolkiendebatten rasar vidare." *Aftonbladet* (Kultur), 11 January 2002.

———. "Tolkiens farliga tankar" and "En dåres försvarstal." *Aftonbladet* (Kultur), 20 December 2001 and 11 January 2002. Archived on the World Wide Web at http://www. aftonbladet.se.

Tolkien, Michael. "J.R.R. Tolkien—The Wizard Father," *Sunday Telegraph*, 7 September 1973, 654.

Tolley, Clive. "Tolkien's 'Essay on Man': A Look at *Mythopoeia*." *Inklings-Jahrbuch* 10 (1992): 221–35.

The Two Towers. Directed by Peter Jackson. New Line Cinema, 2002.

Ueding, Gert, et al., eds. *Historisches Wörterbuch der Rhetorik*. Vol. 4. Tubingen: Max Niemeyer, 1998.

Vance, Eugene. *Mervelous Signals: Poetics and Sign Theory in the Middle Ages*. Lincoln: University of Nebraska, 1986.

Wadstein, Elis. "The *Beowulf* Poem as an English National Epos." *Acta Philologica Scandinavica* 8 (1925): 273–91.

West, Richard C. "The Interlace Structure of *The Lord of the Rings*." In Lobdell, ed., *A Tolkien Compass*, 77–94.

———. *Tolkien Criticism: An Annotated Checklist*. Kent, Ohio: Kent State University Press, 1970.

———. "Túrin's *Ofermod*: An Old English Theme in the Development of the Story of Túrin." In Flieger and Hostetter, eds., 233–45.

White, Michael. *Critical Lives: J.R.R. Tolkien*. Indianapolis. Ind.: Alpha, 2002.

Whitelock, Dorothy. *Sermo Lupi ad Anglos*. 3rd ed. London: Methuen, 1966.

Wicher, Andrzej. "The Artificial Mythology of *The Silmarillion* by J.R.R. Tolkien." *Kwartalnik Neofilologiczny* 28 (1981): 399–405.

Wine, Sherwin T. *Judaism beyond God*. Farmington Hills, Mich.: Society for Humanistic Judaism, 1985.

Wytenbroek, J.R. "Apocalyptic Vision in *The Lord of the Rings*." *Mythlore* 54 (summer 1988): 7–12.

Young, Kimball. "Language, Thought, and Social Reality." In *Social Attitudes*, edited by Kimball Young, 100–35. New York: Henry Holt, 1931.

Young, Robert J.C. *Colonial Desire: Hybridity in Theory, Culture, and Race*. London and New York: Routledge, 1995.

Zaslavsky, Robert. *Platonic Myth and Platonic Writing*. Washington, D.C.: University Press of America, 1981.

CONTRIBUTORS

MICHAELA BALTASAR is in her last semester of the M.F.A. program in fiction at the University of Maryland—College Park. She is currently at work on her first novel.

ALEXANDRA BOLINTINEANU is currently completing her M.A. at the University of Toronto's Centre for Medieval Studies. Her research interests include Anglo-Saxon narrative poetry, the English monastic reformation, and modern speculative fiction. Her paper "The Ancestry of Gollum" was published in *Concerning Hobbits and Other Matters* (Conference Proceedings, University of St. Thomas, 2001).

MARJORIE J. BURNS has been on the faculty of Portland State University for thirty years and has lectured widely on Tolkien throughout the United States, as well as in Australia, Norway, England, and The Netherlands. She has also lived in Norway (once as a Fulbright professor). She teaches Norse and Celtic mythology, as well as Tolkien's literature and that of the Victorian writers he knew. Her publications on Tolkien include four journal articles, two essays in conference proceedings collections, and one book chapter. She has recently completed a book, "Perilous Realms: Celtic and Norse in J.R.R. Tolkien."

JANE CHANCE, professor of English, teaches medieval literature, medieval studies, and women and the study of gender at Rice University. She has taught a course on Tolkien at Rice, off and on, since 1976. A specialist in medieval mythography and general editor of three series, the Library of Medieval Women, Greenwood Guides to Historic Events in the Medieval World, and Praeger Series on the Middle Ages, she has published eighteen books, editions, and translations. Among them are revised editions, in 2001, of *Tolkien's Art: A Mythology for England* (1979) and *The Lord of the Rings: The Mythology of Power* (1992), also translated into Japanese in 2003; and a collection of essays, *Tolkien the Medievalist* (2002). She has served as guest editor for two issues of *Studies in Medievalism*, on the twentieth century (1982) and the Inklings (1991). Her essay revising Tolkien on *Beowulf*—"The Structural Unity of

Beowulf: The Problem of Grendel's Mother"—has been published seven times, most recently in the Norton Critical Edition with the Seamus Heaney translation. Her book *Medieval Mythography: From Roman North Africa to the School of Chartres, 433–1177 A.D.* won the SCMLA Best Book Prize of 1994.

ANDY DIMOND, after a childhood of having *The Hobbit* read to him (and reread, and reread), first experienced *The Lord of the Rings* at the age of twelve and was immediately entranced by its depth and power. Now, eight years later, he is immersed in Tolkien as part of the Century Scholars undergraduate research program at Rice University. He has also served as an editorial assistant for this collection and in part for *Tolkien the Medievalist*, edited by Jane Chance (2002).

MICHAEL D.C. DROUT is associate professor of English at Wheaton College, Norton, Massachusetts, where he teaches Old and Middle English, fantasy, and science fiction. Drout is the editor of *J.R.R. Tolkien's "Beowulf" and the Critics* (2002) and the author of *How Tradition Works: A Descriptive Culture Poetics of the Anglo-Saxon Tenth Century* (forthcoming, 2004, Arizona Medieval and Renaissance Texts and Studies). He has also published articles on Anglo-Saxon literature, *Piers Plowman*, Ursula Le Guin's *Earthsea* novels, and Susan Cooper's *The Dark is Rising*. Drout is the director of the Tolkien Research Group and one of the founding editors of *Tolkien Studies*.

KATHLEEN E. DUBS is currently on the humanities faculty of Pázmány Péter Catholic University in Piliscsaba, near Budapest, Hungary. She teaches courses in medieval literature, the history of the English language, and Old and Middle English, as well as in American literature before the twentieth century. She has lectured on Tolkien, recent interest in whom has resulted in the revival of courses about his work. She is a member of the newly founded Hungarian Tolkien Society.

VERLYN FLIEGER is a professor in the Department of English at the University of Maryland, where she teaches courses in medieval literature, comparative mythology, and the work of J.R.R. Tolkien. She has published two books on Tolkien, *Splintered Light: Logos and Language in Tolkien's World* (1983; rev. ed., 2002) and *A Question of Time: Tolkien's Road to Faërie* (1997). She is the editor with Carl Hostetter of *Tolkien's "Legendarium": Essays on the History of Middle-earth* (2000).

DAVID ELTON GAY teaches folklore in the School of Continuing Studies at Indiana University. His research is primarily in Indo-European studies (especially Germanic and Lithuanian folklore and mythology) and in Finno-Ugrian studies (especially Finnish and Estonian mythology and folklore). His recent publications include articles on the editing of oral traditions, on the *Kalevala*, and on Lithuanian incantations and legends.

JOHN R. HOLMES is chair of the English Department at Franciscan University of Steubenville, where since 1985 he has taught, among other things, medieval literature, Old English language, and Tolkien. Most of his published articles have been in the field of early American literature (he is currently editing the letters of Charles Brockden Brown), but his recent discovery of the delightful fellowship of Tolkien scholars has encouraged him to write more on J.R.R.T.

DAVID LYLE JEFFREY, Distinguished Professor of Literature and the Humanities and provost at Baylor University—Waco, received his B.A. from Wheaton College in 1965 and his Ph.D. from Princeton in 1968. Previously chair of two English Departments (University of Victoria, University of Ottawa), he has taught also at the University of Rochester and the University of Hull (U.K.) and has been a visiting faculty member at Notre Dame and at Regent College (University of British Columbia). He was elected Fellow of the Royal Society of Canada in 1996. He has published eleven monographs and editions, among them *The Early English Lyric and Franciscan Spirituality* (1975); *Chaucer and Scriptural Tradition* (1984); *Toward a Perfect Love: The Spiritual Counsel of Walter Hilton* (1986; 2000); *English Spirituality in the Age of Wesley* (1987; 1994; 2001); *The Law of Love: English Spirituality in the Age of Wyclif* (2000); *People of The Book: Christian Identity and Literary Culture* (1996); *Houses of the Interpreter: Reading Scripture, Reading Culture* (2003); and *Jack Hodgins and his Works* (1990). With B.J. Levy he has published *The Anglo-Norman Lyric* (1990), and with D. Manganiello, *Rethinking the Future of the University* (1998); he has also served as general editor and coauthor of *A Dictionary of Biblical Tradition in English Literature* (1992).

ANDREW LAZO is a graduate student in the English Department at Rice University and a collector of rare books by and about C.S. Lewis. He plans to write his dissertation on myth in C.S. Lewis. He has published several essays and reviews on Tolkien and Lewis.

CATHERINE MADSEN is a contributing editor to the interreligious journal *Cross Currents* and the author of a novel, *A Portable Egypt* (2002). She received the M.F.A. in Writing and Literature from Goddard College in 1990. She converted to Judaism in the same year and serves as a lay cantor in Amherst, Massachusetts. She has published widely on liturgy and is at work on a book on problems in contemporary liturgical prose style.

GERGELY NAGY is a junior assistant professor at the Institute of English and American Studies, University of Szeged, Hungary. He is writing his doctoral dissertation on Tolkien and poststructuralist literary theory. He teaches courses in medieval English literature, Tolkien, and Plato. He has published essays on Tolkien, Chaucer, and Malory. Nagy is also a founding member and the academic vice president of the Hungarian Tolkien Society.

TOM SHIPPEY is Walter J. Ong Chair at Saint Louis University. He has previously held appointments at the universities of Leeds, Oxford, and Birmingham in England, and been Visiting Professor at Harvard and the University of Texas in the United States. His publications include two books on Tolkien, *The Road to Middle-earth* (1982, rev. ed. 1992) and *J.R.R. Tolkien: Author of the Century* (2000), three on Old English, and a number of edited collections and anthologies. He is currently editor of *Studies in Medievalism* and is preparing a volume on Tolkien's predecessor, Jacob Grimm.

JEN STEVENS is a reference librarian at Washington State University, where she works with the English and Foreign Language Departments. She did her B.A. and M.A. in English and American Literature at the University of Colorado at Boulder, where she studied English medieval and Renaissance literature and wrote an undergraduate thesis on the narrative structure of Tolkien's *The Lord of the Rings* trilogy. Her current research interests include Tolkien's and C.S. Lewis's deployment of earlier literatures in their own literary works.

SANDRA BALLIF STRAUBHAAR, a lecturer in Germanic studies at the University of Texas at Austin, can date her obsession with Tolkien to the first appearance of the Ballantine paperbacks. She researches and teaches a number of topics, including medieval Scandinavia, the heroic archetype, the Indo-European folk tale, women's poetry, and postmodern popular medievalism. Lately she has published on Saint Birgitta of Sweden;

trollwomen in the legendary sagas; women skalds; historical sagas and Norwegian nationalism; the Cambridge Celticist Nora K. Chadwick; and Swedish popular novelist Jan Guillou.

RICHARD C. WEST has graduate degrees in both medieval literature and librarianship. He is the compiler of *Tolkien Criticism: An Annotated Checklist* (1970, 2nd ed. 1981) and has published several articles on Tolkien and other authors. He is currently the Assistant Director for Technical Services at the Kurt F. Wendt Library at the University of Wisconsin–Madison. He and his wife and occasional collaborator, chemist Perri Corrick-West, live in Madison, Wisconsin.

MARY E. ZIMMER is a Presidential Fellow at Rice University, where she is writing her doctoral dissertation on seventeenth-century British literature. She has previously published on St. Catherine of Siena in *Studia Mystica* and on John Donne in *Christianity and Literature*.

INDEX

Adderley, C.M., 258
Adventures of Tom Bombadil, The, 25, 158, 300
Ægir (Norse sea figure), 172
Ælfwine/Eriol, 12, 86, 165, 230–32, 239, 243n4
Aesir (Norse gods), 150, 166, 168, 177n11, 179, 180, 188n5
Aftonbladet (Stockholm evening newspaper), 112, 114
Ainulindalë, 2–3
Ainur, 9–10, 24, 53, 94, 166, 175–76, 177n11. *See also* Valar
Alboin (in "The Lost Road"), 105, 246n39
"Aldarion and Erendis," 107
Alfred, King, 133, 230–31
Allan, Jim, 249
allegory, 4, 5, 26–27, 61–67, 123, 185, 238; and applicability, 20–22, 26, 64, 117n12
Althusser, Louis, 98n15
anamnesis, 7, 87, 88, 94
Anderson, Douglas A., xiii, 2, 4
Anderson, Rasmus Bjorn: *Norse Mythology*, 185
Angles, 229, 231, 234
Anglo-Saxon Chronicle, 235
Anglo-Saxons, 4, 11, 195; literature of, 11, 133; pseudohistory for, 11, 239–40, 229–42; words of, 62, 76n34
Ansen, David, 111
Apolausticks, 200, 205
applicability, 20, 21, 26, 64, 109, 111–12, 117n12
Aragorn, 27, 30, 40, 42, 43, 119; ancestors of, 76n16; and Arwen, 38, 71, 119, 272; and boasting,

259; as Christ figure, 181; and Oathbreakers, 251; etymology of name, 6, 70–74, 76n27, 77; events in life of, 72–73, 112; on legend and reality, 267; and magic, 51; mortality of, 272; and oaths, 251, 253, 254, 256, 257–58; on Rohirrim, 102
Aristotle, 136, 142n5
Arthurian legend, 1, 37, 110, 121, 282, 292; Lancelot and Guinevere, 120, 131n14
Arwen, 38, 42, 43, 71–72, 77, 119, 272
Asgard, 70, 165–72 passim, 182, 183
athelas, 72, 76n34, 77, 86
"Athrabeth Finrod Ah Andreth," 26–27
Auden, W.H., 13, 183, 280, 285, 287
Augustine, Saint, 24, 63–64, 68, 97n3, 134; *De Genesi*, 24
Aulë, 151, 168, 172, 173

Balrog, 26, 77, 180, 188n5
Barfield, Owen, 66; *Poetic Diction*, 22, 29; *Saving the Appearances*, 75n11
barrow-wight's incantation, 51
Battle of Brunanburh, The, 250, 252
"Battle of Maldon, The," 1, 250, 252, 253, 258
Battle of Unnumbered Tears, 290
Bede, The Venerable, 231, 244n11; *Ecclesiastical History of the English People*, 234–35
Beleg, 290
Beornings, 109
Beowulf, 151, 234, 237, 240, 259, 266, 268–69
Beowulf, 5, 27, 145, 148; adaptation of language in, 85; boasting speech in 258, 259; comparison with *The*

327